ASIAN LAW SERIES

School of Law

University of Washington

Number 5

Asian Law Series

School of Law, University of Washington

The Asian Law Series was initiated with the cooperation of the University of Washington Press and the Institute of Comparative and Foreign Area Studies in 1969 in order to publish the results of several projects under way in Japanese, Chinese, and Korean law. The members of the editorial committee are: Herbert J. Ellison, Director of the Institute of Comparative and Foreign Area Studies; John O. Haley; and Dan Fenno Henderson, chairman.

1. *The Constitution of Japan: It's First Twenty Years, 1947–67*, edited by Dan Fenno Henderson
2. *Village "Contracts" in Tokugawa Japan*, by Dan Fenno Henderson
3. *Chinese Family Law and Social Change in Historic and Comparative Perspective*, edited by David C. Buxbaum
4. *Law and Politics in China's Foreign Trade*, edited by Victor H. Li
5. *Patent and Know-how Licensing in Japan and the United States*, edited by Teruo Doi and Warren L. Shattuck

PATENT AND KNOW-HOW LICENSING IN JAPAN AND THE UNITED STATES

Edited by

TERUO DOI

and

WARREN L. SHATTUCK

UNIVERSITY OF WASHINGTON PRESS

SEATTLE AND LONDON

Printed in the United States of America

Library of Congress Cataloging in Publication Data
Main entry under title:

Patent and know-how licensing in Japan and the United States.

(Asian law series; no. 5)
Includes bibliographical references and index.
1. Patent licenses — United States — Addresses, essays, lectures. 2. Patent licenses — Japan — Addresses, essays, lectures. 3. Foreign licensing agreements. I. Doi, Teruo. II. Shattuck, Warren Locke, 1908–
III. Series.
Law 346'.52'0486 76-7785
ISBN 0-295-95513-9

Foreword

The plan for this volume, as a joint effort of the Japanese Institute of International Business Law in Tokyo and the Asian Law Program at the University of Washington, goes back about ten years. The project was intended to fill a considerable gap in the literature for lawyers and licensing executives in a field of enormous intricacy and public importance to both Japan and the United States—Japanese/United States technology transfers. Scarcity of bilingual and bilegal talent suggested to us that binational teamwork might expedite publication. Actually, as it turned out, prompt publication was not one of our achievements for numerous reasons, but happily the volume is still timely and unique in its bilateral focus. If anything, its importance is enhanced by the increase in two-way, transpacific traffic in technology over a decade ago.

The dialogue between the two groups of authors—Japanese and American—began in September 1968, with a very rewarding five-day conference in Tokyo and Hakone. Arrangements made by the Japanese Institute enabled American authors to work over manuscripts with their Japanese counterparts in the congenial surroundings of the Industrial Club in Tokyo and in the mountain atmosphere of Hakone. The experts in attendance from Japan were: Sadanao Amemiya, Michiko Ariga, Teruo Doi, Yutaka Kubota, Kazuko Matsuo, Keiko Someno, Yoshinobu Someno, Yasuhara Nagashima, and Koe Toyosaki; and from the United States: John J. Cooper, Wilbur L. Fugate, Eugene H. Lee, John D. Lyon, Stephan H. Philbin, Robert A. Stenzel, and William R. Woodward; and from the sponsoring groups: Takeo Suzuki, Kazushige Ushimaru, Roy L. Prosterman, and Dan F. Henderson.

Since the conference was held, all manuscripts have been updated and revised twice. The volume has experienced the usual problems encountered in multiauthored books compounded by bilingual difficulties and bilateral aspects of a technical subject. Changes in American editorial responsibility and tardy authors on both sides have further slowed up publication. Nevertheless, this updated version comes at a good time because Japanese regulations of foreign licensing have further been liberalized. In addition, the outflow of Japanese technology reached a new stage in 1974, having increased to the point where there were more new Japanese licensors worldwide than licensees, though total Japanese licensees' royalty payments (including old licenses) were still much higher than those received by Japanese licensors.

Special thanks go to the Asian Foundation and the Ford Foundation which provided some of the funds for the Japanese and American sides, respectively. As sponsors, we add our thanks to the authors for their efforts and expertise. They are indeed a select group of contributors. Finally, we owe much to the editors, Teruo Doi and Warren L. Shattuck for seeing this project through.

August 1976

TAKEO SUZUKI
Chairman, Japanese Institute of International Business Law

DAN F. HENDERSON
Director, Asian Law Program
University of Washington

Preface

This project was designed to provide practitioners engaged in licensing transactions between Japan and the United States with basic information concerning both substantive and procedural aspects of the patent systems, particularly, legal protection of know-how, law governing remedies, antitrust, and taxation, as well as the basics of licensing agreements.

The first chapter, jointly written by United States and Japanese authors, is a comparative sketch of the patent systems of the two countries. The second chapter, jointly written, discusses legal protection of know-how in the two countries. The authors point out that in the United States there is a body of case law giving remedies against misappropriation of trade secrets including know-how, but in Japan that law is still not fully established.

The third and fourth chapters, written separately by United States and Japanese authors, deal with the filing and examination of patent applications and other procedural matters. These two chapters show interesting differences in the two patent systems attributable to differences in the legal systems, practices, and tradition.

The fifth chapter, also a joint work by United States and Japanese authors, provides models and guidelines for drawing up licensing agreements under the law of both countries. Important provisions usually inserted in international licensing agreements are discussed, and sample provisions are listed at the end.

The sixth chapter, also jointly written, gives a broad survey of the law of both countries concerning remedies and dispute settlement procedures relevant to licensing transactions.

The seventh and eighth chapters, written separately by a United States author and a Japanese author, discuss regulation of restrictive practices in licensing transactions under United States antitrust law and the Japanese antimonopoly laws. Since the Japanese Antimonopoly Law is modeled after the United States antitrust law, the reader will find that the basic principles are similar, but enforcement measures differ greatly.

The last two chapters, also written separately, deal with tax aspects of licensing transactions between the two countries. This is an important addition to the book, because treatises on licensing usually do not cover this subject.

The funding and sponsor organizations, their representatives and staff, and especially the authors on both sides deserve credit for persevering and seeing this volume through to completion. Writing in English was, of course, an extremely arduous task for some of the Japanese experts. This in turn cast burdens on the editors of both countries, who spent much time checking and rewriting some of the manuscripts, and in corresponding with each other and with the authors. Mr. Donald Swisher, presently a member of the Washington bar, deserves our thanks for his initial review of many of the manuscripts as an editorial assistant to the Director of the Asian Law Program.

TERUO DOI
Professor, Faculty of Law
Waseda University

WARREN L. SHATTUCK
Professor Emeritus
School of Law
University of Washington

Contents

PATENT AND KNOW-HOW LICENSING IN JAPAN AND THE UNITED STATES

A Comparative Study of the Patent Laws of the United States and Japan

MARCUS B. FINNEGAN
KOE TOYOSAKI
DAVID G. CONLIN

I. Introduction

Both the United States and Japan are highly industrialized nations and major economic forces in the world community. The advanced technology of both nations has been a significant factor in their industrial growth. Contributing substantially to the technological development of both the United States and Japan—respectively, the first and the third largest economies in the world—have been their systems of patent law.

The patent system of each nation has been important to its own progress and prosperity, but it has become increasingly important to the other country as well. The extensive economic interaction between Japan and the United States, including the presence of a large market in each country for the products of the other, is largely responsible for the increasing instances of patent procurement by nationals of one country in the other.[1]

Both the United States and the Japanese governments have recognized the importance of a working relationship in the area of patents. The two nations are joined by patent provisions in the Treaty of Friendship, Commerce, and Navigation.[2] They are both members of

1. See Asuo Hiraku Tokkyo (published by The Japanese Patent Office in 1968) at p. 204 for statistics showing the number of patents held in Japan by aliens in representative years during the period 1909–67. In United States Chemical and Pharmaceutical Patent Practice (published by the Practicing Law Institute in 1972) at pp. 161–65, statistics are given showing the activity of aliens in filing and obtaining patents in the United States during the period 1965–69.

2. Treaty of Friendship, Commerce and Navigation with Japan, 15 September, 1953, 4 U.S.T. 2063, TIAS No. 2863.

the Paris Union,[3] and each is a signatory to the 1970 Patent Cooperation Treaty.[4]

In light of the increasing numbers of American and Japanese inventors who are attempting to secure protection for their discoveries, domestically as well as in foreign nations, an understanding of the patent laws of the United States and Japan, particularly their similarities and differences, is virtually essential. It is the need for such understanding that has prompted a comparative study of the fundamental principles of the patent laws of the two nations.

II. A Comparative Overview of the Japanese and American Patent Systems

The heart of the patent systems of both Japan and the United States is the body of patent laws enacted by the legislative branch of each country. Although there are striking similarities, as well as marked differences, in various provisions of the respective laws, the patent statutes of both countries spring from a singular perception of the role that a strong and viable patent system ought to possess in the overall economic, industrial, and material well-being and wholesome growth of the economy and populace of each nation.

Japan and the United States both maintain patent systems because each country has concluded that creative endeavors in the useful arts inject a vital and continuous flow of technological innovations into the industrial mainstream. Moreover, it has been determined that the granting of exclusive rights to a discovery is a just reward and a necessary incentive for inventors to persist in expending their time, effort, and money in such creative indeavors.

The United States Constitution empowers the Congress to "promote the progress of . . . useful arts, by securing for limited times to . . . inventors the exclusive right to their . . . discoveries."[5] Thus, the objective of the United States patent system is to promote progress in the useful arts. The method of realizing that objective is to secure to inventors, for limited times, the exclusive right to their discoveries.

The Patent Law of Japan[6] expresses a similar purpose. The object of

3. Convention of Paris for the Protection of Industrial Property, signed March 20, 1883, 25 Stat. 1372 (1887), T.S. No. 379.

4. A copy of the Patent Cooperation Treaty appears at 876 O.G. [U.S. Patent Office Gazette] 341 (1970).

5. U.S. Const., art. 1, §8, cl. 8.

6. All references herein to the Patent Law of Japan are to the Foster-Ono translation of Articles of Law No. 121 of 13 April, 1959, as amended, Law No. 140 of 1962, Law No. 161 of 1962, Law No. 148 of 1964, Law No. 81 of 1965, Law No. 91, of 1971, in R. Foster and M. Ono, The Patent and Trademark Laws of Japan (1970). The Patent Law of Japan is to be distinguished from the Utility Model Law of Japan which is concerned with "devices" rather than "inventions" and defines "device" as "the creation

the Patent Law is "the promotion of the protection and utilization of inventions, with a view to encouraging inventions and thereby contributing to the development of industry."[7]

The common essence of both the American and Japanese patent systems can be found in these expressions of objective. Any philosophical discussion of either system, as well as any practical inquiry into the statutory structure of each system, must begin with an understanding of this essence. From it emanates several broad principles and concepts that are shared by the patent systems of both Japan and America.

The important concepts derived from the objective of both patent systems are that the nature of the inventions that relate to the purpose of the patent systems are those that fall in the fields of the useful arts or pertain to industry in its broadest sense; that inventors who make discoveries in these fields that relate to the purpose of the patent systems are to be given protection against unauthorized appropriation of their inventions by others; and that such protection is warranted where an invention can be expected to contribute to the progress of the useful arts or the development of industry. These three broad concepts translate into particular provisions in the patent laws of the United States and Japan directed to the nature of subject matter that may or may not be patented, the rights of the inventor and the enforcement of these provisions, the standards of patentability to be used to determine whether a particular invention deserves patent protection, and the requirements of public disclosure necessary for the realization of the full benefit of inventive discoveries. In some cases, there is correspondence between the provisions of the patent laws of the two countries, whereas in others there is divergence.

There is at least one major conceptual difference in the way in which the patent laws of the two countries have been drawn. United States statutes have been drafted with a view toward broadly defining the elements of the American patent system and leaving the courts to imprint the fine texture of the system by statutory interpretation on a case-by-case basis. The Patent Law of Japan is a comparatively more rigorous legislative effort. The difference is one of practice, which would be reflected in other areas of law as well, but it is one that should be appreciated at the outset, for it does have an impact.

The current patent law in force in the United States is the Patent

of a technical idea utilizing natural laws." *See* Foster and Ono, at 105–12; A. Kukimoto, Summary of Japanese Patent Law 29 (1971). The present paper does not deal with utility model registrations.

7. Article 1.

Act of 1952, which is actually Title 35 of the United States Code.[8] Within the last ten years there has been mounting pressure for revision, but no new patent legislation has thus far been enacted.

A. The Rights Conferred by Patents

An appropriate starting point for a comparative evaluation of the patent laws of the United States and Japan is an analysis of the nature of patent rights afforded under the respective laws of each nation. An understanding of patent rights provides a suitable perspective against which to view the prerequisite conditions that must be fulfilled in order to obtain a patent.

The cornerstone of the rights conferred by a patent in either country is the vesting of the exclusive right to the invention in the patentee.[9] Under the Patent Law of Japan, a patentee has the exclusive right to work the patented invention as a business[10] for a period of fifteen (15) years from the date of publication of the application, but not longer than twenty (20) years from the filing date of the patent application.[11] A United States patent has a term of seventeen (17) years from the date of issuance of the patent and affords the patentee the right to exclude others from making, using, or selling the invention throughout the United States.[12]

No payment of post-issuance annuities is required in the United States. In contrast, Article 107 of the Patent Law of Japan prescribes a schedule of fees that must be paid in order to maintain the patent in force.

Unauthorized use of a patented invention constitutes an infringement under the laws of both nations. In fact, where a patented invention is such that it utilizes an earlier patent, Article 72 of the Patent Law of Japan and judicial interpretation of the United States statute both prohibit the use of the later patented invention, absent the license to do so, from the owner of the earlier, more comprehensive patent.

In both nations, upon evidence of infringement, the infringer can be ordered to cease use of the patented invention.[13] The infringer can

8. All references to the United States Patent Statute are to sections of Title 35 of the United States Code, designated as 35 U.S.C.

9. References herein to the "patentee" or "inventor" are understood to include more than one patentee or inventor as the case may be and to refer to the assignee, heir, or other successor of the patentee or inventor if ownership of the application or patent has been transferred.

10. Article 68.

11. Article 67.

12. 35 U.S.C. §154.

13. *See* Article 100 of the Patent Law of Japan and 35 U.S.C. §283. *See generally* Nakamura, *Patent Infringement—A Comparison of the United States and Japan*, 56 J.P.O.S. 504 (1974); Yoshii, *Patent Infringement Litigation in Japan*, 54 J.P.O.S. 383 (1972).

also be compelled to pay damages to the patentee adequate in compensation for the patentee's loss, and in no case will the award be less than that of a reasonable royalty for the use.[14]

The patent systems of Japan and the United States are therefore fundamentally similar in the benefits afforded. These patent rights are granted to induce practical, industrial innovation and its disclosure. The right to bar other members of the public from using an invention is a substantial and significant endowment by the respective governments of these two nations, and is given only in those classes of cases in which the desired inducement can be expected to be realized. The various requirements for patentability imposed by each country, discussed in detail below, are designed to insure that patent rights are only conferred where the public benefit is commensurate with the public sacrifice that accompanies the granting of patent protection.

In Japan, the infringing manufacture or use of a patented invention must be in connection with a business and not, for example, for a household purpose.[15] In addition, the patent right does not extend to permit prohibition of the use of a patented invention for the purpose of test or research, or to vessels or aircraft merely passing through Japan or equipment used therein, or to things that existed in Japan prior to the time the patent application was filed.[16]

Direct infringement in the United States is constituted by the making, using, or selling of the patented invention without authority.[17] Non-business use and experimental use are not exempted from actionable infringement by either statute or judicial interpretation. However, a charge of infringement has rarely, if ever, been brought against an ordinary, individual consumer. Also, damages are not normally recoverable for experimental use unless the use is for a commercial purpose.[18] The United States Patent Statutes exempt vessels, aircraft, and other vehicles, temporarily within the United States, from patent infringement.[19]

Where direct infringement is shown, one who knowingly and intentionally causes, encourages, or otherwise actively induces another to commit that direct infringement can also be held liable as an infringer,[20] as can one who contributes to the direct infringement by

14. *See* Article 102 of the Patent Law of Japan and 35 U.S.C. §284. Note that in the United States, interest and costs are awardable, 35 U.S.C. §284, as well as reasonable attorney fees, although the latter applies only in "exceptional" cases.

15. Article 68.

16. Article 69.

17. 35 U.S.C. §271(a).

18. Northill Co. v. Danforth, 51 F.Supp. 928, 58 U.S.P.Q. 575 (N.D.Cal. 1942); Radio Corp. of America v. Andrea, 90 F.2d 612, 34 U.S.P.Q. 312 (2d Cir. 1937).

19. 35 U.S.C. §272.

20. 35 U.S.C. §271(b). *See* Fromberg v. Thornhill, 315 F.2d 407, 137 U.S.P.Q. 84 (5th Cir. 1963).

providing a material part of the invention, knowing it to be specially adapted for use in infringement.[21]

In determining whether a particular product, machine, or process infringes a particular United States patent claim, the first step is to assess whether there is "literal" infringement, i.e., whether the product, machine, or process that allegedly infringes falls within the meaning of the terms of the claim.

In the interpretation of claims, the language used is of primary importance. In his patent specification, the inventor is permitted to define the terms he uses in the claims, even if his definitions are slightly at variance with the established meanings of the terms.[22] However, while the claims will be interpreted in light of the specification in order to ascertain their meaning and scope, the specification may not be used to change or expand the meaning of the claims.[23]

If there is no literal infringement, the patentee will still have an action of infringement if the elements of the suspect product, machine, or process perform substantially the same function in substantially the same way to achieve substantially the same results as the patented invention.[24] This is known as the "doctrine of equivalents."

The doctrine of equivalents is an important aspect in determining whether or not there has been an infringement, since it is often the case that a literal infringement of a claim has been avoided. One limitation on the application of the doctrine of equivalents is the principle of "file wrapper estoppel." This principle comes into play when the patentee has amended his claims to avoid a rejection during the prosecution of his application in the patent office. The patentee may be precluded from asserting that his pre-amendment claim, which the accused infringer is now infringing, embraces equivalents entitled to protection.

Although the application of the doctrine of equivalents and the rule of file wrapper estoppel depends upon the circumstances of each individual case; as a general proposition, the scope of the patentee's protection can extend beyond the literal language of the claims to cover equivalent modes of operation, but does not include those modes that have been given up and sacrificed in order to obtain the patent.

The Japanese interpretation of the scope of the patent is similar to

21. 35 U.S.C. §271(c). *See* Aro Mfg. Co. v. Convertible Top Replacement Co., 377 U.S. 476, 141 U.S.P.Q. 681 (1964).

22. *See, e.g.*, Chicago Steel Foundry Co. v. Burnside Steel Foundry Co., 132 F.2d 812, 56 U.S.P.Q. 283 (7th Cir. 1943).

23. United States v. Adams, 383 U.S. 39, 49, 148 U.S.P.Q. 479, 482–83 (1966); Seymour v. Osborne, 78 U.S. (11 Wall.) 516, 547 (1870).

24. Graver Tank & Mfg. Co. v. Linde Air Products Co., 339 U.S. 605, 85 U.S.P.Q. 328 (1950).

that of the United States. Under Article 70 of the Patent Law of Japan, the technical scope of a patented invention is determined in light of the specification and the claimed scope. Although the Patent Law of 1921 lacked such a provision, it had been the general practice of the courts in Japan to determine the scope of the patent in the light of the specification, particularly the description of the scope of the claims to the patent, together with the drawings.

Under Japanese law, the doctrine of equivalents is recognized,[25] as is the concept of the doctrine of file wrapper estoppel.[26] Recourse to the latter is infrequent in the Japanese courts, whereas it is very often raised in patent infringement litigation in the United States.

The interpretation of the scope of a patented invention is a critical facet of determining patentability, validity, and infringement. Under Japanese patent law, anyone can make a request to the patent office for an interpretation of the technical scope of a patented invention.[27] Upon receipt of such a request, the patent office will designate three trial examiners to render an interpretation. Under United States patent law, however, there is no comparable provision that allows for interpretation of the scope of a patent either by the United States Patent Office or by the courts.

Infringement is conduct against which the patent right may be enforced. However, there are limitations on the patent right, notwithstanding the existence of an infringement.

Only a valid patent can be infringed. Under 35 U.S.C. §282, every claim in an issued patent is presumed to be valid. However, this is not a conclusive presumption, and §282 also affords the accused infringer the right to assert, as a defense, the invalidity of the patent on the grounds that the patentee has failed to comply with the requirements of patentability. There are additional grounds on which a patent may be held to be unenforceable, such as laches;[28] fraud practiced in obtaining the patent;[29] and patent misuse which can include various antitrust violations such as illegal price-fixing arrangements,[30] resale

25. Badische Anilin und Soda Fabrik A. G. v. Sekisui Kagaku Kogyo K. K., 12 Kakyū Minshū 937 (Osaka Dist. Ct. 1961).

26. *See* Muranaka v. K. K. Daiwa Gomu Seisakusho, 247 HANREI TAIMUZU 263 (Tokyo Dist. Ct. 1970).

27. Article 71.

28. *See* Gillons v. Shell Co. California, 86 F.2d 600, 32 U.S.P.Q. 1 (9th Cir. 1936), *cert. denied*, 302 U.S. 689, 37 U.S.P.Q. 842 (1937); Pierce v. International Telephone & Telegraph Co., 147 F.Supp. 934, 112 U.S.P.Q. 175 (D.N.J. 1957).

29. Walker Process Equip., Inc. v. Food Mach. & Chem. Corp., 382 U.S. 172, 147 U.S.P.Q. 404 (1965); Beckman Instruments, Inc. v. Chemtronics, Inc., 428 F.2d 555, 165 U.S.P.Q. 355 (5th Cir. 1970), *on remand*, 328 F.Supp. 1132, 170 U.S.P.Q. 466 (W.D.Tex. 1971).

30. *See, e.g.*, United States v. Univis Lens Co., 316 U.S. 241, 53 U.S.P.Q. 404 (1942).

territorial limitations,[31] tying arrangements,[32] and pooling arrangements.[33]

Unlike the Patent Law of Japan,[34] the United States Patent Statute does not provide for publication of an application and opposition to its issuance as a patent. In addition, under Japanese law a patent can be invalidated within five years of its issuance.[35]

While there are certain circumstances under United States law in which a "declaratory judgment" suit can be brought against a patentee essentially for the purpose of invalidating a patent, there is no time limit for bringing such a suit. Furthermore, declaratory judgment suits can be brought only where there is an actual controversy between the patentee and a potential infringer. Accordingly, there is no procedure in the United States that is truly analogous to the Japanese provisions for opposition and demand for invalidation. The United States Patent Office makes the determination of patentability in the first instance, subject to court review,[36] and the validity of an issued patent can be fully tested in the course of patent infringement litigation whenever such litigation may arise.

In addition to the general limitations on property rights under Article 29(2) of the Japanese Constitution and Article 1(1) of the Japanese Civil Code, which subordinates the enjoyment of property rights to the public welfare, the Patent Law of Japan provides for a number of limitations on patent rights. The most notable of these are the compulsory licensing provisions.

A patent right under Japanese law is subject to a non-exclusive license for any person who, having made the invention without knowledge of the contents of the pending patent application, or having learned the invention from an independent inventor, has been engaged in the business of working the invention or has made preparations for such business in Japan at the time of filing the patent application.[37] In addition, the non-working of a patented invention

31. *See, e.g.*, Keeler v. Standard Folding Bed Co., 157 U.S. 659 (1895); American Industrial Fastener Corp. v. Flushing Enterprises, Inc., 362 F.Supp. 32, 179 U.S.P.Q. 722 (N.D.Ohio 1973).

32. *See, e.g.*, International Salt Co. v. United States, 332 U.S. 392, 75 U.S.P.Q. 184 (1947).

33. *See, e.g.*, American Securit Co. v. Shatterproof Glass Corp., 268 F.2d 769, 122 U.S.P.Q. 167 (3d Cir. 1959).

34. *See* Articles 51, 52, 55, 65-2 and 65-3.

35. Articles 123–24.

36. 35 U.S.C. §§141–45.

37. Article 79. However, in an action for confirmation of the right to exploit a patent, it was held that the mere preparation of a drawing of an electric motor-operated movie camera was not sufficient preparation for its manufacture under Article 79. Konishiroku Kogyō K. K. v. Yashica K. K., 162 HANREI TAIMUZU 164 (Tokyo Dist. Ct. 1964).

makes that invention subject to a compulsory license.[38]

The Patent Law of Japan provides for compulsory license where it is necessary for the public interest,[39] although it does not appear that a request for license under this provision has ever been made. Compulsory licenses may also be obtained in certain special circumstances under Articles 80, 81, and 175.

By contrast to the practice in Japan, there is no general compulsory licensing provision under the United States Patent Statute, although there are compulsory licensing provisions in certain statutes covering specific situations.[40] In addition, the United States does not have working requirements for a patent.

In general, statutory restrictions on patent rights, outside of the antitrust area, are relatively few in the United States. However, the broad powers of the federal courts and agencies have sheltered non-statutory compulsory licensing, or the equivalent, in some situations where necessary to correct fraud, misuse, or antitrust violations.[41]

The patent systems of the United States and Japan are essentially alike in the rights afforded the patentee, although some differences in procedure and limitations are important to remember. In exchange for the exclusive right to the invention granted to the patentee, various conditions must be satisfied. Here again the two systems are fundamentally similar, but there are some significant areas of divergence that are developed more fully below.

B. The Nature of Subject Matter Which May be Patented

Article 29 of the Patent Law of Japan provides that "anyone who has made an invention that can be utilized in an industry may obtain a patent therefor," subject to the other requirements of the Patent Law. It follows that inventions that *cannot* "be utilized in industry" do not constitute proper subject matter for the protection of the patent laws. In *Tsuda* v. *Director-General of the Patent Office*,[42] the Japanese Supreme Court held that an invention must be technically and industrially workable to be patentable. In that case, telegraph codes, which consist of combinations of letters, numbers, and certain symbols, were declared unpatentable.

Likewise, methods of advertising have been held unpatentable on

38. Article 83.

39. Article 93.

40. *See, e.g.*, The National Air Quality Standards Act of 1970, 42 U.S.C. §1857h-6; the Atomic Energy Act, 42 U.S.C. §2183; Sease, *Common Sense, Nonsense and the Compulsory License*, 55 J.P.O.S. 233 (1973).

41. *See, e.g.*, Charles Pfizer & Co. v. Federal Trade Commission, 401 F.2d 574, 159 U.S.P.Q. 193 (6th Cir. 1968); *Sease, supra*, note 40, 55 J.P.O.S. at 239–50.

42. 7 Minshū 461 (S.Ct. 1953).

the same grounds.[43] Methods of raising vegetables, cultivating pearls, and storing or transporting goods are examples of inventions that have been found to have industrial utility. The requirement of industrial utility has also been held to be satisfied with respect to chemical inventions that have the possibility of being utilized in the future, even though the level of technology existing at the time of application does not specifically show the capability of using the invention.[44]

The United States Patent Law is similarly directed to the protection of inventions in the "useful" arts. Section 101 of Title 35 provides that a patent may be obtained for "any new and useful process, machine, manufacture, or composition of matter, or any new and useful improvements thereof," subject to the other requirements of patentability set forth in the statute.

Certain types of inventions have been judicially excluded from patent protection. Scientific truths, phenomena of nature, mental processes, and similar abstract or intellectual concepts are unpatentable.[45] Patents may not be granted for mere methods of executing business or financial schemes.[46]

An area that has been the subject of much controversy in the United States is the protectability of computer programs under the patent laws. At one time, processes comprising a series of steps governing the internal operation of a computer were held to be unpatentable as mere mental processes. The United States Court of Customs and Patent Appeals, which is the judicial body that decides an appeal by a patent applicant from Patent Office refusal to allow the application,[47] later held that such processes, which perform technologically useful functions, are patentable,[48] although processes for simply solving mathematical equations are not considered patentable.[49] More recently, the United States Supreme Court, in the case of *Gottschalk* v. *Benson*,[50] cast doubt on the patentability of any process for controlling the internal operation of a computer.

The requirement of utility in 35 U.S.C. §101 has been a limiting

43. Ōmura v. Director-General of the Patent Office, 7 Gyōsei Reishū 3157 (Tokyo High Ct. 1956).

44. Tokkyochō, Shinsakijun No Tebiki §3.13 (4th ed. 1970).

45. Gottschalk v. Benson, 409 U.S. 63, 175 U.S.P.Q. 673 (1972); Funk Bros. Seed Co. v. Kalo Inoculant Co., 333 U.S. 127, 76 U.S.P.Q. 280 (1948); O'Reilly v. Morse, 56 U.S. (15 How.) 62 (1853).

46. Loew's Drive-In Theaters, Inc. v. Park-In Theaters, Inc., 174 F.2d 547, 81 U.S.P.Q. 149 (1st Cir. 1949), *cert. denied*, 338 U.S. 822, 83 U.S.P.Q. 543 (1949); In re Sterling, 70 F.2d 910, 21 U.S.P.Q. 519 (C.C.P.A. 1934).

47. *See* 35 U.S.C. §141.

48. *See* In re Waldbaum, 457 F.2d 997, 173 U.S.P.Q. 430 (C.C.P.A. 1972); In re Musgrave, 431 F.2d 882, 167 U.S.P.Q. 280 (C.C.P.A. 1970).

49. *See* In re Christensen, 478 F.2d 1392, 178 U.S.P.Q. 35 (C.C.P.A. 1973).

50. 409 U.S. 63, 175 U.S.P.Q. 673 (1972).

factor in the field of chemical inventions.[51] It has been held that a chemical process lacks utility, unless the product produced by the process itself possesses utility.[52] In addition, where the only known utility of a chemical compound is in the production of other chemical compositions, the resultant compositions must have a practical utility of their own in order for the starting chemical compound to be considered useful within the meaning of the statute.[53]

It can be seen, therefore, that the nature of subject matter that may be patented under both the United States and Japanese patent laws is governed broadly by a requirement for industrial or practical utility. In the case of each nation's patent system, the utility requirement imposes a limitation on the types of inventions that can be protected.

The judicial bodies of each country have played a key role in applying the utility requirement to specific classes of inventions, and as indicated, there are particular areas, such as methods of doing business and abstract intellectual concepts, that have been held to be unpatentable under both patent systems. In other fields, particularly in the chemical area, the interpretation of utility or usefulness has been more stringent in the United States than in Japan.

In addition to the broad industrial utility requirement, the Patent Law of Japan expressly excludes certain fields of invention. Article 32 provides that patents cannot be obtained with respect to (1) an invention of an article of food or drink, or of an article of taste; (2) an invention of a medicine, including diagnostic, preventative, and curative medicines, as well as a method of mixing two or more medicines to manufacture one medicine, but not including instruments, things not directly applied to the human body, cosmetics, or processes in the manufacture of medicines;[54] (3) an invention of a substance to be manufactured by a chemical process;[55] and (4) an invention of a substance to be manufactured by a method of transformation of atomic nuclei. (1), (2), and (3) were repealed by the revision of 1975.

By contrast, the United States Patent Law affords patent protection

51. *Compare* Callison v. Dean, 70 F.2d 55, 21 U.S.P.Q. 240 (10th Cir. 1934), *with* Brenner v. Manson, 383 U.S. 519, 148 U.S.P.Q. 689 (1967).

52. Brenner v. Manson, 383 U.S. 519, 148 U.S.P.Q. 689 (1967).

53. In re Kirk, 376 F.2d 936, 153 U.S.P.Q. 48 (C.C.P.A. 1967); In re Joly, 376 F.2d 906, 153 U.S.P.Q. 45 (C.C.P.A. 1967).

54. TOKKYOCHŌ, SHINSAKIJUN NO TEBIKI §3.14 (4th ed. 1970). *See also* Jarkovsky, *A Comparative Review of Japanese and U.S. Patent and Related Laws*, 50 J.P.O.S. 76, 82 (1968); Otani, *Introduction to the Japanese Patent System*, 7 P.T.C. J.Res. & Ed. 13, 16 (1963); Yamashita, *Some Aspects of Pharmaceutical Patents in Japan*, 44 J.P.O.S. 291 (1962); Kukimoto, *supra*, note 6, at 39–40.

55. In enacting this exclusion, the legislature believed that to allow the granting of a patent on a new chemical compound could be detrimental to the progress of industry. Similar arguments are fully answered in Godenhielm, *The Scandinavian Patent Community*, 4 IND. PROPERTY 10, 11 (1965).

for chemical compositions of matter that have the requisite degree of utility discussed above, including articles of food, medicines, and substances made by chemical processes.[56] In fact, the United States Patent Statute contains virtually no specific exclusions of classes of invention from the operation of the patent laws.

Article 32 of the Patent Law of Japan additionally excludes "an invention that is likely to be detrimental to public order, good morals, or public health." There is no corresponding exclusion in the United States statute, but inventions that offend public law and morals have been judicially held to be unpatentable in the United States,[57] as they are in most countries.[58] As might be expected, this issue has not arisen frequently in the history of United States patent jurisprudence.

Overall, United States patent law has proven to be relatively liberal when compared to that of other countries with respect to the nature of the subject matter that may be patented. This is particularly true in the field of chemical, including pharmaceutical, inventions. However, with the exception of chemical compounds, and compositions of matter, the United States and Japanese patent laws bear more similarity than difference as regards the nature of patentable subject matter.

C. The Standards of Patentability

Assuming that an invention is of such a nature as to be patentable as discussed in the previous section, it cannot be protected by a patent in either the United States or Japan unless it is (1) different from what has been publicly known or done before; and (2) *sufficiently* different from what has been publicly known or done before.

In the United States these two requirements are termed, respectively, "novelty" (35 U.S.C. §102), and "nonobviousness" (35 U.S.C. §103). These conditions, or standards of patentability, find similar expression in the Patent Law of Japan, which excludes from patent protection inventions that lack novelty[59] and those that are obvious.[60]

By and large, although there are important differences between the American and Japanese standards of novelty and nonobviousness, the conditions of patentability in the two nations are quite similar. Underlying both patent systems is a common appreciation that the private protection afforded in order to promote invention must be balanced

56. In this respect, United States law is relatively liberal as compared to the laws of many other countries. *Compare* Note, *Patentable Subject Matter Under National and Multinational Systems*, 2 Law & Pol. Int'l. Bus. 479, at 487–92 (1970).

57. Fuller v. Berger, 120 F. 274 (7th Cir. 1903), *cert. denied*, 193 U.S. 668 (1904).

58. *See* Note, *Patentable Subject Matter Under National and Multinational Systems*, 2 Law & Pol. Int'l Bus. 479 (1970).

59. Article 29.

60. Article 29.2

against a public interest in the freedom to use knowledge that is in the public domain. These competing interests are reconciled under both systems by limiting patent protection to those inventions that meet a minimum level of difference from what is already known to the public.

1. The Requirement of novelty. Section 102 of Title 35 United States Code, has seven (7) subparagraphs that define events concerning the invention to be patented, the occurrence of which will preclude it from obtaining patent protection. Three of these subparagraphs have been primarily relied upon by the patent office and courts when determining whether the novelty requirement has been met. These novelty-defeating, or anticipating, "prior art" provisions read as follows:

> (a) the invention was known or used by others in this country, or patented or described in a printed publication in this or a foreign country, before the invention thereof by the applicant for patent. . . .
>
> (b) the invention was patented or described in a printed publication in this or a foreign country or in public use or on sale in this country, more than one year prior to the date of the application for patent in the United States. . . .
>
> (e) the invention was described in a patent granted on an application for patent by another filed in the United States before the invention thereof by the applicant for patent. . . .

Sections 102(a) and (e) relate to art existing before the *date of invention* of the subject matter. Under United States practice, the patent applicant would have to prove that he actually made the invention earlier than the date of the prior art.

Section 102(e) makes the filing date of a United States patent the effective date of the patent as a reference against another patent application.[61] However, it has been held that the convention filing date of a United States patent based on a foreign patent application cannot be relied on as the effective date of the reference patent.[62]

Section 102(b) refers to the date in which the United States application was *filed* rather than the date of invention. That section of the statute bars issuance of a patent for an invention that was known more than one year prior to the date of filing. Considering §§102(a), (b), and (e) together, it can be seen that an inventor generally has no more than one year from the time that his invention becomes known to the

61. This provision is based on the Supreme Court case of Alexander Milburn Co. v. Davis-Burononville Co., 270 U.S. 390 (1926). *See also* Hazeltine Research, Inc. v. Brenner, 382 U.S. 252, 147 U.S.P.Q. 429 (1965).

62. In re Hilmer, 359 F.2d 859, 149 U.S.P.Q. 480 (C.C.P.A. 1966); In re Hilmer, 425 F.2d 1108, 165 U.S.P.Q. 255 (C.C.P.A. 1970).

public within which to file an application for a patent. In this connection, it is to be noted that public use referred to in §102(b) does not include experimental use.[63]

The novelty requirement imposes a condition that an invention sought to be patented must be new. It must differ in some respect from what has been known or done before. Lack of novelty, or "anticipation," is a very technical defect and requires that the invention for which a patent is sought finds exact correspondence in the prior art alleged to be anticipatory.[64]

In addition, the prior art must be "enabling," i.e., it must be sufficiently clear and complete as to enable one skilled in the art to make and use what is described.[65] If the prior art is a machine or product that was actually made, it must have been at least minimally operable, or useful, before a later invention will be declared anticipated.[66]

The broad "known or used by others in this country" prior art provision of §102(a) relates to public knowledge and public use. This section of the statute was intended to adopt the previously existing body of case law under which prior knowledge or use had to be public knowledge or use.[67] In general, the prior art provisions of §§102(a), (b), and (e) prevent the issuance of a patent on an invention where the knowledge of the invention is in the public domain.

The novelty requirement of the Patent Law of Japan is contained in Article 29. A patent may not be obtained in Japan if the invention was publicly known or publicly operated in Japan prior to the effective filing date of the application. In addition, an applicant is not entitled to a patent on an invention that was described in a publication anywhere in the world prior to the effective filing date.

The requirement that the invention must not have been known, operated, or described in a publication makes the Japanese "novelty" requirement very similar to the United States requirement under §§102(a) and (b) in the sense that the same types of prior art are involved. However, in the United States the date of invention may be

63. *See, e.g.*, Egbert v. Lippman, 104 U.S. 333 (1881); In re Yarn Processing Patent Validity Litigation, 498 F.2d 271, 183 U.S.P.Q. 65 (5th Cir. 1974).

64. Seymour v. Osborne, 78 U.S. (11 Wall.) 516 (1870); Bates v. Coe, 98 U.S. 31 (1878).

65. *See* In re Moore, 444 F.2d 572, 170 U.S.P.Q. 260 (C.C.P.A. 1971); In re Le Grice, 301 F.2d 929, 133 U.S.P.Q. 365 (C.C.P.A. 1962).

66. *See* General Electric Supply Corp. v. Maytag Co., 100 F.2d 218 (8th Cir. 1938), *rev'd. on other grounds*, 307 U.S. 243 *reh. den.* 308 U.S. 631 (1939); A. B. Dick Co. v. Simplicator Corp., 34 F.2d 935 (2d Cir. 1929); In re Dowty, 118 F.2d 363, 49 U.S.P.Q. 99 (C.C.P.A. 1941).

67. H.R.Rep.No. 1923, 82nd Cong., 2d Sess. 6, 17 (1952); *See* Pennock v. Dialogue, 27 U.S. (2 Pet.) 1 (1829); Gillman v. Stern, 114 F.2d 28, 46 U.S.P.Q. 430 (2d Cir. 1940), *cert. denied*, 311 U.S. 718 (1941).

of critical importance, while in Japan, only the application date is pertinent to determining novelty.

By itself, Article 29 imposes a rather strict rule. However, some exceptions are provided in Article 30. These exceptions have an effect somewhat similar to the one-year grace period provided under United States law during which certain types of disclosures can be made without defeating patent rights. The period in Japan is, however, only six months.

Under Article 30 of the Japanese law, a person who otherwise has the right to obtain a patent for a particular invention may conduct an experiment and publish the results, or make a public disclosure at a meeting or academic society designated by the director-general of the patent office, without losing the right to a patent, so long as the patent application is filed within six months after such an event.[68] Under §§102(a) and (b) of the United States law, an inventor may make a public disclosure of his invention and still obtain a patent, provided the application is filed within one year of the disclosure.

Article 30 also provides that display of the invention at certain types of exhibitions does not result in loss of rights, if the application is filed within six months.

A patent applicant desiring to take advantage of the exceptions in Article 30 of the Patent Law of Japan must submit a paper with his patent application indicating his desire to take such advantage, as well as a paper certifying that the experiment, publication, or display falls under the Article 30 exception.[69] There is no specific statutory provision under United States law that corresponds to this requirement. However, patent applicants are under an obligation imposed by the United States courts to disclose to the patent office any information regarding prior art, acts, or disclosures that is relevant to the determination of patentability of the invention.[70]

In recent years, there has been much controversy and activity in this area. A number of courts have dealt with the question of whether or not a patent applicant has been properly candid and open in his dealings with the patent office during the pendency of his application.[71] There have been instances in which a patent has been held to be unenforceable because the patent applicant failed to advise the

68. Article 30(1).

69. Article 30(4).

70. *See, e.g.*, Beckman Instruments, Inc. v. Chemtronics, Inc., 428 F.2d 555, 564–65, 165 U.S.P.Q. 355, 362–64 (5th Cir. 1970), *cert. denied*, 400 U.S. 956, 168 U.S.P.Q. 1 (1970); Precision Instrument Mfg. Co. v. Automotive Maintenance Machine Co., 324 U.S. 806, 65 U.S.P.Q. 133 (1945).

71. *See, e.g.*, Monsanto Co. v. Rohm & Haas Co., 456 F.2d 592, 172 U.S.P.Q. 323 (3d Cir. 1972); Smith, *Fraud Upon the Patent Office as a Violation of the Sherman Antitrust Law*, 53 J.P.O.S. 337–73, 423–38 (1971).

patent office of pertinent information known to him that might have led to the denial of the application if the patent office had been aware of such information.[72]

The direction of the case law has been toward increasing strictness in this area.[73] Although it is not precisely analogous to the Japanese requirement that an applicant must advise the patent office that he wishes to take advantage of the Article 30 exceptions, it is certainly a somewhat related aspect of United States practice of which Japanese inventors and patent agents should be aware.

A final exception under Article 30 to the requirements of Article 29 of the Patent Law of Japan is that patent rights are not lost in a case where an invention has been made publicly known, or publicly worked in Japan, or published anywhere in the world, contrary to the will of the person who has the right to apply for a patent on it, if that person files an application within six months.[74]

Even though the invention is not in the public domain as defined in 35 U.S.C. §§102(a), (b), or (e), a patent applicant may lose the right to a United States patent or may not be entitled to a patent under certain circumstances specified in subparagraphs (c), (d), (f) and (g) of §102.

Under §102(c), an inventor cannot obtain a patent if he has abandoned his invention. The inventor in such a case has forfeited his right to a patent.

If a patent applicant has (1) filed an application in a foreign country more than twelve months before the filing of the application in the United States, and (2) the foreign application has issued as a patent in the foreign country prior to the United States filing date, §102(d) bars the issuance of a United States patent on the same invention.[75]

A patent applicant who did not himself invent the subject matter sought to be patented may not obtain a United States patent on that subject matter under §102(f). This is known as "derivation" of the invention by the patent applicant from another.

In the United States, in the case of two bona fide inventors of the same subject matter, the one entitled to a patent on the invention is the one who first actually made the invention. This is set forth in §102(g), which states in part that "a person shall be entitled to a patent unless . . . before the applicant's invention thereof the invention was made in this country by another who had not abandoned, suppressed,

72. *See* Chromalloy American Corp. v. Alloy Surfaces Co., 339 F. Supp. 859, 173 U.S.P.Q. 295 (D.Del. 1972); Charles Pfizer & Co. v. F.T.C., 401 F.2d 574, 159 U.S.P.Q. 193 (6th Cir. 1968).

73. *See generally*, Smith, *supra*, note 71; Ram, *Patent Fraud: A New Defense?*, 54 J.P.O.S. 363 (1972); Dodds, *Fraud on the Patent Office*, 56 J.P.O.S. 345 (1974).

74. Article 30(2).

75. *See, e.g.*, Ex parte Iizuka, 171 U.S.P.Q. 50 (P.O.Bd.App. 1970).

or concealed it." In contrast to United States law, most countries, including Japan, consider the first inventor to be the one who has first filed his application for a patent.

Out of §102(g) arises the fairly complicated interference practice in the United States, through which the first inventor of the subject matter claimed by two or more applicants is determined. An "interference" is a proceeding conducted in the United States Patent Office that resembles an actual trial and is conducted for the purpose of establishing priority of the invention or earliest inventorship.

Determining the first actual inventor involves many considerations and is much more difficult than basing the right to a patent on earliest filing date. An invention is considered to have been made when there has been both "conception" and a "reduction to practice."[76]

"Conception" generally relates to the formulation of a complete idea of the whole invention in the inventor's mind,[77] while "reduction to practice" is either the actual successful construction and operation of the invention,[78] or the filing of the United States patent application directed to the invention.[79] The respective dates on which conception and reduction to practice occur for each of the competing parties must be established to ultimately determine which of the parties is entitled to the patent.

Although §§102(a), (b), and (e) are quite different from §§102(c), (d), (f), and (g), they all are part of the novelty requirement of the United States Patent Statute. They are similar in that in each case something has occurred, with respect to the identical subject matter sought to be patented, before either the filing of the patent application or the time at which the invention was made, which places the invention in the public domain, or places the patent applicant in the position of being ineligible for a patent on the invention.

2. *The requirement of nonobviousness.* Because the novelty requirement of the United States Patent Law is satisfied if there are any differences between the subject matter sought to be patented and the prior art specified in §102, instances in which a claimed invention is anticipated by prior art acts or disclosures are unusual. Differences typically do exist between what has been known or done before and an invention upon which a patent application is filed.

However, while the existence of such differences is sufficient to

76. *See* 35 U.S.C. §102(g.)

77. *See* Mergenthaler v. Scudder, 11 App. D.C. 264, 1897 C.D. 724 (D.C.Ct.Appls. 1897).

78. *See* Corona Cord Tire Co. v. Dovan Chemical Corp., 276 U.S. 358 (1928); Field v. Knowles, 183 F.2d 593, 86 U.S.P.Q. 373 (C.C.P.A. 1950).

79. *See* Automatic Weighing Machine Co. v. Pneumatic Scale Corp., 166 Fed. 288 (1st Cir. 1909).

satisfy the novelty requirement, the statute additionally requires a minimum level of innovation or a substantial degree of difference from the prior art before a patent may be granted. This is the requirement that an invention must be nonobvious in order for it to be patentable. The most common reason that the later invention would be held ineligible for patent protection is a determination that the invention, though different from the prior art, would nevertheless have been obviously suggested by the prior art.

The requirement of nonobviousness evolved in judicial opinions.[80] It was incorporated into the 1952 Patent Act as §103 of Title 35. Section 103 reads in part as follows:

> A patent may not be obtained though the invention is not identically disclosed or described as set forth in Section 102 of this Title, if the differences between the subject matter sought to be patented and the prior art are such that the subject matter as a whole would have been obvious at the time the invention was made to a person having ordinary skill in the art to which said subject matter pertains.

The reference to §102 in §103 indicates that the prior art to be considered in determining whether or not an invention is obvious comprises the types of prior art described in §102. It is certain from the relevant court decisions that the prior art acts and disclosures set forth in §§102(a), (b), and (e) constitute prior art that can be considered in determining patentability under §103.[81]

There has recently been a great deal of controversy over the question of whether §102(g) defines prior art that may be used to hold an invention obvious. The United States Court of Customs and Patent Appeals in one case attempted to decide the very complex legal question posed by the action of the patent office in rejecting an application on the ground that the invention was obvious from the prior invention of another patent holder.[82] The lengthy opinions by different judges on the court presented the many considerations pro and con. Although no conclusive holding on that difficult issue of law emerged from the court's decision, it does appear that the Court of Customs and Patent Appeals leans toward the view that any prior art described in any provision of §102 is prior art that may be relied upon in refusing a patent under §103, where the differences are only obvious.

It can be expected that this question will again be put before the courts in the United States. A firm decision either way could have an

80. *See* Rich, *Laying the Ghost of the "Invention" Requirement*, 1 A.P.L.A. Q. J. 24 (1972); Mintz & O'Rourke, *After Black Rock: New Tests of Patentability—The Old Tests of Invention*, 39 G.W.L. Rev. 123 (1970).

81. *See* Hazeltine Research, Inc. v. Brenner, 382 U.S. 252, 147 U.S.P.Q. 429 (1965); In re Harry, 333 F.2d 920, 142 U.S.P.Q. 164 (C.C.P.A. 1964).

82. In re Bass, 474 F.2d 1276, 177 U.S.P.Q. 178 (C.C.P.A. 1973).

important impact upon United States practice in the area of the application of the statutory nonobviousness requirement of 35 U.S.C. §103.

Despite the reference in §103 to the time the invention was made, the times set forth in the pertinent provision of §102 apply in determining whether a prior art, act, or disclosure is available in determining obviousness. Thus, if an application is directed to an invention that differs in only an obvious way from an invention described in a printed publication more than one year prior to the date of the application, the applicant is not allowed to show that his invention was made prior to the printed publication. The one-year bar of §102(b) discussed above applies equally to §103, where the differences are such that the application claims only an invention obvious over the prior art.[83]

In the usual case involving the issue of obviousness, the determinative question is whether or not the differences between the prior art and the invention sought to be patented are such that the subject matter claimed in the application would have been obvious to a person having ordinary skill in the pertinent art. The test of obviousness under United States law has never been defined with absolute precision, and since it is a relative concept, it really cannot be set forth with any kind of accuracy. It is a legal conclusion that must be drawn by the patent office or a court based on the particular facts of the individual case.

In *Graham* v. *John Deere Company*,[84] the Supreme Court of the United States set forth a general approach to determining obviousness:

> . . . under §103, the scope and content of the prior art are to be determined; differences between the prior art and the claims at issue are to be ascertained; and the level of ordinary skill in the pertinent art resolved. Against this background, the obviousness or nonobviousness of the subject matter is determined. Such secondary considerations as commercial success, long felt but unsolved needs, failure of others, etc., might be utilized to give light to the circumstances surrounding the origin of the subject matter sought to be patented. As indicia of obviousness or nonobviousness, these inquiries may have relevancy. See Note, Subtests of 'Nonobviousness,' 112 U.Pa. L.Rev. 1169 (1964).

Following the guidelines of the Supreme Court, prior patents, publications, and other prior art constituting evidence of obviousness or nonobviousness are analyzed to determine the differences between

83. In re Foster, 343 F.2d 980, 145 U.S.P.Q. 166 (1965), *cert. den.*, 383 U.S. 966, 149 U.S.P.Q. 906 (1966). *See also* In re Collins, 462 F.2d 538, 174 U.S.P.Q. 333 (C.C.P.A. 1972).

84. 383 U.S. 1, 17–18, 148 U.S.P.Q. 459, 467 (1966).

the invention and the prior art, and to assess the level of ordinary skill in the pertinent art.[85] The inventor may be able to provide evidence tending to show that the prior art does not make the invention obvious. For example, evidence of unexpected and improved results flowing from the use of the invention often weighs heavily in favor of a conclusion of nonobviousness.[86]

In addition, such factors as the satisfaction of a need long felt by an industry, commercial success indicating acceptance of the invention by the industry as an advance, and radical departure from the direction of previous attempts to solve a long standing problem are considerations that, as indicated in the Supreme Court's opinion in the *Graham* v. *John Deere* case, can lead to a conclusion that the invention would not have been obvious to one of ordinary skill in the pertinent art.[87]

The final conclusion as to whether or not an invention is obvious is one that must be based upon all of the available evidence, including the relevant prior art and any evidence provided by the inventor, such as discussed above, that may tend to indicate nonobviousness.[88] In the end, patentability under §103 of the United States Patent Statute must be decided on the basis of all the facts of each individual case, and it has proven very difficult to establish specific guidelines useful in a broad range of fact situations.

Under Article 29-2 of the Patent Law of Japan, inventions that "could have easily been accomplished prior to the patent application" on the basis of the prior art, are not patentable. No comparable provision existed in the Patent Law of 1921, but in actual practice under the earlier law, a similar test had been applied by the patent office in judging whether an idea amounted to a patentable invention or whether an invention was novel.[89] The evolution of the additional requirement of patentability, that an invention must not only be new, but also must attain a minimum level of difference, into a statutory condition is comparable to the development of §103 in the United States Patent Law.

85. *See* In re Fielder, 471 F.2d 640, 176 U.S.P.Q. 300 (C.C.P.A. 1973); In re Palmer, 451 F.2d 1100, 172 U.S.P.Q. 126 (C.C.P.A. 1971).

86. *See* In re Orfeo, 440 F.2d 439, 169 U.S.P.Q. 487 (C.C.P.A. 1971); In re Fenton, 451 F.2d 640, 171 U.S.P.Q. 693 (C.C.P.A. 1971).

87. *See* Ingersoll-Rand Co. v. Brunner & Lay, Inc., 474 F.2d 491, 177 U.S.P.Q. 112 (5th Cir. 1973); Reeves Instrument Corp. v. Beckman Instruments, Inc., 444 F.2d 263, 170 U.S.P.Q. 74 (9th Cir. 1971), *cert. den.*, 404 U.S. 951, 171 U.S.P.Q. 641 (1971).

88. In re Freeman, 474 F.2d 1318, 177 U.S.P.Q. 139 (C.C.P.A. 1973); In re Fielder, 471 F.2d 640, 176 U.S.P.Q. 300 (C.C.P.A. 1973).

89. Koike Sanso K. K. v. Director-General of the Patent Office, 10 Gyōsei Reishū 774 (Tokyo High Ct. 1959); Dow Chemical Co. v. Director-General of the Patent Office, 14 Gyōsei Reishū 326, Tokyo High Ct. 1963).

Although the language of Article 29-2 of the Patent Law of Japan differs from the language of 35 U.S.C. §103, in operation the test of patentability is quite similar. In the application of Article 29-2, the patent office compares the purpose, construction, and effect of the invention and the prior art. The patent office considers an invention obvious if it consists of an easily accomplished aggregation, mere conversion, or mere replacement of known technology, or if it consists of an easily made change of use or form of known technology and the effects of the change can be anticipated, or if it consists merely of a readily accomplished change of factors such as measurements, temperatures, or conditions, the effects of which can be anticipated.[90]

Despite these broad negative tests for obviousness, the details actually considered in determining patentability under Article 29-2 are substantially similar to those considered under the United States law of obviousness. Patents are granted where there are substantial differences in results,[91] where simple expedients give substantial benefits,[92] and where troublesome steps can be omitted without changing the results.[93]

In arguing for patentability in the United States, the vocabulary, emphasis, and form of the argument or evidence may be somewhat different from that used in Japan. However, because the patent systems of the two nations are so much alike in their philosophical bases, an invention that is novel and that differs sufficiently from the prior art to advance the industry to which it is connected may usually be expected to be patentable in both nations.

Where there is a marginal case involving an invention that is very close to the prior art, and where the significance of the innovation may be doubtful or difficult to prove, disparities can develop. In addition, differences in the nature of the prior art under the laws of Japan and the United States, discussed above in connection with the novelty requirement, could lead to differences in the determination of patentability of the same invention in the two countries. By and large, however, it would appear that the similarities in application of 35 U.S.C. § 103 and Article 29-2 of the Patent Law of Japan far outweigh the differences.

90. Tokkyōchō, Shinsakijun No Tebiki §3.3 (4th ed. 1970).

91. Temler Werke Vereinigte Chemische Fabriken v. Director-General of the Patent Office, 3 American Chamber of Commerce in Japan, Digest of Japanese Court Decisions in Patentability and Patent Infringement Cases 8 (Tokyo High Ct. 1966) (hereinafter referred to as Japanese Patent Digest); Yonehara v. Director-General of the Patent Office, 9 Gyōsei Reishū 234 (Tokyo High Ct. 1958).

92. Kato v. Director-General of the Patent Office, 3 Japanese Patent Digest 5 (Tokyo High Ct. 1966).

93. Toyo Koatsu, K. K. v. Director-General of the Patent Office, 2 Japanese Patent Digest 1 (Tokyo High Ct. 1964).

D. Disclosure Requirements

Under the patent systems of both the United States and Japan there must be a disclosure of the invention, so that the public can ultimately realize a benefit from the grant of patent rights. This disclosure is embodied in the patent application and the laws of each nation include provisions governing the type of disclosure that must be presented in the patent application. In general intent, the disclosure requirements of the patent laws of the two nations are substantially the same.

Section 112 of the United States Code requires a patent specification that is adequate to enable any person skilled in the art to make and use the invention. Likewise, Article 36 of the Patent Law of Japan mandates that the patent application explain the invention in sufficient detail so that any person having knowledge in the art can "easily effect the working thereof."

Both 35 U.S.C. §112 and Article 36 of the Patent Law of Japan also require the patent application to set forth the scope of the invention sought to be patented. The demands or claims of the patent are the measure of the rights that the patentee acquires. A clear description of the invention in the claims affords the critical working definition of the invention and thereby informs both the patent owner and the public of the bounds of the patentee's rights.

The adequacy of the patent specification and the definitiveness of the patent claims have always been matters of importance under United States law, and are particularly significant during the period when the application is being examined by the patent office. At this stage, the opportunity exists either to improve the language of the specification or claims by amendment, or to file a new application having an expanded disclosure, if necessary, without an unduly long period of time passing after the filing of the initial application. Satisfaction of the disclosure requirements of the United States Patent Law has also been important in determining whether an issued patent is valid and can be enforced in court against an accused infringer of the patent.

In recent years, the United States Court of Customs and Patent Appeals, in its review of patent office decisions refusing to allow patents, has commented extensively upon the requirements imposed by 35 U.S.C. §112. Its opinions have clarified considerably the various aspects of these disclosure rules. Some of the details are of particular interest to applicants for United States patents, who are nationals of other countries.

The Court of Customs and Patent Appeals has held that, for an applicant to be entitled to the filing date of a foreign application, the disclosure of the *priority* application must satisfy the United States disclosure requirements as set forth in §112.[94] This means that an inventor in a country foreign to the United States who intends to file in his own country and later file in the United States must be aware of, and actually comply with, United States disclosure requirements in his earliest application in his own country if he hopes eventually to obtain the benefit of his earliest filing date in the United States.

The first paragraph of 35 U.S.C. §112 deals with the type of disclosure necessary to provide a satisfactory patent specification. According to the first paragraph of §112, the specification must contain (1) a written description of the invention, (2) a written description of the manner and process of making the invention, (3) a written description of the manner and process of using the invention, and (4) the "best mode" contemplated by the inventor for practicing his invention.

The descriptions of the invention and the manner of making and using it must be in "such full, clear, concise, and exact terms as to enable any person skilled in the art . . . to make and use . . ." the invention. Generally, under both the United States Patent Law and the Japanese Patent Law, a person skilled in the art is a person having common knowledge in the field of technology to which the invention relates.

The specification must fulfill the conditions imposed by §112 as of the filing date,[95] and the addition of "new matter" to the application after its filing date is prohibited.[96] The Court of Customs and Patent Appeals has stated that "an important purpose of Section 112, first paragraph . . . is the definition of the attributes which a patent specification must possess as of the filing date to be entitled to that filing date as a *prima facie* date of invention."[97]

The first requirement of §112 is that there be a written description of the invention. This has been called the "description requirement."[98] Claims are presented with the application as filed, but often, and in fact, usually, the claims undergo amendment during prosecution before the patent office. The requirement that there be a written description of the invention really means that claims presented after the filing date must comport with the original specification disclosure.

There does not have to be a literal correspondence between a subsequently presented claim and language in the original specification

94. Kawai v. Metlesics, 480 F.2d 880, 178 U.S.P.Q. 158 (C.C.P.A. 1973).

95. Tummers v. Kleimack, 455 F.2d 566, 568, 172 U.S.P.Q. 592, 593 (C.C.P.A. 1972).

96. 35 U.S.C. §132.

97. In re Smith, 481 F.2d 910, 914, 178 U.S.P.Q. 620, 623 (C.C.P.A. 1973).

98. Martin v. Johnson, 454 F.2d 746, 172 U.S.P.Q. 391 (C.C.P.A. 1972); Fields v. Conover, 443 F.2d 1386, 170 U.S.P.Q. 276 (C.C.P.A. 1971).

to satisfy the description requirement.[99] Rather, a subsequently presented claim has sufficient support when the "specification as originally filed . . . conveys clearly to those skilled in the art the information that the applicant has invented the specific subject matter later claimed."[100]

The description requirement is of special significance to applicants outside the United States. Where a patent applicant needs to rely upon the convention date, or the date of an earlier filed United States application, the earlier disclosure must be sufficient to teach the invention claimed at a later time. Where claims undergo amendment and the incorporation of new language, it is possible for the original application to lack the necessary support. If this necessary support is absent in the original application, the benefit of the earlier filing date of that application is lost.

One controversial aspect of the requirement for a description of the invention has led to disagreement among different courts. The Second Circuit Court of Appeals has held that §112 requires disclosure of properties of a chemical composition upon which the patentee relies for patentability.[101] In that case, the court gave no weight to evidence that was asserted to prove unexpected results because of the failure of the patent to disclose the unexpected properties and results. Presumably, this would also apply to other types of advantages flowing from inventions other than chemical compositions.

The Court of Customs and Patent Appeals has held that §112 imposes no requirement that an applicant disclose all properties of chemical compounds or chemical compositions in his application.[102] The court agreed with the patent office that it was reasonable to require the applicant to include in his application statements regarding the properties relied upon for patentability, but only so long as inclusion in the application would not be at the sacrifice of the filing date. This conflict over disclosure of properties or results relied upon for patentability has yet to be resolved. As a matter of proper practice, the patent application as filed should disclose all of the advantages, properties, and results of the invention of which the inventor is aware.

The specification must be "enabling" both as to how to make and how to use the invention. These are the second and third requirements of the first paragraph of §112. The explanation is addressed to

99. In re Lukach, 442 F.2d 967, 169 U.S.P.Q. 795 (C.C.P.A. 1971).

100. In re Smith, 481 F.2d 910, 914, 178 U.S.P.Q. 620, 624 (C.C.P.A. 1973). *See also* In re Smythe, 480 F.2d 1376, 178 U.S.P.Q. 279 (C.C.P.A. 1973); In re Ruschig, 379 F.2d 990, 154 U.S.P.Q. 118 (C.C.P.A. 1967).

101. Carter-Wallace, Inc. v. Otte, 474 F.2d 529, 176 U.S.P.Q. 2 (2nd Cir. 1972), *on rehearing*, 474 F.2d 529, 176 U.S.P.Q. 452 (2nd Cir. 1973).

102. In re Davies, 475 F.2d 667, 177 U.S.P.Q. 381 (C.C.P.A. 1973).

those persons skilled in the art and therefore things which are known in the art related to the invention need not be spelled out in the specification. In fact, an applicant can submit prior art publications to establish that the specification as originally filed is adequate, if faced with a rejection of his application on the ground that it is not sufficient to enable one skilled in the art to make and use the invention.[103] The general test is whether one skilled in the art could make or use the invention, given the specification disclosure, "without undue experimentation."[104]

Where the patent specification sets forth in sufficient detail the way to make the invention and the way to use the invention, the patent office must accept the truth of the statements made in the specification unless it has some evidence suggesting that the invention cannot be made or used in the manner asserted in the application.[105] To respond to a patent office decision that the invention cannot be used as set forth in the specification, the patent applicant may be required to prove that it has utility where the patent office says it does not, or he may be able to meet the examiner's objection by limiting the scope of the claims to a point where the patent office believes that the utility is commensurate with the more limited scope.

The "best mode" requirement is designed to prevent the patent applicant from concealing, and thereby preserving for himself, the most advantageous manner of using the invention while presenting to the public less desirable modes.[106] The requirement means that the applicant must present what he believes to be the best mode. This aspect of §112 does not come into question frequently.

The second paragraph of §112 of Title 35 of the U.S. Code provides that the specification must contain claims that point out with particularity and distinctness the "subject matter which the applicant regards as his invention." This requirement is satisfied so long as the claims of the application are free of vagueness or lack of definiteness,[107] and so long as there is no conflicting evidence suggesting that the inventor actually regards as his invention something different from, or narrower than, the invention as defined in the claims.[108]

Article 36-2 of the Patent Law of Japan requires a patent applicant

103. *See* In re Brebner, 455 F.2d 1402, 173 U.S.P.Q. 169 (C.C.P.A. 1972).

104. *See* In re Eynde, 480 F.2d 1364, 1370, 178 U.S.P.Q. 470, 474 (C.C.P.A. 1973).

105. *See* In re Gardner, 475 F.2d 1389, 177 U.S.P.Q. 396 (C.C.P.A. 1973); In re Marzocchi, 439 F.2d 220, 169 U.S.P.Q. 367 (C.C.P.A. 1971).

106. *See* In re Gay, 309 F.2d 769, 135 U.S.P.Q. 311 (C.C.P.A. 1962).

107. In re Wakefield, 422 F.2d 897, 164 U.S.P.Q. 636 (C.C.P.A. 1970); In re Borkowski, 422 F.2d 904, 164 U.S.P.Q. 642 (C.C.P.A. 1970).

108. In re Borkowski, 422 F.2d 904, 164 U.S.P.Q. 642 (C.C.P.A. 1970); In re Prater, 415 F.2d 1393, 162 U.S.P.Q. 541 (C.C.P.A. 1969).

to submit, together with the application, a specification stating the title of the invention and containing a brief explanation of the drawing (if necessary), a detailed explanation of the invention, and a description of the scope claimed for the patent. As noted above, Article 36-4 provides that the detailed explanation of the invention must contain a statement of the purpose, composition, and effect of the invention so that those having the ordinary skill of the art to which the invention pertains can easily work the invention.

It would appear that the United States requirements are to some extent more stringent than the comparable Japanese patent law requirements for disclosure, but certainly the overall purpose is similar. For those who intend to file first in Japan and then in the United States, compliance with United States requirements should satisfy Japanese requirements and also afford the benefit of the Japanese filing date to the United States application.

In the description of the scope claimed for the patent "only the matter indispensable to the construction of the invention described in the detailed explanation of the invention shall be stated."[109] In the United States, it is generally preferred practice, where possible, to restrict the claims similarly to the crux of the invention. Indeed, the second paragraph of §112 requires that the claims "particularly point out and distinctly claim" the invention. However, the inclusion of what might be considered superfluous matter in the claims does not ordinarily give rise to a rejection of the claims.

The rights afforded under the patent systems of both Japan and the United States do not flow automatically from the creation of a patentable invention. A full and clear expression of the invention in writing in accordance with the disclosure requirements of the patent laws of both countries is an essential step in the acquisition of patent rights. Satisfaction of the disclosure requirements is a matter that deserves meticulous attention, and its importance should not be underestimated.

III. Conclusion

In any given country, the area of patent law is ordinarily a distinct, and unique field within its general body of laws. However, minimization of the differences between the patent laws of one country and of others throughout the world is beneficial in promoting advantageous international economic and political interactions.

Comparison of the patent systems of the United States and Japan

109. Article 36-5.

reveals that, although there are differences, the overall contours of the respective patent systems are fairly similar. The development of an invention, application for a patent on the invention, and rights flowing from the grant of the patent are sufficiently alike that, in the majority of instances, harmony can be expected between an inventor's posture, from a patent law standpoint, both in Japan and in the United States.

The Protection of Unpatented Know-how and Trade Secrets in the United States and Japan

JOHN LYON AND TERUO DOI

I. INTRODUCTION

The United States and Japan both have highly industrialized economies based on technology. In both countries industrial technology has become highly complex and is becoming more so. "New" areas of industrial enterprise, such as oceanography, space technology, and atomic energy, dramatically embody this trend. Equivalent changes mark "older" technological industries, such as aviation, chemical, electronics, and others.

Two corollaries of this change are of special importance to attorneys who counsel industrial clients in the United States and Japan. First, the value of the clients' technologies is increasingly likely to be substantial, either in its importance to the individual client's operations, or in its earning power when licensed, or both. The value of technology to competitors likewise increases, and there has been a corresponding growth in efforts to learn, one way or another, what secrets the competition has. The need for protection of technology is correspondingly increased, and the lawyer plays a major role in that protection.

The second corollary of the growth in technological complexity is that "know-how," or, the methods and techniques by which inventions are reduced to practice, or the bridging of theory and application, correspondingly grows in complexity, and so provides an increasingly valuable competitive advantage to its possessor. Know-how is, in general, unpatentable, because it is not sufficiently novel or inventive. It must be protected by secrecy rather than by statutory monopoly.

Even patentable technology may, of course, be kept secret by choice. If it appears that its importance will extend substantially beyond the statutory term of a patent, and if it seems feasible that its secrecy may be preserved indefinitely, or if its patentability is doubtful, so that an issued patent may be highly vulnerable to successful attack in the courts, secrecy may be preferable.

Technological know-how of these types is the subject of this study. In both the United States and Japan such know-how is a highly developed and essential part of the industrial base, and there is and will continue to be an important interchange of know-how between the two countries.[1] Yet the difference between the legal status accorded know-how in the two countries is striking.

The authors of this paper have attempted to set forth a summary of the relevant law of each country that will serve as a useful introduction to lawyers of both countries. Some of the discussion may accordingly seem elementary to the domestic reader, although novel and valuable to the foreign reader.

For example, it is important to note that in the United States, a common-law country, the law in the area of technological know-how is largely judge-made law discoverable only by a critical reading of a multitude of decisions. Also important is the federal system in the United States. The legal problems of our area of concern are usually governed by state law, which is not uniform in the fifty states, and are resolved sometimes by state courts and sometimes by federal courts applying state law. The predictable confusion, conflict, and lack of uniformity exists on many points. In the United States, in short, there is a great deal of relevant law, but because it is embodied in numerous decisions made by diverse tribunals, it is often difficult to determine the controlling principle in a particular situation.

On the other hand, Japan is a civil-law country, and its codes and statutes do not deal at all with know-how. Indeed, it appears that the entire body of Japanese know-how law consists of a single case of inconclusive result. It is as difficult to predict results in Japan as it is in the United States, but for the reason that there is too little law, rather than too much.

The legal terminology of one country may also sometimes be puzzling to a foreign lawyer. The authors have attempted to clarify the meaning of various words in the text which follows. At the outset, it must be explained that in contrast to most other countries, the United

1. An interesting economic discussion appears in U.N. Dept. of Economic & Social Affairs, *The Role of Patents in the Transfer of Technology to Developing Countries* (Report of the Secretary General) U.N. Doc. E/3861/Rev. 1 (1964). Concerning the protection of know-how in Belgium, Czechoslovakia, Federal Republic of Germany, Italy, Japan, the Netherlands, Poland, Rumania, Spain, Sweden, Switzerland, United States and Yugoslavia, *see* THE PROTECTION OF KNOW-HOW IN THIRTEEN COUNTRIES (Jehoram, ed. 1972).

States does not have a category of law clearly labelled as "know-how law." The term does not even appear in most general indexes, digests, dictionaries, or other research aids. Instead, "know-how" is governed by the law of "trade secrets." However, a contract that involves disclosure of technical information on a license basis is commonly referred to as "know-how" licensing, rather than "trade secrets" licensing. It may be said, subject to qualification depending on the intention of the parties, that the term "know-how licensing" implies a continuous flow of information from the licensor to the licensee, while the term "trade secrets licensing" implies transfer of the licensor's existing technical information.[2]

The term "trade secret" is broader than "know-how," and the law of trade secrets long antedates the new technology. Practically everything a businessman might want kept confidential for one reason or another—customer lists, sources of supply, plans for new or changed products, advertising campaigns, etc.—has been denominated a trade secret and protected. These nontechnological assets are not of direct interest in this study. In the United States, however, they are included in the term "trade secret." This inclusion has influenced the law and cannot be ignored. Notice for example this typical definition of "trade secret":[3] "A trade secret may consist of a formula, process, device or compilation which one uses in his business and which gives him an opportunity to obtain an advantage over competitors who do not know or use it."

A modern attempt to delineate a narrower area of technological trade secrets is made in this statute:[4]

> "Secret scientific material" means a sample, culture, microorganism, specimen, record, recording, document, drawing or any other article, material, device or substance which constitutes, represents, evidences, reflects, or records a scientific or technical process, invention or formula or any part or phase thereof, and which is not, and is not intended to be, available to anyone other than the person or persons rightfully in possession thereof or selected persons having access thereto with his or their consent, and when it accords or may accord such rightful possessors an advantage over competitors or other persons who do not have knowledge or the benefit thereof.

2. *See* the discussion, Eckstrom, *Industrial Foreign Licensing Agreements*, in A LAWYER'S GUIDE TO INTERNATIONAL BUSINESS TRANSACTIONS 127 (W. Surrey & C. Shaw ed. 1963).

3. RESTATEMENT OF TORTS §757, comment (b) at 5 (1939). This definition has been frequently cited in opinions: *see, e.g.*, Sun Dial Corp. v. Rideout, 16 N.J. 252, 108 A.2d 442 (1954).

4. N.Y. PENAL LAW §155.00(6) (McKinney 1967). The statute defines the physical embodiment of the secret, not the secret itself; a wise limitation in a penal code. Theft of "secret scientific material" is a felony, *id.* §155.30(3), as is its unauthorized copying with intent to appropriate the use thereof, *id.* §165.07.

For the purposes of our discussion, this definition adequately describes the interests to be considered. While the term "trade secret" will frequently be employed, our study deals with the narrower area of technological know-how, save for occasional illustrative references to other kinds of trade secrets used to show their influence on the development of the law.

We have not attempted to give a definitive treatment of trade secret law in the United States. Such an effort would requre, at the least, a lengthy treatise. Several such books, of good quality and relatively recent publication, are available to persons desiring a more detailed coverage of the field.[5]

This study is limited to the parts of the law of trade secrets most likely to be of concern to a Japanese or United States attorney working for a client on the licensing and protection of technology. It emphasizes the problems and issues that must be recognized. The solutions are of course shaped by the particular circumstances.

II. Basis of Protection of Know-how

In the United States the theoretical basis for the protection of know-how has evolved on a case-by-case basis, and the general theory can be learned only from a study of the many relevant decisions. As will be evident, there is a substantial quantity of applicable United States case law, and, although confusion or uncertainty exists on many points, there is no doubt that the owner of unpatented know-how or trade secrets enjoys substantial legal protection.

To what extent an owner of unpatented know-how or trade secrets is protected under the existing Japanese law is uncertain. Japan has no legislation squarely dealing with the subject matter as does Germany in the German Law of 1909 concerning Prevention of Unfair Competition.[6] Nor does Japan have a body of case law such as the United States law, which is discussed in the following pages.[7] That there are problems in this area is well recognized. The increase of know-how transactions with foreign countries, including licensing

5. For example, R. Milgrim, Trade Secrets Rev. 1974; A. Turner, The Law of Trade Secrets (1962), which also covers British law; E. Ellis, Trade Secrets (1953). The special case of employees is covered in J. Costa, The Law of Inventing in Employment (1953). A shorter but good treatment appears in 2 R. Callman, Unfair Competition and Trade-marks Ch. 14 (2d ed. 1950). A survey of industrial practices in the area is found in Harris & Siegal, *Protection of Trade Secrets: Initial Reports*, 8 P.T.C.J. Res. & Ed. (now Idea) 360 (1964).

6. *Gesetz gegen den unlauteren Wettbewerb* (U.W.G.). *See* Krasser, *Protection of Know-how in Germany* in The Protection of Know-How in Thirteen Countries (Jehoram, ed. 1972).

7. For comparative study of know-how protection including Japan, *see* T. Doi. Nou-hau (Know-how) (1966).

and investment in exchange for shares of a newly organized corporation, has induced much discussion of know-how in recent years. This is an age of severe competition in technology, and Japanese industries have become keenly aware of the danger of industrial espionage.[8]

The authors will first discuss the theoretical basis of know-how protection as it has evolved in the United States and will then examine the aspects of Japanese patent law and the general tort principles that are relevant to the problem in Japan.

A. Theory of Protection of Trade Secrets in the United States

The basic theory of judicial protection of trade secrets in the United States is not at all clear. It is not that discussions of theory do not exist, but rather that there are too many. Various cases contain a number of explanations, supporting seemingly incongruous if not contradictory theories, none of which adequately explains the results of all the cases. From time to time some doughty clearer of underbrush attempts to restore or, rather, to create simplicity and unity. Mr. Justice Holmes, for example, made one such attempt, with his revelation that it was all nothing more than a matter of confidential relations.[9] But trade secrets are protected where no sort of confidential relation existed between the parties;[10] and no effort to unify the law of trade secrets has won universal acceptance.

The real obstacle to clarity is one which is not unique to the law of trade secrets. It is the slippery and elusive nature of ideas considered as things. The law is not yet able to deal sensibly and consistently with "intellectual property" because, by and large, there is no adequate language to be employed in such dealing. Philosophers and logicians, having developed their own jargon, may be comfortable in the area, but the rest of the world, including lawyers, deals with ideas by analogy, as though they were only another sort of personalty like automobiles or furniture. It is straightforward enough to provide a measure of protection to the paper and ink that are the corporeal manifestation of, say, a secret process. Traditional principles prohibit the theft of the paper and ink or their copying, support an order for their return by a wrongful possessor, regulate their transfer, and, in short, deal conventionally and predictably with them. The law of trade secrets, however, is really concerned with the ideas expressed in

8. Illustrative is *Sangyo supai o umu mono* (Causes for industrial espionage), Asahi Shimbun, 16 Nov. 1967, P. 3, Col. 1.

9. *See* his opinion in E.I. du Pont de Nemours Powder Co. v. Masland, 244 U.S. 100, 102 (1917).

10. *E.g.*, Cincinnati Bell Foundry Co. v. Dodds, 10 Ohio Dec. Reprint 154 (Super. Ct. Cincinnati 1887).

these physical embodiments, and not, except peripherally, with the paper and ink. Here both jurisprudence and the English language falter. If *A* conceives a valuable idea, and keeps it secret, *A* "owns" it; it is his "property", or, at least, so say some of the cases. If *B* independently conceives the identical idea, and keeps it secret, *B* "owns" his idea as well. If the ideas are identical, are there one or two? If there is only one, do *A* and *B* each own it—intellectual tenants by the entirety, as it were—or do they each own an undivided one-half? When, in preparation for licensing, *A* discloses his idea to *C* (under appropriate safeguards), and *C* understands it, are there now one, two, or three ideas?

These questions are of course absurd. If they are reminiscent of the medieval concerns of the Scholastics, it is not coincidental; for it is from them that we derive, with only slight modification, our unexamined notions of these matters. So long as we persist in thinking of an idea as a thing comparable to a chair or an acre of land, confusion will persist. A new generation of lawyers, exposed to analytic philosophy and the new math, may come to terms with the ultimate mystery of trade secrets. For the present, the prudent practitioner will so order the protection of his client's trade secrets that any or all of the theories can be made to fit, as the occasion dictates.

Only rarely will the theory make any predictable difference, and this fact is a further reason for the continuing confusion. In general, no one's rights or obligations are likely to turn on the question of which theory is invoked (indeed, if anything, the contrary is true: the rights of the parties may determine which theory is invoked), and, accordingly, no one has a reason to press for the establishment of clarity.

Nevertheless, there exists an occasional transaction in which results are mandated by the choice of theory. Different statutes of limitation may govern under different theories.[11] If the wrongful use of a trade secret by the United States government is a tort, one remedy is available,[12] but if it is a breach of contract, there is another.[13]

Good cause, therefore, exists to survey the various theories which the courts have considered in cases involving the protection of trade secrets.

1. The Property Theory. The senior theory of trade secret law is that they are a form of property, comparable to real or tangible personal

11. *See, e.g.*, Petnel v. American Tel. & Tel. Co., 280 App. Div. 706, 117 N.Y.S. 2d 294 (1952): Sachs v. Cluett, Peabody & Co., 265 App. Div. 497, 39 N.Y.S. 2d 853 (1943), *aff'd*, 291 N.Y. 772, 53 N.E. 2d 241 (1944).

12. Aktiebolaget Bofors v. United States, 194 F.2d 145 (D.C. Cir. 1951).

13. Aktiebolaget Bofors v. United States, 153 F.Supp. 397 (Ct. Cl. 1957).

property, and will be protected as such. The classic American exposition of this theory is in *Peabody* v. *Norfolk*,[14] which is noteworthy also for the court's reliance on most of the other theories. The plaintiff, an inventor of certain machines and the process for making them, sought an injunction against a former employee and another defendant. The former employee had agreed in a written contract to act as the plaintiff's engineer and to keep confidential all information concerning the subject machinery and its method of manufacture. When he left the plaintiff's employ, however, he agreed to build for the second defendant, who knew of the nondisclosure contract, a factory, disclosing and using the secret information. The court affirmed the grant of an injunction saying:[15]

> If he [plaintiff] invents or discovers, and keeps secret, a process of manufacture, whether a proper subject for a patent or not, he has not indeed an exclusive right to it as against the public or as against those who in good faith acquire knowledge of it; but he has a property in it, which a court of chancery will protect against one who in violation of contract and breach of confidence undertakes to apply it to his own use, or to disclose it to third persons. The jurisdiction in equity to interfere by injunction to prevent such breach of trust, when the injury would be irreparable and the remedy at law inadequate, is well established by authority.

The court principally relied upon the theory that a secret process constitutes property. An important right associated with the concept of property is the right of the owner to exclude others from the use of the property. While this right may be limited, regulated, or circumscribed, some vestige of it must remain to justify the use of the word "property." Here, in the court's conception, the process idea is reduced to ownership by the act of rightfully acquiring possession of it, in the first instance by inventing or discovering it. Ownership is then preserved by keeping it secret. Unrestricted communication of the idea would destroy its exclusivity and thus its status as property.

It is therefore a necessary corollary of the property theory that to preserve the property, the idea must be communicated, if at all, accompanied by restrictions on its further transfer or use. The restrictions may be explicit as in an express contract, or they may be implicit as in the "confidential" relationship of inventor and engineer, which is discussed in detail below.

Another illustrative decision is *Cincinnati Bell Foundry Co.* v. *Dodds*.[16] The opinion is by Judge, later Chief Justice, Taft, who saw the property theory as important because the plaintiff was a purchaser rather

14. 98 Mass. 452 (1868).
15. *Id.*
16. 10 Ohio Dec. Reprint 154 (Super. Ct. Cincinnati 1887).

than the "inventor or discoverer" of a process. Plaintiff bought a bell foundry and with it a secret process used in the manufacture of bells. An employee of the selling company, who had learned the secret process while in the latter's employ, proposed to use and to disclose the secret. Plaintiff sued for and obtained a preliminary injunction, which the defendant moved to dissolve, arguing that, as he did not have and never had had a confidential relation with the plaintiff, it followed that the plaintiff had no direct rights against him. Instead, he claimed, the plaintiff was relegated to a sort of derivative action, suing the employer–vendor who would in turn sue him. Taft rejected this defense, relying on the theory that the alleged secret process was a property that could be sold with its attendant rights:[17]

> The principles of law governing the consideration of this case therefore are:
>
> *1st.* That the inventor of a secret process has a property right in it which he may call upon a court of equity to protect him in against the use or disclosure of the secret by any person acquiring knowledge of it in confidence.
>
> *2nd.* That the inventor may sell the secret and all his property in it and thereby vest in the purchaser as full rights as he himself has to protection against its use or disclosure by any one who may have acquired knowledge of it in confidence from the inventor or himself.

In this case, while other theories could have been employed to reach the same result, the property concept was an undoubted convenience. For the same reason, it may be employed where the question involves the status of a trade secret of a bankrupt[18] or the suitability of a trade secret as a contribution to the capital of a newly formed corporation.[19]

17. *Id.*

18. It is property which passes to the trustee: *In re* Bettinger Corp., 197 F.Supp. 273 (D. Mass. 1961).

19. Durand v. Brown, 236 F. 609 (6th Cir. 1916), held that capital stock was properly issued in exchange for the contribution of trade secrets. But the issue usually arises only when the corporation has failed, and the more common outcome is the opposite: *see, e.g.*, Trotts v. Metalmold Corp., 139 Conn. 668, 96 A.2d 798 (1953). In the United States, the usual corporate law is that the directors or incorporators of a newly formed corporation may accept property (or services) for stock, and may fix a monetary value therefor. The directors' action is not subject to review save where a lawsuit is brought by a shareholder, creditor, or other interested party. The value fixed by the directors will be upheld if "reasonable." Japanese readers are cautioned that these principles may vary considerably from one state to another.

In Japan, know-how is treated as property under the Commercial Code and is made subject to the examination of a court-appointed inspector to determine whether it is a proper contribution in kind in exchange for newly issued shares of an existing corporation or shares to be issued by a new corporation. Where contribution of know-how involves a promise to supply future technical information and services, theoretical justification should be supplied under applicable provisions of the Commercial Code. Such a promise is an obligation to the corporation the performance of which depends on the ability and intention of the promisor. In addition, the value of know-how, which

It appears to be the most commonly employed theory at this time.

2. *The Confidential Relation Theory.* A "confidential relation" theory is often separately identified in the United States cases. Obviously, it is not normally inconsistent with the property theory. The two may usually be, and often are, invoked simultaneously.[20] But the "confidential relation" theory has its ardent partisans, of whom Justice Holmes was one. He proclaimed the supremacy of this theory in a leading case, *E.I. du Pont de Nemours Powder Co.* v. *Nasland.*[21] Du Pont sued a former employee, seeking to enjoin him from using processes alleged to be secret and to have been learned by him while in du Pont's employ. In the course of preparation for trial, defendant wished to disclose du Pont's processes to experts aiding his defense, which was that they were not secrets but were well known in the trade.[22] The district court forbade the disclosure; the court of appeals reversed; and the Supreme Court in reversing the court of appeals, which had analyzed the issue in property terms, said:[23]

> We approach the question somewhat differently. The word "property" as applied to trade-marks and trade secrets is an unanalyzed expression of certain secondary consequences of the primary fact that the law makes some rudimentary requirements of good faith. Whether the plaintiffs have any valuable secret or not the defendant knows the facts, whatever they are, through a special confidence he accepted. The property may be denied but the confidence cannot be. Therefore the starting point for the present matter is not property or due process of law, but that the defendant stood in confidential relations with the plaintiffs, or one of them. These have given place to hostility, and the first thing to be made sure of is that the defendant shall not fraudulently abuse the trust reposed in him. It is the usual incident of confidential relations.

It is not likely—since no such question was presented—that Justice Holmes meant to say that trade secrets would be protected only

depends on the maintenance of secrecy, can be destroyed by improper disclosure as well as by independent discovery by third parties. Despite these difficulties, know-how has been consistently accepted as property and a proper subject of a contribution in kind in exchange for shares. No case has been reported which involves disputes as to the appropriateness of know-how contribution. The practice is supported by commentators. *See* Koseki, *Tokyo chisai ni okeru nou-hau no toriatsukai jisseki* (Treatment of know-how in the Tokyo District Court), SHŌJI HŌMU KENKYŪ (no. 191) 7 (1960). The relevant provisions of the Commercial Code are arts. 168(5), 172, 173, 181 and 280–2.

20. *See, e.g.*, Peabody v. Norfolk, 98 Mass. 452 (1868).

21. 244 U.S. 100, 102 (1917).

22. As a matter of procedure, it is normally possible to conduct trade secret litigation in the United States in such a way that confidentiality is not lost, by taking testimony *in camera*, "sealing" or not reproducing critical parts of the record, and other methods. In Japan, however, there is no procedure for nonpublic trial of such cases, accordingly, prospective plaintiffs must face the probable loss of secrecy if they bring suit. For this reason, the *inclusion in licenses of arbitration provisions* is desirable.

23. 244 U.S. at 102.

against abuse of confidential relations. If protection were so circumscribed, there would be no relief against the outright thief or spy, for example, or against anyone who wrongfully or unfairly comes into possession of trade secrets outside of a relation of confidence or trust. The "property" theory more readily fits these cases, and its more universal applicability probably explains its continued supremacy.

There are situations in which "confidential relations" is more apt than "property," and in those situations the appropriate "theory" will be employed. The most common instance is that in which the defendant could have learned the secret process legitimately, albeit with some expenditure of effort, but chose instead to obtain it easily and wrongfully from the plaintiff. For example, in *Smith* v. *Dravo Corp.*,[24] the parties negotiated for the sale of plaintiff's freight-container business to defendant. In the course of the negotiations, which ultimately terminated because the parties could not agree on a selling price, plaintiff disclosed to defendant the construction secrets of its containers. Afterward, defendant commenced the manufacture of similar containers, and plaintiff sued. Defendant, among its other defenses, denied that the matters in question were secret, claiming that they had been disclosed to the public by the public sale of the containers. The court of appeals, reversing a judgment for the defendant, emphasized the theory of confidential relations. The publicly sold containers were not like some simple object that revealed all its details "at a glance." Defendant could have learned all the secrets by painstaking investigation and analysis of the publicly sold containers, which the court agreed would have subjected it to no liability. But it did not thus learn the secrets; instead it wrongfully used the information imparted to it in confidence.

On facts like these, the operation of the property theory is far from obvious. If plaintiff "owned" the construction know-how embodied in its containers, it had a readily defeasible title as against anyone willing to take the trouble to study them. The conscience of the court was shocked by defendant's free ride on plaintiff's efforts, and it somehow seems fairer that defendant, too, should be compelled to invest some labor as a prerequisite to commercial reward. What is really operating here is a sense of outrage at an unjust enrichment, and the confidential relation theory is a convenient rationale.

These two theories, the property theory and the confidential relations theory, are in great part only different points of view. One focuses on the right of plaintiff, the other on the wrong of defendant. They are thus more complementary than contradictory.

24. 203 F.2d 369 (7th Cir. 1953).

Other theories stated in the opinions of American judges are special subdivisions or extensions of one of these two outlooks, particularized in terms of such peculiar circumstances of the individual transaction as an express agreement, an employment relation, or the like.

This discussion has outlined in a general way the theoretical basis of protection in the United States. As previously noted, the law in Japan in this area is much less developed. However, it is helpful to discuss the relevant aspects of the Patent Law of Japan and of the general tort principles.

B. Protection of the Owner of Unpatented Know-how in Japan

1. Under Patent Law. The basic principles of know-how protection in Japan can be best approached by first noting that the general principles provided in Part II of the Model Law for Developing Countries on Inventions[25] are applicable to Japan, except for the provisions concerning remedies. Section 53 of the Model Law (Conditions of Protection of Technical Know-How) provides in Subsection (1) that "Subject to any right conferred by patents in force and the provisions of subsection (2) of the present Section, manufacturing processes or knowledge concerning the use and application of industrial techniques shall be in the public domain." Subsection (2) however states an important exception: "Nevertheless, provided that if these processes and knowledge have not been published or made available to the public, they shall be protected against unlawful use, disclosure or communication by third parties, on condition that the person who has developed them has taken the necessary steps to preserve their secret character."[26] Section 54 (Unlawful Use) defines tortious acts concerning know-how as follows:[27]

> Any use, disclosure, or communication, without the consent of the owner, of the processes and knowledge referred to in Section 53(2) by any person who is aware of their secret character as referred to in Section 53(2), or who could not fail to be aware of such character, shall be deemed to be unlawful.

Section 55 (Independent Acquisition) provides an important exception to this principle as follows:[28]

> Any person who has developed, by his own means, manufacturing processes or knowledge concerning the use and application of industrial

25. United International Bureaux for the Protection of Intellectual Property (B.I.R.P.I.), Model Law for Developing Countries on Inventions Pt. II: Technical know-how (1965) (hereinafter cited as Model Law).

26. *Id.* sec. 53.

27. *Id.* sec. 54.

28. *Id.* sec. 55.

techniques and any person who has legally acquired those processes or that knowledge from the former shall, even if another person has kept secret the same processes and knowledge, be free to use, or communicate them.

If these principles were not recognized in Japan, the patent system would become ineffective. A number of provisions in the Patent Law of Japan[29] are however founded upon these principles. First, an invention that is not kept secret by the inventor lacks patentability; Article 29 provides that an inventor cannot obtain a patent involving the following:[30]

(1) An invention which has been publicly known in Japan prior to a patent application;

(2) An invention which has been publicly worked in Japan prior to a patent application;

(3) An invention which has been described in a publication distributed in Japan or in any foreign country prior to a patent application.

Pending applications are kept secret by the patent office. Officials of the patent office are obligated not to impair the secrecy of inventions under application for patent, and such disclosure would subject them to criminal liability under article 200.[31]

Secondly, article 39(6) indicates:[32]

Any patent application or utility model registration application made by a person who is neither an inventor or originator nor a successor of the right to obtain a patent or utility model registration shall, in respect of the application of the provisions of paragraphs 1 to 4 inclusive, be deemed not to be a patent application or utility model registration application.

To enforce this provision, an examiner is required to refuse approval where the applicant is neither the inventor nor the successor to the right to obtain a patent (art. 49[4]). A person whose invention was wrongfully appropriated by the applicant may file an opposition to the latter's patent application (art. 55).

Thirdly, after a patent is issued to a person who has wrongfully appropriated the invention, the true inventor or the owner of the

29. *Tokkyohō* (Patent Law) (Law No. 121, 1959), in 6 EHS No. 6850A.

30. *Id.* art. 29 (EHS translation).

31. Patent Law art. 200 reads as follows: (*Offense of divulgence of secrecy*) Art. 200. In case any person who is or was an official of the Patent Office has divulged, or has made a surreptitious use of, any secrecy relating to an invention under a patent application that has come to his knowledge in the course of performance of his duty, he shall be punished by penal servitude for not more than one year or by a fine of not more than fifty thousand yen.

32. *Id.* art. 39(6).

invention may demand a trial hearing for invalidation of the patent in accordance with article 123.[33]

Upon publication of a patent application in accordance with article 51, the secret character of the invention is lost, but the applicant will enjoy "the exclusive right to work the invention under such patent application as his business."[34]

In addition, a person who invented first and has been working the invention without losing the secret character of his invention will be entitled to continue working it after a patent is issued on the same invention to a person who made the invention independently and applied for a patent. Article 79 provides:[35]

> Any person who, by making without knowledge of the contents of the invention under a patent application such invention by himself, or by learning without knowledge of the contents of the invention under a patent application from the person who made such invention, actually is engaged in the business . . . in Japan at the time of the patent application . . . shall have a nonexclusive license with respect to the patent right under such patent application within the scope of the invention and the purpose of business under such working or preparation.

Upon publication of the application filed by an independent inventor of the same invention, the owner of know-how changes his status to that of a nonexclusive licensee by prior use.

2. *Under General Tort Principles.* Unlike the German law mentioned above,[36] there is no provision in the Japanese Law to Prevent Unfair Competition[37] that specifically deals with know-how or trade secrets. The director-general of the patent office, testifying before the House of Representatives, Committee on Commerce and Industry was asked about the then recent Toray case involving industrial espionage between rival companies. He stated on 10 November, 1967: "There is no law directly regulating 'industrial espionage.' The Patent Office is considering the submission of a proposal to insert a provision in the present Law to Prevent Unfair Competition in order to suppress acts of unauthorized use of know-how (technical information) of competitors."[38]

33. *Id.* art. 123. It reads as follows: (*Trial hearing for invalidation of patent*) "Art. 123. If a patent falls under any one of the following items, a trial hearing may be demanded in respect of making such patent invalid. In this case, with regard to any patent, the claim for which covers more than two inventions, the demand may be made for each invention: . . . (4) If the patent has been granted to a patent application of a person who is not the inventor and does not succeed to the right to obtain a patent on such invention."

34. *Id.* art. 52(1).

35. *Id.* art. 79.

36. Note 6 *supra*.

37. *Fusei kyōsō bōshihō* (Unfair competition prevention law) (Law No. 14, 1934), in 6 EHS No. 6895.

38. Asahi Shimbun, Nov. 11, 1967, P. 1.

The only case in Japan which mentions the legal status of know-how is *Deutsche Werft Aktiengesellschaft* v. *Chūetsu–Waukesha Yūgen Kaisha*, decided by the Tokyo High Court on 5 September, 1966, in a special appeal from a ruling of the Tokyo District Court that denied a petition for a temporary injunction.[39]

The claimant, Deutsche Werft Aktiengesellschaft, a German company with its principal office in Hamburg, concluded a contract with Waukesha Bearings Corporation, a Wisconsin corporation, by which the claimant granted an exclusive license to manufacture and sell oil-lubricated stern tube sealings for propeller shafts of ships in the United States and Canada using the claimant's know-how. Waukesha agreed to keep the process secret. Waukesha, for the purpose of manufacturing and selling the stern tube sealings in Japan, signed a joint-venture agreement with Chūetsu Metal Works, Ltd., a Japanese corporation, and organized the respondent corporation, Chūetsu–Waukesha Yūgen Kaisha, each party contributing 45 percent of the capital. The respondent started operations, and the claimant filed a petition for a temporary injunction against the respondent, contending that the latter's act of manufacturing and selling the stern tube sealings constituted violation of the contract between the claimant and Waukesha, and that therefore the claimant was entitled to an injunction against both the respondent and Waukesha. The Tokyo District Court denied the injunction, and the claimant appealed, seeking cancellation of the ruling of the Tokyo District Court. As the ground for appeal, the claimant contended:[40]

> [The joint venture company] cannot simply be said to be a third person. It is an alter ego of Waukesha under the veil of a separate corporate personality; it is a dummy of Waukesha Corporation. The Waukesha Corporation has been wrongfully using the corporate veil of the respondent company which it organized and over which it has been exercising control in order to perform an act which violates Waukesha's duty of forbearance towards the claimant under the contract. Hence, it can be properly concluded that the act of the respondent constitutes an act of Waukesha. . . . Since Waukesha and the respondent company jointly performed a tortious act, it must be considered that the claimant company has the right to enjoin such act against the respondent company in the same manner as against Waukesha Corporation.

The Tokyo High Court in dismissing the appeal held as follows:[41]

> No matter how know-how is to be considered under the law, know-how

39. 17 Kakyū minshū 769 (Tokyo High Ct., Sept. 5, 1966); digested in T. Doi, Digest of Selected Japanese Trademark and Unfair Competition Cases with Comments (1971). For comment on this case see, T. Doi, Kokusai torihikiho Hanrei kenkyū (The law of international transactions: Comments on selected cases) 137 (1967).

40. 17 Kakyū minshū at 772–73.

41. *Id.* at 770–71.

> has property value and yet it has not been recognized as a legal right. Under the know-how contract (technological assistance contract), the other contracting party, the licensee (as to the know-how), owes the duty of not disclosing the know-how that it obtains under the contract outside the scope limited by the contract, and such a duty is a contractual obligation. The obligor (not the respondent in this petition) which has revealed the know-how to outsiders in violation of the contract is clearly liable to pay damages under contract law. But if a third person who is not the contracting party is informed of the said know-how by the obligor or obtains the knowledge of it accidentally and engages in manufacturing by using the know-how, it is proper to construe that the claimant is not entitled to an injunction, since there is no specific provision under the present statutes. Although know-how has property value, it cannot be considered, at the present moment, that the law recognizes the effect of a right (whether it is an incorporeal right or a right of obligation) which is enforceable against a third party. Protection of know-how can only be achieved by the effort of the owner to maintain it as an industrial secret and prevent disclosure to others. The respondent Chūetsu–Waukesha Yūgen Kaisha has the obligor as one of its members, and the latter is a party to the aforementioned contract (contributing 45 percent of the capital), and two of the directors were appointed by the obligor company. But the respondent is a third person in a legal sense with regard to the said contract, as admitted by the appellant. Hence, even if it is admissible that the respondent has committed an illegal act by assisting the obligor company in the nonperformance of the latter's duty, the cause for a temporary injunction in the instant petition is not clearly stated.

Although the Tokyo High Court admitted the property value of know-how, it clearly denied injunctive relief against a third party who willfully misappropriated the know-how on the ground that there is no statutory provision to this effect. We must therefore consider to what extent know-how can be protected under the existing provisions of the Civil Code.

The general tort principle is set out in Article 709 of the Civil Code as follows: "A person who, wilfully or negligently, has injured the right of another is bound to compensate him for the damage which has arisen therefrom."[42]

The first question is whether article 709 is available to an owner of know-how who seeks damages for losses caused by its misappropriation. If article 709 is strictly interpreted, an injured party can recover damages only where he can prove that he has a right and that this right was injured. But by a liberal interpretation, it is considered that if the injured party can prove that he has an inviolable interest and this was injured by an illegal act, he can recover. The liberal theory suggests that "injury of right" should be interpreted to mean the

42. Civil Code Art. 709.

existence of "illegality" in the defendant's act.[43] Thus, the owner of know-how can recover damages under article 709 according to this theory.

Kenichiro Osumi, associate justice of the Supreme Court, has written:[44]

> We should recognize the creation of a tort (unlawful act) for infringements of know-how. As already stated, know-how itself possesses an independent property value, but it is not something which is the subject of specific rights; moreover, Civil Code art. 709 makes an "infringement of rights" the requisite for tortious conduct. However, this so-called "infringement of rights" is nothing more than a symbol for illegality, and if we rely on the modern theories which consider a tort to have been created in the case where one has inflicted damage upon another by an illegal act regardless of whether or not a specific right has been infringed, the unlawful infringement of know-how must be recognized as constituting a tort. If one insists on making a problem out of the infringement of right, let us say that people have the right not to be hindered in the pursuance of their business by another as a "right of personality" and that infringement of know-how is an infringement of this right of personality, but I do not feel that it is worthwhile to stretch the argument that far.

As to an injunctive remedy, there is no express provision in article 709, but article 198 provides that "if a possessor is disturbed in his possession, he may by an action for maintenance of possession demand discontinuance of the disturbance as well as reparation in damages."[45] As a proper extension of this provision, injunctive remedy can be granted where the claim is based on ownership or other exclusive rights. The basis for the remedy is considered to be the inviolability of the right in question, and thus the remedy is extendable to certain exclusive rights other than real rights. As to know-how, Justice Osumi, in the same article, states:[46]

> Consequently, for the protection of know-how there is really no alternative in cases where there has been an infringement but to look for a remedy in the general provision of the Civil Code. Yet, even in those instances where there has been a theft of know-how by someone else or some other such unlawful infringement, the right to petition for an injunction is not recognized on this point, since the right to petition for an injunction is also not recognized (where a patent has been applied for), even though after the publication of the patent application the right to receive a patent constitutes the same kind of right of exclusive use as a patent (Patent Law art. 52), this situation probably must be accepted.

43. I. KATO, FUHŌ KŌI (Torts) 30–38 (1957).
44. Osumi, *Know-how and Its Investment*, 1 LAW IN JAPAN 92, 102 (1967).
45. CIVIL CODE Art. 198.
46. Osumi, *supra* note 44, at 101–2.

Justice Osumi's reluctance to conclude that an injunctive remedy is available under the existing law, a view which coincides with the position taken by the Tokyo High Court in the *Chūetsu–Waukesha* case, is based on the absence of a specific code provision granting such a remedy and the fact that the existing law cannot be construed to give exclusive control to the owner of know-how. But if an injunctive remedy is not given to an owner of know-how whose secret information was acquired by some unlawful means such as those provided under the Criminal Code, justice will not be achieved. In many instances, damages do not give the owner of know-how an adequate remedy.[47]

III. The Meaning of "Secret" in the United States Cases

The importance of secrecy in relation to the theory of know-how protection in the United States was mentioned earlier. This element must now be explored in greater detail.

Whatever theory is invoked by the court, the decisions are agreed on the proposition that to be protectible, a secret must indeed be "secret." Here unanimity ceases. It is not possible to discern a uniform rule governing the required degree and quality of secrecy or the effect of change and the passage of time on secrecy. Moreover, from time to time the issue of secrecy is presented in disguise under the rubric "novelty." Finally, some of the more down-to-earth decisions in recent years suggest that secrecy and novelty discussions are really efforts to get at the question of value.

The cases discussed below have been selected for the purpose of presenting a cross-section that should give the reader some "feel" for the area. It is important to note that a reading of the full opinions in these and many other cases will probably leave the reader with the viscerally satisfied feeling that justice has been done. This reaction is significant because it results from the way the facts were stated in the opinions. The facts are critical in any litigation, but are especially important in trade-secret cases. The hoary rule of advocacy, to the effect that a court convinced that the facts favor one side will find the law to confirm that side's position is particularly applicable in this area. The principles of law are sufficiently vague and flexible, and there are so often contradictory principles—protection of property versus freedom of competition, for example—that in most disputes

47. Although it seems that Japanese courts are reluctant to give protection to nonstatutory rights, the Tokyo District Court recognized an individual's right of privacy and granted damages to the injured party, Arita v. Hiraoka (Yukio Mishima), 15 Kakyū minshū 2317 (Tokyo Dist. Ct., Sept. 28, 1964). The principle, that protection can be accorded to nonstatutory rights, which this case necessarily involved, could usefully be extended to the protection of know-how. Know-how can be regarded as a kind of industrial "privacy."

arguable enough to be litigated by sensible men, either result can be justified by precedent. Persuasive presentation of the facts is of paramount importance.

This observation is of concern not only to an advocate, but also to a counselor who is guiding the establishment of a trade-secret protection program, or conducting negotiations, or handling other business related to this field. Counsel will be wise to reserve a small place in his planning for the litigation he expects will not come, and to remember the evidentiary potential of the letters, memoranda, drafts, and other minutia of the transaction.

A. Secrecy and the Confidential Relationship

A secret process or technique is most secret at its conception. Perfect and absolute secrecy would require that the secret go no further, but, of course, there is no such requirement. As one court indicated:[48]

> Secrecy is a relative term. What is known to several persons may no longer be secret in the strict sense. But we are concerned with the meaning in the legal and equitable sense. Was it secret in the sense that a disclosure by an employee would lessen its value? Was it secret in the sense that third parties would be willing to pay for a breach of trust to ascertain its nature?

A secret may be disclosed to a number of persons and not lose its legal character as a secret if it is disclosed in confidence.[49] The most common instance is the disclosure to employees, as is illustrated by *Peabody* v. *Norfolk*, a leading American case discussed above.[50] Plaintiff had disclosed his secret to his engineer-employee. His right was protected against "one who in violation of contract and breach of confidence undertakes to apply it to his own use, or to disclose it to third persons."

The disclosure to employees is confidential, whether or not there is a written contract of employment specifically imposing a duty to treat

48. L.M. Rabinowitz & Co. v. Dasher, 82 N.Y.S. 2d 431, 437 (Sup. Ct. 1948).

49. A case which might appear to carry this principle to the boundary of the absurd is Kernel Cutter, Inc. v. Fawcett Publications, Inc., 284 F.2d 675 (7th Cir. 1960). Plaintiff appealed from the dismissal of its complaint by the District Court for failure to state a claim. The complaint alleged that plaintiff had originated and advertised a confidential method for bass fishing; when it stopped advertising in defendant's magazine, defendant published an article disclosing the method, as a result of which, it was alleged, plaintiff lost all the value of its secret. The complaint alleged that the secret method had been disclosed—presumably in confidence—to more than 25,000 purchasers. The court of appeals reversed, reinstating the complaint. The probable actual holding of the case is that in the federal courts almost any combination of words and figures arranged on a piece of paper will be held to state a claim, at least when the question arises under Fed. R. Civ. P. 12(b) (6).

50. 98 Mass. 452, 458 (1868). *See* text accompanying note 14 *supra*.

the information as confidential.[51] One court stated the proposition as follows:[52]

> It is implied in every contract of employment that the employee will hold sacred any trade secrets or other confidential information which he acquires in the course of his employment. [Citations omitted.] This is a duty that the employee assumes not only during his employment but after its termination. It is an absolute and not a relative duty.

It is not wise, however, to rely upon this principle in all circumstances. Unrestricted disclosure to a large class of employees, for example, without any indication that secrecy is desired, may be taken as evidence that the matters in question were not secret at all.[53] Where the employee himself is the originator of the alleged trade secret, the absence of any express agreement may weigh against the employer.[54]

The implied obligation of confidentiality applies not only to employees but to any agent[55] and continues despite termination of the agency.[56] It applies also to other fiduciaries, such as corporate directors.[57]

The duty of nondisclosure will also be imposed, where circumstances warrant, on independent contractors. In one early case,[58] the inventor-manufacturer of a pump sent out for repair certain "patterns" used in the manufacture of the pump. The repairman, who seems to have been an independent contractor, surreptitiously copied

51. However, a written contract is highly desirable as to any employee who has access to sensitive information. Such employee agreements, and their status under both Japanese and United States law, will be discussed in some detail below. *See* notes 145–49 and accompanying text *infra*.

52. L.M. Rabinowitz & Co. v. Dasher, 82 N.Y.S. 2d at 435. The court said that a written contract only "fortified" the duty. Also in point is Junker v. Plummer, 320 Mass. 76, 67 N.E. 2d 667 (1956).

53. Excelsior Steel Furnace Co. v. Williamson Heater Co., 269 F. 614 (6th Cir. 1920).

54. Wexler v. Greenberg, 399 Pa. 569, 160 A.2d 430 (1960).

55. Restatement (Second) of Agency §395 (1957).

56. *Id.* §396.

57. Vulcan Detinning Co. v. American Can Co., 72 N.J.Eq. 387, 67 A. 339 (Ct. Err. & App. 1907); Fairchild Engine & Airplane Corp. v. Cox, 50 N.Y.S. 2d 643 (Sup. Ct. 1944) (Vice President and Director). Japanese Civil Code art. 644 states the duty of diligence of a mandate as follows: "A mandatary is bound to manage the affairs entrusted to him with the care of a good manager in accordance with the tenor of the mandate." This proposition has never been applied to a case involving unauthorized disclosure or misuse of know-how. A similar provision is found in Commercial Code Chap. 4, Corporations, art. 254–2. In addition, Commercial Code art. 264 provides the duty of corporate directors not to compete with their corporation. The rule can cover the situation where directors during the term of their office conduct a competing business using various trade secrets belonging to the corporation. But again there is no judicial precedent dealing with a situation where directors during the term of their office made necessary preparation for a competing business and began its operation after resigning from the corporation.

58. Tabor v. Hoffman, 118 N.Y. 30, 23 N.E. 12 (1889).

the patterns and sold them to defendant, who used them to manufacture pumps. Defendant was enjoined at the suit of the inventor-manufacturer.

In *Kamin* v. *Kuhnau*,[59] plaintiff, the proprietor of a garbage collection service, devised garbage truck bodies using hydraulic devices to pack the garbage. He retained defendant as an independent contractor to construct the bodies for him. When defendant began making and selling the bodies in competition with plaintiff, suit was brought. One of the several defenses was that there was no confidential relationship. Affirming a judgment for plaintiff, the court held that there was no need to show any express agreement to keep secrets, or to stand in a confidential relationship; such a relationship could be implied. "And the implication may be made not simply as a product of the quest for the intention of the parties but as a legal conclusion recognizing the need for ethical practices in the commercial world."[60]

A duty of nondisclosure may also be imposed on a variety of other persons having contractual or business relationships with the discloser. The apparent intent of the parties, judged from all the circumstances, seems to be a major determining factor in these cases, although the courts do not usually speak in terms of intent. The importance of intent has, however, been pointed out.[61] Needless to say, a clear record of intent contemporaneous with the transaction would be of great value in preventing disputes.

A dispute will on occasion arise from disclosure to a supplier. *Kamin* v. *Kuhnau*[62] is such a case. Another is *Allen-Qualley Co.* v. *Shellmar Prods. Co.*[63] Plaintiff's employees invented a novel candy wrapper and a method for making it. Officers of plaintiff entered into discussions with defendant, a candy-wrap manufacturer, looking to defendant's manufacturing the wrapper for plaintiff, and, on the basis of an oral agreement of confidentiality, disclosed the process. Defendant subsequently commenced production of the wrappers for its own account, and was enjoined at plaintiff's suit. Here the intent to preserve confidentiality was reasonably clear.

By contrast, the lack of clear intent brought an opposite result in another supplier case, *Mycalex Corp. of America* v. *Pemco Corp.*[64] Plaintiff was a manufacturer of glass-bonded mica, a component of electronic devices. One of the defendants was a supplier of "frit," an

59. 232 Ore. 139, 374 P.2d 912 (1962).
60. *Id.* at 919.
61. *See, e.g.*, 2 R. Callman, Unfair Competition and Trademarks 803 (2d ed. 1950); 64 Harv. L. Rev. 976, 978 (1951).
62. 232 Ore. 139, 374 P.2d 912 (1962). (See text at n. 59 *supra*.)
63. 31 F.2d 293 (N.D. Ill. 1929), *aff'd*, 36 F.2d 623 (7th Cir. 1929).
64. 159 F.2d 907 (4th Cir. 1947).

ingredient used in plaintiff's manufacturing process. Plaintiff experienced production difficulties and on several occasions invited officers of defendant to visit plaintiff's plant, study the process and problem, and make recommendations. Later defendant commenced production of glass-bonded mica itself, and incorporated the second defendant to handle that part of its business. Plaintiff sued and lost; the court of appeals affirmed. Particularly damaging to its case was the testimony of an officer of plaintiff, on direct examination by plaintiff's attorney, that "we didn't bind them by any agreement of secrecy. That is not customary between manufacturers . . . and a supplier . . ."[65] Other important evidence included proof that at about the time plaintiff first sought defendant's help, defendant was carrying on "extensive research and experimentation with the idea of entering the field."[66] Plaintiff made a weak showing concerning what defendant's representatives learned, or might have learned, during the visits and discussions; whether the information was generally available in trade literature; and what defendant's process was or whether it was substantially equivalent to plaintiff's. Some facts that seemed to the court to be adverse to plaintiff are not necessarily so, suggesting the probability that plaintiff's case was not as fully prepared as it might have been. For example, the court thought it significant that defendant's plant visits were at plaintiff's invitation, although it is hard to imagine how it would be possible to visit the plant, short of trespass, without the proprietor's invitation. Similarly, the visits were for a "legitimate purpose." This is not relevant except where there is an alleged preconceived fraudulent scheme; the usual trade-secret case involves misuse of information rightfully acquired, not the less common wrongful acquisition of information. Plaintiff did not protest immediately after learning of defendant's entry into the business, although the duration of the elapsed interval is not clear; the court states in one part of its opinion that it was several months, and in another that it was two years. The former is not an excessive time to consult counsel, ascertain the facts, and reach a decision. Finally, the court thought it significant that plaintiff continued to buy frit from defendant, although this was presumably an independent economic decision not related to the controversy. This marshaling of seeming irrelevancies emphasizes the effect of an inadequate record of intent, of content of disclosure, and of other conduct related to the protection of confidentiality.[67]

Somewhat surprisingly, a number of trade-secret cases deal with the

65. *Id.* at 912.
66. *Id.* at 909.
67. And *see* Speciner v. Reynolds Metals Co., 177 F. Supp. 291 (S.D.N.Y. 1959).

question of whether a licensee was in a confidential relationship with his licensor. These cases result from the licensor's extraordinary lapse of judgment in failing to provide for nondisclosure in the license. Normally, a confidential relation will be implied, as in *Hyde Corp.* v. *Huffines*.[68] Plaintiff, inventor of a hydraulic garbage compressor, granted an exclusive manufacturing license to defendant. Defendant subsequently repudiated the license but continued the manufacture. Plaintiff sued for an injunction and damages, and won. The court held that the relationship of licensor and licensee was confidential despite the absence of an express provision in the license prohibiting manufacture after its termination.

There are a variety of other business relations that give rise to confidentiality disputes. One example involves what was described as a lease of personality. Plaintiff was the licensed manufacturer of a magnetic "fishing tool" used to retrieve metallic objects from oil wells. Defendant "leased" the tools from plaintiff and "subleased" them to users. The contract between plaintiff and defendant prohibited defendant from disassembling the tools, to keep secret their construction. Defendant disassembled a tool and commenced manufacture of a similar one. At plaintiff's suit, it was enjoined.[69]

Misunderstandings concerning confidentiality often arise after abortive business negotiations.[70] The best-known case is *Smith* v. *Dravo*.[71] Plaintiff, a manufacturer of cargo and freight containers, entered into negotiations to sell its business to defendant. In the course of negotiations it disclosed substantial information concerning its business, including pending patent applications, blueprints and models of containers, and customer lists. After negotiations terminated on failure to agree on price, defendant commenced the manufacture of containers similar to plaintiff's. Judgment for defendant was reversed. The court recognized that there was no express undertaking of confidentiality. But, it said, the information was disclosed for one purpose, to aid defendant's appraisal for considering a purchase, and defendant knew and understood that purpose. Trust was reposed that the information would be received by defendant for that purpose only.[72]

There is sometimes an aroma of deliberate fraud in preliminary

68. 158 Tex. 566, 314 S.W.2d 763, *cert. denied*, 358 U.S. 898 (1958).

69. K & G Oil Tool & Serv. Co. v. G. & G. Fishing Tool Serv., 158 Tex. 594, 314 S.W.2d 782, *cert. denied*, 358 U.S. 896 (1958).

70. Such misunderstandings can best be averted by entering into a preliminary secrecy agreement before any disclosures are made. A form of agreement is set forth and discussed below. *See* pp. 673–74 and appendix *infra*.

71. 203 F.2d 369 (7th Cir. 1953). *See* text accompanying note 24 *supra*.

72. *See also* Schreyer v. Casco Prods. Corp., 190 F.2d 921 (2d Cir. 1951).

negotiation cases, as in *Franke* v. *Wiltschek*.[73] Plaintiff developed and manufactured a compressed face cloth, which the user soaked in water to expand to its original size. Defendants saw the product in a store and approached plaintiff with the proposition that they become sales representatives. Plaintiff at first was not interested, but defendants persisted, and negotiations commenced. Defendants greatly misstated the size of their sales force, and requested that plaintiff show them the factory, and explain the process, costs, and other details of the business. After disclosures a contract was signed, but in a few weeks defendants terminated it and almost immediately, through a related corporation, began to make and sell a competing product. Judgment for plaintiff was affirmed.[74]

The outside inventor, submitting suggestions to a potential buyer, is a perennial problem for corporate counsel. Unless dealt with outrageously, the idea submitter is usually on the losing side of litigation. Often the courts will find that the submission lacked novelty,[75] but sometimes it is held that no confidential relation was established.[76]

B. The Degree and Quality of Secrecy

Process and know-how information that, at the relevant time, is generally known by the public or by the trade will not be protected as a trade secret; similar significant information known only to the originator and those in a confidential relation with him will normally be protected. Between these two extremes lie the greater number of the litigated cases. No simple test is available to determine whether protection will be afforded information in this middle zone. An educated weighing of various factors should indicate, but will not assure, a correct answer.

The factors commonly considered are:[77]

1. Extent to which the information is known or available;
2. The originality or novelty of the information;
3. The value of the information;
4. The cost of acquiring the information and the cost and difficulty of independently duplicating the information; and
5. Efforts of the claimant to protect the information.

73. 209 F.2d 493 (2d Cir. 1953).

74. A fraud even more blatant gave rise to Spiselman v. Rabinowitz, 270 App. Div. 548, 61 N.Y.S. 2d 138 (1946).

75. *E.g.*, Juliano v. Hobart Mfg. Co., 200 F. Supp. 453 (D. Mass. 1961), *aff'd mem.*, 303 F.2d 830 (1st Cir. 1962); Houser v. Snap-on Tools Corp., 202 F. Supp. 181 (D. Md. 1962).

76. *E.g.*, Sachs v. Cluett, Peabody & Co., 265 App. Div. 497, 39 N.Y.S. 2d 853 (1943), *aff'd*, 291 N.Y. 772, 53 N.E.2d 241 (1944); Newell v. O.A. Newton & Son Co., 104 F. Supp. 162 (D. Del. 1952).

77. *See* Restatement of Torts §757, comment (*b*) at 5 (1939).

Each of these factors will be explored by analysis of illustrative decisions.

In the background is another aspect that is common to almost all the cases, sometimes explicitly recognized and sometimes not. This factor, which is really the most important of all, is the extent to which the court feels the defendant has wronged the plaintiff through breach of trust or confidence. The strongest influence on the ultimate decision is not the nature and extent of plaintiff's right, but the nature and extent of defendant's wrong. Although, as the earlier discussion has shown, the theories of trade-secret protection and of the confidential relationship must not be neglected, counsel can anticipate that the principal focus of the court's attention will be on the defendant's conduct. The degree of wrongness of his behavior will tend to determine the degree of protection. This principle should be kept in mind as the following material is read.

1. Extent to Which the Information is Known or Available. A common defense in a trade-secret action is the claim that the information was widely known, or at least widely available. It is normally stated that the person claiming the secret has the burden to disprove public knowledge or availability.[78]

General knowledge in the trade of the alleged secret will ordinarily render it unprotectible.[79] Illustrative is *National Starch Products, Inc.* v. *Polymer Industries*,[80] an action against former employees. The court upheld as stating a valid defense defendant's answer pleading that the allegedly secret processes were known to at least ten of plaintiff's competitors and were generally available to the trade, without charge, from raw material suppliers.[81]

No protection will be afforded an alleged secret against a disclosee who already knew it at the time of disclosure.[82]

More than merely theoretical public availability is required. In *Ben-*

78. *See, e.g.*, Sarkes Tarzian, Inc. v. Audio Devices, Inc., 166 F. Supp. 250 (S.D. Cal. 1958), *aff'd*, 283 F.2d 695 (9th Cir. 1960), *cert. denied*, 365 U.S. 869 (1961); Bickley v. Fritchey Bean Co., 173 F.Supp. 516 (E.D. Mich. 1959), *aff'd*, 279 F.2d 685 (6th Cir. 1960); Houser v. Snap-on Tools Corp., 202 F.Supp. 181 (D. Md. 1962).

79. *See, e.g.*, Fairchild Engine & Airplane Corp. v. Cox, 50 N.Y.S. 2d 643 (Sup. Ct. 1944); Mycalex Corp. of America v. Pemco Corp., 159 F.2d 907 (4th Cir. 1947) ("Clear and convincing" proof required).

80. 273 App. Div. 732, 79 N.Y.S. 2d 357 (1948).

81. The opinion does not indicate whether the allegedly secret information was as widely known at the time it was disclosed to defendants. The legal position of a disclosee of a valid trade secret, when the "secret" has subsequently become public is a particularly vexing problem on which there is a substantial split of authority and which will be separately treated. *See* notes 112–29 and accompanying text *infra*.

82. Great Lakes Carbon Corp. v. Continental Oil Co., 249 F. Supp. 468 (W.D. La. 1963).

ton v. *Ward*,[83] plaintiff sued for recission of a contract under which he had bought into defendants' business, claiming, *inter alia*, that defendants had misrepresented that they had a secret metal-treating process, and that the process was in fact covered by an old, expired patent. The court held for the defendant, saying:[84]

> As already stated, it does not appear that the use of the metal had been introduced under that [expired] patent, and, so far as the public were concerned, the process remained unknown. It was therefore open to anyone who should rediscover the process to enter upon the manufacture of metal under that process, and, by guarding the secret of manufacture, reap all the benefit possible therefrom.

Rejecting plaintiff's contention that defendants did not and could not "own" the process because of its earlier patenting, the court said that defendants by knowing the process and having the equipment to apply it owned it as well as any nonpatented invention could be owned.[85]

Geographic factors may be relevant. In one of the hydraulic garbage-packer cases discussed previously, the court held as irrelevant the fact that the device was known and used in other parts of the country, because it was not known in the area where plaintiff independently thought of it and disclosed it to defendant.[86]

A trade secret is not rendered unprotectible by being made the subject of a patent application, as such applications are confidential.[87] Nor is a secret lost if independently developed (but kept confidential) by others.[88]

One who receives a trade secret in confidence will often be bound to respect the confidence even though the secret might have been available to him from other, including public, sources. A striking illustration is *Allen-Qually Co.* v. *Shellmar Products Co.*[89] Plaintiff's employees

83. 59 F. 411 (N.D. Iowa 1894).

84. *Id.* at 414.

85. Judgment for defendants was also based in part on a conflict of testimony as to whether they had made the alleged misrepresentations.

86. Kamin v. Kuhnau, 232 Ore. 139, 374 P.2d 912 (1962). *See* text accompanying notes 59–60, *supra*. This principle has obvious significance for international transactions, when an item of technology is public in one country but unknown in the other. The co-authors have found no case directly dealing with this point. Under the patent laws of both countries, however, public use abroad is no bar to patent, while foreign publication is a bar. This can be taken to indicate a policy that foreign technology is not considered relevant unless it is readily available domestically, and some such principle might well be applied in know-how litigation.

87. *E.g.*, A.O. Smith Corp. v. Petroleum Iron Works Co., 73 F.2d 531 (6th Cir. 1934), *modified on rehearing*, 74 F.2d 934 (6th Cir. 1935).

88. *E.g.*, Sandlin v. Johnson, 141 F.2d 660 (8th Cir. 1944). This principle might not extend to cover a situation in which each company in the industry has independently discovered the secret.

89. 31 F.2d 293 (N.D. Ill. 1929), *aff'd*, 36 F.2d 623 (7th Cir. 1929).

invented a novel candy wrapper and a process for making it. Shortly thereafter, a patent issued to a stranger covering a similar or identical invention. After the issuance of the patent, plaintiff commenced discussions with defendant, a candy-wrap manufacturer, concerning a proposal that defendant manufacture the wrap for plaintiff. Defendant orally agreed to respect plaintiff's confidence and the wrap and process were disclosed to it. At this time neither plaintiff nor defendant knew of the stranger's patent. Following the disclosure by plaintiff, defendant instructed its employees to construct a machine to use the process, and instructed its counsel to make a patent search. The search disclosed the patent, which defendant promptly bought. It then broke off discussions with plaintiff and commenced the manufacture of the wrapper for its own account.

Plaintiff sued, seeking an injunction. The court held that the defendant's patent was no defense. It was not material, as between these parties, whether the patent was valid and covered the wrap and process. Defendant had been led to acquire it only by violating its confidential relation. Had there been no such relation, defendant could have done what it did, but there was, and it could not. The court held defendant to be a trustee *ex maleficio* of the patent, ordered its assignment to plaintiff, and enjoined defendant from continuing in the business.

This case is an excellent illustration of the effect of defendant's wrongful conduct. If, as defendant claimed, the issued patent validly covered the wrap and process, there could have been no trade secret under a strict "property" analysis; but the court's emphasis on defendant's wrongful actions made that irrelevant.

2. *The Originality or Novelty of the Information.* Investigation of the originality or novelty of the alleged trade secret may be no more than another approach to the question of public knowledge or availability. A wholly novel and original idea, not disclosed by the originator, will also be unknown and unavailable to the public; a widely known process or technique will not be novel.

Originality may also be used as an indication of value. Novelty is a variable rather than an absolute quality, and the degree of novelty may be considered when a court sets a value on a trade secret.[90]

Used as a tool for measuring secrecy or value, novelty has its place in trade-secret litigation. However, novelty may sometimes be considered in a trade secret case because of a mistaken, and usually unspoken, attempt to apply principles derived from the law of patents. Novelty as an independent factor has no proper place in trade-secret

90. *E.g.*, Kamin v. Kuhnau, 232 Ore. 139, 374 P.2d 912 (1962).

cases. Trade secrets need not be patentable inventions.[91] It is sometimes asserted that while "invention" and patentability are not required, a lesser thing called "discovery" is necessary. In one case[92] in which protection was granted to the secret process, the court first rejected the defense that the processes were "within the realm of mechanical skill," and then insisted on and found a showing of discovery:

> We do not accept the plaintiff's contention that, regardless of whether processes are novel . . . (they) will be protected against use by anyone who obtains knowledge of them by means of a confidential relation. . . .
>
> Quite clearly discovery is something less than invention. . . . Discovery may be the result of industry, application, or be perhaps merely fortuitous.[93]

While its explanation is less then pellucid, the court appears to be striving for a standard that requires a protectible trade secret to be something more than a vague idea and to have the quality of "know-how." Other courts have pursued a similar goal in a different way. Lack of novelty or originality is sometimes given as the reason for refusal to protect vague or general ideas, *e.g.*, the idea of a loose-leaf foreign tax service,[94] or for refusal to enjoin former employees from applying their skill and general knowledge of the trade.[95]

Further indicating that a bastardized version of patent law is sometimes applied in trade-secret cases, a sort of primitive "felt need" test has been applied to uphold trade secrets, protection being granted because plaintiff has been able to do what others tried but failed to accomplish.[96]

3. The Value of the Information. There is a growing tendency to cut through the intricacies encountered in an attempt to ascertain the precise degree of secrecy or novelty of an alleged trade secret, by emphasizing its value.[97] This approach, applying realistic economic

91. *E.g.*, Fairchild Engine & Airplane Corp. v. Cox, 50 N.Y.S. 2d 643 (Sup. Ct. 1944), Sandlin v. Johnson, 141 F.2d 660 (8th Cir. 1944); Junker v. Plummer, 320 Mass. 76, 67 N.E.2d 667 (1946); Benton v. Ward, 59 F.411 (N.D. Iowa 1894).

92. A.O. Smith Corp. v. Petroleum Iron Works Co., 73 F.2d 531 (6th Cir. 1934); *modified on rehearing*, 74 F.2d 934 (6th Cir. 1935).

93. *Id.* at 538.

94. Irizarry y Puente v. President and Fellows of Harvard College, 248 F.2d 799 (1st Cir. 1957), *cert. denied*, 356 U.S. 947 (1958).

95. *E.g.*, Sarkes Tarzian, Inc. v. Audio Devices, Inc., 166 F.Supp. 250 (S.D. Cal. 1958); *aff'd*, 283 F.2d 695 (9th Cir. 1960); Kaumagraph Co. v. Stampagraph Co., 235 N.Y. 1, 138 N.E. 485 (1923); *see* Bickley v. Fritchey Bean Co., 173 F.Supp. 516 (E.D. Mich. 1959), *aff'd*, 279 F.2d 685 (6th Cir. 1960).

96. *See* Junker v. Plummer, 320 Mass. 76, 67 N.E.2d 667 (1946), and L.M. Rabinowitz & Co. v. Dasher, 82 N.Y.S. 2d 431 (Sup. Ct. 1948).

97. One respected commentator suggests that the "secrecy" and "novelty" tests are really similar inquiries into value. A. TURNER, THE LAW OF TRADE SECRETS 24 (1962).

criteria, seems likely to become more common in cases where relative rather than absolute secrecy is present.

A good example of the approach is *Kamin* v. *Kuhnau*. Defendant said that the plaintiff's alleged trade secrets (embodied in a hydraulic garbage-packer) were not protectible because they were already known elsewhere and were not novel or inventive. The court rejected these contentions.[98]

> Essentially, the question is whether the idea which is disclosed has such value that it may reasonably be implied that the disclosee is not privileged to use it for his own profit. The fact that the idea was already developed by others at the time of disclosure may make it less valuable in the market. Yet the information or knowledge may give to the possessor a commercial advantage over his competitors. This advantage constitutes value, and the disclosure of the information which creates the advantage may be sufficient to raise implied agreement not to appropriate it.

Japanese readers will note the court's use of the term "appropriate." The usage is typical in the United States.[99]

The economic-value approach is particularly useful in dealing with aggregations of proprietary data and know-how accumulated by a technological industrial enterprise over a period of time in the course of meeting and solving a succession of technical problems. Many or all of the individual solutions may be relatively simple, mechanical stratagems, or slight adaptations of known techniques. But the aggregation considered as a whole will nevertheless often be of considerable value, both as an indispensable asset in the business of the proprietor, and as a thing that competitors would pay to learn. Where the competitor seeks to acquire such an aggregation of proprietary data by hiring the proprietor's senior technical personnel, he and the employees are highly vulnerable to litigation.[100]

4. The Cost of Acquiring the Information, and the Cost of Independently Duplicating It. Closely related to value is the cost (and effort) expended in the proprietor's original acquisition of the trade secret, and the cost

98. 232 Ore. 139, 374 P.2d 912, 917 (1962).

99. In the United States one "infringes" a patent, but not know-how. Know-how is "misappropriated," "wrongfully appropriated," "used or disclosed in breach of trust," and so on, but is never said to be "infringed."

100. This situation seems to have been involved in a well-known case, B.F. Goodrich Co. v. Wohlgemuth, 117 Ohio Ct. App. 493, 192 N.E.2d 99 (1963). When International Latex Corp., with little prior experience in the field, received the Project Apollo subcontract for space suits, it hired defendant, the engineer in charge of space-suit research at B.F. Goodrich, which had extensive experience and know-how developed over almost thirty years. Defendant was enjoined from disclosing any trade secrets to his new employer. Eastman Co. v. Reichenbach, 20 N.Y.S. 110 (Sup. Ct. 1892), *aff'd mem.*, 29 N.Y.S. 1143 (1894), and Harold v. Herold China & Pottery Co., 257 F. 911 (6th Cir. 1919) are earlier cases involving senior technicians privy to aggregations of proprietary data.

and difficulty the competitor would incur in independently duplicating it. A process or technique produced only with considerable cost and effort is more likely to be valued highly than one costing nothing,[101] although, of course, effort may be misdirected or fruitless, while accident may sometimes produce a cheap answer to a problem. The wrongful acquisition or misuse of an expensive secret is likely to seem more wrong and to produce a stronger sense of unfairness.

The question of cost is more often approached from the other side. The inquiry is, Would substantial cost and effort be necessary to duplicate the information independently? If so, the courts are likely to restrain and even penalize the defendant who has wrongfully acquired or misused an alleged trade secret. This most clearly appears in the cases in which the defendant pleads that his action has not actually been harmful, because he might have learned the same things by analysis of and experimentation based on publicly available information, particularly the information provided by the publicly available product of the proprietor of the trade secret. In short, he argues that by means of what is known in the modern jargon as "reverse engineering," he could have achieved his goal. This defense is very unlikely to be accepted, and the defendant may find that his attempted shortcut has stopped him from doing what anyone else remains free to do.

Illustrative is *Stone* v. *Grasselli Chemical Co.*, an action against a defendant that hired an employee of its competitor and, with knowledge that the employee had agreed to confidentiality, induced him to reveal the secrets of plaintiff's manufacture of depilatories. The court said:[102]

> The injunction should not be refused, because the process was such that it would probably have been disclosed by independent experiments in the manipulation of the ingredients of which the products of both parties were alike composed. The Grasselli Company, by its own conduct, has put itself in such a position that it may even lose the advantage of future independent experiments. It would be quite impossible hereafter to decide how much of the improvement in the product of the Grasselli Company would be attributable to its own independent efforts and how much to the knowledge of Stone's process fraudulently acquired by it. Every doubt must be resolved against the parties to a fraudulent act.

Numerous cases support this principle.[103]

101. In Smith v. Dravo Corp., 203 F.2d 369, 373 (7th Cir. 1953), the court said that although a trade secret need not be an invention, it must "represent in some considerable degree the independent efforts of its claimants."

102. 65 N.J.Eq. 756, 55 A. 736, 762 (Ct. Err. & App. 1903).

103. *See, e.g.*, Smith v. Dravo Corp., 203 F.2d 369 (7th Cir. 1953); Franke v. Wiltschek, 209 F.2d 493 (2d Cir. 1953); K & G Oil Tool & Serv. Co. v. G & G Fishing Tool Serv., 158 Tex. 594, 314 S.W.2d 782 (1958), *cert. denied*, 358 U.S. 896 (1958);

Where the "reverse engineering" is simple and easy, as in the case of a publicly sold product that reveals its "secrets" on casual inspection, protection is not likely to be afforded.[104]

5. Efforts of the Claimant to Protect the Information. A factor sometimes considered by courts is the extent of the efforts made by the party claiming a trade secret to protect it. Where the claimant posted KEEP OUT signs and provided a visitors' register imprinted with an agreement of nondisclosure and nonuse,[105] or barred visitors and kept plans locked up,[106] the court tended to be favorable to the claimant. A claimant that did not restrict "common employees" from observing the process[107] or did not mention to visiting suppliers, because it was "not customary," that the process should be regarded as a secret,[108] has drawn an unfavorable judicial reaction.

Public sale of a product simple enough to reveal all its secrets on casual observation ends protectibility of the secrets.[109] In *Houser* v. *Snap-on Tools Corp.*,[110] the court found this rule so admirable as to justify its absurd extension to a case in which the product had not yet been marketed, on the theory that "[t]he secret is worthless unless the device is marketed; and, once the device is marketed, the secrecy evaporates." And, of course, an application for a patent ends secrecy when and if the patent issues; the purpose of the patent system is to encourage publication of secrets in exchange for a limited statutory monopoly.

It has been persuasively suggested that the real significance of efforts to protect secrecy, or the lack of such efforts, is the light shed by this evidence on the intent of the claimant of the alleged secret.[111] The lawyer can play an important role in advising a client about the evidentiary value of such precautionary steps.

IV. The Effect of Loss of Secrecy on Remedies in the United States

Loss of secrecy has consequences, which have not received detailed attention in the foregoing discussion. Secrecy is on occasion lost, and

Tabor v. Hoffman, 118 N.Y. 30, 23 N.E. 12 (1889); *cf.*, Kaumagraph Co. v. Stampagraph Co., 235 N.Y. 1, 138 N.E. 485 (1923).

104. *See* cases cited in note 109 *infra*.

105. Sun Dial Corp v. Rideout, 16 N.J. 252, 108 A.2d 442 (1954).

106. Ernst Slide Fastener Co., Inc. v. Stamberg, 120 N.Y.S. 2d 311 (Sup. Ct. 1953).

107. Excelsior Steel Furnace Co. v. Williamson Heater Co., 269 F. 614 (6th Cir. 1920).

108. Mycalex Corp. of America v. Pemco Corp., 159 F.2d 907 (4th Cir. 1947).

109. *See, e.g.*, Carver v. Harr, 132 N.J.Eq. 207, 27 A.2d 895 (Ch. 1942) (*semble*); Juliano v. Hobart Mfg. Co., 200 F. Supp. 453 (D. Mass. 1961), *aff'd*, 303 F.2d 830 (1st Cir. 1962); Speciner v. Reynolds Metals Co., 177 F.Supp. 291 (S.D.N.Y. 1959).

110. 202 F.Supp. 181, 187 (D. Md. 1962).

111. 64 HARV. L. REV. 976 (1951).

this eventuality should be anticipated and planned for. Processes and know-how, in the usual course, are independently discovered by others, are patented or published, are slowly "leaked" at conferences and conventions, or are otherwise subject to gradual erosion of secrecy. While it is possible that a trade secret may continue to be secret indefinitely, legal planning must encompass all alternatives reasonably likely to occur.

Loss of secrecy must be considered at three stages in connection with confidential disclosures: before disclosure, after disclosure but before any alleged breach by the disclosee, and after disclosure and after alleged breach by the disclosee. In the first situation, if the information in question was not secret at the time of disclosure, a purportedly confidential disclosure will not be protected.[112]

The second situation, loss of secrecy after a confidential disclosure but before any alleged breach by the disclosee, is almost as straightforward. The general rule is that the disclosee who remains faithful to his obligations so long as secrecy continues will be as free as anyone else to use the information once it becomes public.[113] This result probably coincides with normal business expectations, and perhaps for that reason the question has not often arisen in reported litigation.

It is possible, however, to contract for a contrary result. The famous "Listerine" case, *Warner-Lambert Pharmaceutical Co.* v. *John J. Reynolds, Inc.*,[114] illustrates this principle. Defendant's predecessor disclosed to plaintiff's predecessor the secret formula for Listerine in return for a promise to pay royalties based on the quantity produced or sold. Gradually the once-secret formula became publicly known, and the plaintiff brought this action seeking a declaratory judgment that it was no longer liable to pay the royalties, and that it also sought the return of a portion of past royalties. It analogized its position to that of the licensee under a copyright, or a patent that expired or was held invalid, in which cases no further royalties could be collected. The court, rendering judgment for defendant, rejected this argument, saying that the patent and copyright cases relied upon by plaintiff all dealt with statutory limited monopolies, on the expiration of which it was intended that public use should be unrestrained. In this area, however, the parties were free to contract as they chose; the contract

112. Cases cited *supra* notes 79 and 82. As previously discussed, the meaning of "secret" in this context is influenced by a variety of circumstances. *See* notes 48–76 and accompanying text *supra*.

113. L.S. Donaldson Co. v. LaMaur, Inc. 299 F.2d 412 (8th Cir. 1962), *cert. denied*, 371 U.S. 815 (1962); Northup v. Reish, 200 F.2d 924 (7th Cir. 1953).

114. 178 F.Supp. 655 (S.D.N.Y. 1959), *aff'd*, 280 F.2d 197 (2d Cir. 1960).

provided for no cessation of royalties in the event secrecy was lost, and there was no reason to imply such a provision.[115]

The doctrine of this case suggests a possible means by which a United States owner of an invention patentable in the United States but not in Japan[116] can nevertheless obtain at least some Japanese licensing revenue. While the United States patent application is still being drafted, and during the period between its filing in and its issuance by the United States Patent Office (which may be several years), the invention will remain secret. The right to practice it during this period is a valuable right that may be licensed. Moreover, the licensee will obtain valuable lead time, a head start over its competitors, which independently may support a contractual promise to continue to pay royalties for at least some period after the United States patent issues and secrecy is lost.[117]

A contract intended to impose perpetual obligation with respect to use of a trade secret should be clear and explicit, since courts will not lightly infer that such a result was intended by an ambiguous or vague agreement.[118] And even an unmistakably clear agreement may not be enforced to the letter in all circumstances; for example, where a former employee had executed an agreement "for all time" not to disclose his employer's secrets, the court enjoined him from disclosure or use for ten years, saying that this "broad restraint was adequate for plaintiff's protection."[119]

The third situation, where secrecy is lost after confidential disclosure and after breach, is the most troublesome and has produced a sharp division of authority. It is clear that breach, while secrecy still exists, is wrongful; the disagreement concerns the appropriateness of injunction as a remedy.

One line of cases, following a principle known as the *Conmar* rule,

115. If plaintiff had stopped *using* the secret formula, it would probably not have had to continue payments. Montgomery v. Kalak Water Co. of New York, 196 F.Supp. 173 (S.D.N.Y. 1961).

116. *See* Chap. 1, Finnegan et al., *supra*, which discusses various categories of inventions, such as medicines, foodstuffs, and products of chemical processes, which are not patentable in Japan.

117. The value of such lead time has been recognized in some United States cases: *see, e.g.*, Schreyer v. Casco Prods. Corp., 190 F.2d 921 (3d Cir. 1951), discussed at notes 123–125 and accompanying text *infra*. In addition, there may be valuable know-how associated with the patent, but not disclosed by it, which can be licensed. It is important, however, to be aware of possible antitrust or patent misuse problems, if it can be charged that the patent did not make the full required disclosure and hence represented an attempt to extend the patent monopoly unlawfully, or that the value of the lead time did not support the continued obligation to pay royalties after loss of secrecy. *See* the discussion of antitrust and know-how in Chap. VIII, Fugate, *infra*.

118. *See, e.g.*, Dollac Corp. v. Margen Corp., 164 F.Supp. 41 (D.N.J. 1958).

119. Ernst Slide Fastener Co., Inc. v. Stamberg, 120 N.Y.S. 2d 311 (Sup. Ct. 1953).

denies injunctive relief. The "leading" case—but neither the first nor the best illustration of the rule— is *Conmar Products Corp.* v. *Universal Slide Fasteners Co.*[120] It dealt with a number of issues, and the factual situation is unfortunately somewhat confused. The portion of the case that came to be known as the "*Conmar* rule" involved what the court (by Judge Learned Hand) construed as an action by plaintiff based upon defendant's allegedly having induced plaintiff's former employees to breach their nondisclosure agreements. After the acts allegedly constituting this tort, but before entry of judgment, patents issued disclosing the alleged secret. Judge Hand noted that some courts had held that in such a case the defendant would be restrained from using the once-secret information, even though the public was free to do so (subject to the patent). He, however, denied injunctive relief, saying:[121]

> We have twice refused to follow this doctrine;[122] and we adhere to our decisions. Conceivably an employer might exact from his employees a contract not to disclose information even after the patent issued. Of what possible value such a contract could be, we find it hard to conceive; but, if an employer did exact it, others would perhaps be obliged to turn to the specifications, if they would use the information. Be that as it may, we should not so construe any secrecy contract unless the intent were put in the most inescapable terms; and the plaintiff's contract had none such. In their absence we do not see why a wrongful inducement to divulge the disclosure before issue should deprive the wrongdoer of his right to avail himself of the patentee's dedication; for, as we have just said, the contract is to be construed as imposing secrecy only until issue. The doctrine must rest upon the theory that it is a proper penalty for the original wrong to deny the wrongdoer resort to the patent; and for that we find no support in principle.

The actual holding of the *Conmar* case is limited. As the foregoing extract shows, the opinion enunciates a rule of contract interpretation applicable in actions for inducing breach of contract. The case itself appears to have been tried principally as an action for patent infringement (the patents were held invalid). The acts allegedly constituting inducement of breach of contract were mainly or wholly innocently done.

The *Conmar* rule, however, in its usual formulation is not an interpretation rule. Informative is *Schreyer* v. *Casco Products Corp.*[123] In a suit for patent infringement and unfair competition, plaintiff alleged

120. 172 F.2d 150 (2d Cir. 1949).

121. *Id.* at 155–56.

122. Judge Hand cited Picard v. United Aircraft Corp., 128 F.2d 632 (2d Cir. 1942) and Pennington Eng'r. Co. v. Houde Eng'r. Corp., 136 F.2d 210 (2d Cir. 1943) neither of which is "on all fours" with the situation in *Conmar*.

123. 190 F.2d 921 (2d Cir. 1951).

that in the course of negotiations concerning a license for defendant to manufacture plaintiff's electric steam iron, plaintiff disclosed in confidence various detailed information, blueprints and manufacturing know-how. No license was agreed upon, but defendant nevertheless commenced manufacture. Prior to the trial of plaintiff's action, a patent issued to him, which was held to be invalid; but, the court said, the confidential information learned by defendant in the licensing negotiations "was substantially disclosed by the issuance of the patent on 5 July, 1949, and the use of that source of information would not, apart from the risk of infringement, have been wrongful (citing *Conmar*)."[124] Accordingly, the court held, injunction was properly denied.

The opinion in this case also has its puzzling features. If the court correctly described the information disclosed in negotiations as detailed information, blueprints, and manufacturing know-how, it seems unlikely that a patent would contain such information. Moreover, the court based its reasoning on the notion that it would not have been wrongful of defendant to use the patent as a "source of information"; but that should be irrelevant, as it does not appear that defendant did use the patent as a source of information.

Whatever the shortcomings of the opinions, it is clear that in the Second Circuit and some other jurisdictions, no injunctive relief will be granted where the information has become public.[125] Other relief, where appropriate, is available; in Schreyer the plaintiff won an accounting for defendant's profits resulting from its having been able, through its breach, to produce and market sooner than if it had waited until the information became public.

Other jurisdictions—probably constituting a majority—have not followed the *Conmar* rule. An illustrative case is *Hyde Corp.* v. *Huffines*,[126] in which plaintiff licensed defendant to manufacture while a patent application was pending. Defendant repudiated the license but continued to manufacture, whereupon plaintiff sued for an injunction and damages. A patent was issued after the trial commenced. The Supreme Court of Texas affirmed a judgment for plaintiff, including injunctive relief, expressly refusing to follow *Conmar*.

The courts granting injunctive relief do so primarily because they emphasize the defendant's wrongful conduct, and find no appropriate remedy for the wrong except injunction (and an accounting, dam-

124. *Id.* at 124.

125. *See, e.g.*, Carter Prods., Inc. v. Colgate-Palmolive Co., 130 F.Supp. 557 (D. Md. 1955), *aff'd*, 230 F.2d 855 (4th Cir. 1956), *cert. denied*, 352 U.S. 843 (1956). *See also* Sachs v. Cluett, Peabody & Co., 265 App. Div. 497, 39 N.Y.S. 2d 853 (1943), *aff'd*, 291 N.Y. 772, 53 N.E.2d 241 (1944); Speciner v. Reynolds Metals Co., 177 F.Supp. 291 (S.D.N.Y. 1959).

126. 158 Tex. 566, 314 S.W.2d 763 (1958), *cert. denied*, 358 U.S. 898 (1958).

ages, or other relief if called for). The defendant, in effect, will not be heard to speculate that he might have used the public sources when they became available, because he did not in fact use such sources; his wrongful conduct deprives him of whatever rights an innocent party would have.[127] This reasoning is comparable to that in the opinions granting relief even though defendant could have, but did not, learn the confidential information by independent experimentation,[128] or by analysis of plaintiff's publicly marketed product.[129]

It is possible that the *Conmar* rule is a special rule applicable only where the disclosure of the secret has come about through issuance of plaintiff's patent, and that it is an expression of a policy designed to prevent extension of the patent monopoly. It is suggestive that the bastion of the *Conmar* rule, the Second Circuit, is also notoriously likely to find litigated patents invalid for want of invention. However, until some further resolution of the present conflicting authorities occurs, this aspect of *Conmar* must remain mere speculation. Meanwhile, it is advisable to accept Judge Hand's advice to evidence the parties' intent in secrecy contracts "in the most inescapable terms."

V. Federal Preemption of State Trade-Secret Laws

At the outset of this chapter, it was noted that the law of the United States governing trade secrets was primarily embodied in the case law of the several states, rather than in federal statutes. Recently, it appeared that there was a substantial possibility that all state-law protection of trade secrets might be held to be barred by the federal constitution; had that come to pass, there would have been few or no enforceable rights in trade secrets in the United States.

This threat to trade-secret protection, which had caused considerable apprehension in commercial and legal groups, was eliminated (for the time being, at least) by the United States Supreme Court's landmark decision in *Kewanee* v. *Bicron*.[130]

Kewanee reversed a lower court decision holding that the patent system created by federal law pursuant to the United States Constitution was the sole and exclusive means for protecting technology, preempting the field, and thus permitting no state legal protection of

127. This reasoning is explicit in, *e.g.*, Adolph Gottscho, Inc. v. American Marking Corp., 18 N.Y. 467, 114 A.2d 438 (1955), *cert. denied*, 350 U.S. 834 (1955), and underlies, *e.g.*, A.O. Smith Corp. v. Petroleum Iron Works Co., 73 F.2d 531 (6th Cir. 1934), *modified on rehearing*, 74 F.2d 943 (6th Cir. 1935); Allen-Qualley Co. v. Shellmar Prods. Co., 31 F.2d 293 (N.D. Ill. 1929), *aff'd*, 36 F.2d 623 (7th Cir. 1929).

128. Stone v. Grasselli Chem. Co., 65 N.J.Eq. 756, 55 A. 736 (Ct. Err. & App. 1903). *See* text accompanying note 102 *supra*.

129. Smith v. Dravo Corp. 203 F.2d 369 (7th Cir. 1953).

130. Kewanee Oil Co. v. Bicron Corp. 414 U.S. 818 (1974).

trade secrets.[131] *Kewanee* held that patent law and trade-secret law coexisted, each with its particular role to play, and that the states were free to protect trade secrets.

Although *Kewanee* appears to have laid to rest the broad issue of federal preemption of trade-secret law, it is likely that the federal–state jurisdictional issue that produced the controversy will continue to surface in other ways. Accordingly, a brief summary of the area is warranted, particularly as a cautionary addition to the checklist of the Japanese practitioner.

The problem had its origin in the 1964 *Sears* and *Compco* cases.[132] These cases involved state unfair competition laws prohibiting, among other things, the copying of manufactured articles. State courts had granted relief to the owners of patents (one for a pole lamp and one for fluorescent lighting fixtures) that had been held invalid against copiers of the manufactured articles described in the patents. The Supreme Court held that the state courts could not grant such relief, because the patentees would thereby gain a monopoly in excess of that available to them under the patent system. The cases had nothing to do with trade secrets, as no secrets were involved; the copying was of obvious, open features of the manufactured articles. However, some understood the Court to be saying that no form of legal protection of industrial property, secret or not, could be constitutionally made available outside the patent–trademark–copyright system.

The confusion arising from these cases was compounded by questions raised, but not answered, by the Supreme Court in *Lear* v. *Adkins*.[133] In *Lear*, the licensee under a patent was sued for royalties and in defense asserted that the patent was invalid; the licensor–patentee urged that the licensee was prohibited from asserting invalidity under the doctrine of "licensee estoppel," to the effect that one who accepts the benefits of a patent license will not be heard to assert that the licensed patent is invalid. The Supreme Court, eliminating the licensee estoppel doctrine, reversed the decision of the court below. An incidental question was raised as to license royalties accrued during the period after the commencement of the license agreement but prior to the issuance of the questioned patent. The Court indicated that settlement of the question would involve consideration of the basis of state protection of "unpatented inventions" and whether such

131. Kewanee Oil Co. v. Bicron Corp., 478 F.2d 1074 (6th Cir. 1973).

132. Sears, Roebuck & Co. v. Stiffel Co., 376 U.S. 225 (1964), *rehearing denied*, 376 U.S. 973 (1964); Compco Corp. v. Day-Brite Lighting Inc., 376 U.S. 234 (1964), *rehearing denied*, 377 U.S. 913 (1964).

133. Lear, Inc. v. Adkins, 395 U.S. 653 (1969).

protection could lawfully be provided. The Court declined, however, to resolve the question, pending further consideration by the state court of the relevant state law.

This asked but unanswered question soon led to conflicting cases in the lower federal courts. In *Painton* v. *Bourns*,[134] a federal district court in an alternative holding, relying on a very broad reading of *Lear* v. *Adkins*, held that compensation could be sought by an "inventor" of an "idea" who had not filed a patent application. The court of appeals reversed,[135] holding that there was no basis for refusal to enforce royalty provisions of trade-secret license agreements (at least where no patent application had been filed), distinguishing *Sears*, *Compco*, and *Lear* as not dealing with trade secrets (except possibly inventions subject to pending patent applications).

The issue was finally posed most clearly in *Kewanee*, where the developer of the trade secrets had a very appealing case. Kewanee had spent more than one million dollars over a seventeen-year period developing techniques and processes for growing a type of crystal used in radiation detectors. As a result of this sustained effort and substantial expenditure, it had what the trial court found to be twenty trade secrets, not generally known. Shortly after Kewanee commenced commercial production of the crystals, a number of its employees, all of whom had signed agreements to preserve the confidentiality of their employer's trade secrets, left and formed Bicron Corporation, which promptly (less than a year) commenced competitive production and sale of the crystals. Kewanee sued Bicron and the former employees for damages and injunctive relief against use or disclosure of the trade secrets. Defendants lost in the trial court, which granted an injunction, and they appealed to the court of appeals. That court reversed, holding that the Ohio state trade-secret laws under which relief had been granted were in conflict with the federal patent laws, which had preempted the field. It relied heavily on a statement by Kewanee's counsel in oral argument that it construed as an admission that Kewanee's trade secrets were patentable inventions and that Kewanee had elected not to file patent applications with the intent to extend its monopoly in the crystals beyond the seventeen-year term of a patent. The court reasoned that the central purpose of the patent system was to encourage inventors to make their ideas public in exchange for the limited monopoly of a patent, and that this purpose was subverted by permitting them instead to keep inventions secret indefinitely while still reaping the economic benefits.

134. Painton & Co. v. Bourns, Inc., 309 F.Supp. 271 (S.D.N.Y. 1970), *reversed*, 442 F.2d 216 (2d Cir. 1971).

135. Painton & Co. v. Bourns, 442 F.2d 216 (2d Cir. 1971).

Kewanee obtained review in the United States Supreme Court. The opinion of that Court (written by Chief Justice Burger) first reviewed the Ohio trade-secret law and the proceedings in the lower courts, and then analyzed the objectives of the patent law and of trade-secret law. The purpose of patent law was said to be the inducement of additions to knowledge by offering, in return for public disclosure of new inventions, a right for a limited period to exclude others from their use. The purposes of trade-secret law, by contrast, were to maintain commercial ethics and to encourage research, development, and invention.

The Court then pointed out that trade-secret law protected matter that did not meet the requirements of patentability, and that abolition of trade-secret protection would not lead to increased disclosure of such unpatentable matter. The more difficult problem was in the area of items of the type that might be patentable. The Court distinguished three situations: trade secrets believed to be patentable, trade secrets known to be unpatentable, and trade secrets of dubious patentability. Trade secrets known to be unpatentable presented no conflict, because the patent system was not available as an alternative to secrecy. On the contrary, the availability of secrecy would encourage invention in areas not covered by the patent system. The absence of secrecy protection would induce lessened research, fragmentation of research, and increased costs. Moreover, the absence of enforceable licensing would lead to lesser utilization or redundant and duplicative manufacturing facilities or both, and to the promotion of industrial espionage.

The category of trade secrets of doubtful patentability was analyzed somewhat differently. The Court said that the absence of trade-secret protection would encourage filing of marginal patent applications, some of which would cover nonpatentable discoveries. Where no patent issued, the time expended in the prosecution of the application would have been wasted, when otherwise some benefits could have been made available through trade-secret licensing. On the other hand, an overburdened patent office might well grant some of the applications, resulting in invalid patents with the attendant restriction of ideas belonging in the public domain, unnecessary litigation, and the like.

The final category was that of patentable inventions. The Court said if state protection of such inventions caused a substantial risk that inventors of patentable inventions would not seek patents, it would be compelled to hold such state protection incompatible with the federal patent system; but trade-secret law created no such risk. Trade-secret law does not protect against independent discovery, reverse engineering, or other honest means by which others may come into possession of the secret; nor does it offer effective protection in many cases of wrongful acquisition, because of the difficulties in proving such acquisition. Thus most inventors will seek the relative security of a patent. Even those who do not do so cause little risk to technical progress because of the likelihood of independent discovery by others.

The Court therefore concluded that none of the three categories involved such conflict with federal patent law that that law should be held to have preempted the field.

VI. Miscellaneous Governmental and Statutory Regulation of Trade Secrets in the United States

As we have observed, the substantive law of trade secrets in the United States remains primarily judge-made and is, in general, state rather than federal law. Statutes and governmental regulation (other than antitrust regulation and tax law, discussed in other chapters of this book) constitute a sparse miscellany. Nonetheless, the possible applicability of a statutory law or government regulation must be considered in each situation as it arises. Some examples merit a brief survey here.

The proprietor of a trade secret may be required to make it public where a legitimate regulatory interest is served thereby, as, for example, in the case of a Board of Health regulation requiring certain food products to bear labels showing the proportions of the various ingredients.[136]

In a few jurisdictions it is a crime to steal or wrongfully use certain types of trade secrets or their physical embodiments.[137]

As a result of "cold war" policies aimed at communist countries, the export of technical information has for many years been the subject of federal regulation under the Export Administration Act of 1969[138] and its predecessors. Currently, however, the act is scheduled to expire and is being extended on a month-to-month basis.[139] Accordingly, no description of the complex regulatory scheme is presented, but the current status of such regulation should be reviewed by the United States practitioner in connection with export transactions.

136. Corn Prods. Ref. Co. v. Eddy, 249 U.S. 427 (1919).

137. *See, e.g.*, N.Y. Penal Law §§155.00(6), 155.30(3) and 165.07 (McKinney 1967) and note 4 *supra*. Generally, as in the New York law, these statutes deal with theft of tangible articles rather than ideas themselves. This treatment conflicts with the usual European codes, which deal with misuse as well. Relevant provisions of the Japanese Criminal Code are discussed below.

138. 50 U.S.C. App. §§2401 *et seq.*

139. P.L. 93–327, 93rd Cong., 2nd Sess., 88 Stat. 287.

The foreign filing of patent applications is also subject to certain restrictions.[140]

VII. Criminal Sanctions for Unauthorized Disclosure or Misuse of Trade Secrets in Japan

Unlike many European countries, Japan does not have any provision in its Criminal Code that punishes acts of unauthorized disclosure, misuse of trade secrets, or industrial espionage. However, provisions of the Criminal Code (arts. 222, 233, 235, 246, 247) concerning intimidation, obstruction of another's business, theft, fraud, breach of trust, and the like may be applicable to such conduct.

The first industrial espionage case in Japan was decided in 1965. *Japan* v. *Telenchef*[141] grew out of a battle between two leading printing companies, one of which enlisted the staff of a private detective agency operated by defendant George Telenchef. The Court held the defendants were guilty of intimidation, trafficking in stolen property, and obstruction of another's business.

In *Japan* v. *Himei*,[142] the defendant, a member of the technological department of a leading chemical company in Osaka, left his employment, carrying with him a material developed for use in the manufacture of vinyl chloride. He took also a document file containing a report concerning a new process for the manufacture of vinyl chloride. All of the things taken were kept secret by the company. The court recognized the value of such materials and documents to the company and applied article 253 of the Criminal Code concerning embezzlement in the conduct of business.

In addition, the Criminal Code punishes persons in certain professions who disclose secrets of their clients or customers:[143]

> A person who is or has been a doctor, pharmacist, druggist, midwife, lawyer, defense counsel, or notary and who without due cause discloses a secret which has come to his knowledge in the performance of his profession, shall be punished with penal servitude for not more than six months or a fine of not more than one hundred yen.

Laws which regulate various professions contain similar provisions. For attorneys, the Lawyers Law provides as follows:[144] "A lawyer or a person who was previously a lawyer shall have the right and responsibility of maintaining the secrecy of any facts he came to know in

140. 35 U.S.C. §181–188.
141. 7 Kakyū minshū 1319 (Tokyo Dist. Ct., June 26, 1965).
142. In Hanrei Taimuzu (No. 209) 260 (Osaka Dist. Ct., May 31, 1967).
143. Criminal Code art. 134.
144. *Bengoshihō* (Lawyers Law) art. 23 (Law No. 205, 1949), in 2 EHS No. 2040.

performing his business, provided that this shall not apply when otherwise provided by laws."

VIII. The Lawyer's Responsibility

This brief survey of the substantive law of trade secrets and know-how has shown that the value of proprietary know-how and unpatented inventions may be lessened or lost by failure to safeguard properly its continued secrecy. Many safeguards, such as plant security, controlled access to confidential information, and the like, are obvious and normally known to persons who possess trade secrets.

Other pitfalls are not so obvious to the layman, and an attorney undertaking general representation of any enterprise to which trade secrets are important must carefully review his client's protective practices. And he must be constantly on the alert. Dangerous omissions in the protective system can develop as personnel or processes change. Particularly difficult are international transactions, as to which the foreign legal context will probably include a number of surprises for the uninformed.

A situation calling for special care is the important preliminary negotiation, whether for licensing, selling, or merger of the business, or other purposes in which technology may be of importance. It is easy, when the negotiation is important and expectations are high, to reveal more than is prudent. If the negotiations fail, the disclosed information may or may not be protected. One remedy is a preliminary secrecy agreement making unmistakably clear the continuous confidentiality of the information. One such form of agreement is set forth in this chapter as an appendix. It is not intended as a model or as a definitive form, but as an illustration of one possible variant of such an agreement. It does not go as far as it could in restricting the disclosee, and thus represents an attempt at a reasonable compromise of the conflicting interests of the disclosee and discloser.

For use in international transactions, the form must be elaborated in several respects. Because the final agreement will likely vary in each case and require substantial negotiation, no attempt to draft definitive provisions for these points has been made.

Paragraph 1 could be expanded to describe in detail the precautions that the disclosee of the confidential material shall take. It should be obvious, however, that if the prospective disclosee is not clearly responsible and honorable, no disclosures should be made regardless of how detailed and strict the agreement, as remedies against the reckless or dishonest are not adequate for the real damage that can be sustained by the owner of know-how made public in breach of contract.

No provision is made in the form, as to the burden of proof concerning the exclusions from confidentiality, Paragraph 1(a), (b), and (c). Each party will normally wish the other to have the burden; most negotiations between parties of equivalent power are likely to leave the question to the general law.

The "public knowledge or literature" exclusion (Paragraph 1[b]) is quite ambiguous in an international transaction, and the agreement should be expanded to express the intent of the parties on the question of whether the "public" is that of one or the other country, or both; and where appropriate, there should be specified a more precise definition of the meaning of "public knowledge or literature," which may be different in each country.

In view of the virtual absence of statutory protection of know-how in Japan, a choice-of-law provision referring to the law of an appropriate state of the United States is desirable. In aid of the enforceability of this provision, the contacts with this state should be recited, including, where applicable, the fact of execution of the agreement within the state.

Similarly, because of the previously noted absence of a procedure in Japan for non-public court-litigation of trade secrets, it may be desirable to select a forum. Arbitration is a solution. Representative arbitration provisions are set out in those portions of this book that are concerned with license agreements and with assignment of interests in technology.

Preliminary secrecy agreements cannot satisfactorily be ready-made forms, but must be carefully developed for each transaction. The form in the appendix, and this discussion, may be a useful stimulus to further thought, but are hardly a substitute for it.

Confidentiality agreements with employees will also on occasion engage counsel's attention. An employer in Japan or the United States can by contract bind his employees not to disclose information that the latter acquire during the course of employment.[145]

In addition, an employer in Japan or the United States may restrict the conduct of employees after termination of employment, at least for a limited period. For example, the following clause was used in a secrecy agreement between a Japanese joint-venture company and their employees:

145. In the United States, as discussed above, an obligation of nondisclosure is implied; but a formal agreement strengthens and clarifies the obligation. *See* notes 50–54 and accompanying text *supra*.

> In addition to the limitations imposed by law upon the use or disclosure to others by me of Confidential Information, I further agree that, if my employment by Employer shall terminate for any reason, I will not for two (2) years thereafter, without first obtaining the written permission of Employer, directly or indirectly perform services for: (a) any person, firm or corporation engaged (or about to become engaged) in the production and/or sale of any product with which at any time during my employment by Employer my work has been concerned or in respect to which I have acquired Confidential Information as a result of my said employment; or (b) any firm or corporation which is the parent, subsidiary or affiliate of such firm or corporation; provided, however, that in the event I am unable to engage in suitable gainful occupation solely by reason of my agreement set forth in this paragraph (5) and not because of the restrictions otherwise imposed by law, the same shall be binding upon me only for so long as Employer shall make payments to me as provided in Exhibit A.

An agreement restricting the activity of employees after termination of the employment may run afoul of a public policy (in both the United States and Japan) against unreasonable limitations on the right to earn a livelihood by the practice of one's trade or profession. In Japanese agreements, quoted in part above, the restrictions are limited to a term of two years. Moreover, the employee's economic security is strengthened by the provision for payment in the event of inability to be employed because of the restrictions. The payments usually provided are almost equal to the employee's regular compensation, although the fringe benefits so important in Japan are lost.[146]

In the United States, post-employment payment is rare and is usually found only in agreements involving very senior executive personnel which provide payments for "consulting." This may explain why American courts have strictly limited the scope of post-termination restrictions on employment. This is an area primarily of case law which varies from jurisdiction to jurisdiction. The outcome in each case very much depends on the facts.[147] Restrictions are more likely to be enforceable when their term is short (one year is standard): when the scope of the proscribed employment is limited and reasonably related to the activities of the particular employee and to the nature of the employer's business and needs; and where it can be shown that the employee possesses important and substantial trade secrets of the employer as distinguished from normal professional skill and knowledge.

146. The validity of such a holdover provision has never been adjudicated in Japan.

147. For a detailed treatment, *see* J. COSTA, THE LAW OF INVENTING IN EMPLOYMENT (1953).

Appendix: Secrecy Agreement

JOHN LYON AND TERUO DOI

THIS AGREEMENT entered into on the ___ day of ________, 19___, between TECHNICAL WIDGETS, INC., hereinafter called "TECHNICAL," and APEX WIDGETS CORPORATION, hereinafter called "APEX."

WHEREAS, TECHNICAL has conducted research and development in the field of widget manufacture and control; and

WHEREAS, TECHNICAL possesses confidential information, data, and documents relating to the above subjects; and

WHEREAS, TECHNICAL and APEX are desirous of entering into discussions with respect to the above subjects under such circumstances that the confidential nature of the disclosures made is maintained;

NOW, THEREFORE, in consideration of the foregoing and the mutual covenants herein contained, the parties hereto agree as follows:

1. APEX agrees that it will treat as confidential any and all information disclosed or transmitted by TECHNICAL pursuant to this agreement and will not divulge any such information to third parties without the prior written consent of TECHNICAL. APEX agrees that it will take all reasonable precautions to insure that it and any of its employees receiving information disclosed by TECHNICAL pursuant to this agreement will maintain the confidentiality thereof. It is agreed, however, that such information:

(a) which was in the possession of APEX prior to receipt of any disclosure by TECHNICAL pursuant to this agreement and not heretofore directly or indirectly derived from TECHNICAL;

(b) which is or lawfully becomes part of the public knowledge or literature; or

(c) which otherwise lawfully shall become available to APEX from sources other than TECHNICAL;

shall not be subject to the provisions of this agreement.

2. APEX agrees that it will not make any commercial use whatsoever of any of the confidential information furnished by TECHNICAL pursuant to this agreement without the prior written permission of TECHNICAL.

3. APEX agrees that it will not make copies or reproductions at any time of any reports, compilations of data, brochures, drawings, blueprints or other documents furnished by TECHNICAL pursuant to this agreement, or any part thereof, and will return all such materials to TECHNICAL promptly upon request.

4. APEX agrees that it will comply with any and all applicable laws regulating the exportation of technical information as from time to time in force.

5. Confidential information disclosed hereunder by TECHNICAL to APEX shall be in writing and marked "Confidential," or if orally disclosed, shall be reduced to writing and delivered to APEX, marked "Confidential," within thirty (30) days of the oral disclosures.

TECHNICAL WIDGETS, INC.

By ______________________________

APEX WIDGETS CORPORATION

By ______________________________

United States Patent Law Application Procedures

ROBERT A. STENZEL

I. Introduction

This chapter describes the procedure an inventor must follow if he is to obtain a patent right in the United States. A governmental agency such as the patent office, which handles a large volume of very complex and technical work, must develop procedures for the efficient conduct of its affairs. An understanding of these procedures as well as some of the philosophy of the basic legislation is essential to the party who seeks to obtain or enforce a patent.

The central idea underlying the patent system is that it is in the public interest to encourage the development of new ways to solve the many problems which beset mankind. This, it has been found, is best done by granting to the innovator a limited period within which he is given exclusive rights in his ideas.[1] Thus, a United States patent is a grant by the government to the inventor and to his heirs and assigns, for a period of seventeen years from the date of grant, of an exclusive right to make, use, and sell the subject matter of his invention in the United States.[2] The rights set forth by congressional enactment find their basis in Article 1, Section 8 of the Constitution which states that the Congress shall have the power "to promote the progress of science and useful arts, by securing for limited times to authors and inventors the exclusive right to their respective writings and discoveries." In

1. The first patent law was enacted 10 April, 1790 (1 Stat. 109), but the patent office as a distinct bureau, in the Department of State, dates from the year 1802, when an official who became known as the Superintendent of Patents was placed in charge. The general revision of the patent laws enacted 4 July, 1836 (5 Stat. 117), reorganized the patent office and designated the official in charge as commissioner of patents. Another general revision of the patent laws was made in 1870, and since that date numerous acts of Congress relating to patents were passed, until they were revised and codified, effective 1 January, 1953, as title 35 of the *United States Code*.

2. 35 U.S.C. §154 (1964).

1790, Congress enacted the statute which is the progenitor of the present Patent Act.[3] In the United States system of jurisprudence the "law" on a given topic includes both legislation and the judicial decisions construing it. Of the latter there is no shortage.

Responsibility for the accomplishment of the constitutional and congressional mandates that invention shall be encouraged rests on the patent office. The administrative head of this agency is the commissioner, and Congress has given him the power to promulgate regulations not inconsistent with the law.[4] These regulations are set forth in the *Rules of Practice in Patent Cases* (referred to hereafter as the *Rules*).[5] A loose-leaf reference work setting forth the examining procedure is the *Manual of Patent Examining Procedure* (hereafter, *Manual*).[6] All changes in patent office policy and procedure are promptly reported in the *Manual* by means of supplements that are periodically incorporated into the text.

All patent office notices are also published in the *Official Gazette* (hereafter, *OG*),[7] a patent office publication appearing each Tuesday and including descriptions of all of the patents and trademarks being granted that week.

It will have been observed that patent law is a complex of a constitutional provision, a federal statute, innumerable administrative regulations, and thousands of decisions construing or interpreting all of these. One of the most important resources for the patent practitioner in assessing the decisions is the *United States Patent Quarterly*,[8] a weekly publication of the privately owned Bureau of National Affairs. It includes well-indexed and head-noted reports of nearly all of the patent, copyright, and trademark decisions of all the courts throughout the country, as well as current patent office notices. The same organization also publishes a weekly *Patent, Trademark, Copyright Jour-*

3. Note 1, *supra*. Title 35 U.S.C. is a codification of the current law, which is substantially the same as when it came into effect 1 January, 1953. Many proposed revisions have been pending in the Congress since 1966 but no general revision has been forth coming.

4. 35 U.S.C. §6 (1964).

5. The rules are officially cited herein in 37 C.F.R. (Code of Federal Regulations). The rule concerned is the number following the decimal point in the citation e.g. 37 C.F.R. §1.52 concerns rule 52.

6. Superintendent of Documents, U.S. Government Printing Office, Washington D.C. 20402, third edition, 1961. Over 40 revisions. $24.50 mailed to a foreign address.

7. Superintendent of Documents, U.S. Government Printing Office, Washington D.C. 20402. Available in two parts. The Patent O.G. has on annual foreign subscription $111.25 Catalog No. C21.5 and Trademark O.G. annual foreign subscription $21.25 Catalog No. C21, 5/a3.

8. Bureau of National Affairs, Inc., 1231 25th St. N.W. Washington D.C., 20037. Annual subscription: $250.00 first year and $240.00 per year thereafter. Air Mail Delivery $32.50 per year additional.

nal,[9] which aims to discuss the full range of the latest developments in all aspects of patent law, including pending legislation. The journal is in newsletter format and includes full-text reproductions of significant judicial opinions, legislation, speeches, and other relevant material.

Decisions of the federal courts are available in various compilations,[10] and these, together with the annotations to the United States Code,[11] the law reviews,[12] the specialized patent-law periodicals,[13] and the textbooks[14] are aids in the search for information about patent law.

II. Organization of the Patent Office

A. An Agency of the Department of Commerce

The patent office is a Department of Commerce agency,[15] and the commissioner, who is the highest official in the office, reports to the secretary of commerce through the assistant secretary for science and technology. The individuals in this chain of command, as well as the four assistant commissioners of patents, are appointed by the President with the advice and consent of the Senate and serve at his pleasure.[16] Patent office policy accordingly varies with the changes in the attitudes of incumbent appointees.

9. Bureau of National Affairs, Inc. 1231 25th St. N.W. Washington D.C. 20037.

10. West Publishing Co., St. Paul Minnesota, publishes the "Federal Supplement" (F.Supp.) which includes all District Court decisions; the "Federal Reporter" (Fed. or F.2d) which includes all courts of appeals, court of claims and court of customs and patent appeals decisions; and Supreme Court Reporter (S.Ct.) which includes all of the Supreme Court decisions. The government publishes Supreme Court decision in the official "United States Reports" available from the Superintendent of Documents Government Printing Office Washington D.C. 20402. Publication of an annual "Decisions of the Commissioner of Patents" has been discontinued.

11. *United States Code Annotated* (USCA) published by West Publishing Company, Inc., St. Paul, Minnesota, and *Federal Code Annotated* published by Bobbs-Merrill Company, Inc., New York, N.Y.

12. Particularly the following: *American University Law Review,* Washington, D.C. *Georgetown University Law Journal*, Washington, D.C. *George Washington University Law Review*, Washington, D.C. *New York University Law Review*, New York, New York.

13. Journal of the Patent Office Society (JPOS) Box 685, Washington, D.C 20044, $6.00/year, $7.00 foreign; *Idea,* published by the Patent, Trademark and Copyright Research Institute, George Washington University, Washington, D.C. 20006; Dunner, Gambrell and Kayton, Patent Law Perspective, Matthew Bender, 235 E. 45th Street, New York, New York, 10017.

14. Deller's Walker on Patents, 2nd Edition, 1964, Baker, Voorhis & Co., Inc., Mt. Kisco, New York, U.S.A. Seidman and Horwitz, Amdur Patent Office Rules & Practice, Matthew Bender 235 E. 45th Street, New York, New York 10017. Smith, Patent Law, Overbeck Co., publishers, Ann Arbor, Michigan, 1964. The following are examples of books available from the Practicing Law Institute; 1133 Avenue of the Americas, New York, New York 10036: Davis, Jr., Practical Patent Licensing; Landis, The Mechanics of Patent Claim Drafting; Jackson and Morris, Art of Drafting Patent Claims; Navin, Patents.

15. 35 U.S.C. §1 (1964).

16. *Id.* §3.

B. Administrative Officers

Four assistant commissioners and various lesser civil service officials are the commissioner's staff and directly help him in the discharge of his responsibilities. These include: (1) the granting and issuing of patents and the registration of trademarks; (2) general supervision over the detailed work of the patent office; (3) formulation of the rules which (subject to approval of the secretary of commerce) govern the day-to-day operations of the patent office, including the review-procedure regulations; (4) recognition of attorneys and agents authorized to appear in patent office proceedings; (5) deciding in certain cases issues that are brought to him by petition under the rules; and (6) performing other duties necessary for the accomplishment of patent office responsibilities.[17]

The commissioner may assign the details of his office among an assistant commissioner for patents, an assistant commissioner for trademarks, an assistant commissioner for legal affairs, and an assistant commissioner for administration.

C. Examining Operation

1. Examiners. To make the examining process more efficient, the work is divided among specialists whose particular areas of expertise are chemical, electrical, and mechanical matters. For each of these areas there are five groups, each headed by a director. Subdivisions known as "art units" specialize still further within each group. The patent office presently employs about twelve hundred examiners and administrators.

Examiners are a highly proficient cadre. Each has a technical education and many are also lawyers. The Patent Office Academy provides training in both patent law and office procedures.[18]

2. Patent office workload. Impatience with patent office delays is common enough, although the delays are readily explained by a volume of applications well above 100,000 per year, of which some 80 percent actually work through to the patent-issuance stage.[19] Couple this workload with difficulties in recruitment of examiners of requisite quality and the result is, currently, an average of fifteen months between filing and the initial patent office action. In individual cases the period of delay varies from six to thirty months. Six months more may pass before the patent actually issues. This situation represents an improvement over previous years, and the

17. *Id.* §6.

18. The Patent Office Academy is open to qualified members of the public. Inquiries should be addressed to the Commissioner of Patents, Washington, D.C. 20231.

19. Industrial Property, World Intellectual Property Organization, Geneva, Switzerland. Published monthly with yearly statistics in each December issue.

eighteen-month filing-to-issuance program contemplated by the Patent Cooperation Treaty signed on 19 July, 1970 by the United States and Japan and eighteen other nations may, in time, be an actuality.[20]

Within the patent office, an examiner's rating (which affects his pay and promotion) is in substantial part based on his ability to bring an application to a conclusion, either issuance or rejection. Examiners are efficient, and a special quality-control section regularly reviews samples of patent-issued applications to ensure continued high quality. An examiner's responsibility is a heavy one. The patent law states a rebuttable presumption that a patent is valid.[21]

3. Patent office facilities. The patent office occupies new and well-planned space in Arlington, Virginia, across the Potomac River from Washington, D.C. Each examiner has an office near a search room, which contains the data on the classes and subclasses of the "prior art" which is so critical to his investigation.[22] This data includes both domestic and foreign information. Centrally located in the building is a duplicate set of classified United States patents, a numerically arranged set of United States patents, and bound sets of patents from foreign countries, as well as over 200,000 textbooks and periodicals.

D. Board of Appeals

The patent office organization includes an administrative board of appeals consisting of the commissioner, the assistant commissioners, and nine examiners-in-chief.[23] If additional manpower is needed, a primary or supervisory examiner can be recruited to the appellate board for a limited period.[24] Examiners-in-chief typically have both legal and scientific competence.[25]

A disappointed applicant can appeal an examiner's decision, rejecting a patent application to an appellate panel that will include at least three members of the board of appeals.[26]

20. 876 O.G. 341. Additional copies are available at no charge from the Commissioner, Washington, D.C. 20231.

21. 35 U.S.C. §282 (Supp.V, 1970).

22. Nearly four million U.S. patents are classified by subject matter into about 300 separate classes. Each class has from 80 to over 500 subclasses. The applications processed by each examiner usually are limited to those classified in one class and sometimes even one range of subclasses. The examiner's search, however, almost always goes beyond this area of classification and may extend to many classes. In these cases the examiners cooperate with each other by directing others to the areas in their class which will be the most profitably searched.

23. 35 U.S.C. §3 Provides for up to fifteen examiners-in-chief.

24. Only one acting examiner-in-chief may sit on each three-man board. *In re* Wiechert, 361 F.2d 482; 149 USPQ 894 (CCPA, 1966). The presence of two may render the decision improper and without effect.

25. 35 U.S.C. §7 (1964).

26. *Id.* §134. This procedure is outlined in text accompanying notes 133–47 *infra.*

E. Board of Interferences

In the nomenclature of patents an "interference" occurs when an issue arises with regard to the time order in which overlapping inventions were developed. Resolution of the interference is the responsibility of the patent office, three-man board of interference examiners, which rules on priority questions.[27] Their work is of particular importance, because in the United States the person who first invents is entitled to patent his idea (if certain conditions are met), even though he may not be the first to apply for a patent on the idea.[28]

III. The Patent Application

A. Persons Who May Apply for a Patent

1. Only original inventors. The constitutional mandate is that patents are to be granted to "inventors," a term construed as meaning the actual inventor, not his assignee or employer. An application for a patent must therefore be executed by the first inventor (or inventors).[29]

Save for a statutory prohibition of application by a patent office employee (they cannot even acquire an interest in a patent except by inheritance or bequest),[30] anyone regardless of age, sex, or citizenship can apply for a patent.

2. Executor, administrator, or guardian. Special provisions are made for the problem arising when an inventor dies or becomes insane, permitting execution of the application by an executor, administrator, or guardian.[31]

3. Joint inventors. If an invention is made by two or more persons, all of them must execute the application save where one refuses to sign or cannot be found. The application must identify all of the inventors.[32]

B. Persons Who May Prosecute an Application Before the Patent Office

An inventor can of course prepare, file, and carry on his application and can communicate with the patent office by correspondence. A foreign national need not appoint a resident agent.[33] Both the application and accompanying correspondence must be in English[34] and legible.

27. 35 U.S.C. §135 (1964).
28. This procedure is set forth in text accompanying notes 148–57 *infra*.
29. 35 U.S.C. §111 (1964).
30. *Id.* §4.
31. 37 C.F.R. §1.47 (1971). Rule 47 per Note 5 *supra*.
32. 35 U.S.C. §116, 37 C.F.R. §1.45 (1971).
33. 37 C.F.R. §1.31–34 (1971). (Rules 31–34).
34. *Id.* §1.52 (Rule 52).

Although the inventor must execute the application, control of its progress will be in the hands of the assignee if the inventor has transferred the entire interest in the invention and the assignment has been recorded in the patent office.[35]

1. Patent attorney or agent. Granted that an applicant can manage his case if he so chooses, such a course may not be in his best interest. Patent office procedures are complex and are the particular province of specialists who must demonstrate their competence before they are admitted to practice before the patent office. If an applicant appears to be insufficiently familiar with the prosecution procedure, the patent office will recommend that he procure the assistance of an attorney or agent, but will not help him identify or select one.[36]

To get on the patent office roster of attorneys and agents an attorney must have been admitted to practice before the courts of a state or territory, or of the District of Columbia; must be in good standing in his bar; must establish his good moral character; and must demonstrate proficiency in the scientific and legal aspects of patent practice.[37] An examination testing knowledge both of patent law and of engineering must be successfully passed. A nonlawyer can become a "patent agent," upon satisfactory attainment of comparable standards. He can practice, of course, only before the patent office.

2. Foreign patent attorney. A foreign patent attorney or agent who possesses the necessary qualifications, who does not reside in the United States, and who is both registered and in good standing in the patent office of the country in which he resides can be admitted to practice before the patent office as an agent. A condition to such admission is a showing that his country grants substantially identical reciprocal privileges to persons who are admitted to practice before the Patent Office of the United States.[38] A foreign attorney so registered can handle only applications for residents of his country. The Japanese Patent Office does not grant reciprocal privileges to American attorneys, and for that reason a Japanese patent attorney cannot be registered in the United States.

C. Parts, Form, and Content of the Application

An application for a patent will be accepted by the patent office, assigned a filing date, and given a serial number only if it is complete. Critical requirements are: (1) petition;[39] (2) oath or declaration;[40] (3)

35. *Id.* §1.36 (Rule 36).
36. *Id.* §1.31 (Rule 31).
37. *Id.* §1.341–348 (Ruls 341–48).
38. 37 C.F.R. §1.341(e) (1971) (Rule 341[e]).
39. *Id.* §1.61; *see* note 53 and accompanying text *infra*.
40. 35 U.S.C. §115 (1964); 37 C.F.R. §1.65 (1971); *see* notes 55–63 and accompanying text *infra*.

tender of the filing fee;[41] (4) specification with a claim or claims;[42] (5) drawings if the subject permits;[43] (6) power of attorney or other proof of authority if someone other than the inventor files or prosecutes an application.[44]

The written material must be in English, typed legibly in permanent black ink on one side of paper 8–8½″ by 10½–13″ in size, double-spaced with margins of 1½″ on the left and top. Photocopies are accepted. A foreign applicant must approach the English requirement with care. It will not be met by material written in a foreign language although accompanied by a sworn translation, nor by grammar and sentence structure so faulty as to inhibit a clear understanding.[45] Even for a native, the English language can be troublesome. A patent office examiner will not proceed if the application does not clearly describe the invention.

Interlineation, erasure, strikeovers and other alterations are not necessarily fatal, if made before the application was signed and the oath administered. Each however must be clearly referred to in a marginal note or footnote on the same sheet, and must be initialed or signed and dated, by the applicant.[46]

Minor defects in an application, such as inadequacies in the drawings, which do not preclude a full understanding of the invention, can be waived by the patent office, subject to correction.[47]

The filing date assigned to an application is of great importance. An application so incomplete as to be denied admission can be given the date of the original filing, upon correction of the defects, only if the applicant shows both that a proper application could not have been submitted in the first instance and that he will suffer irreparable harm if denied the earlier filing date.[48]

An incomplete application and the accompanying fee will be held by the patent office pending correction. The applicant can get them back on request. If he neither so requests nor corrects, the papers will be returned to him after six months. Those parts of an inadequate application which are in proper form can be used together with new material to form a valid application.[49]

41. 35 U.S.C. §§41–42 (1964); 37 C.F.R. §1.21 (1971); *see* note 66 and accompanying text *infra*.
42. 35 U.S.C. §112 (1964); 37 C.F.R. §§1.71–77 (1971); *see* notes 67–98 and accompanying text *infra*.
43. 35 U.S.C. §113 (1964); 37 C.F.R. §§1.81–88 (1971); *see* notes 99–100 and accompanying text *infra*.
44. 37 C.F.R. §1.34 (1971).
45. In re Incomplete application 659 O.G. 917.
46. 37 C.F.R. §1.52 (1971).
47. *Id.* §1.53.
48. *Id.* §1.183. 35 U.S.C. 6 (1964).
49. *Id.* §1.53 and M.P.E.P. §506.01 (1970).

Applications are received by the application branch of the patent office, which verifies compliance with the formal requirements and indicates the filing date and serial number. Serial numbers are limited to six digits, and since over 100,000 applications come in each year a new numbering series must from time to time be established. The current series began in January 1970.[50] Identification of an application is possible only if both the filing date and the serial number are known.

After these procedures are completed, the application moves along to a classification examiner who makes an initial determination about subject-matter classification and thus about the group within which further examination will proceed.[51] At this stage the applicant is sent a receipt showing the serial number, the filing date, and the number of the group to which the application has been assigned. Subsequent correspondence about the application will be expedited if the group number is given. From this point on, the applicant cannot withdraw the application papers, although he can obtain copies.[52]

D. The Petition and Power of Attorney

A petition for a patent is addressed to the commissioner and states a formal request for the grant. The applicant's name and post-office address must appear in the petition if not stated elsewhere in the application. If attached to the specification and oath, the petition need not be signed, otherwise the inventor must sign it.[53] If the applicant expects to use an attorney or agent, this fact is indicated in the petition with a power of attorney or agent authorization, which need not be given in any particular wording.[54]

E. Oath and Declaration

An applicant is obliged to swear (or declare) that he believes himself to be the original and first inventor of the invention.[55] This oath or declaration must also include some other averments which are required by statute and by patent office rules, including a statement about the applicant's citizenship, and residence[56] and a statement that he is a sole or joint inventor.[57] The statutory averment about prior invention includes a statement of belief that the invention was not

50. Previous series started 1 January of 1960 and 1948.
51. M.P.E.P. §903.08 (1971).
52. 37 C.F.R. 1.13, 1.15, 1.21 (1971) (Rules 13, 15 and 21).
53. *Id.* §1.57.
54. M.P.E.P. §601.02 (1970).
55. 35 U.S.C §§25–26, 115 (1964).
56. *Id.* §115.
57. 37 C.F.R. §1.65 (1971).

known or used before his discovery; that it was not in public use or on sale in the United States during the year preceding the application; and that it was not patented, or described in a printed publication, in any country during the year prior to his application.[58]

1. Citation of foreign application in oath. The Patent Act requires a statement concerning applications filed abroad covering the same invention to the effect that no such application has been filed, if this be the case, or that gives the filing dates and serial numbers for applications previously filed. Information concerning plans to file in foreign countries later is not needed. If all of the foreign applications were filed during the twelve months immediately preceding the United States application, the applicant need identify only the earliest of them.[59]

2. Defects in the oath. A mistake in the wording of an oath cannot be cured by an amendment. Neither can an omission, nor a defect in the jurat. For these problems, a new oath is the only remedy. The applicant can usually retain the original filing date despite the delay.[60]

3. Oaths taken in foreign countries. If an oath is made abroad, the authority of the person who purports to administer it (if other than an authorized diplomatic or consular officer of the United States) must be verified by a certificate of a United States diplomat or consul.[61] Verification can be made through an intermediary; a consul certifies the authority and jurisdiction of an official, who in turn certifies the authority and jurisdiction of the officer before whom the oath was taken.

All of the application papers except the drawings and the Rule 68 declaration must be attached together and a ribbon passed one or more times through all the sheets of the application except the drawings, and the ends of the ribbon brought together under the seal before the latter is affixed and pressed, or each sheet must be impressed with the official seal of the officer before whom the oath is taken. If the papers as filed are not properly ribboned or sealed, the application will be accepted for examination, but before it is allowed, duplicate papers properly prepared must be submitted.[62]

4. Supplemental oaths. If an application is amended, Rule 67 requires a supplemental oath to the effect that the subject matter of the amendment was part of his invention. The applicant must as to the new matter make allegations and averments as in the original oath.

5. Declaration. A declaration can be made without an appearance

58. 35 U.S.C. §§115, 102 (1964).
59. 37 C.F.R. §1.65 (1971).
60. M.P.E.P. §602.03 (1970).
61. 37 C.F.R. §1.66 (1971) and M.P.E.P. §604 (1970).
62. 37 C.F.R. §1.66(b) (1971).

before an official empowered to administer oaths, and must be part of the group of papers which together constitute an "application."[63]

F. Applicant's Signature and Name

The application must be signed by the applicant in person using his full name, first name without abbreviation and middle initial or name, if any.[64] The family name comes last, and given name first. If the applicant has only two names, the absence of a third or middle name should be indicated by use of a phrase such as "full name."

To avoid confusion and delay, names should be uniform in all of the application papers. Differences will not however affect the validity of the patent.

G. Filing Fees

Fees are payable at various stages of the patent application process. The Patent Act in Rule 41 sets the fees for filing, for disclaimers, for appeals and for other similar kinds of procedure. Rule 21 sets fees for still other papers.[65] For utility patents, i.e., in all cases except design cases, there is a basic fee of $65.00 that entitles the applicant to present ten claims, and additional fees, $10.00 for each additional claim in independent form, and $2.00 for each claim (whether dependent or independent) in excess of ten. Design cases cost $20.00 to file.

H. The Specification

1. Full, clear, concise, and exact description. The "specification" is that vital part of an application that describes the invention, states the manner and process by which it will be made, and tells how it will be used. This descriptive material must be full, clear, and concise, that is, it must be so detailed and exact that any person skilled in the art to which the invention pertains can make and use it.[66] The rationale is that when the patent grant expires and the invention passes into the public domain, the general public, as represented by one of ordinary skill in the art, will know how to practice the invention.

There are other supplemental description requirements. It is necessary to so describe the invention as to distinguish it from other inventions and from products and processes currently known. The description must include a specific embodiment of the process, machine, manufacturing process, composition of materials, or improvement invented and explain the mode of operation or the princi-

63. *Id.* §1.68.
64. *Id.* §1.57.
65. 35 U.S.C. §41 (Supp.V., 1970) and 37 C.F.R. §1.21 (1971).
66. 35 U.S.C. §112 (1964). See full text in footnote 91, *infra*.

ple. The inventor must also describe the best mode for using the invention, as he sees it.

Failure to properly comply with description requirements is a ground for rejection of an application. Some foreign patent offices do not demand this much information, and it is accordingly necessary to exercise great care in preparing an application for a United States patent when one is working from an application initially submitted abroad.

An inadequate specification can cause a different kind of problem. Issuance of a patent does not preclude an attack on it based on failure to comply with the statute.[67] Thus, it may be expected that an adverse claimant and his counsel will scrutinize the application documents with utmost diligence to ascertain whether the requirements have been strictly complied with.

2. *Directed to a person skilled in the art.* A person "skilled in the art" is one who has ordinary or average knowledge and experience in the particular area. He need not have unusual abilities or excel his colleagues.[68] The knowledge to be imputed to a man skilled in the art depends both on the invention and the art to which it pertains. Whether the invention is described fully and clearly enough is a question of fact to be answered in each instance in light of all of the relevant circumstances.[69] An applicant must provide the public with a full disclosure in return for his patent-monopoly, but the standard is to be reasonably applied with due regard to the subject matter.[70] Thus, a disclosure may be adequate, although a man skilled in the art might have to make several tests or trials before reaching the claimed results.

3. *The best mode must be set out.* Although an applicant must indicate the best mode, as he sees it, for carrying out his invention, he is not restricted to that mode. He is limited only by the scope of his claims as interpreted in terms of the specification. A single preferred embodiment will ordinarily be sufficient in mechanical, electrical and non-chemical cases. In chemical cases, a number of different examples or embodiments may be needed in order to provide a basis for broadly stated claims.[71]

4. *Order of arrangement.* In preparing an application, a particular order should be followed in setting out the details:[72]

67. *Id.* §282.
68. Application of Beach, 152 F.2d 981 (CCPA 1946).
69. Hogg v. Emerson, 11 Howard 587 (1850).
70. In re Hudson, 205 F.2d 174 (CCPA, 1953); In re Rainer, 347 F.2d 574 (CCPA, 1965).
71. M.P.E.P. §608.01(p) (1973).
72. 37 C.F.R. §1.77 (1971).

(a) identification of the inventor and title of the invention; or an introductory passage stating the name, citizenship, and residence of the applicant, and title of the invention

(b) abstract of the disclosure

(c) cross reference to related applications, if any

(d) brief summary of the invention

(e) brief description of the several views of the drawings, if there are drawings

(f) description of the preferred embodiment or embodiments

(g) claim or claims

(h) oath or declaration; power of attorney or agent authorization; petition including the necessary signatures

5. *Abstract of the disclosure.* Under the present United States practice, an abstract of the *disclosure*, setting out in seventy-five to one hundred words the nature of the specification and claims, must be submitted. This abstract and a drawing or the broadest claim will be published in the *OG* when the patent is issued. This notice is intended both to inform others of the disclosure in a new patent and to provide a basis for later retrieval. It may not be used for interpreting the scope of the claims.[73]

6. *References to related applications.* If an applicant is to receive the benefit of the filing date granted to an earlier application he must make specific reference to the prior application (or to all of them if more than one) in the specification. This reference appears in the first sentence of the specification, and cross references to other related applications can be made thereafter wherever appropriate.[74]

If a patent refers to an application that is or becomes abandoned, the application so referred to will be retained by the patent office and may be inspected or copied by any person on written request, without notice to the applicant.[75] It is considered prior art as of the issue date of the patent which refers to it.

7. *Detailed description of the invention and drawings.* Rule 71 of the Patent Act requires a detailed description of the invention with references to the different views of the drawing. Rule 74 requires that the numbers of the figures and the different parts be specified by the use of reference letters or numerals (preferably the latter).[76] This detailed description must be of such particularity as to enable a person skilled in the art to make and use the invention without undertaking an

73. *Id.* §1.72(b).
74. *Id.* §1.78.
75. *Id.* §1.14(b).
76. *Id.* §§1.71 and 1.74.

excessive amount of experimentation.[77] An applicant is usually permitted to use his own terminology so long as it can be understood. Words will be given their ordinary dictionary meaning if the applicant does not specifically indicate otherwise and provided he does not try to give obviously contradictory meanings to the well-known words. The description is in one sense a dictionary for the claims and so should provide a clear support for the terms used by the applicant in his claims.[78]

I. Claims

1. The claim determines the scope of the grant. An applicant must point out with particularity, and distinctly claim, the subject matter of his invention.[79] The "claim" is the most important part of an application, since it defines and limits that for which patent protection is granted. More than one claim can be stated. A patent covers only what is covered by a claim, not what the patentee actually disclosed.[80] This principle has been enunciated by the Supreme Court:[81]

> The scope of every patent is limited to the invention described in the claims contained in it, read in the light of the specification. These so mark where the progress claimed by the patent begins and where it ends that they have been aptly likened to the description in a deed, which sets the metes and bounds to the grant which it contains. It is to the claims in every patent . . . that (a person) must turn . . . to determine what the invention is, the exclusive use of which is given to the inventor. . . . He can claim nothing beyond them.

2. Types of claims. A claim must be limited to a single category of invention, i.e., article, method, apparatus, or composition of matter. An exception to this rule is a "product by process claim" whereby, if an article cannot be described in any other manner, it may be claimed in a single claim directed to the process of making it.[82]

When more than one is presented, claims may be placed in dependent form, or arrangement, in which a claim may refer back to and further restrict a preceding claim. Claims in independent form are construed to include all the limitations of the claim incorporated by reference.[83]

The fact that the independent and dependent claims are in different statutory classes does not in itself render the latter improper. Thus, if claim 1 recites a specific product, a claim for the method of

77. 35 U.S.C. §112 (1964) (see text footnote 91 *infra*); 37 C.F.R. §1.71 (1971); M.P.E.P. §608.01 (1970).
78. M.P.E.P. §608.01(g) (1969).
79. 35 U.S.C. §112 (1964). See text footnote 91 *infra*.
80. Harder v. U.S. Piling, 160 F. 463 (CA 7, 1908).
81. Motion Pictures Patents v. Universal Films, 243 U.S. 502 (1917).
82. M.P.E.P. §706.03(e) (1971). *See also* "Product by Process Claims" 28 JPOS 852.
83. 37 C.F.R. §1.75 (1971).

making the product of claim 1 in a particular manner would be a proper dependent claim, since it could not be infringed without infringing claim 1. Similarly, if claim 1 recited a method of making a product, a claim for a product made by the method of claim 1 could be a proper dependent claim. On the other hand, if claim 1 recites a method of making a specified product, a claim to the product set forth in claim 1 would not be a proper dependent claim if the product might be made in other ways.[84]

A dependent claim can refer back to only one preceding claim. A series of dependent claims is, however, permissible.

3. *Claims are interpreted to include more than just the examples in the specification.* The specification need show only one embodiment of the invention, and it is not necessary to describe in the specification all the forms of the invention that may be embraced within the claims. While the claims of the patent may incorporate the specification or drawing by reference,[85] it is not necessary to embrace in the claims or describe in the specification all possible forms in which the claimed principal may be reduced to practice.

4. *Form of claims.* No particular form of words is necessary in framing claims, so long as the meaning is clear.[86] While there is no set statutory form for claims, the present office practice is to insist that each claim must be the object of a sentence starting with "I" or "We" claim, whether or not the words are stated. The claim begins with a capital letter and ends with a period. Periods may not be used elsewhere in the claim except for abbreviations. Reference numerals may appear in the claim,[87] but must be set off with parentheses.

The patent as printed will follow the applicant's format save where printing difficulties or expense prevent duplication of an unduly complex claim format.[88]

5. *Functional and "means" claims.* The invention or discovery specified in a claim must come within the statutory boundaries,[89] and a claim must be directed to a positive element or structure and cannot depend for its patentability on functional language.[90] A new use for an

84. *See* M.P.E.P. 608.01(n) and the following cases relating to: (1) composition and method of making, In re Bowman, 347 F.2d 905; 146 USPQ 207 (CCPA, 1965); (2) composition and method of using, Ex parte Jacobson, 161 USPQ 436 (Bd. App. 1968); (3) apparatus and method of using, In re Tarczy-Hornoch, 397 F.2d 856; 158 USPQ 141 (CCPA, 1968); (4) article and method of working, Ex parte Budd, 147 USPQ 49 (Bd. App. 1965); and (5) pharmaceutical dosage, Ex parte Rusching, 147 USPQ 46 (Bd. App. 1965).

85. Snow v. Lake Shore Railroad Co. 121 U.S. 617 (1887).

86. Brown v. Guild, 23 Wall. 181 (1874).

87. M.P.E.P. §706.03(d) (1971).

88. *Id.* §608.01(m) (1969).

89. 35 U.S.C. §101 (1964).

90. In re Fuller, 388 O.G. 279 (CCPA, 1929).

old structure, manner or process is not patentable on the theory that the original inventor is entitled to every use to which his invention can be put. A new process is however patentable.

Section 112 of the Patent Act permits a claim for a combination of elements to be stated as a means or step for performing a specified function, without a recital of supporting structure, material, or act in support thereof.[91] This provision is however limited by the fact that a claim that recites only a single means so stated as to encompass all possible means for performing a desired function is not patentable.[92]

6. Restriction and double patenting. Section 121 of the Patent Act states the principles governing restriction:

> If two or more independent and distinct inventions are claimed in one application, the Commissioner may require the application to be restricted to one of the inventions. If the other invention is made the subject of a divisional application which complies with the requirements of section 120 of this title it shall be entitled to the benefit of the filing date of the original application. A patent issuing on an application with respect to which a requirement for restriction under this section has been made, or on an application filed as a result of such a requirement, shall not be used as a reference either in the Patent Office or in the courts against a divisional application or against the original application or any patent issued on either of them, if the divisional application is filed before the issuance of the patent on the other application. If a divisional application is directed solely to subject matter described and claimed in the original application as filed, the Commissioner may dispense with signing and execution by the inventor. The validity of a patent shall not be questioned for failure of the Commissioner to require the application to be restricted to one invention.

"Restriction" as used here includes the practice of requiring an election between distinct or dependent inventions, e.g., election between combination and subcombination inventions, and the practice relating to an election between independent inventions, e.g., an elec-

91. 35 U.S.C. 112 provides: The specification shall contain a written description of the invention, and of the manner and process of making and using it, in such full, clear, concise, and exact terms as to enable any person skilled in the art to which it pertains, or with which it is most nearly connected, to make and use the same, and shall set forth the best mode contemplated by the inventor of carrying out his invention.

The specification shall conclude with one or more claims particularly pointing out and distinctly claiming the subject matter which the applicant regards as his invention. A claim may be written in independent or dependent form, and if in dependent form, it shall be construed to include all the limitations of the claim incorporated by reference into the dependent claim.

An element in a claim for a combination may be expressed as a means or step for performing a specified function without the recital of structure, material, or acts in support thereof, and such claim shall be construed to cover the corresponding structure, material, or acts described in the specification and equivalents thereof. (Amended July 24, 1965, Public Law 89–83, sec. 9, 79 Stat. 261).

92. Ex parte Bullock, 127 O.G. 1580 (1907).

tion of species. The term "independent" means that the inventions have no disclosed relationship, and the term "distinct" means that two or more subjects as disclosed are connected in design, operation, or effect; i.e., they are related, but are capable of separate manufacture, use, or sale as claimed, and are patentable over each other.[93]

A restriction demand may be made in the first patent office action or by telephone at an earlier date. Even though the applicant disputes the demand, he must make an election so the examiner can proceed with the elected claims. Nonelected claims will be regarded as withdrawn, under Rule 142.

A petition can be filed asking for review by the commissioner of an examiner's demand for restriction. If no petition is filed or if one is unsuccessful, the nonelected claims must be made the subject of separate divisional applications.[94] This, however, may be held in abeyance pending the disposition of the elected claims.

The Patent Act has been judicially interpreted to mean that only one patent can be granted on one invention. This prohibition of "double" patenting has been applied in cases involving two or more applications by the same inventive entity, the invention claimed in one application being the same as or not patentably distinct from an invention already claimed. The phrase "the same inventive entity" means the same sole inventor or the same group of inventors, as opposed to instances in which diverse persons were involved. In the latter situation, the applications or patents would be prior art as to each other, and the double-patenting rule would not be applicable.[95]

If two applications by one inventive entity or owner present divergent claims, a terminal disclaimer may be effective to overcome the double-patenting problem. Such a disclaimer includes a provision that the patent shall expire immediately if it ceases to be commonly owned with the other application or patent.[96] If the claims are only superficially, rather than actually, different, the disclaimer technique is inappropriate.[97]

7. *Antecedent basis in specification for claim terminology*. A claim must be in conformity with the invention as described in the remainder of the specification, and each term or phrase used in a claim must have clear support or antecedent basis in the description, so that the meaning of the terms in the claim can be found by referring to the description.[98]

93. M.P.E.P. §802.01 (1968).
94. 35 U.S.C. §121 (1964).
95. M.P.E.P. §804 (1973).
96. *Id.* §804.02.
97. In re Bowers, 359 F.2d 886; (CCPA, 1966); In re Braithwaite, 379 F.2d 594; (CCPA, 1967); and In re Frilette, 412 F.2d 269; 162 USPQ 163 (CCPA, 1969).
98. 37 C.F.R. §1.75(d) (1971).

J. Drawings

1. Generally required. In any instance in which the invention is of a type which permits of the use of drawings, they must accompany the application.[99] An application filed without a drawing is inspected to determine whether one is necessary. If the examiner finds that this requirement has not been met, the application will receive a filing date only if and when the application is accepted. The examiner can demand an illustration under Rule 81 to facilitate his understanding, even though a drawing is not necessary.

2. Photographs not generally allowed. Under the practice set forth in section 608.02 of the *Manual*, a photograph is not acceptable in lieu of a drawing, save where the application relates to crystal structure, metallurgical microstructures, textile fabrics, grain structures, and ornamental effects. Even in these situations, a photograph must show the invention more clearly than would a drawing, and must otherwise comply with the rules which govern drawings. In any application photographs may be included as supplemental exhibits as an aid to the examiner's understanding.

3. Requirements strictly enforced. The drawings-requirement of Rule 84 is strictly enforced by the patent office. A nonconforming drawing may however be admitted for the initial examination process, contingent on later compliance, in which case the applicant will be advised of the need for a correct or new drawing. Once filed, the drawings cannot be returned. However, new drawings or necessary corrections in a drawing can be made by the patent office if the applicant so requests, and at his expense. Correction can be accomplished by means of a separate letter to the chief draughtsman referring to a photostatic copy of the original on which the changes are marked in red.

Where the drawings that are part of a new application are to be identical with those in an earlier application filed by the same applicant, or with part of such drawings, the old ones or any sheets thereof may be used if the prior application has been or is about to be abandoned, or if they are cancelled in the prior application.[100]

Once a drawing has been submitted no change in it may be made except upon permission of the patent office. Substitute drawings will not ordinarily be accepted except where required by the patent office.

4. Models, exhibits, and specimens. Models are no longer generally required as the application demands such a full description of the invention in both the specification and in the drawings. A model will

99. 35 U.S.C. §113 (1964).
100. M.P.E.P. §608.02 (1969).

not be officially accepted for permanent inclusion in the file unless it has been requested. Models however may be effectively used at interviews to demonstrate features to the examiner.

IV. Examination and Prosecution of the Patent Application

According to the Patent Act, the commissioner shall cause an examination to be made of an application and if on examination it appears that the applicant is so entitled the commissioner shall issue a patent.[101] There are however several conditions precedent to the issuance.[102]

A. Order of Examination

An application filed and accepted as complete is assigned for examination to the group responsible for the class of inventions to which the application relates, which takes applications up, in their group, in their order of their filing.[103] Thus, backlog periods may vary from short periods in the singular arts to long periods in the more complex fields.

An application covering subject matter the disclosure of which might be detrimental to national security is designated a "secret order" case and is examined by a "security group."[104] Once so designated, foreign filing is not allowed as a matter of right.

B. One Complete Action on Merits and One Final Action

The basic legislation has been interpreted by the patent office as requiring only one full search and one nonfinal office action or letter. Unless it can be shown that the first action was not complete, the second office action will be "final." Once the examination has been concluded to this stage, no changes in it will be permitted except for changes to correct defects in the application, reduce the issues on appeal, or put the case in condition for allowance.[105]

C. Examination Procedure

An examiner's first step is a careful reading of the application with particular attention to formal matters and to the completeness and clarity of the disclosure.[106] If defects in the disclosure and claims are found, the burden will be on the applicant to correct them. After thoroughly familiarizing himself with the subject matter of the appli-

101. 35 U.S.C. §131 (1964).
102. *Id.* §§101–03, 112 (1964).
103. 37 C.F.R. §1.101 (1971).
104. 35 U.S.C. §181 (1964); M.P.E.P. §1107 (1970).
105. 37 C.F.R. §1.116 (1971) M.P.E.P. §714.12 (1973).
106. M.P.E.P. §702 (1970).

cation the examiner will search the prior art, which is a detail more fully discussed below.

In the United States the concept of "universal novelty" is important. With few exceptions, any printed matter available to the public anywhere in the world is "prior art" and relevant in determining whether the applicant's invention is truly first.[107] To aid in the investigation the examiner has not only the extensive scientific library in the patent office but also the facilities of the Library of Congress.

Any material which supports an inference of prior invention by someone else is a "reference." An already issued United States patent is a reference as of its United States filing date rather than as of the date of issuance.[108] There is controversy over whether a patent having a foreign filing should be effective as prior art as of its United States or foreign filing date.[109]

D. Basis of Classification of Prior Art

The concept of utility is the keystone of the classification system in the United States. It is the function of a process or means or product, or the effect it produces, which governs. Utility as a basis of classification must be taken in the sense of direct, proximate, or necessary function, effect or product rather than remote or accidental use and application as in industry or trades. This basis results in the collecting together of similar processes or means that achieve similar results by the application of similar natural laws.[110]

A complete listing of the classes and subclasses with which the examiners work can be had from the patent office in the *Manual of Classification*.[111] Also available is an *Index of Classification*, which is an alphabetical subject-matter index of classifications.[112] To aid in the use of this material, the patent office has prepared extensive definitions of the classes and subclasses.[113]

107. Woodcock, *What is prior art* in Dynamics of the Patent System 286 (1960).

108. Alexander Milburn v. Davis Bournonville, 270 U.S. 390 (1926).

109. The case of *in re* Hilmer, 359 F.2d 859; 149 USPQ 480 (CCPA 1966) held that only the U.S. filing date may be relied upon by a third party as the effective prior art date. See Stenzel, *Effective Prior Art Date of an United States Patent as of the Foreign Filing Date*, 16 AM U. L. Rev. 335 March, 1967.

110. *Development and Use of Patent Classification Systems*, 1966, U.S. Government Printing Office, Washington D.C. 20402. $1.50, 202 pp.

111. Superintendent of Documents, U.S. Government Printing Office, Washington D.C. 20402, 834 pp. Foreign subscription $21.75.

112. Superintendent of Documents, U.S. Government Printing Office, Washington D.C. 20402.

113. *Id.* 111 The Index includes a chart or schedule for each class showing titles and relationships of subclasses. The definitions must be read in combination with the schedule and refer the reader to areas of related art in other subclasses and classes.

E. Scope of Initial Search

A first search by the examiner will cover the invention as described and claimed, including the inventive concepts toward which the claims appear to be directed. This search thus is determined by the scope of the claims and will also cover the entire claimable subject matter in the case.[114] When references are uncovered, the examiner is called upon to cite against the claims only those references which in his judgment are the best.[115] The examiner, however, will note on the file wrapper the classes and subclasses in which he searched. Knowledge of these facts is important in future litigation of a patent, to determine whether different references which may be cited in defense of the patent were in fact considered by the examiner but discarded.

F. Allowance

If the examiner is unable to find references that would provide a proper basis for rejecting the claims, and if the formal matters are proper, an examiner with proper authority signs a blue allowance slip indicating the original classification and any cross references.[116] The application is then sent to the issue branch, which in turn sends a "Notice of Allowance" and demand for the final fee to the applicant.

G. Communication Notifying Applicant of Reasons for Refusal

In a majority of applications, the examiner's investigation uncovers formal defects or pertinent prior art that require rejection of one or more claims. In this event, he will prepare a communication known as an "Office Action" so notifying the applicant, stating the reason for rejection together with such information and references as may be useful to the applicant in evaluating the wisdom of continued prosecution of his application.[117] Each claim is considered to be a separate entity and is specifically referred to in the examiner's letter.

H. Period for Response

The examiner's letter will also indicate the period within which the applicant must respond if he so wishes. Failure to respond will result in the abandonment of his claim. Currently, three months is the period allowed for a response, on the merits, to an Office Action. Shorter or longer limits may be set in other situations, but in no event will a period for response be more than six months.[118]

114. 37 C.F.R. §1.106 (1971); M.P.E.P. §704, §706 (1970).
115. M.P.E.P. §706.02 (1970).
116. *Id.* §1302.10.
117. 35 U.S.C. §132 (1964); 37 C.F.R. §§1.104–08 (1971); M.P.E.P. §706 (1970).
118. 35 U.S.C. §133 (1964); M.P.E.P. §710.02 (1970).

Whenever a period for response ends on a Saturday, Sunday, or a District of Columbia holiday, the next working day is the terminal date.[119]

I. Abandonment

An applicant faced with an adverse Official Action can either abandon his application or take whatever steps may be necessary in order to continue its prosecution.[120] Failure to amend, submission of an amendment which is not responsive, or refusal by the examiner to admit an amendment results in abandonment.[121]

If an applicant makes a bona fide effort to advance the case to final action, in a substantially complete response to an adverse examiner's action, but fails inadvertently to satisfy some part, an opportunity to explain and to remedy the omission may be given.[122]

J. Requirements of Applicant's Reply

If an Office Action is adverse to the applicant, he must, if he wants to pursue his application, reply and request reexamination or reconsideration, with or without an amendment to the application.[123]

This review process requires of the applicant a written request pointing out with clarity and specificity the alleged errors in the Official Action. He must meet every ground of objection or rejection.[124] He may however request that defects in form be held in abeyance pending the disposition of substantive issues.

In an amendment made in response to rejection, the applicant must clearly indicate the patentable novelty he thinks the claim presents when viewed against the state of the art disclosed by the references cited or the objections made by the examiner. He must also show just how his amendment counters the examiner's points.[125] For an amendment, the requirements as to form, language, and paper are the same as for the original application.[126] Telegraphic amendments are permitted, but must be followed by a confirming letter.[127]

If an amendment states an extra claim, it will not be held nonresponsive if the additional fee is not tendered. The new claim will not be entered until the fee is paid.[128] New matter, that is, matter without a

119. *Id.* §21; 37 C.F.R. §1.7 (1971); M.P.E.P. §710.05 (1970).
120. 35 U.S.C. §141–146 (1964); M.P.E.P. §1200 (1970).
121. M.P.E.P. §714.03 (1970); 35 U.S.C. §133 (1964); 37 C.F.R. §1.135.
122. *Id.*
123. 35 U.S.C. §132 (1964); 37 C.F.R. §1.111 (1971).
124. M.P.E.P. §714.02 (1970).
125. 37 C.F.R. §1.111 (1971); M.P.E.P. §714.04 (1970).
126. M.P.E.P. §714.07 (1970).
127. *Id.* §714.08.
128. *Id.* §714.03; §714.10.

basis in the original application, cannot be the subject matter of an amendment. Nor will an amendment be allowed after a final rejection save where it clearly places the case in condition for allowance, or reduces the issues on appeal.[129]

Amendments after allowance may be made only by permission.[130] Affidavits and sworn statements of fact may be submitted to secure this permission. An affidavit may be submitted along with the amendment under Rule 131, swearing back of a reference date, or under Rule 132, traversing a ground of rejection.

A Rule 131 affidavit is limited to proof of acts within the United States, and therefore a foreign applicant is usually limited to his Convention Priority date.[131]

A Rule 132 affidavit may be directed to one or more comparative tests or results, facts of operability of applicant's disclosure, facts of inoperability of the references, facts of commercial success, and facts of sufficiency of disclosure.[132]

K. Reexamination and Reconsideration

If the applicant responds under Rule 111, the application will be reexamined and reconsidered, and the applicant will be notified if claims are rejected, or objections or requirements made, in the same manner as after the first examination.[133] The applicant may respond to such Office Action in the same manner as provided for under Rule 111, with or without amendment, but any amendments after the second Office Action should ordinarily be restricted to the rejection or to the objection or requirements made in the last Office Action, and the application will be again considered, unless the examiner has indicated that the action is final.

Personal and telephone interviews with the examiner are permitted under Rule 133 upon arrangement and after the first office action. Normally, only one interview is permitted after final rejection.[134]

L. Appeal to the Board of Appeals

An applicant can appeal from a final rejection of a claim by the examiner, to the Patent Office Board of Appeals, by filing a notice of appeal signed by the applicant or his attorney and paying the required fee.[135] This must be done within the period for response set in

129. 37 C.F.R. §1.116 (1971), and M.P.E.P. §714.12 (1970).
130. 37 C.F.R. §1.312 (1971), and M.P.E.P. §714.16 (1969).
131. 37 C.F.R. §1.131 (1971).
132. *Id.* §1.132.
133. *Id.* §1.111.
134. M.P.E.P. §713 (1973).
135. 35 U.S.C. §134 (1964); M.P.E.P. §1200 (1972); 37 C.F.R. §1.191–1.198 (1970).

the last office action, usually three months.[136] Two months after his appeal notice is filed, an additional fee must be paid[137] and a brief filed stating the reasons and authorities on which the appeal is grounded.[138]

The applicant's brief goes to the examiner who handled the application. After reviewing the brief, he will conduct an appeal conference with at least two associates, one of whom will be a primary examiner. If this conference supports the examiner he will prepare an answer to the brief,[139] responding to the applicant's allegations or arguments and stating the examiner's position in such detail that the Board of Appeals and the applicant will be fully informed. The examiner may be persuaded by the applicant's brief that some or all rejected claims should be allowed, in which instance, the applicant will be so advised. An examiner can in his answer state a new reason for rejection and if he does the applicant can file a rebuttal reply.[140]

An examiner's objection to an application on the basis of its form is reviewed by the commissioner on petition by the applicant or by the board of appeals in some instances, along with substantive matters.[141]

In general, the board of appeals considers the case on the basis of the written record and pleadings. An applicant can, however, request oral arguments when he files his brief,[142] and, if he does, can present an oral argument either in person or by an attorney or agent, duly authorized of record prior to the hearing.[143] To this argument, for which a half an hour is normally allocated,[144] the primary examiner can present a fifteen-minute, oral counter argument.[145]

Upon the conclusion of its deliberations, the board of appeals will hand down a memorandum decision that can affirm the examiner's position in whole or in part, can reverse him, or can state a new ground for rejection.[146] Each of the contested claims is separately discussed in the memorandum decision, and the reasons for the board's action on each claim will be stated. A disappointed applicant can petition the board for a rehearing, and if this is denied, his administrative recourse is exhausted. Cases which have been decided by the board of appeals will not be reopened or reconsidered by the

136. M.P.E.P. §1200 (1972).
137. 37 C.F.R. §1.192.
138. *Id.*
139. *Id.* §1208 (1970).
140. 37 C.F.R. §1.193(b) (1971), and M.P.E.P. §1208.01 (1970).
141. M.P.E.P. §608.04(c) and §706.01 (1970).
142. 37 C.F.R. §1.192 (1971).
143. *Id.* §1.34. § M.P.E.P. 1209 (1973).
144. *Id.* §1.194.
145. M.P.E.P. §1209 (1973).
146. 37 C.F.R. §1.196 (1971); M.P.E.P. §1213 (1970).

primary examiner, except where a new ground of rejection has been relied upon by the board of appeals.[147] In such cases, the appellant may submit an appropriate amendment and arguments to avoid this rejection. This response will be considered by the primary examiner and/or the board of appeals. Judicial review of the patent office administrative appellate action can be had. The details are discussed below.

M. Interference Proceedings

1. The "first-to-invent" system. In the United States, the first inventor has a right to patent an invention even though someone else files the first application. There can be only one patent for one invention, and if applications claiming the same invention are before it, the patent office must determine which inventor shall prevail, using a procedure known as an "interference."[148] An interference can also exist if a pending application covers an invention already patented.

2. Between pending applications. To declare an interference between applications, the examiner must first decide whether the alleged invention is in fact patentable and whether the two applicants are in fact claiming the same invention.[149] On these issues it is the claims that are to be considered. Mere disclosure in an application of an invention for which no claim is made does not allow the creation of an interference.[150] In such cases the application will be allowed to issue, and the other party or parties may then copy this claim in their application and request that an interference be declared. Applications by different inventors are not in interference if the ownership is in common, as there is no real conflict of interest.[151]

3. Between an application and a patent. Interference proceedings between an application and a patent already issued may be instituted, provided the patent has not been issued for more than one year prior to the filing of the conflicting application, and provided that the conflicting application is not barred from being patentable for some other reason.[152] Thus, an inventor who has kept his invention secret may file an application within one year from the issuance of a patent that he believes claims his invention and was invented after he made his invention. Such later-filed applicant will, however, be subject to intervening prior art which, while not good against the inventor who filed first, would be good against him. Examples of such prior art are

147. 37 C.F.R. §1.181 and §1.197 (1971).
148. 37 C.F.R. §1.201 (1971); M.P.E.P. §1100 (1970).
149. 37 C.F.R. §1.203 (1971); M.P.E.P. §1101 (1970).
150. 37 C.F.R. §1.205 (1971); M.P.E.P. §1101.02(a) (1969).
151. 37 C.F.R. §1.78 (1971); M.P.E.P. §1101.01(b) (1971).
152. 37 C.F.R. §1.201 (1971); M.P.E.P. §1101.02 (1970).

public use in the United States by anyone more than one year prior to his filing and other patents issued more than one year prior to his filing.

4. Evidence of first invention. Once an interference is declared, each party must submit evidence to the patent office concerning the date on which he made the invention.[153] This involves of necessity clear and convincing evidence about the making of the invention. If such evidence is not submitted, the applicant's earliest date will be the date on which he filed his application. Difficulties of proof, differences in practice, and other practical considerations dictate restriction of an inventor to inventive acts within the United States. In the case of applications by foreigners who file under the Paris Convention, only the earliest date of priority can be used.[154]

Evidence relevant to the inventive process will show conception of the invention, its reduction to practice, and due diligence from the time of conception to the time of reduction to practice.[155] "Conception of the invention" refers to the completion of the means for accomplishing the result. "Reduction to practice" refers to the actual construction of the invention in tangible form. In the case of a machine, reduction to practice would include the actual building of the machine. In addition, actual operation, demonstration, or testing for the intended use is also usually necessary. The filing of an application for patent that completely discloses the invention is regarded as an equivalent or "constructive" reduction to practice.[156] Usually, the inventor who proves he was the first to conceive the invention will be held to be the first inventor if he exercised due diligence in reducing it to practice.

Priority of invention is determined by a board of three highly skilled interference examiners who review the evidence submitted by the parties. During the initial stages of an interference, the identity of the parties and their invention dates is classified information. It is only after the evidence has been received that identities are revealed. If the claims differ from each other only slightly, the examiner may suggest the broadest patentable claim; and if the parties agree, it forms a "common count" so each party will be assured of having the broadest protection possible if he prevails.[157]

A decision of the Board of Patent Interferences can be appealed to the Court of Customs and Patent Appeals. Or, the losing party can file a civil action against the winning party in the appropriate United States District Court.

153. 37 C.F.R. §§1.215–28 and 1.271–86 (1971).
154. *Id.* §1.217; M.P.E.P. §201.13 (1970).
155. 37 C.F.R. §§1.271–86 (1971); *see* M.P.E.P. §715 (1970).
156. M.P.E.P. §715.07 (1970).
157. 37 C.F.R. §1.203 (1971); M.P.E.P. §1101.01(j) (1969).

N. Allowance and Issue

1. Final review by the examiner. When a patent application has come to a favorable conclusion, either after allowance by the examiner or by the board of appeals, or by a court, the examiner will undertake a final review of the disclosure in preparation for issuance of the patent.[158] He will check formal matters, conformance of the descriptive matter to the claims, the notation and status of copending applications, conformance of the title to the invention as finally allowed, together with such matters as misspelled words and grammatical errors. He will then determine the exact classification on the basis of the allowed claims and make such cross-reference classifications as are appropriate. Finally, he will conduct an interference search, inspecting all the pending prints and drawings or invention digests, in the relevant subclasses of the class in which the application has been put, and all other pertinent classes whether in his group or elsewhere, in order to ascertain whether some other applicant claims substantially the same subject matter as is being allowed in the case at hand. Interfering cases will be duly noted; however, an interference would be proposed only as to an application filed within three months of the filing of the allowed application.[159] If the search does not disclose any interfering application, the examiner will prepare the case for issue by signing the file wrapper and forwarding the application to the Issue and Gazette branch.

2. Issue and Gazette Branch. The Issue and Gazette Branch will notify the applicant or his attorney or agent in writing that the application has been allowed, and will request payment of the issue fee within three months from the mailing date of the notice.[160] An estimated fee of $100.00 plus $10.00 for each page or portion thereof, of the specification as printed, and $2.00 for each sheet of drawings will be then charged.[161] On payment, the patent will issue. If payment is not timely made, the application will be regarded as abandoned or forfeited. Any remaining balance of the final fee as determined by the printed patent must be paid within three months from the sending of notice of the balance due, and, if it is not paid, the patent will lapse at the termination of this three-month period.[162] An abandonment for nonpayment can be set aside by the commissioner if the applicant tenders a defaulted payment together with a late-payment charge, within three months after default, and shows sufficient reason for the de-

158. M.P.E.P. §1302.01 (1972).
159. *Id.* §1101.01.
160. *Id.* §1303.
161. 35 U.S.C. §§41 and 151 (1964); M.P.E.P. § 1306 (1973).
162. 37 C.F.R. §1.316 (1971).

lay.[163] This statutory period of, in the aggregate, six months, may be extended only by a specific act of Congress.

When the estimated issue-fee is paid, the Issue Branch assigns a tentative patent number and an issue date, which is usually two to three months thereafter. After these steps are taken, withdrawal of the application is allowed only if permission is obtained from the Commissioner.[164]

3. Issuance. The patent office maintains the application in secret until the time of issuance. Each Tuesday at 12:00 noon Eastern Standard time, some 1500 to 1800 patents are officially issued by publication of the abstract or claim, together with a figure of drawing, in the *Official Gazette*, and distribution of the printed patent. The original patent grant, bearing the signature of the issuing officer and of the commissioner, is deposited in the mail or by arrangement can be picked up in person at the patent office.[165] Copies are also made available to the public at this time.

Allowed applications that are subject to a "secrecy order,"[166] are withheld from issue until such time as disclosure of the subject matter will not be detrimental to national security. The seventeen-year period of exclusive right begins when the patent is finally issued. Withheld applications are reviewed periodically to determine whether continued secrecy is necessary.

Each patent identifies the references cited against it, the classifications of the references, as well as the names of the examiner or examiners and the applicant's attorney, if any.

4. Grant of the original patent. Each patent is issued in the name of the United States, bears the seal of the patent office, and recites the following formal grant:

"TO ALL TO WHOM THESE PRESENTS SHALL COME:

WHEREAS, THERE HAS BEEN PRESENTED TO THE

Commissioner of Patents

A petition praying for the grant of Letters Patent for an alleged new and useful invention the title and description of which are contained in the specification of which a copy is hereunto annexed and made a part hereof, and the various requirements of Law in such cases made and provided have been complied with, and the title thereto is, from the records of the Patent Office in the Claimant(s) indicated in the

163. 35 U.S.C. §41(a) and 151 (1964); 37 C.F.R. §1.317 (1971).
164. 37 C.F.R. §1.313 (1971).
165. M.P.E.P. §1309 (1973).
166. M.P.E.P. §1304 (1970).

said copy, and Whereas, upon due examination made, the said Claimant(s) is (are) adjudged to be entitled to a patent under the Law.

Now, therefore, these Letters Patent are to grant unto the said Claimant(s) and the successors, heirs or assigns of the said Claimant(s) for the term of Seventeen years from the date of this grant, subject to the payment of issue fees as provided by Law, the right to exclude others from making, using or selling the said Invention throughout the United States."

This inscription is on a stiff-paper cover to which a copy of the patent is bound with a blue ribbon, affixed with the patent office seal. "Soft" copies of the patent can be purchased from the patent office for fifty cents apiece.[167] An *Official Gazette* notice that includes a single figure from the drawings and recites the abstract or broadest claim is released when the patent is issued.

O. Correction of Patents

Errors in a patent can be corrected in three ways: by reissue of the patent, by the issuance of a certificate which becomes a part of the patent, and by means of a disclaimer.[168]

1. Reissue of the patent. A patent that is, through error and without deceptive intention, invalid wholly or in part because of a defective specification or drawing or of a claim of more or less than the applicant had a right to claim, can be reissued by the commissioner on surrender of the original patent and on payment of a fee.[169] A reissued patent will have a term equal to the unexpired term of the original patent.

An application for reissue must include the entire specification and claims of the patent. This is accomplished by cutting up copies of the original patent and mounting each column on a separate sheet. The matter to be deleted is enclosed in square brackets and additions are underlined.[170] Examination will start on receipt of (1) the corrected patent; (2) an offer to surrender the original patent; (3) a reissue oath or declaration; and (4) a filing fee the same as that for an original application. The applicant retains his original filing date, but is subject to any newly discovered prior art having an earlier effective date. Restriction or division will not be required;[171] but upon request by the applicant, the reissue may result in separate patents for distinct and separate parts of the patented product.

167. 37 C.F.R. §1.21 (1971).
168. M.P.E.P. ch. 1400.
169. 35 U.S.C. §251 (1964); 37 C.F.R. §§1.171–79 (1971); M.P.E.P. §1401 (1970).
170. 37 C.F.R. §1.173 (1971); M.P.E.P. §1401.06 (1970).
171. M.P.E.P. §1401.10 (1970).

Reissue may be sought at any time prior to expiration of the patent save where the reissued patent will enlarge the scope of the claims stated in the original patent, in which case the application for reissue must be filed within two years from the date of the original patent.[172]

Patent office procedures in the case of a reissue application are the same as those for an original application. The same standard of patentability is applied, an interference may be declared, and appeals may be taken.[173] If the patent is reissued, matter deleted from the original patent is enclosed in heavy brackets, and matter added is printed in italics. A reissue application receives a new number beginning with "Re" and is printed in the *Official Gazette* in the same manner as is an original patent, and copies of the original patent are marked with a notice of reissue.

2. *Certificate of correction.* If a mistake in a patent occurs through the fault of the patent office, a certificate of correction will be issued without charge and recorded on all printed copies of the patent.[174] If the mistake is of such a nature that the intended meaning is obvious from the context, the patent office may decline to issue a certificate and will merely place the correspondence regarding the error in the patent file.[175] Certificates of correction are reported numerically in the *Official Gazette*.

Clerical or typographical errors in an application can carry through to the patent. On a showing that the mistake was made in good faith and on payment of a fee, the applicant can obtain a certificate of correction, provided the correction will not add new matter to the patent or otherwise require reexamination of the application.[176] An illustration of this kind of venial mistake is a patent issued on an application naming joint inventors when in fact one of the persons named was not an inventor but was included by mistake and without fraudulent purpose.[177] It should be noted that although deletion of an inventor is no problem, the addition of an inadvertently omitted inventor is much more difficult.

3. *Disclaimer practice.* At the common law, if any claim of a patent were held invalid, the entire patent was void. This harsh result has been avoided by section 253 of Title 35 United States Code which provides that whenever, without any deceptive intention, a claim of a patent is invalid, the remaining claims shall not thereby be rendered

172. 35 U.S.C. §251 (1964).
173. 37 C.F.R. §1.176 (1971); M.P.E.P. §1401.09 (1970).
174. 35 U.S.C. §254 (1964); 37 C.F.R. §1.322 (1971).
175. M.P.E.P. §1402 (1973).
176. *Id.* §1402.01 (1973).
177. 35 U.S.C. §256 (1964); 37 C.F.R. §1.324 (1971).

invalid.[178] A patentee, whether of the whole or any sectional interest in the patent may, on payment of the fee required by law, disclaim any complete claim stating therein the extent of his interest in such patent. Such disclaimer must be in writing and be recorded in the patent office. In like manner, any patentee or applicant may disclaim or dedicate to the public the entire term, or any terminal part of the term, of the patent granted or to be granted.

VI. Appeal to the Courts from a Patent Office Decision

An applicant dissatisfied with a decision of the board of appeals or the board of patent interferences has a choice between appealing to the Court of Customs and Patent Appeals (CCPA)[179] or filing a civil action against the commissioner of patents in the United States District Court for the District of Columbia.[180]

A. Appeal to the CCPA

Within sixty days after an adverse decision by the board of appeals or the board of patent interferences, an appeal may be taken to the CCPA by giving notice thereof to the commissioner and filing in the patent office, in writing, the specific reasons for the appeal.[181] The commissioner, through the office of the solicitor, will acknowledge receipt of the notice and transmit to the court certified copies of all the necessary original papers in evidence in the case.[182] In an *ex parte* case, the appellant submits a printed brief setting forth his authorities and arguments on the issues set forth and the reasons for appeal. The commissioner in turn furnishes the court with the grounds of the decision of the patent office, touching all the points raised by the reasons of appeal.[183] The review of the CCPA is confined to the points set forth in the reasons of appeal and must rely entirely upon the written record made in the patent office.[184] The CCPA cannot base its decision on prior patents which an applicant includes in his record if they were not considered by the examiner or the board in connection with the rejection, and the court has no authority to pass upon patentability of claims allowed. The CCPA has pointed out that the question of patentability of an alleged invention is an *ex parte* issue between the applicant and the patent office, with the patent office representing

178. 35 U.S.C. §253 (1964). *See* 37 C.F.R. §1.321 (1971) and M.P.E.P. §1403 (1969).
179. 35 U.S.C. §§141–44 (1964); 37 C.F.R. §§1.301–02 (1971).
180. 35 U.S.C. §§145–46 (1964); 37 C.F.R. §§1.303–04 (1971).
181. 37 C.F.R. §§1.301–02 and 1.304 (1971).
182. M.P.E.P. §1216.01 (1970).
183. 35 U.S.C. §143 (1964).
184. 35 U.S.C. §144 (1964), Dreyfus v. Lilienfeld, 9 USPQ 507 (CCPA, 1931).

the public, whereas the issue of priority of invention in interference proceedings is an *inter partes* matter.[185]

The jurisdiction of the CCPA in a patent interference is limited to a review of the decision of the board of patent interferences. No appeal lies from the refusal of the patent office to declare or reform an interference.[186]

Within forty days after the record has been printed, the appellant must file a printed brief setting forth the facts, the errors relied upon, and a statement of authorities and arguments. The patent office ordinarily will file a reply brief.[187]

All five judges of the CCPA consider each case either after oral hearing or on brief. An oral hearing requires the applicant or his attorney to appear at the Court House located across Lafayette Square from the White House in Washington, D. C. In *ex parte* cases one-half hour for oral argument is allowed each party. After consideration of the issues and arguments, the court renders a written memorandum opinion stating the reasons for its reversal or affirmance of the Patent Office decision, and in some instances remanding the case to the patent office. A decision reversing the patent office will command the commissioner to issue the patent.[188]

If either the commissioner or the appellant is dissatisfied with the decision of the CCPA, each or both may petition the United States Supreme Court to grant a writ of certiorari ordering the court below to send up the certified record so they may review the case.[189] This review is not a matter of right, but is solely at the discretion of the Supreme Court justices. Because of the very heavy load of that court, few petitions for review are granted. In fact, until the Supreme Court decided the case of *Brenner* v. *Manson*,[190] many thought the Supreme Court had no authority to review cases from the CCPA.

B. Civil Action in the District Court

An applicant's suit against the commission[191] is an *ex parte* matter in which the refusal of the patent is alleged for cause of action. The relief sought is an order to the commissioner to issue the patent.

An action against the prevailing party in an interference[192] is an

185. Gowen v. Hendry et al, 4 USPQ 161 (CCPA, 1930); 35 U.S.C. §§36, 52, 59 (1964).
186. Ewing v. U.S. ex rel Fowler Car, 244 U.S. 1 (1917).
187. M.P.E.P. §1216.01 (1970).
188. 35 U.S.C. §144 (1964).
189. 28 U.S.C. §2101 (1964).
190. 383 U.S. 519 (1966), 148 USPQ 689.
191. 35 U.S.C. §145 (1964).
192. *Id.* §146.

Chart illustrating appeals from the decisions of the Examiner

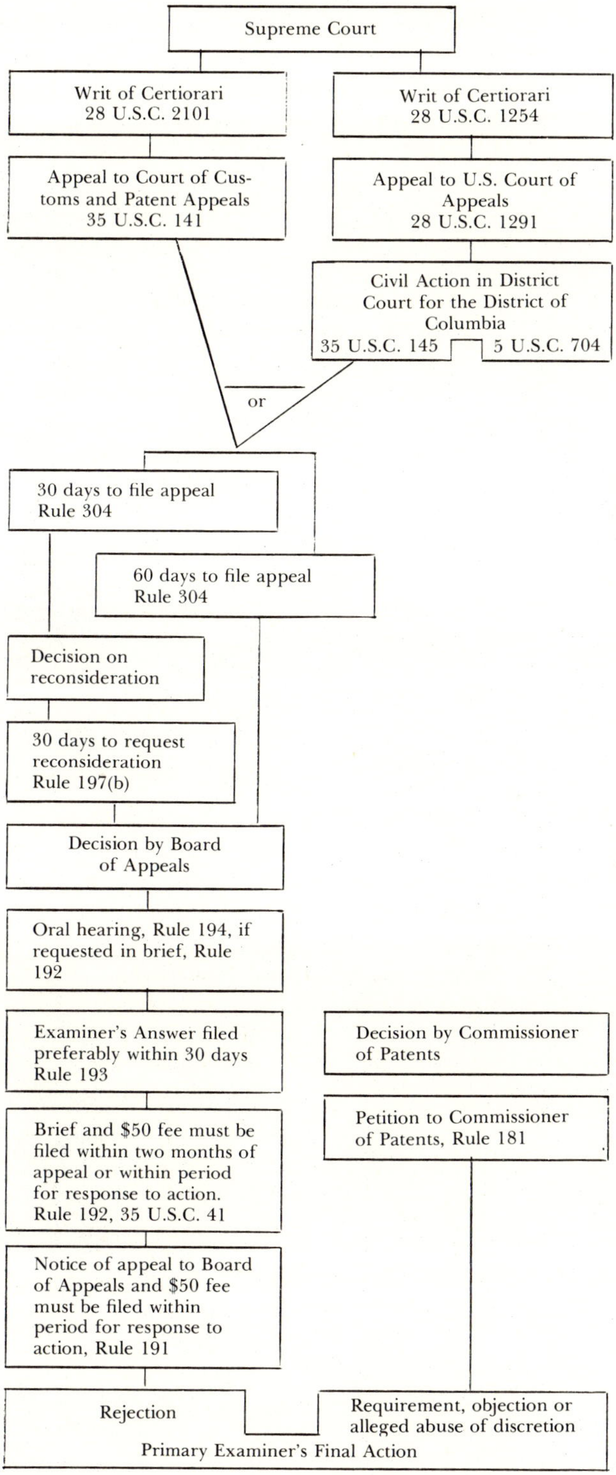

inter partes suit claiming a right to patent on the basis of priority of invention.

When an action is started against the commissioner, the solicitor of the patent office signs a notice of the proceeding and this is placed in the application file, which is kept in his office pending termination of the action. A statement indicating the final decision of the court is entered on the original notice, and the application is returned to the examiner, whose subsequent procedure is the same as that following an appeal.[193]

The court will have, at the time of trial, a certified copy of the file wrapper and contents.[194] If the action is dismissed before trial, no disclosure of the application, to the public, necessarily occurs. The court's decision will however remove any hope of secrecy. Unlike an appeal to the CCPA, the filing of a civil action does not require the immediate filing of a transcript of the application. The complaint will be open to the public. Patent office files subpoenaed by the court are transmitted in care of a patent office employee with a certified copy, under stipulation that the copy be retained by the court and the original returned.

In an action against the commissioner, venue is always in the District of Columbia. A suit based on interference is really between competing applicants, and the commissioner is not a necessary party. Venue will usually be in the district of the defendant's residence.[195] If one of the parties is a foreigner, however, suit must be brought in the district court for the District of Columbia.[196]

Actions by an applicant in the district court are sometimes denominated "trials de novo" because expert testimony and evidence of commercial success may be admitted. Nevertheless, the administrative record of the patent office forms the nucleus of the evidence before the court.[197] The court has no authority to remand the matter to the patent office for consideration of new evidence offered at the trial and therefore must act on its own. Patentability is always in issue, and the court may consider any and all evidence bearing on patentability.[198]

There is a presumption of regularity in a decision of the patent office and the burden of demonstrating that the decision was wrong is on the party challenging the administrative action.[199] This doctrine

193. M.P.E.P. §1216.01 (1970).
194. 28 U.S.C. §1744 (1964).
195. *Id.* §§1391 (Supp. V, 1970) and 1392 (1964).
196. *Id.* §113 (1964).
197. Minnesota Mining & Mfg. Co. v. General Electric Co. 167 F.Supp. 37, 40 (D.C. D.C. 1958).
198. Hill v. Woster, 132 U.S. 693 (1890).

applies both to the review of a denial of an application and to interference.

An appeal may be taken as a matter of right from the district court to the appropriate Court of Appeals,[200] which will review only errors of law and a decision which is clearly contrary to the facts.[201] This appeal must be based on the record in the district court. After briefs have been submitted, an oral hearing may be had before a panel of three judges.[202] A decision of the court of appeals will be in the form of a ruling directing the district court to enter judgment in accordance therewith. If one of the parties is dissatisfied, he can petition the United States Supreme Court for a writ of certiorari.[203] Few such petitions are granted.

VI. Protest and Public Use Proceedings

The patent statutes do not provide for opposition by a member of the public to the grant of a patent. Nevertheless, the idea is currently being tested in a voluntary program. Otherwise, protests to the patent office are usually merely acknowledged and are filed after being referred to the examiner in charge of the application involved.[204]

If a member of the public believes that an invention that is part of an interference or claimed in an application has been in public use or on sale for a year before the application was filed or before the date alleged by an interfering party in his preliminary statement or the date of invention asserted, a "public use proceeding" can be initiated before the commissioner. Such a proceeding is rare and requires a petition supported by affidavits or declarations filed by the person who purports to have the derogatory information.[205]

199. Morgan v. Daniels, 153 U.S. 121, 125 (1894).
200. 28 U.S.C. §§1291, 1292 (1964).
201. FED. R. CIV. P. 52(a).
202. 28 U.S.C. §46 (1964).
203. *Id.* §1254.
204. 37 C.F.R. §1.291 (1971).
205. *Id.* §1.292.

Patent Office and Court Procedures in Japan

YOSHINOBU SOMENO AND KEIKO SOMENO

I. Introduction

The relevant procedures of the Japanese Patent Office may be classified into four categories: (1) examination of applications and granting of patents; (2) trial to invalidate, correct, or amend patents; (3) determination of the technical scope of patents; and (4) determination of the conditions for compulsory licensing.

The rules and regulations of the patent office were drastically changed by the Patent Law of 1959, the main features of which can be summarized as follows: more than one invention can be covered by a single application; publications in foreign countries are included in the prior art for the determination of novelty; detailed rules are provided to restrict amendment of specifications and drawings both for applications filed and patents granted; procedures for appeal within the patent office from judgment in trial are abolished; trial for the confirmation of the scope of patent right is abolished; additional rules are provided for infringement procedures to meet the needs of special cases; and provision is made for a recording system covering exclusive licenses. In addition, the 1970 revision of the patent law established a new system under which a patent application is publicly disclosed within a certain time after the filing date (early disclosure), and examination of an application begins only when the applicant or other person demands it (deferred examination).[1] A similar system was adopted by the Federal Republic of Germany in 1967, when its patent law was amended.[2]

1. *Tokkyohō* (Patent Law) (Law No. 121, 1959, *as amended*, Law No. 91, 1970), in 6 EHS No. 6850A. The translation principally relied upon for this chapter appears in The Patent and Trademark Laws of Japan (2d ed. R. Foster and M. Ono trans., 1970). References in this chapter to individual sections of the Patent Law will normally appear by article number inserted in the text, without further reference in the footnotes.

2. Patentgesetz (Patent Law) 1967.

II. Powers and Organization of the Patent Office

A. Powers of the Patent Office

The Japanese Patent Office, established as an extraministerial bureau of the Ministry of International Trade and Industry (MITI), is empowered to handle a wide range of matters. These include examination of applications for patents and utility models,[3] and for registration of trademarks and industrial designs; trial of appeal cases and invalidation cases; adjudication of the technical scope of patented inventions; determination of the conditions under which compulsory nonexclusive licensing of patents will be ordered; publication of the official gazette; examination of patent attorneys; and other matters related to the protection of industrial property, including encouragement of inventive activities.

The power of the patent office is restricted by article 76(2) of the Constitution of Japan, which prohibits administrative agencies from trying cases as a tribunal of last resort. Any person who regards a patent office act or disposition to be improper can file a court action to contest its validity.

Civil and criminal jurisdiction over patent infringement cases belongs to the regular courts of justice. The patent office is empowered to determine the technical scope of a patented invention which is in dispute, but its finding is only advisory and will not bind the court.

Issues concerning the validity of a patent are, however, within the exclusive jurisdiction of the patent office. If the defendant in an infringement action raises a defense of invalidity of the patent alleged to have been infringed, the court has to stay the proceeding until the patent office determines the issue of invalidity.[4]

B. Organization of the Patent Office

The patent office is headed by a director–general and consists of seven departments: the general affairs department, five examination departments, and the trial department. The first examination department receives applications of all kinds, classifies them properly, examines them as to the formal requirements, and conducts substantive examinations for registration of trademarks and industrial designs. The other examination departments conduct substantive examinations of patent and utility model applications in the area of technology assigned to each. The second and third examination de-

3. Utility models (*jitsuyōshinan*) are devices of less creative level which are registered and protected for ten years from the date of publication in the PATENT GAZETTE under *Jitsuyōshinanhō* (Utility Model Law) (Law No. 123, 1959, *as amended several times*).

4. Patent Law art. 123 provides the grounds and the patent office procedure for invalidating patents, and art. 168(2) provides that the court, when necessary, may stay the litigation proceeding until the patent office adjudication has become finally binding.

partments examine machinery; the fourth examination department, chemistry; and the fifth examination department, electrical engineering. The trial department hears and decides cases submitted for its adjudication. At present, the patent office has 1,100 examiners and 195 adjudication examiners.

III. Applications for Patent

A. Persons Entitled to File An Application for Patent

Any person residing in Japan who has the legal capacity to perform juristic acts can file a patent application. An alien who resides in Japan or a juridical person who has a place of business there can apply for a patent if the applicant's country accords Japanese nationals a like privilege or is a party to a treaty with Japan providing for reciprocity or national treatment in the enjoyment of patent rights (Patent Law art. 25). The Paris Convention for the Protection of Industrial Property is such a treaty.[5]

The applicant must be the inventor or his successor in title (art. 33), and a patent issued to anyone else is subject to invalidation (art. 123[1][iv]). If the applicant is a transferee of the invention, he must file with the patent office a document certifying that he has obtained the right to apply for a patent by succession or assignment. A joint application is necessary if the right to obtain a patent is co-owned (art. 37).

The patent application may be filed either by the applicant himself or by his appointed agent. Under the Patent Attorneys Law,[6] only an attorney at law or a patent attorney may represent the applicant. A nonresident applicant must appoint a patent administrator in order to file an application in Japan (Patent Law art. 8).

B. Documents Required for Application

An application must be in a form specified by regulation and filed with the director–general of the patent office. The following particulars are covered: (1) name and domicile or residence of the applicant; (2) date of filing; (3) title of the invention; and (4) name and domicile or residence of the inventor (art. 36). The application must be accompanied by a specification containing the following: (1) title of the invention; (2) brief explanation of the drawings; (3) detailed explanation of the invention; and (4) the scope of the claim for patent. Drawings should also be submitted where necessary.

Normally, an application must be limited to one invention, but

5. Convention of Paris for the Protection of Industrial Property, Oct. 31, 1958, [1962] 13 U.S.T. 1, T.I.A.S. No. 4931. Revised 1967, 21 U.S.T. 1583, T.I.A.S. 6923.

6. *Benrishihō* (Patent Attorneys Law) (Law No. 100, 1921), in 6 EHS No. 6890.

there are exceptions. A single application can cover other inventions having any of the following relationships to the invention described in the claim for patent:[7]

(1) an invention that utilizes the whole or the essential part of the matter indispensable to the construction of the specified invention as the essential part of the matter indispensable to the construction thereof, and that achieves the same object as that of the specified invention;

(2) in the case where the specified invention is an invention of a thing, an invention of a method of producing such thing, or an invention of a machine, implement, apparatus, or any other thing for producing such thing;

(3) in the case where the specified invention is an invention of a method, an invention of a machine, implement, apparatus, or any other thing which is used directly in working the invention of the method.

The "detailed explanation of the invention" in the specification must contain a statement of the purpose, composition, and effect of the invention in such a way that any person having ordinary knowledge in the technical field to which the invention belongs may easily work the invention (art. 36[4]). The applicant must state in "the scope of claim for patent" only matters indispensable for the composition of the invention as stated in the detailed explanation of the invention (art. 36[5]). If the applicant fails to state any of the required information, his application will be rejected, and if a patent is by mistake issued on the basis of a nonconforming application, such patent will be subject to invalidation by an adjudication of the patent office (art. 123 [1][iii]).

The technical scope of a patented invention is limited to the scope of claim as described in the specification (art. 70). If the statement of claim does not fully state the matters that are indispensable for the construction of the invention, the application will be rejected.[8] Such a deficiency is fatal even though other parts of the specification are clear and complete.

C. Filing of An Application

Unlike the United States Patent Law, the Japanese statute adopts the first-to-file system. If two or more applications for the same invention are filed on different dates, the one first filed will be valid (art.

7. Patent Law art. 38.

8. Comissariat à la Energie Atomique v. Tokkyochō chōkan (Director General of the Patent Office), 14 Gyōsei reishū 1532 (Tokyo High Ct., Sept. 26, 1964), *aff'd*, 23 Minshū 54 (Sup. Ct., Jan. 28, 1969).

39[1]). The later applicant is not entitled to a patent even though he completed the invention first (art. 49[1][i]).

An applicant must pay a filing fee of ¥2,000 per case. Prior to 1 January, 1971, the fee was ¥1,000 per case, plus ¥1,000 per invention. Under the 1970 Patent Law, the patent office commences examination only when the applicant or another person demands it and pays an additional fee of ¥7,000 per case, plus ¥1,000 per invention (i.e., per claim) is paid. For instance, if an application involves seven claims, the applicant must pay a total of ¥16,000 (¥2,000 filing fee, ¥7,000 basic examination fee, plus ¥7,000 additional examination fee). By 1975 revision these fees were further raised as follows: ¥2,000 to ¥4,000, ¥7,000 to ¥14,000, and ¥1,000 to ¥2,000.

If an applicant mails his application from any district in Japan, it is deemed to have been filed with the patent office as of the date of mailing. Confirmation of the filing date is important not only in the examination of novelty, but also in the handling of various other matters, that include the following:

1. If another application covering the same invention is subsequently filed, it will be rejected.

2. If an applicant is to avail himself of his priority under the Paris Convention, he must submit a document supporting his assertion of priority within three months after the date on which the competing application is filed (art. 43).

3. An applicant can supplement or amend his specifications and drawings only if he does so within one year and three months from the filing date (art. 17-2). Thereafter, he can supplement or amend only at the time he demands examination, or in response to a notice that the application has been rejected.

4. Eighteen months after the filing date, the director–general will disclose the contents of the application to the public by a notice in the *Patent Gazette* (art. 65-2). The details are further discussed below.

5. If an applicant does not demand examination of the application within seven years after the filing date, the application is deemed to have been withdrawn (art. 48-3[4]).

6. The patent will be lost at the end of the twentieth year from the date of application, even though its fifteen-year life has not yet expired (art. 67[1]).

D. Examination as to the Formality of the Application

Applications filed with the patent office are received by the application section of the first examination department. The clerk in charge of this section stamps the receiving date on the first page of each application and gives a serial number to it according to the order of receipt. The applicant will be notified of this number and must use it on all subsequent communications with the patent office concerning the application.

The application then goes to an examiner, who conducts an examination as to compliance with the formalities. He will, for example, ascertain (1) whether necessary documents such as specifications and drawings are complete; (2) whether the application fee has been paid; (3) whether a certificate to prove the applicant's nationality or corporate personality has been submitted, where the applicant is a foreign person or corporation; (4) whether an administrator to handle patent matters has been appointed, if the application was filed by a nonresident; and (5) whether a document to prove his power-of-attorney has been submitted, if the application was filed by the applicant's agent or patent attorney.

If the examiner finds any formal defect in the application, he may order the applicant to remedy the defect, and if the applicant fails to do so, the application will be rejected. An applicant may voluntarily correct any deficiency in his application. If the application is considered by the applicant to have been wrongfully refused, he can demand a trial. The details of this procedure are discussed below. A dissatisfied applicant may further appeal to the Tokyo High Court.

When an application is found to be complete and in order, it is given a classification designation according to the area of technology to which the invention belongs and is then ready for examination as to substance.

The examination as to substance normally begins after public disclosure of the application in the *Patent Gazette*, which occurs eighteen months after the date of filing. If, however, the applicant demands examination at the time he files the application, examination may begin before such public disclosure.

E. Early Disclosure of Applications

The 1970 revision inserts Chapter III-2, Public Disclosure of Application after the existing Chapter III, Examination.[9]

Under article 51 of the Patent Law before the 1970 revision, a patent application was disclosed to the public when the examiner found that there was no ground for rejection, upon a ruling by the examiner that publication should be made. The increasing complexity of technology, the increase of applications, and the limited manpower of the patent office naturally resulted in a delay in the publication of

9. Chapter III consists of articles 47 to 65, while Chapter IV includes articles 65–2 and 65–3.

applications. This led to duplication of inventive efforts and wasted investment in the development of new technology. In addition, late disclosure of applications increased the number of duplicate applications on the same invention.

It was accordingly considered necessary to adopt a system under which all applications are disclosed to the public within a certain period of time after filing, regardless of the stage of examination. The early disclosure system will also enable the public to challenge applications at an earlier stage. The new eighteen-month rule went into force on 1 January, 1971, and was made applicable to applications filed after that date.

Article 65-2(2) not only calls for public disclosure by publication in the *Patent Gazette*, but also specifies the details which must be disclosed. They are (1) name and domicile or residence of the applicant; (2) number and date of the application; (3) name and domicile or residence of the inventor; (4) matters stated in the specification, and contents of the drawings attached to the application, except material the director-general considers likely to harm public order or good morals if published; (5) number and date of the public disclosure; and (6) other necessary matters.

The effect of public disclosure is covered by the statute. Article 65-3(1) provides that[10]

> An applicant for patent, when he has given warning by presenting a document describing the contents of the invention under patent application after public disclosure of application has been made, may, of a person who worked such invention as a business after such warning but before publication of application, demand payment of a compensation in an amount corresponding to the amount of money which would normally be received for the working in the case such invention were a patented invention. The same shall apply even in the case where the warning concerned has not been given, as against a person who, being aware that the invention was under a patent application of which public disclosure of application had been made, worked the invention concerned as a business before publication of application.[11]

The applicant can make such a demand for compensation only after publication of his application (art. 65-3[2]). The exercise of the right

10. Patent Law art. 65–3(1).

11. The terms publication of application (*shutsugan kōkoku*) and public disclosure of application (*shutsugan kōkai*) are specific terms of art. Foster and Ono define them as follows: *Publication of Application*. . . . Insertion in the Official Patent . . . Gazette of the contents of an application when no reason for rejection is found in examination, etc. Also called "second publication." Not to be confused with the term next below. . . . *Public Disclosure of Application*. . . . Automatic insertion in the Official Patent Gazette of the contents of a patent application one year and six months after the application date. Also called "first publication." Not to be confused with the term next below. Foster-Ono, *supra* note 1, at x.

to demand compensation does not affect the exclusive right of the applicant to work the invention after his application is published under article 52(1) or his patent right (art. 65-3[3]).

F. Examination Based on Demand

Before the 1970 revision, all applications were subject to examination by examiners. There are good reasons for the change to an examination-on-demand system. As the drafters of the revision noted[12]

(1) An inventor may not want to obtain a monopoly right even though his invention is patentable, and files an application solely to exclude another from obtaining a patent monopoly which would interfere with the inventor's use of his invention;

(2) An inventor may not be sure about the patentability of his invention due to the uncertainty of the standard of examination, and files an application to avoid the risk that he will have to challenge an application filed by another person;

(3) An inventor who wanted to obtain a monopoly right, when he filed an application, may later abandon this intention, due to the appearance of superior technology or the loss of commercial value for his invention.

When a patent application is filed with the patent office for one of the above reasons, the applicant might not care to have his invention examined or to have a patent issued, so long as he can be assured that no other person can obtain a patent for the same invention.

Thus, the drafters of the revision considered it appropriate to adopt a system under which examination is to be conducted only if the applicant demands examination within a certain period after his application. Under this system, an applicant obtains priority even though examination is not sought. An applicant after filing his application may consider whether it is necessary to demand examination, or whether application alone is sufficient to protect his interests. The patent office is relieved of the burden of examining all the applications, including those for which applicants do not wish to obtain a patent. This system reduces the delay in examinations to a considerable extent.

In order to implement a system of deferred examination, the 1970 revision incorporated new provisions after article 48 in Chapter III, Examination.[13] The law now provides that the examination of a pat-

12. Kōgyōshoyūkenshingikai (Industrial property council), *Kōgyōshoyūken seido no kaisei ni kansuru tōshin* (Proposals concerning reform of industrial property system), JURISUTO (No. 415) 67 (1969). Explanation of the 1970 revision in this chapter relied largely on Doi, *Patent Law Reform in Japan*, 1 LAWASIA 109 (1970).

13. Patent Law arts. 48–2 to 48–6, Law No. 91, 1970, amending Law No. 121, 1959.

ent application shall be carried out only upon demand (art. 48-2). Any person may demand examination of an application within seven years from the date of filing the application (art. 48-3[1]). In addition, an applicant who filed a new application based on the division of a previous application under article 44(1), or based on change of a previous application under article 45(1) or (3) or article 46(1) or (2), or after an amendment under article 53(4) in which the applicant submitted a statement that he wishes this provision to apply, may demand examination even after the lapse of the seven-year period. He must however move within thirty days after such division or change of the application, or the filing of a written statement that he wishes the provisions of article 53(4) to apply (art. 48-3[2]). A demand for examination once made can not be withdrawn (art. 48-3[3]). An application for a patent shall be considered to have been withdrawn if no demand is made within the stipulated period (art. 48-3[4]).

A demand for examination is made by a letter sent to the director-general, reciting (1) name and domicile or residence of the person demanding examination and, if the demand is made by a juridical person, name of its representative; (2) date of demand; and (3) identity of the patent application for which demand for examination is made (art. 48-4). The director-general will publish the demand in the *Patent Gazette* at the time of or immediately after public disclosure, if demand is made before public disclosure, or immediately after the demand for examination if the demand is made after public disclosure (art. 48-5[1]). If the demand is made by a person other than the applicant, the director-general will also notify the applicant (art. 48-5[2]). If the director-general finds that a person other than the applicant has been working the invention as a business after public disclosure and before publication of the application, he may, if he considers it necessary, order the examiner to give priority to this application (art. 48-6).[14]

An examiner may reject an application upon a ground set out in article 49: (1) the invention lacks novelty (art. 29); (2) the invention relates to unpatentable subject matter (art. 32); (3) the right to obtain a patent is co-owned, but the application is not filed jointly by all the co-owners (art. 37); (4) another person has filed an application earlier than the one under examination (art. 39); (5) the detailed explanation of the invention in the specifications is insufficient in that a person skilled in the field to which the invention belongs can not easily understand it or in that matters indispensable for the construction of the invention are not described in the claim (art. 36[4] and [5]); (6) the

14. *See* note 12 *supra*.

application covers more than one invention, and does not fall under article 38[15]; and (7) the applicant is neither the inventor nor his successor in title to the invention (art. 49[4]).

G. Publication of Applications, Opposition, and Patent Office Decision

If as to an application not previously published, the examiner finds no reason for rejection, he will direct publication and the director-general will have it published after serving the applicant with a transcript of the examiner's decision. Publication is made in the *Patent Gazette* by inserting the following information:
(1) name and domicile or residence of the applicant and the name of its representative in the case of a juridicial person; (2) number and date of the application; (3) name and domicile or residence of the inventor; (4) matters stated in the specification and contents of the drawings attached to the application; (5) number and date of the public notice of the application; and (6) other necessary matters (art. 51).

Publication confers upon the applicant a provisional right to work the invention exclusively (art. 52). Later, a full patent right is granted to the applicant covering a period of fifteen years from the date of publication (art. 67). This becomes effective on registration (art. 66).

Within two months after publication of an application, any person may file with the director–general an objection to the grant of patent (art. 55). This objection must be in writing and state that the application fails to meet specified statutory requirements for patentability stated in article 49.[16] The examiner will notify the applicant, who can file a reply (art. 57). The examiner will render a decision on the objection (art. 60), and if he sustains it, the application will be rejected.

If in the course of his examination prior to publication the examiner finds the invention under application is unpatentable, he will reject it and notify the applicant of the reasons for rejection. The applicant can then, within a reasonable period fixed by the examiner, file a counter-statement (art. 50). When the examiner notifies the applicant of the reasons for rejection, he simply states his conclusion under the relevant provisions of the law, and does not furnish the applicant with a copy of the citation. Accordingly, the applicant has to obtain a copy of such citation for himself in order to prepare the counter-statement mentioned above. If the examiner finds the applicant's counter-statement strong enough to overcome the reasons for rejection, the examiner will grant the patent.

15. *See* note 7 and accompanying text *supra*.
16. *See* text accompanying note 16 *supra*.

An applicant, in order to counter grounds for rejection, may divide or alter his application. An applicant who intends to divide the application must file a new application with respect to the invention thus severed (art. 44). Division of an application can be made at any time before a final decision has been rendered.

Under article 8 of the Utility Model Law, an applicant for a patent may alter his application into an application for utility model registration,[17] if he moves within thirty days after the date on which a transcript of a rejection decision is served. If the applicant takes this course, his original application for a patent is deemed to have been withdrawn.

IV. Trial at the Patent Office

A. Adjudication on the Decision of Rejection

An applicant, when he receives a notice of rejection, may demand a trial[18] if he moves within thirty days after the receipt of the notice (art. 121). Normally, the trial is conducted on the basis of written statements, but the chief trial judge may require the applicant to appear and argue orally before the trial judges (art. 145[2]). If the trial judges find for the applicant and reverse the decision of the examiner, they will render a trial decision ordering publication of the application, or if the application has been published already, they will render a decision to grant a patent to the applicant without further publication of the application (art. 159[4]).

There have been more demands for trial under article 121 than can be handled promptly. A trial judge must have experience as an examiner; therefore the supply of the necessary manpower is less than the supply of examiners. The drafters of the 1970 revision sought a solution to the delay problem, in three provisions added after art. 161. When a demand for trial is made under art. 121(1), the director–general orders the examiner to conduct an examination concerning the demand, provided an amendment is made to the specifications or drawings attached to the application, within thirty days after the demand (art. 161-2). Article 161-3 makes the statutory provisions regarding examination applicable to such demands. Article 161-4 provides that the examiner, when he renders a decision that a patent be granted under art. 60 or 62 (which is made applicable *mutatis mutandis* by art. 161-3) may rescind the previous decision of rejection upon which the demand was made.

17. *See* note 3 *supra*.

18. This section deals with *shimpan* procedure in the patent office. *Shimpan* is a trial conducted by *shimpankan* (trial judges) headed by a *shimbanchō* (chief trial judge). After the hearing, judges will render *shinketsu* (decision), which is referred to in Foster & Ono translation as "judgment in trial." *Satei* is a decision made by examiners (*shinsakan*).

B. Trials After Issuance of Patent

Trials in the patent office can also be obtained after the issuance of a patent. First, upon demand, a patent duly established by registration may be subject to a trial for invalidation (art. 123). This is the only way in which the validity of a patent can be tested. The principal basis for a trial to invalidate a patent is violation of art. 49, which enumerates the various grounds on which an application is to be rejected.[19] Second, a patentee may demand a trial to correct the specifications or drawings when he seeks to reduce the scope of his claim, to correct an erroneous description, or to explain an ambiguous description (art. 126). If the specifications or drawings have been corrected in violation of art. 126, a trial-type hearing may be demanded to invalidate the correction (art. 129).

The law does not specify the persons who can demand a trial under these provisions and is construed to permit any person to demand one, except that a trial to correct or amend the specifications or drawings can only be demanded by the patentee. A person who demands a trial must submit a demand in writing to the director–general setting forth the name and domicile or residence of the party and his representative, name of the representative in case of a juridical person; the designation of the trial case; and the nature of the demand and reasons therefore (art. 131).

A trial is conducted by a panel of three to five trial judges named by the director–general (art. 136), one of whom is designated as the chief trial judge (art. 138). When a trial is demanded, the chief trial judge must serve the defendant with a copy of the written demand and give him an opportunity to submit an answer in writing (art. 134).

In a trial for invalidation of a patent, the parties are usually required to appear before the trial judges for oral argument (art. 145). The trial judges may inquire into matters not asserted by the parties and render a decision on such matters, but are required to notify the parties to give them an opportunity to respond (art. 153).

Upon termination of the trial, a decision is made (art. 157). A decision to invalidate a patent would indicate, e.g., that "the patent under trial is declared to be null and void." If such a decision becomes final and conclusive, the patent thus invalidated is deemed not to have existed from the beginning (art. 125). Any correction to amendment allowed by a trial decision has a retroactive effect (art. 128). A party who is dissatisfied with the decision can appeal to the Tokyo High Court.

19. *See* text accompanying note 16 *supra*.

V. Other Procedures at the Patent Office

A. Determination of the Technical Scope of a Patented Invention

In infringement cases, parties often ask the patent office to determine the technical scope of the patented invention under dispute. The prescribed procedure provides that a request for a determination as to the technical scope of a patented invention may be made to the patent office (art. 71). Upon such a request, the director–general designates three trial judges to hear the matter.

B. Grant of a Nonexclusive License on a Compulsory Basis

The director–general of the patent office can order a patentee or his exclusive licensee to grant a nonexclusive license to a party desiring to use the patented invention, under the following circumstances: (1) where the patentee has not worked his invention for more than three consecutive years in Japan (art. 83); (2) where a patented invention would utilize another person's patented invention, registered utility model or registered design, and the patentee or his exclusive licensee wants to work his invention, but is prevented from working it by the existence of such other person's interest (arts. 92 and 72); and (3) where the working of a patented invention is particularly necessary for the public interest (art. 93).

A person who wants to work a patented invention in a situation falling under (1) or (2) above may, with the permission of the director–general, request the patentee or his exclusive licensee to negotiate regarding the granting of a nonexclusive license. In a situation falling under (3), an interested party may so negotiate with the permission of the minister of international trade and industry. If negotiation does not result in an agreement, or if the patentee or his exclusive licensee refuses to negotiate, the interested party may petition the director–general to render an award setting out the terms of a nonexclusive compulsory license.

VI. Jurisdiction and Procedure of Courts

A. Tokyo High Court

A party who is dissatisfied with a ruling or decision of the patent office may appeal to the Tokyo High Court when a trial decision refuses a patent; when a trial decision rules on a motion to dismiss a demand to supplement or amend the specifications or drawings; when a trial decision concerns invalidation of a patent; when a trial decision rules on a demand to correct the specifications or drawings; when a trial decision invalidates a correction previously made; when a trial decision is on a demand for retrial; when a ruling is for dismissal of a demand for correction of the specifications or drawings; and when a ruling is made dismissing a demand for a trial.

If the patent office awards a nonexclusive compulsory patent license, this action may be reviewed by the minister of international trade and industry, whose decision can be appealed to the Tokyo High Court (art. 184-2). If the objection is devoted only to the terms of compensation, the appeal is made directly to the Tokyo High Court.

The director-general of the patent office is made the party defendant when review in the Tokyo High Court is sought under article 178 (art. 179). If an appeal is from a trial decision rendered on a demand to invalidate a patent or to correct specifications or drawings, the prevailing party in the trial is made the party defendant.

The Tokyo High Court will examine the legality or illegality of the patent office decision or ruling and will inquire into the facts upon which the decision or ruling below was based. There is a conflict of opinion between the Tokyo High Court and the Japanese Supreme Court as to the admissibility of new evidence in such an appeal. The Tokyo High Court refuses to admit new evidence. The Supreme Court holds otherwise.[20]

Action in the Tokyo High Court on the patent matters listed above are subject to the Code of Civil Procedure. The court can only uphold or cancel the contested decision or ruling of the patent office (art. 181[1]).

B. Supreme Court

A party dissatisfied with a decision of the Tokyo High Court in this type of contest can request the Japanese Supreme Court to review the matter. That court will do so only where the appellant alleges unconstitutionality, or deviation from Supreme Court precedents, or a violation of law in the judgment rendered by the Tokyo High Court. Error in the determination of facts by the Tokyo High Court does not constitute grounds for Supreme Court review.

20. Someno, *Shinketsu torikeshi soshō* (Action to cancel trial decisions), 5 Jitsumu Minji Soshoho Koza (Lectures on the law of civil procedure) 199 (1969).

Drafting License Agreements in Japan and in the United States

WILLIAM R. WOODWARD AND KAZUKO MATSUO

Many of the problems encountered in drafting license agreements both in Japan and in the United States are discussed in this chapter with illustrative clauses, which are collected into an appendix. The examples used have been taken (sometimes with modification) from diverse sources, which are not identified because they are, for the most part, actual agreements. They are, of course, written in a variety of styles, and some of the details cover relevant or incidental matters not worthy of text discussion.

I. The Preamble

In a license agreement, the preamble or introductory clause should name the contracting parties, specify the type of contract (such as "a nonexclusive license agreement regarding patents" or "an exclusive license agreement for trademarks and technical information"), and then lead to the body of the agreement with a suitable phrase, such as "agree as follows" (Example I-1). In an international agreement, the American practice of identifying in the preamble the state or country of incorporation of the parties should be followed, but that information alone is not sufficient identification from the international point of view. It is essential that the parties' official addresses be stated. In the American practice these are often stated in the preamble, whereas in the Japanese domestic practice addresses are more commonly on the signature page. Either place will serve the purpose. The notice provision (discussed below) may also specify addresses, but these do not necessarily coincide with the official addresses.

The preamble should also specify short names of the parties to be used in the body of the agreement. Preferable for such designations is some part or a condensation of a party's name, or the party's initials. Sometimes it can be a functional designation such as "licensor" or "licensee." It is desirable to put the party's short name in distinctive type or full capital letters wherever it appears in the body of the agreement to make it easier to find provisions referring to one party or the other. Other stylistic details that make an agreement easier to use are headings for sections and paragraphs and an index or table of contents for a long agreement. To avoid the necessity for screening the language of headings in order to ensure full consistency with the text, a clause something like Example I-2 may be useful.

A statement, in the preamble, of the circumstances under which the agreement is made is common in the Anglo-American "whereas" clause usage (Example I-3), but rarely, if ever, does this appear in Japanese agreements. A statement of this kind has a certain usefulness in international agreements, particularly if a reference to a circumstance such as or related to a prior agreement or a companion agreement will foster a better understanding or more certain interpretation of the present agreement.

Some general background facts must be stated in the application to the Japanese government for validation. These need not be repeated in the agreement in order to get them into the official record.

II. Dates and Places

Various dates are essential in a license agreement. The effective date, which may not precede the final governmental approval, should be stated (Examples II-1, 2). The dates of execution may be important in connection with the authority of a signer to act for a party. Although the date of execution may be recited in the effective-date clause (Example II-1), it is more appropriately placed on the signature page along with an identification of the place of signing, particularly if the parties sign at different times and places. The place of signing may be important in relation to governing-law principles—a matter discussed more fully below.

With Japanese license agreements, it is common to make the "effective date" the day on which the Japanese government approves the agreement (Examples II-1, 3), or on a day an indicated period after the day on or month in which governmental approval is given (Example II-2). This kind of provision may be combined with a clause that defers effectiveness until other conditions are met. Approval by the government within a stated period is not uncommonly a condition (Example II-4).

The agreement can also provide for certain limited and noncommiting preliminary acts, such as market tests using imported products, to be done by the parties prior to the effective date, without impeding approval of the transaction (Example II-4).

In order that both parties may know the effective date, it is advisable to use a provision requiring the party responsible for obtaining approval to inform the other party promptly when such approval has been obtained. Useful too is a sentence reciting that such notification (rather than approval per se) makes the agreement binding (Examples II-2, 4).

III. Grants of Licenses

A. Scope

1. Exclusive or nonexclusive and recording. A license can of course be either exclusive or nonexclusive, and the grant should be entirely clear as to the interest granted.

The recording of license grants is important in Japan and pertinent provisions are often desirable in the document.[1] Both parties must participate in the recording process[2] and a clause obligating the licensor to assist the licensee in recording is desirable if recordation is contemplated.

In practice, many licenses used in Japan do not include a clause regarding recordation. (Notice, however, Example III-A-8, Art. 4.) The omission is typically intentional. Under Japanese law, even if an exclusive license agreement does not contain a clause requiring the licensor to join in recording, he is legally obligated to do so, so long as the parties really intend to conclude an exclusive license agreement.[3] A licensor may prefer to occupy this legal relationship.

Investigation to determine whether a grant of the license under negotiation has previously been recorded is a routinely advisable precaution. Even a nonexclusive license can be recorded, and if recorded, it will prevail over a later conflicting exclusive license.

The application for recordation includes a statement of the scope of the license and a statement covering restrictions, royalty terms, manner of paying royalty, and the duration of the grant. A copy of the license must also be submitted to the patent office to prove the accuracy of the application statement.[4] The copy of the agreement is returned.

In the United States a licensee does not need the assistance of the licensor in order to record. The recording statute, which in terms refers only to patent assignments, is so interpreted as to cover an exclusive license that operates as a transfer. This means that a transfer

1. An unrecorded nonexclusive license is unenforceable against third parties. *Tokkyohō* (Patent Law) §99. (Law No. 121, 1959, in 6 EHS No. 6850A). Exclusive licensing is provided for in *Id.* §77, and cannot be effective as such unless it is recorded. §98, 1(2).

2. Recording is in the patent office. *Id.* §99(1).

3. *Cf.* Imaizumi shokai v. Ochi, HANREI JIHO (No. 205) 23 (Tokyo Dist. Ct. Sept. 23, 1959).

4. Patent Registration Order, art. 30.

license must be recorded to be effective against later competing interests acquired in good faith and for value. The standard used to determine whether a license is a "transfer" for this purpose is, perhaps, narrower than the standard used to determine whether an exclusive license is a transfer for tax purposes,[5] but it would not be safe to assume that any transaction that would qualify as a "sale or exchange" for tax purposes would not be an "assignment" for purposes of the effect of failure to record. To abbreviate the recorded information in the United States, it is necessary to write two companion documents, one a basic grant of the patent rights explicitly or implicitly subject to further terms and conditions of the (unrecorded) companion agreement.

A nonexclusive license is governed by contract-assignment rather than property-transfer principles and is effective against a later licensee of a United States patent even though he does not have either actual or recorded notice of it.[6]

2. *Licensed patent and subject matter.* (i) There are two ways in which the subject matter of a license can be identified: in terms of specific patents or patent applications (Example III-A-1), and in terms of comprehensive patent or patent-application descriptions covering both present and future patents insofar as they relate to a specifically defined process or apparatus (Examples III-A-2, 3, 4, 5). The description details can be covered in the text of the agreement (Example III-A-4), in an attached schedule, which may be amended from time to time (Example III-A-3), or by referring to patents or patent applications later to be specifically identified as having become available (Example III-A-5).

(ii) So long as the subject matter of the license is eventually identified, there is no restriction on the identification technique. If recordation of the license at the Japanese Patent Office becomes necessary, and the patent is not adequately identified in the application and license, the applicant for recordation must submit a petition curing the defect. A separate provision regarding "future rights and applications" or "improvements" is often used and can be helpful. If future patents or patent applications are to be covered, a clause re-

5. 35 U.S.C. §261 (1964). See Ellis, *Validity of Doctrine that a Full Exclusive License is in Fact an Assignment*, 34 J. Pat. Off. Soc'y 643 (1954). *Cf.* Photo-Drama Motion Picture Co. v. Social Uplift Film Corp., 220 448 (2d Cir. 1915); Waterman v. Mackenzie, 138 U.S. 252 (1891).

6. Corbin, 4 Contracts §902 (1951). The so-called English Rule, followed at common law by several states, awards priority to the assignee who first notifies the obligor, of his interest. *Id. See also* Restatement (Second) Contracts §175 (Tentative Draft No. 3, April 18, 1967). Under the Uniform Commercial Code, an interest in a patent is a general intangible, a security interest in which (but not an outright sale) is governed by the filing requirements of the statute. See §§9–102, 9–106, 9–301(1)(d), 9–302(1).

quiring notice when the new patents or applications are described is desirable. At the very least, the licensee should have a right to be informed about the details of applications or patents coming under the agreement, if he later requests such information.

3. Territory of grant. If the antitrust law of the United States can be applied to the transaction, it will be important to avoid contractual geographic restrictions on the sale or use of the licensed products and to state only such territorial limitations as are appropriate to the industrial property rights involved.[7] In the case of patents, where the patents granted in various countries are independent of each other and limited to national territory, it is recognized that a license can be limited to a particular nation. The best way to effect such a limitation, avoiding all semblance of a merely contractual restriction, is to describe the patents under which licenses are granted as patents issued in certain countries (Example III-A-6). Restrictions on exportation are discussed later.[8]

In the case of unpatented technical information and know-how, there seems to be no question but that the licensee can be limited as to the places in which he is permitted to use the information (for making products or practicing a process), either in terms of national or other geographic boundaries or in terms of particular factories or work locations.[9] Licensors frequently desire, however, to limit the countries in which the licensee is permitted to sell products made with the licensed information, and often prefer to exclude the licensor's domestic market from the area of licensed sales. To give this kind of plan the semblance of a property-grant limitation, as opposed to a contractual restriction, language is used such as: "*A* licenses *B* under the . . . patents and technical information to make, use and sell licensed products in countries of the Far East and Latin America as herein defined," or "*A* licenses *B* to make, use, and sell licensed products under A's patent and technical information rights in the licensed area, but not in any other countries."

The effectiveness of this formulation is doubtful. A close analogy is the case of a process patent, which under the United States law, unlike that of a number of other industrial countries, gives no right to prohibit or control the sale of products made by the patented process (although there is a limited right under the Tariff Act[10] to exclude

7. *Cf.* United States v. National Lead Co., 332 U.S. 319 (1947); Timken Roller Bearing Co. v. United States, 341 U.S. 59 (1951); and *cf.* Shin Nippon Koki Co., Ltd. v. Irvin Industries, Inc., N.Y. Sup. Ct. N.Y. City, PTCJ No. 232, p. A–16 (June 12, 1975).

8. Concerning exportation matters see the text at fn 14 *infra*.

9. Milgrim, Business Organizations, Vol. 12, Trade Secrets 605 (7)(b)(ii) (1975).

10. 19 U.S.C. §§1337, 1337 ii (1970). *See* Stark, *Protection for Process Patents Against Imported Goods*, 34 N.Y.U.L. Rev. 1254, 1264 (1959); Kaye and Plaia, *Revitalization of*

importation of such products if unlicensed). It is an established principle in the United States that a limitation on the sale there of products made by a patented process is not to be regarded as a limitation on the scope of a license, but as a contractual restriction that can get no protection from the existence of the patent.[11]

A license granted to the Japanese party can be restricted to Japan, or to a part of Japan that will probably be identified by business areas rather than by administrative districts such as prefectures.

4. *Acts licensed.* (i) According to the Japanese Patent Law, "working" or "practicing" an invention are terms encompassing the following acts:[12]

1. In an invention of a thing, acts of *manufacturing, using, transferring, leasing, exhibiting* for the purpose of transfer or lease, or *importing* the thing;
2. In an invention of a process, acts of *using* the process;
3. In an invention of a process of manufacturing a thing, acts of *using, transferring, leasing, exhibiting* for the purpose of transfer or lease, or *importing* the thing produced by the process in addition to those mentioned in the preceding items.

This definition is different from that used in the United States, which reads "make, use, and sell," and under which process claims give no exclusive right to use or sell the product of the process.[13] Moreover, the importation and exhibition of patented products are not acts subject to the exclusive right protected by a United States patent. In order to describe practice of the invention comprehensively, the phrase "make, have made, use, sell, lease, and otherwise dispose of the licensed products" is sometimes used (cf. Example III-A-1).

Acts of export are not included in the "practice" of the invention, under Japanese law,[14] but export is one of the most significant activities of the parties, especially with respect to the international balance of payments. Accordingly, "export" is dealt with quite commonly in a separate contractual provision.

The license may cover all acts of practice integrally or separately.

Unfair Trade Causes in the Importation of Goods, 57 J. PAT. OFF. SOC'Y 208, 269 (1975). *Cf.* United States v. Singer Mfg. Co., 374 U.S. 174, 187–88, 195–96 (1963).

11. United States v. General Elec. Co., 82 F.Supp. 753, 814–15 (D.N.J., 1949). *Cf.* Cummer-Graham Co. v. Straight Side Basket Co., 142 F.2d 646 (5th Cir. 1944); American Equip. Co. v Tuthill Bldg. Material Co., 69 F.2d 406 (7th Cir. 1934). *Contra*, Q-Tips, Inc. v. Johnson & Johnson, 109 F.Supp. 657 (D.N.J., 1951). *Cf.* also Shin Nippon Koki Co., Ltd. v. Irvin Industries, Inc., NY Sup. Ct. NY City, PTCJ No. 232, p. A–16 (June 12, 1975).

12. *Tokkyohō* §2(3).

13. *See* Cochrane v. Badische Anilin & Soda Fabrik, 101 U.S. 293, 311 (1884).

14. *Cf.* K.K. Hayashi Seisakusho v. Horikawa Press K.K., 14 Kakyu minshu 979 (Tokyo Dist. Ct. May 18, 1963).

Moreover, it is possible to grant an exclusive license for some acts of practice and a nonexclusive license for other acts. Incidental licenses for manufacturing tools, machines, and processes may be included in general terms in a license to make, use, and sell equipment to be made with such machines or tools or by such processes (Example III-A-7).

(ii) In case of a license for expensive machines having a relatively long, useful life, the licensor may prefer to grant a license only to make, have made, use, and lease, excluding any license to sell. Such a license not only may offer a better opportunity, from a practical standpoint, for a good royalty yield, but also avoids a troublesome question. What kinds of rebuilding of the machine, by a purchaser of the machine from the patentee, or by a purchaser from a licensee authorized to sell, would be within the scope of the patent and which, being merely "repair," would be permissible without license?[15] Moreover, under the circumstances just described, a license to make, have made, and use, without any license to sell, may qualify as a sale of all substantial rights to a patent for United States income-tax purposes.[16] There is no comparable tax question under Japanese law. This type of license is particularly suitable when the licensor holds not only patents on the machine, its components, or its method of manufacture, but also on one or more processes that can be performed with the machine by a user. If a license to sell long-life productive machinery were granted, a question would be raised concerning the extent to which the purchaser might be impliedly licensed, without further royalty, for the process inventions. The answer to this question and drafting language for resolving both the doubt and the problem could then be troublesome.

(iii) Negation of implied licenses is a routine problem solvable only by meticulous description coupled with a recital that the licensor grants to the licensee, expressly or by implication, with respect to any patent, nothing except as specifically provided in the agreement (cf. Example III-A-3 Art. I Sec. 3 [a]).

5. *Sublicensing rights.* (i) If a licensee is to have a right to grant a sublicense, this interest should be specifically granted (Examples III-A-1, 5, 8, 9). If he is not to have this right a disclaimer of it can be used. Such an express disclaimer may help to avoid dispute and is for this reason worthwhile even though, as a matter of law, there is no right to sublicense save where the license permits, except possibly, and doubtfully, in the case of exclusive licenses (on an antitrust basis).

15. Aro Mfg. Co. v. Convertible Top Replacement Co., 365 U.S. 336, *reh denied* 365 U.S. 890 (1961); Aro Mfg. Co. v. Convertible Top Replacement Co., 377 U.S. 476 (1964).

16. Lawrence v. United States, 242 F.2d 542 (5th Cir. 1957); A.E. Hickman, 29 T.C. 864 (1958). *But cf.* Kirby v. United States, 297 F.2d 466 (5th Cir. 1962).

If the licensor recognizes that it is not feasible for the licensee to sufficiently practice the licensed invention and that it is not feasible for the licensor to find another licensee, he may authorize the licensee to grant a sublicense at the licensee's discretion (Examples III-A-1, 4). It is common to impose conditions on sublicensing such as prior written consent of the licensor (Example III-A-8), restricting a sublicense to the exact scope necessary for exercising the license (Example III-A-9) or limiting sublicensing to persons who meet qualifications specified in the license.

(ii) A sublicense is different from a subcontract. In the case of a subcontract, the subcontractor manufactures products and is paid for his labor by the contractor or licensee. Moreover, the licensee manages and controls the subcontractor's purchase of raw materials, the sales of products manufactured and the quality of the products. The subcontractor turns over all products he manufactures to the licensee. A licensee who is prohibited from granting a sublicense may utilize a subcontractor.[17] A subcontract in this sense is exercise of a "have made" right. In other words, under Japanese law, as under American law,[18] a licensee has a right to have a licensed product made for him even if no specific "have made" right is recited in the grant. In Japan, subcontractors are frequently employed and are considered to be normal instrumentalities of the licensee. If the licensor wants to prohibit the licensee from using subcontractors, the limitation must be carefully and precisely stated as it will be in derogation of an implied right.

(iii) Both exclusive and nonexclusive licensees may find it desirable to have a right to grant sublicenses. A sublicense granted by a nonexclusive licensee cannot, however, be recorded in the Japanese Patent Office as can a sublicense granted by an exclusive licensee, who is explicitly authorized by §77 (4) of the Japanese Patent Law to grant sublicenses with the consent of the patentee.

(iv) In addition to being able to grant a nonexclusive license, an exclusive licensee may grant an absolutely exclusive sublicense, thus excluding himself from the right to practice the licensed invention. The latter type of license cannot be recorded under Japanese law.[19]

(v) Even if the right to grant sublicenses is given in the agreement,

17. Yonehara v. Goshi Kaisha Shinko Orimonosho, 17 Minshu 2700 (Gr. Ct. Cass., Dec. 22, 1938).

18. Heywood-Wakefield Co. v. Small, 96 F.2d 496, 502 (1st Cir. 1938). This effect may be limited or overcome by words used in the license agreement. Westinghouse Elec. & Mfg. Co. v. Tru-City Radio Elec. Supply Co., 23 F.2d 628 (8th Cir. 1927).

19. §77(4) of *Tokkyohō* permits a nonexclusive license by an exclusive licensee only. Although an exclusive licensee can grant an exclusive sublicense, this is not subject to recordation under §27(1)(ii).

the actual grant of a sublicense under a Japanese license must be approved by the Japanese government, as the qualifications of a sublicense are important to the national economy.

Since governmental approval is necessary anyway, a sublicensing clause can make such approval a condition to the licensee's right to sublicense (Example II-A-2).

B. Duration of Agreement

1. Specified period. The duration of the agreement is usually fixed in terms of a specified period calculated from a specific date which is also the effective date (Examples III-B-1, 2). The duration of the agreement, as generally understood, is a concept that admits of certain obligations existing and being enforceable after the term of the agreement (see par. VIII A-4C below). Some draftsmen, however, prefer to define a "principal period" of the agreement or define "the five-year period" or the like rather than call that period the term of the agreement.

2. Life of any patent. If there is more than one patent, present or future, the term of the agreement is generally determined by the term of the last expiring patent (Example III-B-3). This technique for setting the expiration date can be employed in combination with a specific period, so that the license expires with the last expiring patent or with the termination of a specific period calculated from the effective date, whichever date is later or earlier as may be agreed. The purpose of this method is to avoid terms which otherwise might be too long or too short depending on when the last patent expires. Needless to say, if the agreement covers only patent rights, its term cannot extend beyond the lives of the patents (Examples III-B-3).

A method may be adopted that will enable the licensee to eliminate from the agreement a patent he later finds unnecessary to his purpose and to relieve himself from all obligation to pay royalty for such a patent (Example III-B-1).

Where United States law applied, it was formerly very important to permit the licensee to surrender his license as to one or more specific patents. This was particularly desirable with respect to patents which had not been issued when the agreement was executed, so that the licensee would not be irrevocably bound to pay royalty or not to contest validity,[20] as to patents the scope and validity of which he could not know when he committed himself to the agreement.[21] Now that a licensee can always free himself from royalty obligation, in the United

20. Concerning an obligation not to contest the validity of a licensed patent, see par. VII-D 4, *infra*.

21. *See* the discussion of patent invalidity, par. III-4 and par. VII-B, *infra*.

States, by showing that the patent in question is invalid, the necessity for a contractual provision of this type is no longer so pressing.

A licensee may obligate himself to pay royalty on invalid patent claims under a United States patent, induced by his desire to be licensed as to valid claims under the same patent. This problem is not apt to arise under a Japanese patent, which normally covers only one claim. For the protection of the licensee a clause permitting surrender of rights under any particular claim, by written notice identifying the patent and claim, seems warranted (Example III-B-4) if only to leave the initiative of a validity controversy with the patent owner.[22]

The examples illustrate a right to surrender a license under a patent issued either before or after the execution of the agreement, although the surrender right could reasonably be limited to future patents on the ground the licensee would normally have had an opportunity to study each of the already-issued patents. Since under American law, as already mentioned, the licensee cannot be deprived of the right to challenge validity even as to patents he has had an opportunity to appraise before entering into the contract,[23] the patent owner may prefer to retain the initiative in precipitating a validity contest by allowing the licensee a right to surrender his license as to any particular patent.

3. Sublicenses. It may be wise to state clearly that the term of any sublicense agreement expires automatically upon termination, for any reason, of the original license agreement (Example III-B-2).

4. Condition subsequent. Invalidation or cancellation of an existing patent, and denial of a pending application for a future patent, should be made a ground for termination, either on notice or automatically, as the parties may prescribe.[24]

IV. Improvements Devised by Licensee or Licensor

In the absence of a specific provision in the agreement, neither the licensor nor the licensee is obliged to furnish the other with information about or rights in improvements made in the subject matter of the licensee. However, the licensor sometimes agrees that the license includes improvements made or obtained by him during the license agreement. The licensee sometimes undertakes to inform the licensee, and may grant to the licensor rights on such improvements. There is, however, no established commercial practice defining "improvements." Nor has there been a court decision concerning this

22. Lear, Inc. v. Adkins, 395 U.S. 653 (1969).

23. Blonder-Tongue Laboratories Inc. v. University of Illinois Foundation, 402 U.S. 313 (1971).

24. Lear, Inc. v. Adkins, *infra* note 47 and discussed in text to which it is cited.

matter in either the United States[25] or Japan. It is important, therefore, to recite, in the license agreement, a definition of "improvements." Alternatively, the parties may agree that each will inform the other of and grant rights in all technology acquired during the life of the license that relates to a specified technical area.

If the parties desire to include all related inventions, they may so provide in the description clause of the license agreement. For this purpose "improvement" alone is not suitable because its meaning is obscure. A phrase like "development or improvement" may have utility (Examples IV-A-1, 2, 3).

A. Title to Improvements

It is a principle of United States and Japanese law that the right to patent an invention shall belong to the inventor or his assignee, and so it is reasonable to provide that the title to improvements made by the licensee should belong to the licensee. If the licensor, however, feels that he is sufficiently clear of the warning expressed in the *Transparent-Wrap* case[26] and similar conditions in Japanese law,[27] he may insist on a transfer of title to or an exclusive license in improvements invented by the licensee, on the ground that such improvements are really extensions of the licensor's invention. It is reasonable and desirable in the more usual case, however, to provide in the license agreement that the respective rights of the licensor and the licensee in the improvements made by the other party shall be substantially reciprocal (Examples IV-A-1, 2, 3).

B. Obligation to File Patent Applications

The application for a patent covering an improvement made or acquired by the licensor during the period of the license agreement will usually be filed by the licensor, or by the licensee under the name of the licensor, in the licensed territory, and the licensee is usually given a license for the improvement patent. It is reasonable to provide that the licensee may file an application for a patent covering improvements made or acquired by the licensee, in the licensed territory, and that the licensor may file in the licensee's name in any other area. If the licensor is granted a patent for the licensee's improvement, it is reasonable to provide that the licensee shall have a license under the licensor's patent. The licensor's right to file a patent appli-

25. It is sometimes contended, for example, that the estoppel should not apply if the patent owner has not chosen the first forum, but had been subjected to a declaratory action in a forum chosen by the infringer. See Fisher Controls Co. Inc. v. Control Components, Inc., 185 USPQ 261, 262 (S.D. Iowa, 1975, Stuart, J.).

26. See the discussion of description techniques, par. III-A 2, *supra*.

27. Transparent-Wrap Mach. Co. v. Stokes & Smith Co., 329 U.S. 637 (1947).

cation covering an invention of the licensee may be limited to cases in which the licensee does not file one on his own behalf, within a specified period, in which case the licensee should be required to give timely notice to the licensor. Since in any application for a patent in the United States, the inventor is the applicant, the license should require his cooperation where one party is to patent an improvement made by the other.

A licensor or a licensee may invent or acquire improvements the licensor does not wish to have disclosed through patent applications. It is therefore important to consider possible provisions in the license agreement covering this contingency. The ramifications of the problem can be highly complex.

It is usual for the licensor to bear the expense of filing patent applications in the licensed territory covering his improvements. The licensee, on the other hand, might well promise to bear such expenses, depending on what seems most appropriate to the parties in the particular transaction. The licensee often agrees to bear the expense of a patent application covering an improvement devised by the licensee although the application is filed for the benefit of the licensor (Example IV-B-1).

C. Period of License on Improvements

It is usually reasonable to provide that a license on improvements made by the other party shall expire with the license granted to such party. However, as to the licensee's license on a patent issued to the licensor, as assignee, covering the licensee's improvements, it is reasonable to provide that the license shall continue during the life of the patent. Sometimes the licensor will demand a royalty-free license on the licensee's improvements during the life of the patent. This produces no great imbalance if the licensor's patents are also licensed for the lives of the patents, since the matter would simply be one of overall price. In other cases, a balance could be struck by providing a royalty to be paid by the licensor on the licensee's improvements after the term of the license under the licensor's patents has expired.[28]

D. Employee and Consultant Agreements

Unless otherwise agreed, title to an invention made by an employee or consultant will usually belong to such employee or consultant, both under United States and Japanese law, depending to some extent on the facts; however, the employer is generally held to acquire a license

28. See the discussion of this and other possible antitrust problems in Chapter VII, Ariga, *infra*.

or shop right.[29] It is, therefore, desirable, where improvement inventions are covered in the contract, to require the parties to conclude agreements with employees (and perhaps with consultants) under which the license-agreement parties will acquire sufficient rights in the inventions of their employees and consultants to support licenses of the scope they have granted in the agreement (Examples IV-D-1, 2).

V. Compensation for the License

A. Royalty

The price of a license is usually called "royalty" at least if it is payable in periodic amounts. Although in some cases a license is granted royalty-free, in most cases the licensee promises to pay a royalty.[30]

B. Royalty Basis

Royalty is most often determined on a fixed-price basis, on a running-royalty basis, or on a combination of these. "Running royalty" can be based on volume of sales, on a specified sum per unit or on profits. Other methods are sometimes used (Example V-B-1).

1. Lump sum. A fixed-price royalty can be paid in a lump sum or in installments (Example V-B-2).

2. Sales basis. Sales-basis royalty can be computed on either gross sales or on net sales. In the former arrangement, royalty is usually imposed on the full selling price including any charge for packing, transportation, insurance, and sales tax.

If net sales are the measure, the deductions from gross sales must be specified with care. Strictly speaking, there is no established practice as to what items should be excluded from the gross selling price in

29. *Tokkyohō* §35(1) gives the employer a royalty-free, nonexclusive license of a patent that his employee has obtained for an invention made in the performance of his duties in the course of the employment. Similar results have been reached by the application of equitable principles in American law (with little, if any, appreciation in the cases that the matter should now be regarded as one of state rather than federal law). United States v. Dubilier Condenser Corp., 289 U.S. 178, 187 (1933), citing Lane & Bodley Co. v. Locke, 150 U.S. 193 (1893) and earlier cases. The state-or-federal aspect of this problem could not have been expected to arise until after the decision in Erie R.R. v. Tompkins, 304 U.S. 64 (1938). The lack of distinct state-by-state doctrines is not surprising in view of a similar growing together of the law of trade secrets recently deduced by R. M. Milgrim and reported in an address before the New York Patent Law Assn., 14 N.Y.P.L.A., Bn. No. 5 (Dec. 1974–Jan. 1975) 1.

30. Royalty is the price for granting a license. More strictly speaking, it is the price for granting a specific right and interest with respect to a patent or technical information, but not items such as the cost of sending licensor's engineer, instructing the licensee's personnel or performing specific engineering, unless the parties reasonably intend to regard such matters as incidental to an unitary transaction, which may be important for tax reasons. Heil Co. v. 38 T.C. 989 (1962), acquiesced-in, 1963–1 Cum. Bull. 4.

calculating the net selling price. It is common to exclude not only separate charges for packing, transportation, and the like, but also to deduct certain costs such as transportation expenses not separately billed (Examples V-3, 4, 5).

3. Sales to affiliated companies and fair market value. If licensed products are used by the licensee, no sales price is realized, and if licensed products are sold to an affiliated company of the licensee, there is a danger that the sales price may be unreasonably low. In these situations it is reasonable to calculate the royalty on the basis of the fair market value at the appropriate market level—manufacturer's market, wholesale market, or retail market—as the transaction dictates, at the time and in the territory of the use or sale of the licensed products (Examples V-B-6, 7).

4. Percent of sublicense fee or lease fee. If a licensee receives a sublicense fee, the royalty to be paid by the licensee to the licensor is sometimes calculated as or increased by a specific percentage of the sublicense fee, and where he receives a lease fee for the licensed product, the royalty is sometimes calculated as a specific percentage of the lease fee. If the licensee is licensed both to sell and to lease patented articles, the royalty for a lease transaction may be based on fair market value as in the case of a sale, or the parties may prefer to fix the royalty as a proportion of the lease payments received by the licensee.

In the case of a license to make, have made or use machinery without any license to sell,[31] all or most of the royalty may be determined by the extent of the use of the machine or by the value of its product (as is commonly done for process patents). If there is also to be a fixed initial payment, especially one against which use-royalties will not be credited, the licensor should consider the advisability of requiring an additional lump sum payment, either a fixed amount or calculated according to a predetermined scale, in the event of a reconstruction of the machine or some capacity-increasing alteration of it. It may be important, according to the nature of the machine, to define in some detail the type of reconstruction, replacement, or capacity alteration that will necessitate an additional payment, as well as the formula to be used in measuring payments. The magnitude of the increase in capacity or the probable extension of the useful life of the machine are often suitable standards.

5. Export sales: discrimination. In view of the possible competitive problems of other licensees in areas outside of the licensee's home country, the licensor will sometimes request the licensee to pay a higher royalty on his license-product export sales. A prohibitive dif-

31. See par. III—A—4(ii) and n. 16 *supra.*

ferential might, however, be seen as a restriction on exports and in conflict with United States antitrust doctrine regarding royalty systems that unfairly discriminate between competing regions or technologies.[32]

6. Applicability of patents or know-how. If royalty is to be related to the use of licensed technology in manufacturing activities the drafting must be handled with particular care. As to patents in this context, see Example V-B-8. As to technical information, see Example V-B-9. As to royalty provisions applying simultaneously and alternatively to patents and know-how, see Examples V-B-1 and 10, read together.

7. Profit basis. Profit-basis royalty is calculated as a percentage of the "profit" derived from technology and the obviously tough problem is getting consensus on the way in which "profit" is to be calculated. Since it is difficult to devise a mutually acceptable formula for overhead and other indirect costs, this method of royalty computation is rarely used. It is perhaps suitable in a joint venture where the licensor has both access to information and a degree of control, through participation in management and ownership of the licensee, a joint-venture corporation.

C. Minimum and Maximum Royalties

1. Minimum royalty. A licensor sometimes requests his licensee to guarantee an annual, minimum running royalty during part or all of the license period, because the amount of the running royalty depends upon the sales or profit of the licensee, and the licensor is not assured of receiving a fixed-sum amount of royalty without such a guarantee (Example V-C-2). Minimum-royalty clauses are more often used in exclusive-license agreements than in nonexclusive ones.

Alternatively, the licensee may be required to make an initial down payment against which royalties will be credited and which may be made nonrefundable (Example V-C-3).

2. Maximum royalty. In some cases, there is a stipulation to the effect that the licensee is relieved of any further charge for the license after the total payments of the licensee have reached a specific amount (Example V-C-4), thus setting a maximum on the royalty obligation.

D. Manner of Payment

1. Advance. A royalty clause can provide for a partial advance payment as either a down payment against which the royalty that accrues will be credited or as an initial payment. Prepayment clauses of these

32. La Peyre v. FTC, 366 F.2d 117 (5th Cir.) 1966; Peelers v. Wendt, 360 F.Supp. 193 (W.D. Wash. 1966) 111; Laitram Corp. v. King Crab, Inc., 244 F.Supp. 9, modified 245 F.Supp. 1019 (D. Alaska 1955).

types are more common in exclusive patent licenses, and in some know-how transactions. Under Japanese law, however, no payment of royalty to a nonresident is permitted until after the license agreement has been approved by the Japanese government.

2. *When due.* An initial payment is usually made within a certain period, such as sixty days, after governmental approval of the transaction. Running royalty is usually calculated for each specified period, for example, for each quarter, half year, or year and paid within a given number of days after the end of the period. It is important to specify in the license agreement when royalty is to be paid (Examples V-B-2 and V-D-1). Care should be taken to avoid stating that royalty "accrues" or becomes "due" any great length of time before the amount is required to be paid, because most corporations in the United States and Japan are on the "accrual basis" of income-tax accounting, and an income tax may accordingly be ruled to be payable by the licensor for the year in which royalty income "accrues" or becomes "due."

3. *Sublicense royalties.* A licensee may be made responsible for its sublicensee's acts and royalties (Examples V-B-8, Sec. 3.01 and V-B-9, Sec. 4.05). If a licensee is permitted to sublicense only its subsidiaries, it may be made responsible for acts and royalties of the subsidiaries whether or not a formal sublicense is granted to them (Example V-B-7). A licensee's obligation with regard to sublicense royalties may be stated as a percentage, with or without a minimum dollar or yen amount (Example III-9).

4. *Published applications.* The exclusive right to work the invention in Japan begins with the publication of the patent application, although the scope of the patent is not finally determined until the patent is actually granted. Whether patent royalties shall begin with publication of the application or upon grant of the patent is a detail the agreement should specify. Indeed, sometimes royalties are made to begin with the date of the application, although the status of the patent at that stage is quite uncertain. This arrangement is also sometimes encountered in the United States, even though the exclusive right conferred by a patent begins there only on the date of grant.

5. *Effect of United States and Japanese taxes.* Royalty paid by a resident licensee to an American licensor is taxed under the Japanese tax system as income having its source in Japan.[33] If the American licen-

33. The Convention between Japan and the United States of America for the Avoidance of Double Taxation and the Prevention of Fiscal Evasion with Respect to Taxes on Income, March 8, 1971, 23 U.S.T. 967, T.I.A.S. 7216, art. 8(5) and art. 14(2). For a discussion of these and other tax details see Chapter X, Nakamura, Toyama, and Dodge, *infra*.

sor has no permanent establishment in Japan, i.e., office, factory, branch, warehouse, the rate is 10 percent. If the licensor has a permanent establishment in Japan royalty received is included in overall Japan-related income, which is taxed the same as the income of a Japanese resident. In each case, the American taxpayer is entitled to a foreign tax credit against his United States income tax, within the rule and limits of Section 904 of the United States Internal Revenue Code.[34]

If an American licensor has no permanent establishment in Japan, the resident licensee must pay the tax on behalf of the American licensor, and the drafting can become complex. The licensee should be required to furnish the licensor with the official tax receipts to facilitate obtaining foreign tax credit, and either required to absorb the tax as additional royalty or permitted to offset it against royalties.

Example V-D-2 is a typical clause regarding taxes. It is intended to impose on the licensee the burden of all domestic taxes. Alternatively, taxes such as sales, turnover, invoice, purchase, transmission, and registration taxes as well as local or regional income taxes can be specified. To the specification a general catch-all clause can be added to pick up types of tax omitted, or later levied.

The tax treaty also limits the United States tax on royalty received from an American licensee by a nonresident Japanese recipient to 10 percent (instead of the higher rates otherwise applicable). A clause such as Example V-D-2 would be suitable for an agreement between a Japanese licensor and an American licensee.

6. *Currency.* Royalty is usually paid in United States dollars to an American licensor and in dollars, yen, or some foreign currency by an American licensee to a Japanese licensor. Types of currency, and exchange rates, are important details in license agreements (Example V-D-3).

7. *Currency conversion.* If the amount of the royalty has to be computed in yen, as by a Japanese licensee obliged to pay on a sales basis or profit basis running royalty, it is necessary to specify in the agreement the ratio of currency conversion and the times at which this ratio is to be applied. The formula of the official rate at the date of the payment (Example V-D-3) has been widely used. It is difficult to use "currency conversion shall be at a ratio agreed upon by both parties," because in such a case it would be necessary to get the approval of the Japanese government for each payment. Moreover, under the present practice, such approval is practically unobtainable. Today it would be wise to provide an alternative, in terms of bank buying rate

34. See the discussion, Chapter IX, Cooper, United States Taxation of Patent and Know-How Licensing, section on Foreign Tax Credit, *infra*.

at some major city, applicable in the event there should be no official rate.

8. Party authorized to receive payment. Only the licensor is entitled to receive royalty due from the Japanese licensee. Under the Japanese Foreign Exchange and Foreign Trade Control Law,[35] a third person cannot be made the payee.

9. Reports. (i) Where the amount of royalty is to be calculated on the basis of the sales of the licensed product, it is important for the licensor to have a right to check the data upon which calculation of the royalty will be based. This clause should require the licensee to submit a periodic report, require the licensee to keep records on the basis of which reports are to be prepared, and authorize the licensor to inspect all relevant records.

(ii) As to reports, the following matters are usually covered in the license agreement:

1. Form of reports—The items to be stated in the report are (a) number or quantity of licensed products produced, sold and used by the licensee during each royalty period; (b) amount of royalty due in each period and method of calculation; (c) name and address of customers, dates of sales, number or quantity of sales.

2. Reports are usually submitted within one or two months from the last day of each royalty period.

3. The report may of course cover royalties arising from sublicenses and do this by requiring copies of the reports of sublicenses save where the licensee insists on restating the relevant substance of sublicense reports in order to avoid disclosing some of their details.

4. Usually the reports are written in English whether the licensee be Japanese or American, signed by the licensee and sent by registered air mail. The licensee is sometimes required to include an oath affirming the accuracy of the report or to attach the verification of a competent auditor or accountant (Example V-D-4).

5. The licensee usually has the obligation to keep records that supply (a) amount of production and sale; (b) consumption of material and parts, if this data affects calculation of royalty; (c) name and address of the customer, and date and price for each sale, and (d) where there are returned products or uncollectable accounts, data concerning the customer, amount of returned goods, and amount uncollectable, if the royalty calculation is thereby affected.

6. The licensor will usually reserve a right to have its own personnel or an independent auditor audit the licensee's records. In this case, it is customary to provide that the audit will be made on the premises of

35. *Gaikoku Kuwase Oyobi Gaikoku Boeki Kanriho* (Foreign Exchange and Foreign Trade Control Law) (Law No. 228, 1949), in 5 EHS No. 5010.

the licensee during reasonable business hours at licensor's expense and that the person who audits the record shall owe the licensee a duty of secrecy (Example V-D-5).

E. Place of Payment

In the absence of specific provisions, royalty will be payable at the general address of the licensor specified in the agreement. If payment is to be made at a place different from the licensor's general place of business, the payment place should clearly be specified. It is not unusual to make royalty payable at a bank or other fiscal agent designated by the licensor.

F. Time Limit for Questioning Royalty Payments

Sometimes provisions are used that limit the period within which the licensor can raise questions concerning royalty accounting. Three years is a typical limitation period.

G. Interest

Under Japanese law, if a licensee fails to pay royalty when it is due he is liable to pay interest on the sum in arrears, at the rate of 6 percent per annum unless otherwise agreed by the parties.[36] A license clause requiring the licensee to pay interest at a specified rate is sometimes considered. However, this arrangement may not be feasible, since the approval of the Japanese government with respect to license agreements does not cover the payment of interest and approval of the government for each contractual interest payment is necessary (Example V-G-1). In the United States, each state has a statute setting the rate of interest on past due liquidated debts, if the parties have not contracted about this detail. Contractual interest is governed by usury statutes the details of which will rarely be relevant in license transactions. There is no problem in the United States with regard to outward remittance of exchange.

H. Royalty Reduction

It is sometimes provided that the royalty shall be reduced for specified causes such as the following:

1. If the licensed product is covered by plural patents, the licensor may promise to reduce the royalty if the number of patents used is decreased through modification of the product or the expiration of some of the patents. The method by which royalty is reduced may be stipulated in the license agreement or left to be determined by the mutual agreement of the parties in each case (Example V-H-1).

2. Sometimes the licensor promises to reduce royalty if the total

36. COMMERCIAL CODE §514.

sales of the licensed products exceeds a stated number of quantity (Example V-H-2).

I. Allocation of Payments

When technical information and know-how are exclusively licensed without any connection to a patent license, it is essential, in order to secure capital gains treatment under the United States Internal Revenue Code, that the licensee have the right to continue using the information after the full royalty payment period of the agreement runs out. Where, however, technical information and know-how, including technical assistance services, are furnished in connection with an exclusive patent license running for the full term of the patent, all the payments to the licensor will receive capital gains treatment even though the right to use that part of the information that remains confidential when the patent and the license expire will then terminate, provided the patent license can properly be regarded as the more significant element of the transaction and the license to use confidential information as an auxiliary item designed to "launch" the patented technology.[37] Although the principle just stated holds when some payment or payments are identified as compensation for technical information and technical assistance and some for patent rights, it is probably wise in this type of case not to allocate payments between technical information and patent rights but to make all payments relate to both kinds of benefits.

Another allocation matter of considerable potential tax significance is allocation of royalty payments according to national source. The question could come up not only when the licensee makes and/or sells the licensed articles in various countries, with or without having a permanent establishment there. The most important problem relates to exclusive licensees and sublicensees of patents licensed by United States companies, because of the capital-gains character the proceeds of such licenses may have for domestic tax purposes, especially in the case of transactions that antedate the 1962 Revenue Act. Under the 1962 and later revenue statutes, a grant that exclusively licenses a controlled foreign company under American-held patents is subject to provisions that limit the availability of capital-gains treatment, and tax the income of controlled foreign subsidiaries to the parent company in various situations.[38]

The national laws of the countries involved may vary as to the amount of sublicense royalties that may be remitted to the licensor (e.g., 50 percent limit in Switzerland). Where exclusive licenses have

37. Heil Co., 38 T.C. 989 (1962), acquiesced in, 1963–1 CUM. BULL. 4.

38. See Kauder, *Taxation of Domestically Controlled Foreign Corporations: A Comparative Study of Subpart F and Section 482*. 14 VILL. L. REV. 260 (1969), discussing INT. REV. CODE §§482, 951–964 and the related Treasury Regulations.

been granted to licensees in several countries, and it is desired to permit sublicensees to make articles in one of these countries and sell them in another, the licensor might advantageously prescribe, according to his own interest, which territorial licensee shall collect and remit the royalty from each sublicensee. In the case of patents it may sometimes be desirable to allocate royalties according to the place of manufacture, sometimes according to the place of sale, or perhaps even half to each. In the case of technical information, it may be more difficult to allocate to any place other than that in which the information is utilized to make licensed products; however, where the information is used essentially to support a patent license, an allocation different from the patent license allocation would not seem to be necessary.

All of these problems will need consideration in a transaction that requires the application of Japanese tax law.

J. Miscellaneous Royalty Clauses

Example V-J-1 is intended to avoid making an export-purchaser an infringer where there is an applicable patent in the country of use but none in the country of manufacture. Example V-J-2 is similar in purpose, except that there the exportation is by the licensee's customer rather than by the licensee. In this case the licensee has the option to pay royalty and bring the products within the license with respect to the country of use.

VI. Litigation with Third Parties

Not many license agreements have provisions regarding infringement problems. The reason seems to be the extreme difficulty encountered in drafting about the action which is to be taken by the parties to prevent infringement. The facts vary widely in different transactions, and future problems are hard to anticipate with specificity.

If an infringement provision is included it will usually recite: (1) an obligation to give notice of existing, imminent or likely infringement or infringement suits by a third party; (2) an obligation or authority to sue for infringement and an obligation to cooperate with or assist each other in preventing infringement; (3) the manner in which the expenses incurred in preventing infringement will be shared; and (4) who can sue and how a money recovery shall be shared.

A. An Obligation to Notify of Infringement or Misappropriation

It is common to require that the licensee, whether exclusive or nonexclusive, shall promptly notify the licensor of any existing or threatened infringement by a third party that comes to the licensee's attention (Examples VI-1, 5, 6, 7, 8). Such a provision is particularly necessary where the licensee solely practices the patent involved, in the territory where infringement might occur. The notice clause can be couched in mutual-obligation form (Example VI-3). The parties may prefer to consult together before either acts, or to act together, and these purposes can be implemented in the license. It will be wise, if only one party is obligated to watch for infringements, to require the other party to inform the obligated party of any relevant facts coming to his attention (Example VI-5). Where confidential technical information is licensed a notice of misappropriation or misuse of it should be required (Examples VI-5, 8).

Some licenses include an agreement with respect to defense of an infringement suit instituted by a third party against the licensee (who shall defend and who bears the expense of defense) and impose an obligation on the licensee to notify the licensor promptly if such a suit is threatened or filed (Examples VI-1, 8). The defense problem can also be approached in terms of a warranty by the licensor, against infringement.[39]

Although a licensor arguably owes his licensee an implied duty to protect him against a claim that the subject matter of the licensed patent infringes another patentee's rights, the point is largely moot. Equally moot is the argument that a licensor impliedly promises that no one will infringe the licensed patent. In practice these are areas to which draftsmen devote considerable attention and leave no room for debate about implied duties.

B. Obligation to Sue

Litigation is expensive, and if undertaken must be prosecuted with vigor and competence. The licensor is often the party most deeply concerned in an infringement controversy and he is very apt to insist on control over the appropriate means for dealing with an infringer or with a claim that the licensed subject matter infringes. Consultation with the licensee may be stipulated (Examples VI-1, 3, 6). Even if the licensee is obligated by the agreement to notify the licensor of an infringement problem, the licensor is usually permitted to determine the measures and time for attacking it (Examples VI-5, 8). In some transactions, a quite different approach may be preferable. If in the affected territory only the licensee practices the licensed patent or know-how, it may be better to leave him free to determine what legal action or other steps are to be taken, perhaps after consultation with or advice from the licensor (Examples VI-3, 6, 8).

39. See par. VII–B–7 and examples there referred to, *infra*.

"Who shall prosecute a suit" is quite different from "who determines the measures and time for counteracting infringement," where the problem is infringement of the licensed patent. The licensee may be required to initiate a legal proceeding as plaintiff, even though the licensor decides when, where, and how the suit shall be prosecuted (Examples VI-1, 6). According to Japanese law, only an exclusive licensee whose license is recorded at the patent office is entitled to bring suit in his own name, independent of the patentee.[40] Therefore, if a licensee who is obligated to prosecute legal actions is a nonexclusive licensee or the holder of an unrecorded "exclusive" license, a provision so obligating the licensee means in practice that legal action will be prosecuted by the licensee in his licensor's name. Regardless of who sues, the other party is in most cases required to cooperate or assist in collecting and providing necessary evidence such as materials and information (Examples VI-1, 5, 8).

C. Manner of Sharing Expenses

How the expenses incurred in removing an infringement shall be borne is a matter of great concern to both the licensor and the licensee. Where the licensor and the licensee have substantially equal rights in determining policy and methods they usually share expenses equally (Examples VI-1, 6, 7; §6 (b)(i)). If, however, the license is nonexclusive, or if legal action is to be taken by one party without the approval of the other or only with the other's consent, there is a different kind of problem. The burden of expenses is usually imposed on the licensor in a nonexclusive license, and on the acting party in the latter case (Examples VI-3, 5, 6(c), 7 § 6(b)(iii), 8).

D. Right to Damages for Infringement

The party who bears the expense of litigation with an infringer is generally entitled to any monetary award obtained. If expenses are shared, so is the award (Examples VI-1, 4, 5, 6, 7, 8).

E. Negation of Obligation regarding Infringement

A general negation of any obligation in the licensor to remove an infringement is common, especially in nonexclusive licenses (Example VI-9).

VII. Miscellaneous Provisions

A. Patent Marking

The primary purpose of patent marking in Japan is to give a warning to potential infringers. In the United States, patent marking serves as a notice to the infringer, thus enabling the patentee to re-

40. *Tokkyohō*, §§98(1), 100(1).

cover damages from the time the infringement was commenced.[41] The United States marking statute is not, however, applicable to process patents. With that exception, therefore, it may be advisable to insert a provision requiring patent marking by the licensee (Examples VII-A-1, 2, 3). Some licensees, however, find marking requirements so burdensome that they refuse to agree to them.

The Japanese Patent Law provides that a patentee, an exclusive licensee, or a nonexclusive licensee shall make efforts to affix a marking on the thing, the invention of which has been patented, or on the product of a patented process. Such marking indicates that the invention of the thing or process has been patented.[42] This provision, like the corresponding United States law, does not make patent marking compulsory. Patent marking in Japan is made by the word *Tokkyo* ("patent") and the patent number in the case of an invention of a thing, or *Hōhō Tokkyo* ("process patent"), and the patent number in the case of an invention of a process.[43] In the United States, statutory marking is effected by the word "patent" or its abbreviation "pat.," followed by the patent number.

If the licensor himself manufactures and sells products, utilizing the patented invention, he may not obligate his licensee to affix patent markings if he does not so mark his own goods.

Under United States law, the benefits of marking are available only if substantially all goods made under the patent are marked.[44] It is not necessary to affix patent markings on things to be exported to a foreign country, because the patent has effect only within the country that granted it. A patent marking relating to Japan or the United States would have no meaning in a third country.

A clause may be used requiring that a patent marking be used together with the trademark and the trade name, on a nameplate to be affixed to products made under the licensed patent (Example VII-A-4).

It is illegal to affix a patent marking to a thing not under patent, or to affix a false patent marking and there are penal provisions in both countries with respect to such acts (cf. Japanese Patent Law §188 and 198 and 35 U.S.C. §292).

B. Warranty

A license agreement may contain warranties as to the following topics:

41. 35 U.S.C. §287 (1964).
42. *Tokkyohō* §187.
43. *Cf. Tokkyohō Shikko Kisoku* (Patent Law Enforcement Regulation) §28 (MITI no. 10, 1960, in 6 EHS No. 6852A).
44. 35 U.S.C. §287 (1964).

(1) Title of the licensor and his right to grant the license; (2) Present and subsequent validity of a patent; (3) Exceptions in terms of prior commitments, and for patents as to which the licensor's right to license is limited or conditional; (4) Correctness and effectiveness of information furnished or contained in patent specification; (5) Noninfringement of patents of third parties; and (6) Negation of implied warranty.

It is desirable that any commitments of the licensor in these respects be clearly expressed and that other commitments be clearly negated, because these terms deal with subjects in which precedents are either few (Japan) or likely to confuse (United States). One way to handle these problems is broadly to negate all warranties (Example VII-B-1). Such a clause will not avoid the statutory warranty under Japanese law, as to prior dispositions by the licensor in favor of third parties.[45]

1. Licensor's title. A general warranty of title is shown in Example VII-B-2. If exceptions are necessary an introductory phrase can be used: "Except for the prior commitments stated in . . . ," the reference being to a schedule or letter listing and identifying the desired limitations on the warranty.

2. Validity of patent. A licensor usually wants to disclaim all warranty obligation as to the scope and validity of the patent. The following are clauses suitable for this purpose: (1) "This agreement shall remain in force irrespective of whether any of the licensed patents is declared invalid," or (2) "The licensor makes no warranty of any kind, either express or implied, as to the scope and validity of any licensed patents."

When such a clause is used in a patent license, the licensor should be able to retain any royalty previously paid, if the patent is declared invalid (by the patent office in Japan or by a court in the United States).

In Japan, invalidation of the only patent involved, or of all the patents involved, will give the licensee the right to refuse payment of future royalties, by terminating the agreement. In the United States a court decision denying validity affects the parties, not the patent, and another court with a different party before it, instead of applying an estoppel, might hold the patent to be valid.[46] The effect of a decision, on future royalties, accordingly varies with the circumstances. The situation under United States law is sufficiently complex to warrant use of a provision for license termination if the only patent or a

45. CIVIL CODE art. 572.

46. Blonder-Tongue Laboratories v. University of Illinois Foundation, *supra*, n. 24; Kaiser Industries Corp. v. Jones & Laughlin Steel Corp., 185 USPQ 343 (3rd Cir. 1975) rev'g 187 USPQ 193 (W.D. Pa. 1974, Rosenberg, J.).

principal patent is held invalid. Termination can be at the licensee's option or automatic. If the licensee has a general right to terminate at will, as is common in nonexclusive agreements, a special clause dealing with invalidation of a patent is unnecessary.

3. Maintenance. In an exclusive license the licensor will usually be made responsible for paying the fees and taxes necessary to keep the patents in force, as these steps protect the licensor's title and right to receive royalties and he will want to control them. In the case of a nonexclusive license, on the other hand, the licensor will probably prefer to avoid all responsibility to his licensee to maintain a particular patent. If the type of royalty provision used makes it unfair to the licensee to leave the question of maintenance to the discretion of the licensor, the licensee can be given a right to cure the defects and perhaps to offset his expenses against royalties.

A licensor's duty to maintain patents may except a patent as to which the licensee waives in writing his right to maintenance. A clause of this type is of little utility save where the agreement also obligates the licensee to reimburse the licensor for the cost of maintaining the patents, as otherwise the licensee has no incentive to execute a waiver.

Another way to divide the responsibility between the licensor and the licensee is illustrated in Example VII-B-3. See also the provisions for filing applications and maintaining patents, discussed in connection with patents on improvements.[47]

4. Obligations not to contest validity. Since 1969 it has been settled[48] that a licensee must not be precluded from contesting the validity of a United States patent, either by an implied obligation resulting under state law from his status as a licensee or by express contract. As a matter of caution, commitments not to contest the validity of patents of other countries should be limited to patents covered by the license, to the duration of the license and to the scope of the license (Examples VII-B-4 and 5). In United States agreements an explicit negation of any obligation of the licensee is sometimes provided as to his conduct regarding the licensor's patents outside of the scope of the license (Examples VII-B-6, 8).

5. Exceptions regarding patents for which licensor's rights are limited or conditional. Where a license covers many patents, especially future patents, a number of exceptions regarding the scope or terms of the license may be necessary to avoid inconsistencies or misunderstandings (Examples VII-B-8 and 10). Particular care is needed if the licensor's interest in a particular patent is or may be in some way less than total or perfect.

47. *See* the discussion in par. IV-B, *supra*.
48. Lear, Inc. v. Adkins, 395 U.S. 653 (1969).

6. Technical correctness and effect. Where no confidential technical information or know-how is supplied with a patent license, the licensor will usually refuse to warrant the correctness or technical effectiveness of the patent specifications. An important element of any license transaction is avoidance of litigation, and these are details particularly apt to engender dispute. The same considerations apply to warranties of quality or utility where technical information is to be supplied by the licensor "if he chooses," i.e., on a voluntary basis with no firm commitment to supply information. Even where the licensor is bound to supply technical information, he will usually use very guarded language in expressing any representations as to the quality or sufficiency of the information supplied (Example VII-B-10).

Three kinds of clauses are appropriate, if the licensor does undertake to warrant technical correctness or effect: (1) The licensor warrants technical effectiveness up to the level achieved in the factory of the licensor or of a normal licensee; (2) The licensor warrants that the products to be made under the license shall be of the same quality as the samples supplied by the licensor; and (3) The licensor warrants that the production capacity, quality of the products, and material consumption given are as described in the specification supplied by the licensor.

The first type of clause has a drawback. The details covered by the warranty are not clear. In the second, no warranty is made as to production-capacity or yield. The third clause is the most effective and meaningful coverage (Example VII-B-11).

Product liability, in all of its many ramifications, is of much current concern in the United States[49] and is beginning to receive attention in Japan. There are problems here which should be considered in license-drafting. In a license context the emphasis is apt to be on a disclaimer of responsibility in the licensor for personal injuries or property damage suffered by the licensee or any customer or sublicensee by reason of defects in the licensed technology (Example VII-B-12).

7. Noninfringement of a third party's patent. A licensor will not often be willing to warrant that a licensed patent does not infringe any third person's patent (Example VII-B-13). Such a warranty may, however, be required by a licensee who has the superior bargaining position, or used at the suggestion of the government (Examples VII-B-14, 15).

49. There is an extensive literature. Illustrative are FRUMER & FRIEDMAN, PRODUCTS LIABILITY (1974) and HURSCH & BAILEY, AMERICAN LAW OF PRODUCTS LIABILITY (1974).

C. Most-Favored Licensee Clause

A "most-favored licensee" clause states that if the licensor later executes a license agreement with a third person on terms more favorable to the licensee than those of this license, the licensor will give the licensee the benefit of the more favorable terms (Examples VII-C-1, 2). This type of clause is appropriate only in a nonexclusive license, as it anticipates the granting of an additional license to another person on the same subject matter.

"More favorable terms" is not an ideally clear phrase. Both words, "favorable" and "terms," require drafting amplification. The objective, of course, is to give the licensee an economic advantage, and the clause can be restricted to such matters as royalty and expense sharing. Other matters, such as sublicensing rights and geographic coverage, may require careful thought. The details can be troublesome. For example, if the royalty rate set in a later license is lower while other terms are the same, there seems clearly to be a "more favorable" term. But if the methods of calculation in the two agreements are different, it may be difficult to decide which term is in fact the more favorable. It may be better in some transactions to provide that the licensee will have an election, to come under the terms of a later license or to continue under his own original agreement, rather than to provide that a "more favorable term" of a later agreement will automatically apply to the earlier license (Examples VII-C-1, 2).

The benefit of more favorable terms should be limited, in time, to the period covered by the more favorable later agreement. If several later licenses are anticipated, the drafting of the duration language must be handled with great care.

The basic problem of competitive equality, at which a "more favorable terms" clause is aimed can be approached in a quite different way. The parties can agree that the licensor will not grant to a third person a license on more favorable terms than those granted to this licensee.

Differences in the subject matter of the licenses granted to different persons can cause dispute if the "more favorable terms" clause is not drafted with an eye to this contingency. How much variation will remove a later license from the coverage of the clause? It seems unlikely that a clause of the usual type will enable a licensee to demand more or different technology just because a later license covers the broader ground. However, it can be provided that the licensee shall be given an opportunity to consult with the licensor regarding extension of his license to the subject matter covered in a later license which is within the same general subject-matter area.

D. Trademarks and Trade Names

A provision concerning the use of a trademark on the licensed products is often included in a license agreement. Several types of clauses are in use: (1) Clauses granting the licensee the right to use the licensor's trademark or trade name, with or without a duty to use it (Examples VII-D-1, 2, 3 and 4[a]); (2) Clauses prohibiting the licensee from using the licensor's trademark or trade name or similar ones (Example VII-D-5); and (3) Clauses requiring use of a specific trademark and that it be registered by the licensee; a duty to register may be made conditional on nonregistration by the licensor (Examples VII-D-5, 6).

Trademark matters are evidently of considerable complexity, not so much in the drafting as in the factual considerations with which the draftsman must cope. From the perspective of a licensee his licensor's trademark can, if well and favorably known, be a valuable asset which the licensee can exploit. But if he uses it, he faces the obvious difficulties posed by the fact that the license must some day come to an end. He may at that time lose his position, in the trade, which he has established through use of the trademark, and be obliged to rebuild his market with a new trademark. And if the reputation of the licensor's trademark is enhanced by the licensee through use on products of good quality and by promotional activity such as advertising, the licensor will be the ultimate beneficiary. Example VII-D-2 may be interpreted as charging the licensee with an obligation to use the licensor's trademark, and this may not be in his best interest considering the effect this practice will have on his business when the license terminates. His problem can perhaps be met by a provision permitting him to use the licensor's trademark for an agreed-on period after termination of the license period. Better for him still may be permission to use the licensor's trademark, rather than a duty to use it.

When an agreement permits or requires use of the licensor's trademark by the licensee, the parties probably intend that the licensee shall take some responsibility for the quality of the goods that will bear the trademark. It can for example be provided that the licensee's methods of manufacture will be the equivalent of those used by the licensor.

If the licensee is prohibited from using the licensor's trademark or trade name or similar ones he will be free to use any other that he chooses. Or it can be explicitly recited that the licensee will use his own trademark on products made by use of the licensed patent or technology (Example VII-D-5). Arrangements of these kinds free the licensor from the risk that his trademark may be degraded by the activities of the licensee. This problem is more fully discussed below.

In third type of clause the trademark to be used by the licensee is specified in the license agreement (Example VII-D-5), and this can be either a new trademark or one already owned by the licensee. If a new trademark is to be devised, it is necessary to decide in whose name the trademark shall be registered (Example VII-D-6). Even where the licensee is free to use any trademark, it is sometimes stipulated that the trademark is not to be identical or similar to any used by the licensor (Example VII-D-5).

Since under the Japanese Trademark Law the first applicant for registration is, as a rule, entitled to the right of trademark,[50] it is of great importance to register the trademark to be used in Japan.

As with patents, a right granted to use a trademark may be exclusive (cf., Example VII-D-4[a], 7) or nonexclusive (cf., Examples VII-D-1, 3). Which type the licensor will grant depends on the terms of, and will conform to, the related patent license.

A license granting a right to use a trademark can in each country be registered in the patent office,[51] and the application for recording will include, as a patent license, a statement of the scope of the license, royalty terms, manner of paying royalty and the duration of the grant. Usually the term and the territory will be the same as those of the accompanying patent license (Examples VII-D-4[a], 7). Also identical will be the patent license and trademark references to goods or products (Examples VII-D-1, 2, 3, 4[a], [c], 7, 8).

Royalty is generally required for a trademark license. A single lump-sum royalty may cover both, if the license to use the trademark is incidental to a patent license.

In order to maintain the business good will, as to which his trademark is a factor, a licensor will usually want to be sure, insofar as he can, that the goods for which his trademark is used are of appropriate quality and design. In the United States this kind of control is an essential element in trademark licenses because it establishes a basic relationship between the licensor and the licensee (that is, they become "related companies" within the meaning of Section 5 of the Trademark Act).[52] This relationship is necessary if the use of the trademark by the licensee is to support the licensor's registration of the trademark (the fifth-year affidavit required by Section 8[a] may, for example, rest on this foundation).[53]

50. *Shōhyohō* (Trademark Law) §8 (Law No. 127, 1957), in 6 EHS No. 6880A.

51. *See* the discussion of patent license-grant recording, par. III–A–1, *supra*. Trademark license recording in the United States is different. When a claim of exclusive right to use is made *in an application* or in a required affidavit, the rights of licensees are to be mentioned as exceptions.

52. Trademark Act of 1946, §5, 15 U.S.C. §1055 (1970).

53. Trademark Act of 1946, §8(a), 15 U.S.C. §1058(a) (1970). This affidavit is made

In Japan, if the use of the trademark by the licensee produces deception or confusion as to the quality of the goods, anyone can initiate a proceeding for cancellation of the trademark registration.[54] It is accordingly vital that a license agreement include a provision concerning quality control of the goods to be manufactured and sold by the licensee under the licensed trademark. For example, the licensee may be allowed to use the trademark only on goods which meet a quality stipulated by the licensor (Example VII-D-9); or the licensee may be required to comply, to the best of his ability, with standards set up by the licensor (Example VII-D-10); or the licensee may be required to submit for licensor approval samples of products, at intervals designated by the licensor (Example VII-D-11). It may further be provided that the licensee shall at once remove the trademark from goods of his which do not meet the indicated quality standards. Most drastic is a clause authorizing the licensor to terminate the license if the licensee does not observe quality standards stipulated by the licensor (Examples VII-D-4, 12).

A trademark can be lost if it becomes a generic term. These risks must be countered by appropriate license clauses. Suitable are provisions allowing the licensor to control the use of his trademark, in all of the relevant details. Included will be particulars as to the design of the trademark as used by the licensee both on goods and in advertising (Examples VII-D-4[b], 8, 9, 13, 14, 15).

Trademark licenses raise contestability and transferability problems and questions about infringement that do not differ materially from those already discussed in relation to patents and that permit of similar solutions (Examples VII-D-5, 16, 17).

When a license agreement terminates, a dispute may arise between the parties concerning subsequent use of the trademark by the licensee. Particularly pressing will be questions about goods bearing the licensor's trademark, which are still in the licensee's inventory. For these problems the license agreement should provide answers, as in Examples VII-D-4[c], 18, 19. Fair to the licensee will be a grace period during which he can sell goods bearing the licensed trademark. A clause of this type can be limited to termination by reason of expiration of the license term, thus excluding termination resulting from cancellation for wrongdoing (Example VII-D-20).

Sometimes a trademark or patent licensee is also permitted to use the licensor's trademark or an abbreviation of it on condition that the

during the fifth year to show use of the mark and thus escape cancellation for nonuse at the end of the sixth year. *Id.*

54. *Shōhyohō* §53.

goods produced and marketed under the license bear a label reading "licensed by (the licensor's trade name)" (Example VII-A-4).

E. Confidentiality Obligation

If the agreement licenses only patented inventions, there is no confidentiality problem because the inventions have already been published. In many cases, however, the agreement also licenses the use of secret material, such as, unpublished patent applications and other technology. Moreover, a license agreement will sometimes cover only unpatented technology with no patent application in prospect. Since the essential value of secret material depends on its being kept secret, the license can properly require the licensee to exercise the necessary security precautions. These benefit the licensee too, and indeed, he may require the licensor to make a similar covenant.

Deliberate wrongful disclosure is a different matter. Even though the license does not contain an express covenant against such disclosure, a licensee who executes a license agreement covering private or confidential technical information of any kind is usually regarded as impliedly undertaking an obligation to protect its confidentiality save where the agreement expressly negates such an obligation. A comparable undertaking by the licensor will not, however, be implied. The license should not, as to these relationships, leave anything in the realm of implication or doubt.

To avoid uncertainty concerning the existence and scope of a confidentiality obligation a detailed clause is normally used in every license agreement as to which it is appropriate (Examples VII-E-3, 4, 6, 8, 9, 10, 12, 14, 15). Some agreements provide broadly that both the licensor and the licensee shall do their best mutually to keep technical information secret (Example VII-E-1).

A license may obligate the licensee to disclose to the licensor technical information gained by the licensee during the term of the agreement. In such a case, it is usually provided (as in Example VII-E-5) that both parties mutually undertake to preserve the secrecy of such information. The last sentence of Example VII-E-5 would be used if the parties fear that the standard of care indicated may be too strict, especially in the United States, where technical employees frequently change employers.

It will usually be expected that the geographic coverage of a confidentiality obligation is worldwide rather than limited to the license-territories. The license should carefully delineate the area coverage.

Also important will be some other confidential-obligation details, such as: (1) a provision to the effect that the confidentiality clause binds both the licensee and his sublicensees (Examples VII-E-4, 7); and (2) that if the licensee contracts with other persons to build a factory, set up a plant, or procure manufacturing machinery and is obliged to disclose to such persons any confidential matter, he will require them to keep such matter secret. Variations of the foregoing can be used. For example, a clause stating that the licensee shall not sublicense, or disclose technical information to third parties, save upon prior written consent of the licensor. Or, a clause stating that the licensee shall restrict the documents and drawings furnished to it in connection with the license to such persons as to whom the information is absolutely essential to accomplish the purposes of the license. Or, that the licensee will disclose to a contractor engaged in the construction of plant or equipment only such information as is absolutely necessary in relation to the work to be performed by him.

Still another approach is illustrated by the commonly used clause which recites that every third person with whom the licensee deals will be subject to the same confidentiality obligation, with regard to technical information furnished to the licensee by the licensor, as is undertaken by the licensee, and that the licensee will take from each such person a written confidentiality undertaking so phrased (Examples VII-E-5, 7, 8, 13, 16).

A license will often particularize about the security measures to be taken by the licensee and by third persons with whom he deals. For example, the licensee may be required to set up office or company routines regulating the safeguarding, custody, and use of secret documents, and the dissemination of secret information (Example VII-E-9). Similar precautions may be required of sublicenses and contractors.

It is understood, as a matter of course, that the officers and directors of the licensee corporation are subject to the same confidentiality obligation as that of the licensee, and drafting about them is not customary. Employees other than officers are the subject of confidentiality clauses in a typical license. The objective is of course to prevent wrongful disclosure of technical information, not to acquire a right to damages from the erring employee. A duty not to divulge secret information obtained in the course of the employment probably exists as a matter of law.[55] What is needed is pressure on the employer. This can be asserted by clauses requiring him to police the release and use of the information, and to include carefully drafted confidentiality clauses in all employment contracts. A breach of this kind of covenant

55. Milgrim, Business Organizations, Vol. 12, Trade Secrets §5.2 (1975).

can be made a ground for termination or other remedies against the licensee. The most rigorous of the security measures a licensor can use is a clause reciting that a breach of such a covenant by an employee is deemed to be a breach of the license agreement by the licensee (Examples VII-E-6 to 10, 13, 15, 16).

The secrecy of technical information is not fully guaranteed unless employees are under a duty not to wrongfully disclose information, not only during the period of their employment but also after its termination. There are accordingly agreements that provide that the licensee must charge his employees with a confidentiality obligation which runs for a given period of time after the termination of the employment, or even with a duty to refrain from accepting employment with another company engaged in a competing business during a given period of time after the termination of the employment (Example VII-E-8). An employment contract of this type is enforceable, provided its geographic and duration provisions are reasonable under the circumstances.[56] In drafting for a transaction in which the need for secrecy is of short duration, care in setting the period of employee-restraint will be necessary.

It is usually important to extend in general language the licensee's obligation of secrecy, for a period after the termination of the license (Example VII-E-8, 11, 12, 14). Secrecy for certain types of technical information, however, may be important only for a limited period, because of the rapid development of the technology. In some transactions, the technical information disclosed to the licensee will become public property or obsolete before the term of the license runs out. In these situations a post-termination type of clause will be unfair to the licensee. It is accordingly desirable in drafting the confidentiality clause to free the licensee from his secrecy burden as soon as the technical information is no longer secret for a cause other than a wrongful act of the licensee, and to limit the period after termination of the license, to a reasonable period. Alternatively, it may be provided that the licensee shall undertake a confidentiality obligation regarding technical information during such period as the information is kept secret by the licensor and no longer (Examples VII-E-6, 9, 16). Obsolescence problems are more complicated, and for them no definitive practice has evolved.

Where unpublished technical information is to be furnished by a United States licensor to a foreign licensee, it is necessary to limit the distribution of products made under the license, in accordance with the laws and regulations of the United States. In point are the Trad-

56. *See* Arnold and McGuire, *The Law and Practice of Corporate Information Security*, 57 J. PAT. OFF. SOC'Y 169, 237 (1975).

ing with the Enemy Act,[57] the Export Administration Act,[58] and the Department of Commerce Export Control Regulations,[59] which impose restrictions on the exportation of technical data (Examples VII-E-17, 18, 19). If the subject matter of the technical data relates to arms and implements of war, within the meaning of the Munitions Control Act,[60] Department of State procedures must also be satisfied. These legislative and regulatory controls may make it unlawful for the licensor to disclose to a licensee, regardless of clauses about confidentiality.

Secrecy problems have another dimension. The nature of the licensed information permitting, it is often better for the parties concerned to seek the protection afforded by a patent rather than to rely on confidentiality safeguards. It will on occasion be necessary to use a confidentiality clause in a license agreement to protect information pending consummation of patent-application procedures, both as protection against public disclosure during that period and also to set a time limit on the secrecy obligation. Example VII-E-2 is illustrative.[61]

F. Technical Assistance

When the subject matter of a license agreement is a patent or patent application, the licensee can learn the details of the invention by reading the data published in the *Official Gazette* or by obtaining a copy of the unpublished data from the licensor (applicant). In a transaction of this kind the parties may or may not feel that the licensor should provide the licensee with technical assistance to aid in working the invention.

In any case, and particularly where the patent is on a highly technical level, information and materials other than those disclosed in the specifications of the patent may be desirable. Thus, it is common to supplement a patent license agreement with an agreement covering related technical information and materials. In many transactions covering know-how the licensee will need technical assistance in order properly to utilize the know-how, and the agreement should contain appropriate provisions.

The kind of assistance a licensee will need and the scope of it will vary widely, and the drafting for each transaction must be carefully tailored to the circumstances. Specificity as to just when, what, and where is highly desirable in a technical assistance clause. Phrases such

57. 50 U.S.C. Ann. §§1–44 (1964).

58. Act. of Dec. 30, 1969, Pub. L. No. 91–184, 83 St. 841, repealing 50 U.S.C. Ann. §2021–31 (1964) (codified at 50 U.S.C. Ann. §§2401–13 (Supp. 1971)).

59. 15 C.F.R. §§368–99 (1971).

60. 22 U.S.C §1934 (1970).

61. *Cf. Tokkyohō* §29.

as "technical information relating to . . ." or "know-how relating to the manufacture of . . ." may be useful. Included may be secret technical specifications, data, and the like, as to which confidentiality will be vital. Mechanical aids such as blueprints, drawings, and flow-sheets may be necessary and the clause may list and describe them (Examples VII-F-1,2,5,6[a],7,9[a],10).

Important too are the timing and duration of particular kinds of technical assistance. Usually, the information should be made available immediately or very soon after the agreement becomes operative. It can be timed to coincide with the initial royalty payment, or even made due on demand (Examples VII-F-6[a],8,9,11[a]).

Information subsequently acquired by the licensor during the life of the license must also be considered by the draftsman. A duty to provide technical help of this kind is often put on the licensor (Examples VII-F-6[a],8,9).

In an international license agreement, it is appropriate to specify the language in which the technical information is to be supplied (Example VII-F-6[a]).

"Technical information" may include both information about manufacturing techniques and information about marketing (Example VII-F-7). It can also include advice about and guidance in the use of such information and data. Particularly important in some transactions will be personnel training. Programs can be set up in the licensor's plant for the instruction of employees of the licensee (Examples VII-F-3, 6[b], 11[c], 12). Useful may be information relating to the construction of the plant which licensee expects to build (Example VII-F-3). Sometimes information about not only the design and building of machines and equipment but also about their installation and layout will be needed (Example VII-F-3). These matters may require help by the licensor's engineers, on the site, rather than just memoranda (Examples VII-F-6[b], 11[b]).

For many forms of technical assistance, the license will provide specific instructions, for example, as to when each type of assistance will be given, about the number of engineers to be sent by the licensor to the licensee's plant, and about the number of, timetable for, housing of and instruction of employees of the licensee who are to receive training in the licensor's plant. Also important will be agreement about the expenses involved in these operations (Examples VII-F-3 and 6[b]). On occasion visa and tax problems may dictate shifting the sites of training from the licensor's plant to that of the licensee, for which purpose independent technicians may be preferable to employees of the licensor (Example VII-F-6[b]).

In some agreements it is stipulated that if the licensee finds it difficult to procure, in his area, the materials needed for construction of a needed plant or the building of needed equipment, the licensor will supply such materials to the licensee (Example VII-F-4).

Technical assistance, like so many other aspects of a license transaction, puts heavy demands on security measures and requires detailed drafting about secrecy.[62]

G. Transferability, Assignability of Licenses, Licensor's Rights and Interests

If a corporate party to a license agreement merges with another corporation, the anticipated development of the license transaction will necessarily be affected. If the license agreement is silent on the matter the license-interest of the merged party will, as a rule, pass to the successor corporation where the survivor of the merger is an entity other than the merged party.[63] This result may or may not be desirable, and the possibility of merger should be considered by the draftsman. Whether a basic clause prohibiting assignment will serve the purpose requires thought. Cf., Examples VII-G-3, 6, 7, 10. A more specific coverage may be preferable. Although assumption of the obligations of the merged corporation, by the successor, is routine the draftsman may choose to specify such assumption, in the license (Example VII-G-8).

Death of an individual license-party, and especially death of the licensee, is also a contingency which the draftsman will want to ponder. If the license does not otherwise provide, the interest of the decedent will pass to his heir or legatee.[64]

All kinds of transfers of the licensee's interests, whether voluntary, upon merger, or upon death pose for the licensor a serious risk. Technology may pass from the licensee to a competitor of the licensor. For this risk appropriate license-drafting is essential. Useful is a clause to the effect that the license agreement and license are non-transferable (Example VII-G-11), but this seems too coarse a tool for the job. Better is language particularly addressed to death or merger or sale that leaves to the licensor an opportunity to evaluate the situation when one of these events occurs (or, in the instances of merger or sale, when the planning is under way). There will certainly be transactions in which the licensor would be benefitted if the licensee's posi-

62. *See* the discussion, par. VII–E, *supra*.

63. In the United States this is a matter of the corporation law of the particular state or states of incorporation and may require close examination to verify the consequences in a particular case.

64. It is common to provide in a license to an individual that the license is "personal" so as to indicate it is to terminate on death of the licensee, as well as to indicate nonassignability.

tion were assumed by a successor in interest. What is probably most needed is discretion in the licensor to approve or disapprove of a prospective transfer by whatever means, and a right to terminate if he disapproves (Examples VII-G-8, 9).

Merger or death of and sale by the licensor may or may not pose equally serious problems for the licensee. The draftsman should at least consider the possibilities.

Assignment. It is usually considered necessary that the licensor obtain the consent of the licensee before assigning his interest in the agreement, even though the license-document contains no explicit provision to this effect.[65] The licensor has not only rights but also obligations, under the agreement, and his duties are in their very nature not transferable without the consent of the obligee-licensee.[66] Drafting for this situation is nonetheless useful. Examples VII-G-7 and 10 are indicative.

A license can recite that it will be binding on and inure to the benefit of the licensor and his assigns. This language will be interpreted to permit assignment by the licensor (Examples VII-G-4, 6, 8) but leaves some questions unanswered. Royalty can surely be assigned, but what of other rights such as a right to be informed of improvements made by the licensee? Some interests of the licensor are arguably too personal to be transferable without specific authorization. If the prospective transferee is a competitor of the licensee, it is by no means clear that the licensee would be obliged to give information on improvements to the competitor.

The parties usually intend that the licensee will have no right to transfer his rights under a license agreement save on consent of the licensor. A licensee's duties are so important a part of the transaction as to make it essential that the licensor have an opportunity to weigh the financial, technical, and moral responsibility of a prospective assignee of the rights, since the assignee will normally be expected to perform the duties. To implement the parties' purpose drafting is necessary. Under the Japanese Patent Law, a license may be assigned without the licensor's consent if it is done together with the business of working the invention.[67] In both countries there is need for agree-

65. The licensee's right to exercise the license is so closely interwoven with the credit risk involved in royalty payments and the personality factor involved in confidentiality and other covenants that assignment can materially impair the position of the licensor. For a discussion of the basic contract principles, see CORBIN, 4 CONTRACTS 66 867, 869, 870 (1951).

66. See the discussion of basic contract principles, CORBIN, 4 CONTRACTS §§865, 866, 867 (1951).

67. Under §§77(3) and 94(1) of the Patent Law, exclusive and nonexclusive licenses can be assigned without the licensor's consent if the assignment includes the business of working the licensed patent.

ment about the various details that might otherwise cause controversy. Examples VII-G-1 and 2 are illustrative.

One aspect of the problem requires particular care. The theory behind the Japanese Patent Law provision mentioned above is that the licensee will build his business around the license and after such business has been established, the licensor's interest will not be harmed only by a change of the carrier of the business and that a licensee who built the business will be unable to dispose of the business if the license cannot go with it.

Few modern license agreements go so far as flatly to forbid transfer of the licensee's rights. Some do, as in Example VII-G-11. Almost all license agreements currently prepared deny assignment by the licensee save on written consent of the licensor (Examples VII-G-3, 6 to 10). Refinements of the latter type of clause may be needed properly to handle the problems present in a particular transaction. Comparatively rare is a provision authorizing the licensee freely to assign the license (Example VII-G-5).

In Japan, if either party to a license agreement is changed a new governmental approval is needed, under the Foreign Investment Law. Until such approval is given the transfer is not effective between the new parties.[68] Examples VII-G-7 and 8 make reference to this regulatory procedure.

H. Severability of Agreement

If part of a license agreement is for any reason invalid or unenforceable under the law that governs the creation of legal relations, there is a question as to how this defect affects the rest of the agreement. For this problem the following provision may provide a solution:

> While it is the belief of the parties hereto that all of the provisions in this agreement are valid and enforceable under applicable law, it is recognized that there is always a possibility that one or more of the provisions may subsequently be declared invalid or otherwise rendered unenforceable by court or administrative decision. Unless the invalidity or unenforceability of any such provision does substantial violence to the underlying sense of the remainder of the agreement, it is the intention of the parties hereto that any such invalidity or unenforceability shall not in any way affect the validity or enforceability of any other provisions of the agreement except those of which the invalidated or unenforceable provisions comprise an integral part or which are otherwise clearly inseparable.

68. *Gaishi ni kansuru horitsu* (Law Concerning Foreign Investment) art. 10 (Law no. 163, 1950), in 5 EHS No. 5410.

This language merely restates the relevant legal principle[69] in a way that should make reasonable dispute unlikely. If the purpose of the remaining portions of the agreement will be defeated by reason of the partial invalidity, the whole must fall, and whether that purpose will be defeated may of course be disputed. There is an area of doubt here, which drafting probably cannot remove.

VIII. Termination of Agreement

A license agreement should come to an end when any of several events occurs: (a) expiration of the licensed patent; (b) abandonment of the licensed patent; (c) cancellation of the licensed patent due to nonpayment of fees; (d) invalidation of the licensed patent by a proceeding in the patent office; (e) expiration of the agreed license period; (f) termination of the license agreement by one of the parties in the exercise of a right to terminate; (g) fulfillment of a condition subsequent; and (h) mutual consent to termination.

As to items (a), (b), (c), and (d), if the license covers only one patent and provides that the duty to pay royalty is contingent on the existence of the patent during the payment period, a termination clause may be considered unnecessary. There will, however, often be more than one patent involved, and many license agreements cover interests other than patent rights. The underlying legal principles may be obscure in application, particularly to a situation in which one of several interests becomes invalid, and may differ from country to country.

The principal concern, as to items (e), (f), (g) and (h), will be drafting coverage of the possible loose ends that may be troublesome after termination. Some of the details are discussed below.

When all of the ramifications are reviewed, it seems wise to carefully consider in each license-drafting assignment the desirability of a carefully tailored termination clause that goes beyond the obviously useful termination-for-cause provision.

A. Termination due to Default or Breach

License agreements usually permit termination by the injured party if either party fails to perform his obligations under the agreement. The drafting may vary considerably in the details since defaults can be of differing degrees of seriousness.

69. Where separation of the lawful part from the unlawful part is on the one hand practicable and on the other hand not productive of a result which is incompatible with the policy behind the illegality, a court may separate them. See Corbin, 6A Contracts §§1390, 1520–1525 (1962).

A license can provide broadly that upon any breach the injured party can terminate. This kind of clause may not serve the parties' best interests. Probably better is a clause that permits termination if one or more specified obligations are defaulted, those specified being of course the more important ones. A variation of this approach may be a grace period during which a default can be cured, or a provision that the injured party can terminate after a default has lasted for a stated period.

A useful supplement to either type of clause is a sentence stating that the injured party can waive his right to terminate, without prejudice to any other remedy available to him under the agreement or under the applicable law. In some transactions the parties have expressly waived any right to cancel conferred by law, reserving other legal remedies (Example VIII-A-1).

1. Effect of Termination. Under the general principles of contract-law cancellation (rescission) for breach ("material breach" in the Common Law vernacular) ends the contract duties of the parties insofar as the contract is at that time still executory.[70] There will remain perhaps other legal remedies, such as a right to damages, because of the breach. These propositions do not work well in some license transactions. Termination of a license whether for breach or some other reason often leaves unresolved details, and for these the draftsman should make proper provision.

The licensee should undertake to return the various physical things such as printed material, drawings, manuals, and blueprints which he has received from the licensor. Just what is to be returned, when, and how should be made clear.

An obligation of confidentiality should continue for an agreed period (Example VIII-A-2).

The licensee should expressly covenant not to use the licensed technology after termination save as may then be authorized or as may be provided in the license agreement (Example VIII-A-2).

2. Notice of termination. It is usual to provide, as in Example VIII-A-4, that a notice of default and a grace period during which the default can be cured, shall precede termination. A warning of this kind is not required by law and a license can if the parties so agree be equally drastic. A license can call for notice and a grace period for certain kinds of default and for immediate termination without prior warning or demand, in the event of an especially serious breach such as intentional disclosure of secret know-how.

A sublicense should direct attention to the termination provisions

70. CORBIN, 4 CONTRACTS §946 (1951).

of the license and state the parties' purpose about the effect, on the sublicense, of such termination. If the main license permits cure of a licensee's default by a sublicensee, the sublicensee should contain a similar clause and authorize the sublicensee to offset his expenses against royalty. Or, the sublicense can obligate the sublicensee to render the performance in question. If it does, the effect of his default, on the sublicense, should be spelled out.

Wherever a person who is not himself the defaulter is affected by a default, notice of it will be especially important. If sublicensing is permitted, a license should require the licensor to give notice to sublicensees of defaults by the licensee, and may perhaps both authorize cure by the sublicensee and give him a grace period within which to render the defaulted performance. The language of the usual notice clause (Examples XI-1, 2, 3) is not adequate for sublicense situations.

Where sublicenses are particularly important to the licensor as a means for broadening the manufacturing or distribution base on which his royalties depend, the drafting can take the appropriate direction. Sublicensing will not only be permitted (or even required), but a sublicensee will be explicitly authorized to render any performance of the licensee should the latter default. Notice of default will be given to the sublicensee, and a grace period allowed him.

It is customary to recite in a sublicense that it will end if the main license is terminated. If sublicensing is permitted only as to subsidiary companies of the licensee, a sublicense should provide for its termination automatically if the sublicensee ceases to be a subsidiary (Example VIII-H-4).

3. Curing a default. Under a clause such as Example VIII-A-5, a party who receives a notice of default can avoid termination by curing his default within the stipulated period, provided the default is of a type which permits of cure. A default in a royalty payment is one thing. Intentional disclosure of secret technology is something else. According to Example VIII-A-4, the party in default can avoid termination, not by curing the default but by paying a sum stated in the agreement or a "reasonable amount" if the parties so stipulate. A clause of this kind can operate on defaults that are not curable. A term such as "reasonable compensation" as used in Example VIII-A-4 has a built-in problem of indefiniteness. Better is a clause stating a standard by which the sum to be paid shall be computed, or provides for valuers or appraisers or arbitrators whose decision as to the amount to be paid will govern.

It should be noted that in Example VIII-A-5, a right to terminate is suspended during the pendency of arbitration proceedings if the existence of a default is in issue before the arbitrators.

4. Right to complete orders on hand. A licensee whose right to use technology has ended because the license has terminated may find himself with orders he cannot fill or with goods, made under the license, which he no longer has the right to sell. Both problems merit attention in the drafting of a license. Sale of articles produced during the period of the agreement may be permissible as a matter of law if the quantity of the articles involved is within reasonable limits and if they are sold within a reasonable period, but to avoid dispute it is wiser to provide for this contingency in the agreement.

Similar problems arise concerning the post-termination performance of repair and other warranty obligations incurred in the sale of goods before termination.

Under Example VIII-A-2 the licensee is authorized to dispose of its stock of the licensed products and parts during the year subsequent to the termination of the agreement.

B. Termination after Trial Period

A license will on occasion provide for a trial period after which either party can withdraw. Careful handling of the drafting about the situation which will appertain, if the license aborts, is needed. Return of technical documents and secret material are routine problems. This type of transaction has some of the aspects of an option and can readily be cast into an option format. There may be a down payment the disposition of which will be a relevant detail.

Trial period or option arrangements are particularly useful where the technical information can be transferred in "two bites." If the proposed licensee, having examined the first lot of technology loses interest in the venture he will have limited his financial commitment and the licensor will have limited his exposure to security risks.

C. Expiration

1. Renewal. If a license expires during the life of a patent or when an agreement covering know-how expires, the licensee may very much want to renew the license. An option to do so can be made a term of the license (Example VIII-C-1). An option to renew "if the parties agree," or "on terms to be agreed on," may be unenforceable.[71] Nevertheless, many licenses prepared in Japan contain renewal clauses worded in one of these ways.

2. Licensee's right to use know-how. Sometimes a licensor wants the licensee's right to use technical information and know-how furnished under the license to end on termination or expiry of the agreement.

71. Corbin, 1 Contracts §§95, 98 (1963).

Such a consequence may be proper in the event of early termination for a breach by the licensee, but quite inappropriate in the case of normal expiration of the license term. The policy of the government of Japan is opposed to cutting off the licensee's right to use the information or know-how in this way.[72] Moreover, for United States tax reasons, it may be desirable to assure the licensee a continuing right to use the information or know-how, in perpetuity.

Physical things like manuals, drawings, and related materials can be distinguished and their return required even though there is no provision prohibiting further use of the information derived from or furnished by them. Exact copying of the licensor's products after the term of the agreement is also distinguishable and may well be forbidden by the contract.

Where the licensor is obligated to provide technical information about current improvements, during the term of the agreement, some of the know-how may be quite new when the agreement ends. He should not be obliged to permit the continued use of this technology without compensation. Finding the right drafting formula by which to work out this problem, within the framework of Japanese governmental policy and United States tax policy is not easy.

D. Termination by Mutual Consent

A clause stating that the parties can terminate by mutual consent serves no useful purpose and is not often used.

E. Insolvency or Bankruptcy

The consequences of insolvency can range from inability to meet current royalty payments to insolvency proceedings such as reorganization (in the United States) or liquidation. Financial troubles can affect either party, with adverse consequences to the other party. License clauses can anticipate many of the eventualities. Basic is a clause permitting termination if the other party becomes bankrupt (Examples VIII-E-1 to 4).

F. Corporate Dissolution

A corporation may dissolve or discontinue its business for reasons other than insolvency, and the license should contain a clause suitable to this contingency. Whether the clause shall operate only if the licensee dissolves, or if either dissolves, is for the parties to agree. Also to be decided is whether termination shall be automatic or upon election (cf., Example VIII-E-2).

72. Rev. Rul. 64–56, 1964–1 C.B. 133.

A clause permitting termination if the other party "undergoes any substantial change in management or control," as in Example VIII-G-1 is too obscure and therefore should be avoided. The objective sought to be achieved by the draftsman may be meritorious but more precise identification of the termination events is needed.

G. "Force Majeure"

The typical license agreement excuses a party who fails to perform an obligation because of war, a strike or a natural catastrophe. Example VIII-F-1 is illustrative (cf., Example VIII-F-2), which permits an extension of the license period if performance is interfered with by *force majeure*, provided the purpose of the agreement is not thereby permanently frustrated.

H. Cross Licenses

Termination of the licenses and rights of the defaulter may be a more appropriate remedy for breach of an agreement calling for cross-licenses than is termination of the agreement (Example VIII-H-1). It should be made entirely clear that the rights and licenses of the injured party are not affected by his use of this remedy (Example VIII-H-2). This mode of attack on the problem is especially useful where one of the parties takes his interest under the agreement free from royalty obligation. A supplemental clause can state specifically that royalty-free licenses are not to be terminated save for breach by the grantee thereof, or upon expiration of the relevant patents (cf., Example VIII-H-3 with Example VIII-A-2).

IX. Settlement of Disputes

Arbitration clauses are common in international license agreements and some of the possibilities are illustrated in Examples IX-1 to 3. The draftsman will want to familiarize himself with the contemporaneous arbitration details, both legal and practical, before undertaking to put his clause in final form.

X. Governing Law

Also widely used are governing-law clauses. A well-drafted license agreement will reflect the considered agreement of the parties identifying the country or state whose law they wish to be applicable to their transaction. This area, too, is beyond the scope of the present chapter. A primary problem is the substantive validity of governing-law provisions, a matter as to which the law, particularly in the United States, is far from stable. Familiarity with the current position of the courts in the relevant localities will be essential.

XI. Notices

Notices *inter se* the parties are routine details of a license transaction and the drafting should answer the questions that can arise about notices. The method by which notices shall be transmitted should be specified, for example, surface mail, registered mail, airmail, cable, or special messenger. The address or addresses to which notices are to be sent should be stated. Also useful is a clause indicating the time when a notice is to be effective upon receipt or upon sending. This clause will serve further to allocate the risk of loss or delay in transmission. See Examples XI-1 to 3.

Appendix: Examples of License Agreements

WILLIAM R. WOODWARD AND KAZUKO MATSUO

I. Preamble

I–1

By this Agreement made and entered into by and between A COMPANY, INCORPORATED, a ______ corporation having its principal office in ______ , ________ , U.S.A., and B-A K.K., a Japanese corporation in formation, being represented by its association of promoters through B MANUFACTURING CO., LTD., a Japanese corporation having its principal office in Tokyo, Japan, the said parties agree as follows:

I–2

(*Effect of Headings*). The headings to Sections and Subsections of this Agreement are for the convenience of reference only, do not form a part of this Agreement, and shall not in any way affect the interpretation hereof.

I–3

This AGREEMENT entered into this ____ day of ______ , ______ , and between M, a corporation organized and existing under the laws of Japan, having its principal place of business at ________, Tokyo, Japan (hereinafter referred to as "Sublicensor"), and N, a corporation organized and existing under the laws of Japan, having its principal place of business at ________, Tokyo, Japan (hereinafter referred as "Sublicensee").

WITNESSETH:

WHEREAS, L (hereinafter called "Licensor") is a manufacturer in the United States of America of X and owns various inventions, patent rights, secret manufacturing processes and formulae and other similar property and rights relating to the manufacture, testing and operation of X, and has, over a period of years, acquired unique experience, skills and knowledge relating thereto, and has in its employ technicians skilled in manufacturing and engineering, and other technological arts and practices incident to the manufacture of X; and

WHEREAS, Sublicensor has entered into as of ______, a Technical Assistance and License Agreement with Licensor in the form attached hereto as Exhibit "A" (hereinafter called "License Agreement") under which License Agreement Sublicensor has the right to grant a sublicense to have manufactured in Japan on behalf of Sublicensor Licensed Products (as hereinafter defined) and is willing to grant to Sublicensee such a sublicense subject to the terms and conditions set forth below; and

WHEREAS, Sublicensee desires to obtain such a sublicense;

Now, THEREFORE, in consideration of the mutual promises hereinafter set forth, the parties hereto have agreed as follows:

II. Effective and Execution Dates

II–1

This Agreement, while executed on ____ day of ______, 19___, shall not become finally effective unless and until it is approved in writing by the appropriate authorities of the Japanese Government, and any other written Government approval shall have been obtained as shall be necessary, in the opinion of Licensor, to make this a valid agreement and to obtain the benefits, with respect to the payments to be made by Licensee to Licensor hereunder, of the provisions of the Income Tax Convention between Japan and the United States of America. Licensor shall notify Licensee promptly upon the receipt of all such approvals.

II–2

This Agreement shall not become finally effective unless and until it and the License Agreement are approved in writing by the appropriate authorities of the Japanese Government, and any other written Government approval shall have been obtained as shall be necessary, in the opinion of Sublicensor and Licensor, to make this and the License Agreement valid and binding, and to obtain the benefits with respect to the payments to be made by Sublicensor to Licensor under the License Agreement, of the provisions of the Income Tax Convention between Japan and the United States of America. Sublicensor shall notify Sublicensee promptly upon the receipt of all such approvals, and this Agreement shall become effective as of the first day of the month immediately following the month in which such notice is given. Said effective date shall be inserted on Exhibit "B" to this Agreement which shall at that time be duly acknowledged by each party.

II–3

Article 15. (*Effective Date and Term*). (a) This Agreement shall become effective from the day on which the Japanese Government approval shall be given thereto, and shall continue in full force and effect for a period of five (5) years from the said day, with the extension of every five years, subject to the Japanese Government approval, unless terminated by either of the parties to this Agreement in accordance with Art. 16.

(b) This Agreement will remain in force irrespective of whether or not any of the Patent Rights of LICENSOR is declared invalid.

(c) Notwithstanding the foregoing (a), the provisions of Art. 11 hereof shall take effect upon the signing of this Agreement, even before the effective date provided for in (a) above.

Article 11. (*Import from LICENSOR*). (a) After the signing of this Agreement, if LICENSEE deems it necessary so to do, LICENSEE may purchase the above products manufactured by LICENSOR directly or through LICENSEE's representative, for the purpose of testing the market, even before the effective date of this Agreement as provided in Art. 15 hereof.

(b) LICENSEE and/or its nominees shall have the right to sell, use, lease and otherwise dispose of the above products purchased from LICENSOR under (a) above in Japan.

II–4

(*Effective Date*). 1. This Agreement shall become effective when the parties shall have obtained approval from the respective governmental authorities to the extent such approval is required by law, including, without limitation, approval by the Japanese Foreign Exchange and Foreign Investment authorities. A shall promptly take steps to obtain such approval and shall promptly notify B of any action taken by the governmental authorities. This Agreement will become effective only after the following conditions have been fulfilled: (1) A has obtained appropriate government assurances, among others, that foreign exchange will be available annually for the payment of dividends to A of at least 20 percent of A's equity capital and, in addition, sufficient exchange will be available to repatriate the capital of New Company paid in by A to New Company within a 5 year period from the date said capital has been paid in; and (2) A has obtained in final contract form commitments previously made to A by ______ permitting fulfillment of the obligations undertaken by A in Exhibit "No. 2" with respect to ______'s patent rights in Japan. The parties shall acknowledge in writing the date when the foregoing conditions have been satisfied and that date (or a later acknowledged date in the event of a difference of opinion) shall be the effective date of this Agreement. In the event the foregoing conditions have not been satisfied by the first day of January, 19___ , or such later date as may be mutually agreed by and between the parties hereto, either party may by notice in writing to the other rescind this Agreement, and thereupon all liabilities of the parties other than the secrecy obligations contained in Section 3 hereof shall absolutely cease and determine without any claims for damages, expenses or otherwise.

III. Grants of Licenses

A. Scope

III–A–1

Article 2. (*License*). (a) Licensor hereby grants to Licensee an exclusive license to manufacture, use, sell, lease and otherwise practice the invention covered by Japanese Patent No. _____ during the term of this Agreement.

(b) Licensee shall have the right to grant sublicenses with respect to the license granted under (a) above.

Article 3. (*Export*). (a) Licensee may further sell _____ exclusively in _______ , and nonexclusively in _______ . Licensee may also sell _____ in other countries of the world provided that a prior mutual agreement therefor shall be made case by case.

(b) Licensor agrees that the right to sell provided for in (a) above may be extended by Licensee to Sublicensees.

III–A–2

Article 2. (*Licensor hereby grants to Licensee*) (a) A nonexclusive license under the know-how and technique of Licensor to manufacture in the Territory the X products developed by Licensor: and, (b) A nonexclusive license to use, sell and dispose of, either within or without the Territory, with the exception of Japan, all the X products manufactured by the use of Licensor's process.

Licensor agrees that the license hereby granted may be extended by Licensee to any and all subsidiaries of Licensee in the Territory, but with the understanding that the operations of each subsidiary of Licensee under the license hereby granted shall be deemed the operation of Licensee. Licensee shall give written notice of each subsidiary of Licensee operating under the license hereby granted and all limitations, terms and conditions of this agreement and license shall apply to and be binding on each subsidiary of Licensee to which the license hereby granted is extended.

III–A–3

Article 1. Section 1. A grants LICENSEE a nonexclusive, nontransferable right and license to make, use, and sell, in the Licensed Territory, in any and all fields, Licensed Products covered by any issued Licensed Patents, and parts therefor, and in connection therewith a right and license to use the Technical Information, but no right or license is granted to export, or sell for export, from the Licensed Territory, or to import, or sell for import, into countries outside of the Licensed Territory, such Licensed Products except as provided, in _____ . *Cf.*, "Licensed Patents" shall mean the patents and applications for patents owned or controlled by A in the Licensed Territory which relate to the Licensed Products hereinafter defined or to the process used in manufacturing the Licensed Products and which are now or may hereafter be included in Schedule A hereof.

Section 3. (a) No rights or licenses are granted by A to LICENSEE, expressly or by implication, with respect to any technical information or patents owned by A, except as provided in Sections 1 and 2.

Section 4. (a) A shall submit to LICENSEE, within five (5) months after it is filed, a copy of each initial patent application owned by A which relates to products of the types licensed hereunder and which A deems of sufficient importance to warrant consideration of filing a corresponding patent application in the Licensed Territory.

(b) In case LICENSEE shall notify A in writing within fifty (50) days after such copy shall have been submitted to LICENSEE, of its desire that a corresponding application or applications be filed in the Licensed Territory, A shall promptly file and shall prosecute in its own name each such corresponding application as LICENSEE shall have elected, and such application shall be included in Schedule A, and when a patent is granted on such application, LICENSEE shall acquire a license under such patent in the field(s) set forth in Section ___ .

(c) If, within fifty (50) days after such submission to LICENSEE of an initial application, LICENSEE has not notified A in writing of its desire that such a corresponding application be filed, LICENSEE shall be deemed to have rejected and abandoned all rights and licenses to make, use or sell products practising the invention or inventions disclosed in such application.

Section 5. LICENSEE shall, by notice in writing, given within fifty (50) days of the filing or obtaining thereof, submit a copy to A of each patent application filed or obtained by or for LICENSEE in any country, during the term of this agreement, covering an invention or improvement applicable to any Licensed Product. LICENSEE shall, by notice in writing given within sixty (60) days of the issuance to or obtaining by it of each applied patent during the term of this agreement and covering an invention or improvement in connection with any Licensed Product, whether or not granted on any of the aforesaid applications, advise A of such issuance or obtaining, and LICENSEE hereby grants to A a free, nonexclusive license thereunder, for the full term of such patent, to make, have made, use and sell products, and parts therefor, practicing the invention(s) of such patent and falling in the same class as Licensed Products.

III–A–4

Article II. (*Grant of License for A Process*). LICENSOR hereby grants to LICENSEE an exclusive, transferable license, including the right to sublicense, under the A Process to manufacture, use and sell the A in Japan under Licensor's technical and operational information and Japanese patents, including applications of Licensor pertaining to the A Process existing upon the Date of Validation.

Article VI. (*Grant of Licenses under Patents*). (A) LICENSOR hereby grants to LICENSEE royalty-free, exclusive, transferable licenses or sublicenses, including the right to sublicense, for the manufacture, use and sale in Japan under any Japanese patents based on the A Process or improvements therein:

1. Which are applied for by issued to or owned by LICENSOR at any time from and after the Date of Validation and during the remaining effective term hereof, or
2. Which are applied for by, issued to or owned by others at any time from and after the Date of Validation and during the remaining effective term hereof, to the extent that LICENSOR has the right to grant licenses or sublicenses thereunder.

(B) LICENSEE hereby grants to LICENSOR royalty-free, exclusive in the United States of America and nonexclusive in all other countries of the world outside Japan, transferable licenses or sublicenses, including the right to sublicense, for the manufacture, use and sale under any patents other than Japanese patents based on the A Process or improvements therein:

1. Which are applied for by, issued to or owned by LICENSEE from and after the Date of Validation and during the remaining effective term hereof, or
2. Which are applied for by, issued to or owned by others at any time from and after the Date of Validation and during the remaining effective term hereof, to the extent that LICENSEE has the right to grant licenses or sublicenses thereunder.

(C) The party granting a license pursuant to this Article . . . shall give the other party prompt notice of the date upon which each said license comes into existence.

Article VII. Obtaining Improvements from Sublicensees. Each party hereto will exert reasonable effort to cause sublicensees to:

1. Disclose to LICENSOR or LICENSEE, as the case may be, with the right to sublicense or otherwise disclose to LICENSEE or LICEN-

SOR, as the case may be, such information as said sublicensee may possess, invent or develop prior to the expiration of such period with the right to sublicense or otherwise disclose to LICENSOR or LICENSEE, as the case may be, concerning the A Process technical and operational improvements in said process.

2. Grant to LICENSOR, or LICENSEE, as the case may be, licenses or sublicenses, including the right to sublicense to LICENSEE, or LICENSOR, as the case may be, under any patents based on the A Process or improvements therein:

(a) Which are issued to said sublicensee on or after the Date of Validation and during the remaining effective term hereof, or

(b) Which are issued to others on or after the Date of Validation and prior to the expiration of said remaining effective term, to the extent that said sublicensee has the right to grant licenses or sublicenses thereunder.

3. Permit personnel of LICENSOR, or LICENSEE, as the case may be, to visit facilities of sublicensees for the production of the A by the A Process.

III–A–5

Article 2. (*Grant of Licenses*). 1. Licensor grants to Licensee for the periods of this Agreement and upon the terms and conditions set forth herein:

(a) A nonexclusive right and license under the Licensed Patents, to manufacture or to grant a sublicense to a third person in Japan to manufacture the Licensed Products only, use and sell the Licensed Products;

(b) To the extent that Licensor may legally do so, a nonexclusive right and license under foreign patents corresponding to Licensed Patents, to sell the Licensed Products for export to countries other than to those countries as to which the sale or shipment of such products is or may be prohibited by the laws, regulations or policies of the Government of Japan or the Government of the United States, and

2. In the event that during the term of this Agreement, Licensee should develop or acquire any patents (other than patents issued in Japan) or inventions relating to the manufacture, maintenance or operation of Licensed Products, Licensee shall offer to Licensor a nonexclusive, royalty-free license to manufacture, use and sell under any such patents and inventions throughout the world for the full term of this Agreement.

Article 7. (*Future Patent Rights*). 1. In the event that Licensor, subsequent to _____ 19___ , but during the term hereof, acquires Japanese patents or patent license rights directed to Licensed Products, but not initially coming within the definition of "Licensed Patents" set forth in Article I above, Licensor shall notify Licensee and negotiate for a reasonable time with Licensee regarding a license to Licensee under such patents and corresponding foreign patents, if any.

Cf. Article 1. (*Definitions*). (b) Licensed Patents shall mean and include all Japanese patents and patent applications directed to Licensed Products which on _____, 1970, were owned or controlled by Licensor or under which Licensor has the right to grant license to third persons, together with any patents based on or arising out of such patents and patent applications, as well as such other Japanese patents and patent applications, if any, as shall hereafter be included within the scope of this definition as hereinafter provided under _______ .

III–A–6

1.04. "ABLE's patents" means the patents listed in Schedule A annexed thereto and also, subject to paragraph 2.02 below, all other patents owned or controlled by ABLE or any of its subsidiaries, issued at any time in any country and resulting from or claiming benefit of an application for patent filed, in any country, prior to the fifth anniversary of the effective date hereof.

III–A–7

1.07. The licenses granted in paragraph 1.01 are licenses to make, have made, use, lease and sell the equipment therein specified. Such licenses include the rights to maintain such equipment, to practice methods and processes involved in the use of such equipment and to make and have made, to use and have used, and to maintain machines, tools, instrumentalities and materials, and to use and have used methods and processes, insofar as such machines, tools, instrumentalities, material, methods and processes are involved in or incidental to the development, manufacture, installation, testing or repair of such equipment. The foregoing expressions "have made" and "have used" mean only that the grantee of such licenses hereunder may contract with a third party or parties to manufacture or use (as the case may be) for such grantee. Notwithstanding the generality of paragraphs 1.04 and 1.05 hereof, no license is granted by this agreement under patent claims for combinations of any licensed equipment with any instrumentality other than another licensed equipment, a battery, a power outlet, or a magnetic record medium.

III–A–8

Article 2. (*Right and License*). (a) LICENSOR hereby grants to LICENSEE an exclusive right and license, limited to the territory as defined herein to manufacture, have manufactured, use, sell and lease the above products for domestic use and not for export during the term of this agreement.

(b) LICENSEE may not sublicense or contract any part of the agreement to others without the written consent of LICENSOR.

(c) Regardless of the provisions in above Art. ___, LICENSOR authorizes and empowers the LICENSEE to grant a sublicense to C, a corporation organized under the Laws of Japan, with principal business at ______, Tokyo, subject to the approval of the Japanese Government, if necessary; provided however that said corporation shall be wholly owned and controlled by LICENSEE and shall assume all of the obligations, terms and conditions of this agreement.

Article 4. (*Registration of Licenses*). LICENSOR agrees to give any assistance to LICENSEE to enable the latter to register the exclusive licenses under the Japanese Patent No. _____ and Japanese patents and trademark registrations which may be obtained by LICENSOR in Japan falling within the scope of this agreement. Registration of license on the Japanese patents which will cover Products B shall be cancelled if LICENSEE decides not to manufacture Products B.

Article 7. (*Royalty*). (a) LICENSEE shall pay to LICENSOR an amount of _____ Dollars within thirty (30) days after the effective date of this agreement.

(b) LICENSEE shall pay to LICENSOR, during the term of this agreement, a royalty of ___ percent calculated as follows on the Products manufactured in the field of technology covered by U.S. Patents listed in Schedule 1 using technical information supplied by LICENSOR (hereinafter referred to as "Products A"), sold, leased or used by LICENSEE, and a royalty of ___ percent calculated as follows on the Products manufactured under Japanese Patent No. _____ and Patent Application No. _____ (filed _____, 1967) and subsequent Japanese Patents which may be later obtained by LICENSOR (hereinafter referred to as "Products B"), sold, leased or used by LICENSEE. In case LICENSEE grants a sublicense, LICENSEE shall pay the royalty to LICENSOR on the Products (A) and Products (B) sold, leased or used by SUBLICENSEE on the same rate as abovementioned. The above amount of _____ U.S. Dollars shall be credited against the said royalty and no additional royalty need be paid until when the amount of accrued royalty shall be equal to the said amount _____ Dollars.

(c) 1. So long as LICENSEE or SUBLICENSEE manufactures, has manufactured, sells, leases or uses the Products A only, LICENSEE guarantees to pay LICENSOR _____ Dollars for the first year and _____ Dollars for each succeeding year, as minimum royalty from the commencement of sale of the above Products A manufactured by LICENSEE, or SUBLICENSEE but if the amount sold is in excess of the above minimum royalty for any annual period, then the additional royalty will be paid as per the rates in Section (b) above.

2. In the event that LICENSEE or SUBLICENSEE manufactures, has manufactured, sells, leases or uses the Products A and B, or the Products B only, LICENSEE guarantees to pay LICENSOR ____ U.S. Dollars for the first and each succeeding year, as minimum royalty from the commencement of sale of the above Products B manufactured by LICENSEE or SUBLICENSEE but if the amount sold is in excess of the above minimum royalty for annual period, then the additional royalty will be paid as per the rates in Section (b) above.

(d) LICENSEE shall notify LICENSOR in writing of the date on which the sale provided for in (c) above is commenced.

(e) The prices at which LICENSEE or SUBLICENSEE sells the Products above that are the basis of royalty calculation shall be the net selling price as defined in Article 1 C.

(f) The amount calculated as in (a), (b), and (c) above shall be paid in U.S. Dollars after deduction of income tax to be levied by the Japanese Government; LICENSEE shall furnish appropriate evidence of such payment of tax to LICENSOR.

(g) The conversion into U.S. Dollars of such royalties shall be made at the official rate of foreign exchange effective at the time of the said conversion.

III–A–9

Article 3. The Licensee may grant a sublicense to others within the scope necessary for exercising the exclusive right, provided the terms of this Agreement have been fulfilled.

Article 4. (*Royalty*). (a) The Licensee shall pay to the Licensor the amount of one-half net of the royalties paid to the Licensee from the Sublicensee; however, a guaranteed minimum of the royalty to the Licensor must be two point five percent (2.5%) net of the retail price charged in each country for each piece.

(b) The Licensee is responsible for payment of full royalty to the Licensor when the Licensee receives the first payment for the products from the Sublicensee, even if it is partial.

(c) The retail price referred to in the preceding paragraph (a) shall not be less than Four Dollars ($4.00) U.S. for each piece without the written consent of the Licensor. However, the Sublicensee can be allowed to sell the products at a lower price, provided the 2.5% royalty due to the Licensor will not be less than 10 U.S. cents per piece.

B. Duration of Agreement

III–B–1

Article 1. (*Disclaimer of Licensed Patents*). LICENSEE may, at any time and from time to time during the term of this agreement, give eighty (80) days notice, in writing, to Licensor that LICENSEE, no longer desires to be licensed under any one or more of the Licensed Patents, and upon the expiration of such eighty (80) days, all rights and licenses of LICENSEE to make, use or sell products practising the invention or inventions of such patents shall terminate.

Article 2. (*Duration of the Agreement*). Section 1. This agreement is effective as of the date it is validated by the Japanese Government and unless sooner terminated as herein provided, shall continue in force for an original term of ten (10) years beginning with said date of validation and thereafter for such additional term for which the agreement may be revalidated by the Japanese Government, unless notice is given by either party to the other by registered letter of termination of this agreement on the expiration of its original term or on the expiration of any one of such additional terms, such notice to be given at least eighty (80) days prior to such termination date.

Section 2. The provisions of the preceding section to the contrary notwithstanding, this agreement shall not become effective nor be binding on the parties hereto on the aforesaid effective date unless and until LICENSEE obtains the approval thereof by the Japanese Government, in the event that such approval, and LICENSOR shall not be obligated to furnish any information under this agreement until such approval is obtained by LICENSEE, but on the receipt of such information by LICENSOR from the LICENSEE this agreement shall become effective and be binding on the parties hereto as of the aforesaid effective date.

III–B–2

Article 1. (*Duration and Termination of this Agreement*). 1. Unless sooner terminated by mutual agreement of the parties or as hereinafter provided, this Agreement shall be in effect for a term of ten years commencing on the date when this Agreement becomes finally effective as provided in Article 15 hereof. It shall be renewed without further action for successive additional terms of one year each thereafter, unless either party shall have, at least eight months prior to the end of any such term, given the other party written notice of its desire to amend or modify the Agreement or its intention to terminate the Agreement at the end of the then current term.

2. This Agreement shall terminate forthwith and automatically upon the termination of the License Agreement.

III–B–3

Article X. The initial term of this Agreement shall be the term of the last expiring patent included hereunder or fifteen (15) years from the date hereof, whichever period is longer, and the Agreement shall continue for successive annual terms unless and until LICENSEE shall give notice to Licensor, or Licensor shall give notice to Licensee, at least twelve (12) months before the end of the initial term or at least ninety (90) days before the end of any succeeding annual term, of intention to terminate the Agreement at the end of that term.

III–B–4

5.06. By written notice to ABLE, specifying any of ABLE's patents by country, number and date of issuance, and any claim or claims thereof if less than all claims thereof are to be affected, BAKU may, effective as of the date of giving said notice, surrender and terminate all licenses and rights granted hereunder to it under such specified patent or patents or particular patent claims thereof; as of said date, such specified patent or patents shall cease to be among ABLE's patents (but only so far as particular claims are concerned, if claims have been particularly specified in the notice) for the purposes of this agreement, without affecting obligations in respect of royalties on equipment manufactured under license prior to the date of the notice.

IV. Improvements Devised by Licensee or Licensor

A. Title to Improvements

IV–A–1

Licensee agrees to place all new developments or improvements including know-how gained by it in connection with the licensed products, at the disposal of Licensor, and authorizes Licensor to extend any and all benefits therefrom to its licensees during the term of this agreement.

IV–A–2

Each party hereto agrees to exchange with the other all technical information acquired by it prior to the termination of this Agreement relating to (products) and further agrees to carry on research and development with respect to _____ and to communicate to the other all information and data obtained therefrom and thereby, including all new _____ inventions conceived during the life of this Agreement. Each party further agrees that designated representatives of the other may at reasonable times visit the laboratories, pilot plants and other installations of the other in which research and operations relating to _____ are being conducted.

The Licensee agrees to disclose to the Licensor any developments or improvements which it may make in the machines, products and processes designed or suggested by the Licensor and to permit the Licensor to use such improvements or developments in the United States and agrees to cooperate with the Licensor in obtaining United States patent or patents on any of such improvements or developments which may be patentable, and agrees to transfer the title to the United States patents for the same to the Licensor upon the Licensor's paying the expenses in connection with the filing and prosecution thereof.

IV–A–3

Each party agrees to keep the other party informed of any developments or improvements relating to A PRODUCTS.

With respect to developments or improvements made by Licensee, Licensee shall have first right to elect, within a reasonable time, to file applications for the registration of patents in Japan and elsewhere at its own expense. In this case, Licensor shall receive a nonexclusive, royalty-free license to use and to permit others to use any resulting patents for the term of this agreement. In case Licensee does not elect to file applications for the registration of patents in Japan or elsewhere, Licensor shall have the right to do so in its own name and at its own expense. In this case, Licensee shall receive a nonexclusive, royalty-free license to use and to permit others to use any resulting patent for the term of the patent.

With respect to developments or improvements made by Licensor, Licensor shall have first right to elect, within a reasonable time, to file application for the registration of patents in Japan and elsewhere at its expense. In this case, Licensor shall receive a nonexclusive license without further payment to use any resulting patents for the term of this agreement. In case Licensor does not elect to file applications for the registration of patents in the licensed territory, Licensee shall have the right to do so in its own name and its own expense. In this case, Licensor shall receive a nonexclusive, royalty-free license to use and to permit others to use any resulting patent for the term of this agreement.

The provisions of this article shall not apply to any developments or improvements relating to products developed and/or manufactured on a confidential or specific order base.

B. Obligation to File Patent Applications

IV–B–1

Except as otherwise expressly provided in this Article VI, all filing expenses and all taxes and charges to maintain in force each of the

Patents under which any said grant is required under this Agreement shall be paid by the party hereto which is the owner of the Patent. Either party shall be relieved of its obligations to bear the maintenance expenses for any Patent from the time that it advises the other party of its intentions not to maintain any longer the protection of such Patent. From that time on, the other party may maintain in force each such Patent at its own expense.

D. Employee and Consultant Agreements

IV–D–1

Each party hereto shall each acquire rights to inventions which relate to the subject matter of licenses granted hereunder and are made, in the course of their employment, by its or its subsidiaries' employees who are employed to do research, development or other inventive work, such that the other party shall receive with respect to patents issued at any time in any country for any such invention on which an application for patent is filed in any country prior to the fifth anniversary of the effective date hereof, licenses and rights hereunder of the scope and upon the terms herein provided by this agreement.

IV–D–2

Nothing in paragraphs 1.04, 1.05, or 2.01 above shall obligate either party to acquire rights heretofore released or assigned in writing by an instrument which before (specific date) is either (a) recorded in a national Patent Office or (b) made available for inspection by the other party.

V. Compensation for the License

B. Royalty Basis

V–B–1

Section 1. (*Payments*). (a) In connection with each Covered Product made by or for, or used, sold or leased by BETA in the Exclusive Grant Area at any time during the term of this agreement, BETA shall pay to ALPHA, except in the event of and for the period of an election pursuant to paragraph (c) of this Section 1, ___ percent (___ %) of the "base amount" (determined in accordance with Section 2 below) as partial compensation for the grants provided for in Section 1 of Article II.

(b) In connection with each Covered Product made by or for, or used, sold or leased by BETA in the Nonexclusive Grant Area at any time during the term of this agreement, BETA shall pay to ALPHA, except in the event of and for the period of an election pursuant to paragraph (c) of this Section 1, ___ percent (___ %) of the "base amount" (determined in accordance with Section 2 below) as partial compensation for the grants provided for in Sections 1 and 2 of Article II.

(c) If, by written notice sent by BETA to ALPHA within ninety (90) days after the Effective Date, BETA shall elect to substitute fixed payments for the payments that would be due hereunder as provided for in paragraphs (a) and (b) of this Section 1 during the first two years following the Effective Date, then BETA shall pay to ALPHA the sums stated below in accordance with the following schedule:

	Due Date	*Amount*
First payment	120 days after the Effective Date	___
Second payment	_____ ___	___

(d) Within eighteen (18) months after the Effective Date, the parties hereto agree to meet and negotiate fixed payments for an additional period of years which BETA may elect to pay in lieu of the payments provided for in paragraphs (a) and (b) for such period, and in the absence of an agreement between the parties resulting from such negotiations, BETA's obligations under paragraphs (a) and (b) of Section 1 shall remain unaffected.

V–B–2

Licensee shall pay Licensor for the drawings, specifications other technical data and the right of manufacture and sale of a lump sum of U.S. $_____ .. This amount shall be payable within 30 days from the effective date of this agreement.

V–B–3

6.02. For purposes of this Section 6.00, "net sales" price shall mean the gross sales price minus trade discounts, returns, the commodity tax, packing, and transportation and insurance costs. A PRODUCTS shall be considered sold when billed or, if not billed, when delivered, or when paid for if paid for before delivery.

V–B–4

Section 2. (*Determination of Base Amount*). The base amount for the computation of the payments called for under Paragraphs (a) and (b) of Section 1 above with respect to each Covered Product shall be the selling price at which customers are billed by BETA in an arm's length transaction in the usual course of business for such Covered Products, f.o.b. place of manufacture. No deductions of any kind shall be made from such price except the following and then only to the extent that such amounts are included in such selling price:

(a) Cost of packing such Covered Product for shipment to customer.

(b) Transportation and insurance charges.

(c) Ordinary installation services supplied to the customer by BETA.

(d) C.I.F. prices of parts and components to be supplied by ALPHA.

V–B–5

3.05. The term "net selling price," as applied to apparatus subject to royalty, means the gross selling price thereof in the form in which it is sold, whether assembled, or disassembled, less the following items, but only insofar as they pertain to the sale of such apparatus by BAKU or any of its subsidiaries and are included in such gross selling price:

(i) usual trade discounts actually allowed (other than cash discounts, advertising allowances, or fees or commissions to any employees of any of the companies described in paragraph 3.07 below);
(ii) packing costs;
(iii) import, export and excise taxes, and customs duties;
(iv) costs of insurance and transportation from the place of manufacture to the customer's premises or point of installation;
(v) costs of installation at the place of use;
(vi) costs of special engineering services not incident to the design or manufacture of apparatus subject to royalty; and
(vii) costs of batteries and magnetic record media which do not include, or the manufacture of which does not employ, any invention of any of ABLE's patents in force at the time and in the country of the manufacture, sale, lease or use of the apparatus subject to royalty; and
(viii) costs of any equipment which if simply resold by BAKU would be relieved of royalty by paragraph 3.04 above.

V–B–6

In case the licensed products are sold to an affiliated company of Licensee or used by Licensee, the Licensed products shall be deemed to have been sold at the "fair market value." The term "fair market value" shall mean the average net selling price at which customers were billed in a bona fide arm's length transaction during the calendar month concerned. If there is no such arm's-length transaction in said calendar month, "fair market value" shall be determined by the mutual agreement of Licensor and Licensee.

V–B–7

3.06. The term "fair market value," as applied to apparatus subject to royalty, means the net selling price which BAKU or any of its subsidiaries, whichever effects the sale, lease or use subject to royalty, would realize from an unaffiliated buyer in an arm's length sale of identical apparatus in the same quantity and at the same time and place as such sale, lease or use, provided, however, that it shall not be lower than complete cost (less the items referred to in paragraph 3.05 above to the extent these items are included in such complete cost) plus the usual profit factor. Complete cost shall consist of all properly allocable direct costs and indirect expenses necessary or incidental to the design, manufacture or distribution of such apparatus as determined in accordance with recognized accounting practices.

V–B–8

3.01. BAKU shall pay to ABLE royalty, at the applicable rate hereinafter specified in this paragraph 3.01, on each equipment, and maintenance part therefor, which is apparatus subject to royalty (as defined in paragraph 3.03 and subject to paragraph 3.02),

(i) which is sold, leased or put into use by BAKU or any of its subsidiaries while any license acquired hereunder by BAKU with respect to such apparatus shall remain in force, or

(ii) which is made by or for BAKU or any of its subsidiaries while any such license shall remain in force and is thereafter sold, leased or put into use by BAKU or any of its subsidiaries,

such royalty rate to be applied, except as provided in paragraph 3.07 below, to the net selling price of such apparatus if sold for a separate consideration payable wholly in money and in all other cases to the fair market value thereof. The royalty rates applicable to equipment licensed by paragraph 1.01 above are as follows:

Equipment	Applicable Royalty Rates (In %)
(1) Industrial magnetic recording and reproducing machines	3
(2) Commercial magnetic recording and reproducing machines	4
(3) Magnetic recording and reproducing heads	5

Any maintenance part which is apparatus subject to royalty hereunder shall bear royalty at the same rate as the equipment in which it is to be used, but paragraph 3.02 below shall not be applicable to maintenance parts.

3.03. The term "apparatus subject to royalty" means every equipment of the kinds specified in paragraph 1.01 above, and any maintenance part therefor, which upon manufacture includes, or the manufacture of which employs, any invention of any of ABLE's patents in force at the time and in the country of such manufacture, or which includes when sold, leased or put into use, or the use of which employs when put into use, any invention of any of ABLE's patents in force at the time and in the country of such sale, lease or putting into use other than

(i) inventions under which the United States Government holds a royalty-free license if such equipment or maintenance part is contracted for by the United States Government, or by another national government with funds derived through the Military Assistance Program or otherwise through the United States Government.

3.04. An equipment, or maintenance part therefor, which is made and sold by BAKU or any of its subsidiaries and which is apparatus subject to royalty hereunder on account of one or more of ABLE's patents, may be treated by BAKU as not licensed and not subject to royalty hereunder if all of the following conditions are met:

(i) the purchaser is licensed under the same patent or patents, pursuant to another agreement, to have said equipment or maintenance part made;

(ii) the purchaser expressly advised said vendor in writing that, in purchasing said equipment or maintenance part, it is exercising its own license or licenses under said patent or patents to have said equipment or maintenance part made; and

(iii) said vendor retains such written advice and makes it available to ABLE at the latter's request.

V–B–9

4.02. BAKU shall pay to ALPHA a fee, at the applicable rate hereinafter specified in this paragraph 4.02, on each article of a kind hereinafter specified in this paragraph 4.02 and defined in Appendix A attached hereto and made a part hereof, and on each maintenance part therefor, which is an item subject to fee as hereinafter defined in paragraph 4.05 below, and which is sold, leased or put into use prior to two years after the expiration of the base period therefore hereinafter defined in paragraph 4.06 below, such fee rate to be applied, except as hereinafter provided in this Section 4, to the net selling price of such item if sold for a separate consideration payable wholly in money and in all other cases to the fair market value thereof. The aforementioned kinds of articles and the fee rates applicable to them are as follows:

Articles	Rates (In %)
Magnetic Recording and Reproducing Heads	1
Intermittent tape devices except service units	3
Service units for intermittent tape devices	5

4.03. Any maintenance part which is an item subject to fee hereunder shall bear a fee at the same rate as the article in which it is to be used.

4.05. The term "item subject to fee" means any article of the kinds specified in paragraph 4.02 above, and any maintenance part therefor, which is manufactured by BAKU or any of its subsidiaries prior to the expiration of the base period with the use of technical information furnished hereunder (including any such article, and any maintenance part therefor, manufactured by any such company with manufacturing facilities made with the use of technical information furnished hereunder), other than demonstration models and articles and maintenance parts produced in the course of, or intended for use in connection with, research, development or experimental undertakings of BAKU or any of its subsidiaries.

4.06. With respect to items subject to fee, the "base period" for all articles designated in paragraph 4.02 above, and for all maintenance parts shall be the five (5) year period commencing on the first day of the month in which occurs the first manufacture by BAKU or any of its subsidiaries of any such article which is an item subject to fee included in such class; provided, however, that if in one or more periods of twelve (12) consecutive calendar months there shall be no production of any article which is an item subject to fee such twelve (12) month period or periods shall not be taken into account in determining the expiration of said five (5) year period.

4.07. An article shall not be an item subject to fee solely because it contains another article of a kind specified in paragraph 4.02 above, which other article is an item subject to fee, or solely because it contains another such article which would be an item subject to fee hereunder except for the expiration of the base period for such other article.

4.08. The term "net selling price," as applied to an item subject to fee, means the gross selling price thereof in the form in which it is sold, whether assembled or disassembled, less the following amounts but only insofar as they pertain to the sale of such item by BAKU or any of its subsidiaries and are included in such gross selling price. . . .

(b) Approvals have been obtained from the appropriate governmental authorities of Japan of the provisions of this Agreement for which such approval is necessary.

V–B–10

Section 2. "Covered Products" shall mean any, but shall be limited to those (1) which utilize or embody, in whole or in part, any of the Technical Information defined in Section 4 below or any disclosures contained in any Patents or covered by any claims in any Patents, with respect to which grants are made by ALPHA to BETA under any of the provisions of this Agreement; or (2) in which the full effect of

_____ could be directly applied, without basic alteration of the fundamental design of the _____ as described in any of the U.S. Patent Applications listed in Schedule A, annexed hereto, to cause

C. Minimum and Maximum Royalties

V–C–1

In consideration of the license granted by Licensor hereunder, Licensee agrees to pay Licensor a fee of ___ percent of the net sales price of the licensed products which in any case shall not be less than ___ per year.

V–C–2

(1) The minimum payment "A" shall guarantee to "B" is as follows:

a. For the first contract year beginning with the effective date of this agreement and ending with the last day of August, 1969. (U.S. $2,000)

b. For the second contract year, full one year ending with the last day of August, 1970. (U.S. $5,000)

c. For the third contract year, full one year ending with the last day of August, 1971. (U.S. $6,000)

d. For the fourth contract year, full one year ending with the last day of August, 1972. (U.S. $6,600)

(2) "A" shall guarantee the amount of minimum payment provided in (1) of this Article. This guarantee shall be made in U.S. Dollars forthwith after the end of each contract year.

V–C–3

4.04. In part payment for the rights granted hereunder by ALPHA to BAKU shall pay to ALPHA, within thirty (30) days after the effective date of this agreement, the sum of _____, which sum shall be credited with respect to fees that may become due pursuant to paragraph 4.02 above, but in no event shall any portion of such sum be refunded to BAKU.

V–C–4

After the total payments of the lump sum and running royalty provided in article X hereunder have reached the amount of _____, Licensee is relieved of any further payment of the running royalty.

D. Manner of Payment

V–D–1

(1) "A" shall pay to "B" an amount of _____ U.S. Dollars in U.S. Dollars as down payment within 30 days after effective date of this agreement.

(2) "A" shall pay to "B", during the terms of this agreement, running royalty of ___ percent of net ex-factory selling price of "Products" sold and applied by "A" less costs of transportation and insurance in U.S. Dollars at the official rate of foreign exchange effective at the date of payment.

(3) Running royalty provided in this Article shall be due and payable semi-annually, and "A" agrees to pay the total amount of running royalty due and payable during the semi-annual calendar period ending with the last days of February and August in U.S. Dollars within 30 days after the end of the each semi-annual period.

V–D–2

Licensee shall bear all taxes imposed as the result of the existence or operation of this agreement, including, but not restricted to, any tax which Licensee is required to withhold or deduct from royalties or other payments to Licensor except

(i) any such tax imposed upon Licensor by the United States or any political subdivision thereof, and

(ii) any such tax on income imposed upon Licensor by the national government of Japan with respect to royalties payable under this agreement because the equipment or maintenance part, with respect to which such royalty is payable, includes, or its manufacture or use employs, any invention of any of Licensor's patents issued in Japan,

provided however, the Licensee shall furnish to the Licensor official tax reports or other evidence issued by the tax authorities sufficient to enable the Licensor to support a claim for a United States Income Tax Credit in respect of any sum so withheld or deducted.

V–D–3

Payment to Licensor under this Section X shall be made in United States dollars at its office above specified or at such changed address as Licensor shall have specified by written notice. If the currency of the gross selling price (when royalty is to be computed on net selling price) or of the fair market value (when royalty is to be computed on fair market value) is other than United States dollars, conversion to United States dollars shall be effected as follows:

(i) if such foreign currency is Japanese yen, at the official rate applicable to payment for the export of goods as quoted by any of the officilaly approved foreign exchange banks in Japan and in effect at the close of business on the day of payment, except as hereinafter provided;

(ii) as to any payment which is overdue, or as to any payment on any equipment or maintenance part therefor which is subject to royalty on account of any of Licensor's patents issued in the United States whether or not such equipment or maintenance part therefor is also subject to royalty on account of other patents), or if such foreign currency is other than Japanese yen, or such foreign currency is

Japanese yen but no such official rate is in force on the date of payment, or in any other case not described above, the applicable rate shall be the rate expressed in United States dollars at which such foreign currency may be bought in New York City for bank transfer to a creditor in the foreign currency country in respect to the export of goods from such country to the United States, quoted on the last day of the semiannual period in respect of which such payment is to be made, by one of the following as Licensee may select: First National City Bank, The Chase Manhattan Bank, or Morgan Guaranty Trust Company of New York. If no such rate has been quoted by any of the above-named banks on such day, such a rate quoted by any of such banks on the most recent prior day on which any of them quoted such a rate during the last three months of such semiannual period, shall be used; and if such rates were quoted by more than one of such banks on such most recent prior day, Licensee may select therefrom the rate to be used.

V–D–4

Within ninety (90) days after the end of each semiannual period ending on June 30th or December 31st, commencing with the semiannual period during which this agreement first becomes effective and continuing thereafter until all royalties payable hereunder shall have been reported and paid, Licensee shall furnish to Licensor a statement, in form acceptable to Licensor, certified by a responsible officer of Licensee, showing all apparatus subject to royalty which was sold, leased or put into use during such semiannual period, the net selling price of such apparatus or (where royalty is based on fair market value) the fair market value thereof and the amount of royalty payable thereon. If no such apparatus subject to royalty has been so sold, leased or put into use, that fact shall be shown on such statement. If royalty is reduced under provisions of paragraph ___ above, such statement shall also identify each equipment by its product type and the patent or patents involved in such royalty reduction. Each such statement shall also identify transactions of the character described in paragraph ___ above. Also within such ninety (90) days Licensee shall, irrespective of terms granted or collections made on account of any apparatus subject to royalty, pay to Licensor the royalties payable hereunder for such semiannual period. Licensee shall furnish whatever additional information Licensor may reasonably prescribe from time to time to enable Licensor to ascertain which equipment (and maintenance parts therefor) sold, leased or put into use by Licensee or any of its subsidiaries are subject to the payment of royalty hereunder to Licensor, and the amount of royalty payable thereon.

V–D–5

Licensee shall keep full, clear and accurate records with respect to apparatus subject to royalty. Licensor shall have the right through its accredited representatives to examine and audit at all reasonable times all such records and such other records and accounts as may under recognized accounting practices contain information bearing upon the amount of royalty payable to it under this agreement. Prompt adjustment shall be made by the proper party to compensate for any errors or omissions disclosed by such examination or audit. Neither such right to examine and audit nor the right to receive such adjustment shall be affected by any statement to the contrary appearing on checks or otherwise, unless such statement appears in a letter, signed by the party having such right and delivered to the other party, expressly waiving such right.

G. Interest

V–G–1

Royalty payments provided for in this agreement shall, when overdue, bear interest at the rate of six percent (6%) per annum until paid. Each of such payments shall be made in compliance with the Japanese Foreign Exchange and Foreign Trade Control Law (Law No. 228 of 1949) when such law is applicable thereto.

V–H–1

If an equipment is apparatus subject to royalty solely on account of one or a limited number of licensor's patents issued in the U.S.A., Licensee may elect to reduce the amount of royalty otherwise payable hereunder on said equipment by a royalty reduction percentage, specified in Schedule A. Upon written request from Licensee identifying the equipment and each relevant patent, Licensor will inform Licensee of the royalty reduction percentage application in respect of said equipment as a patent and the effective date thereof.

V–H–2

The royalty shall be calculated at the following rates per square yards of the licensed products per 12 month period commencing the effective date of this Agreement:

Square yards	Royalty Percent of net sales value
On the first 1,000,000 yds.	5
On the next 2,000,000 yds.	3
On the next 4,000,000 yds.	2
On all over 7,000,000 yds.	1

J. Miscellaneous Royalty Clauses

V–J–1

3.08. If BAKU or any of its subsidiaries sells or leases any equipment of the kinds specified in paragraph 1.01 above, or maintenance parts therefor, in any country for export to another country, and no royalty would be payable with respect to such sale or lease occurring in the former country, but royalty would be payable had the sale or lease occurred in the latter country, then the latter country shall, for the purposes of this Section 3, be deemed the country of the sale or lease.

V–J–2

3.09. With respect to any equipment of the kinds specified in paragraph 1.01 above, or maintenance parts therefor, which is sold in any country by BAKU to any of its subsidiaries, no license or right is granted or agreed to be granted hereunder, expressly or impliedly, under ABLE's patents issued in any other country, to others than BAKU and its sublicensees hereunder, for the sale, lease or use of said equipment or part unless and until BAKU has paid, or become obligated hereunder to pay, royalty on said equipment or part in an amount not lower than as prescribed in this agreement as applicable to the sale, lease or use of such equipment or part in the latter country.

VI. Litigation with Third Parties

VI–1

Article 1. (*Defensive Litigation*). When any actual or threatened suit against Licensee by reason of the manufacture, use, or sale of Licensed Products, Licensee shall forthwith upon receiving knowledge thereof, give a written notice of such suit to Licensor, and Licensor will communicate to Licensee free of charge all information and particulars in its possession which will assist Licensee in defending or otherwise dealing with such suit.

Article 2. (*Offensive Litigation*). Section 1. In case Licensee and Licensor agree, in writing, that a suit should be brought for infringement of one or more of the patents licensed to Licensee, such suit shall be brought promptly thereafter and be prosecuted by Licensee under the joint control of Licensee and Licensor. If Licensor shall have granted an additional license to another Licensee under the patent or patents, and such other Licensee participates in any suit brought under this Section, the expenses arising out of such suit shall be borne equally by Licensor, Licensee and such other participating licensee, but if no such additional licensee exists or if such other licensee does not participate in any such suit, Licensee and Licensor shall each bear one half of all such expenses. Licensee shall render to Licensor at three months intervals during the period of any such suit or the preparation thereof, an account of the expenses thereof. Any sum of money which may be collected in any such suit by judgment or by settlement shall be used first to reimburse Licensee and Licensor and other participating Licensee if any, for the expenses caused by them in connection with such suit, and any balance then remaining shall be divided equally among Licensee, Licensor and such other participating licensee if any. Licensee shall not make any settlement or other disposition of any such suit without the written consent of Licensor.

Section 2. Nothing herein shall preclude Licensor from bringing suit individually or together with another Licensee where Licensee decides not to participate in any suit.

VI–2

Article 11. (*Warranty Excluded*). 1. Licensor makes no warranty of any kind, either express or implied, as to any patents, inventions, developments, data, specifications, plans, drawings, designs, processes, services, or other rights, or assistance granted, or furnished pursuant to this Agreement.

2. It is expressly understood that Licensor does not warrant the validity of the patents licensed hereunder and it does not warrant that the practice of the invention licensed hereunder and the manufacture, use and sale of the Licensed Products thereof will not infringe patent rights of others.

Article 12. (*Indemnity*). 1. Licensee shall indemnify and hold Licensor and Licensor's employees harmless against any loss, expense (other than expense absorbed by Licensor as expressly provided in this Agreement), claims or liability whatsoever arising out of or in any way connected with the performance of this Agreement or the use by Licensee or any sublicensee of Licensee of the Technical Data or Licensed Patents or any act or omissions of Licensee's managers, employees, workers or agents.

VI–3

Each party shall forthwith give notice in writing of the other party of any infringement or threatened infringement of the said Patent Application or any Patent granted pursuant thereto which shall at any time and from time to time come to the knowledge of either party whereupon the parties hereto shall consult together as to what action (if any) should be taken in respect of such infringement. If such infringement shall occur in Japan, Licensee, with the written approval of Licensor, which shall not be unreasonably withheld, shall institute proceedings necessary to prevent such infringement at the expense of Licensee and any damages awarded should be for the benefit of Licensee.

VI–4

Article 14. (*Infringement of Licensor's Patents and Trademark*).

(a) In the case of an infringement of the Patent and Trademark rights of Licensor in Japan, the expenses for prosecution of the infringement should be borne equally by Licensor and Licensee.

(b) If any damages or compensation are collected through the said prosecution of the infringement, such amount shall be shared equally by Licensor and Licensee after deducting all expenses incurred in the said prosecution of the infringement.

(c) In case Licensor and Licensee do not agree as to chance of success of court action, the cost of taking such action will be borne only by one who actually takes such proceedings.

VI–5

Licensee shall notify Licensor promptly upon learning of any unauthorized disclosure or use being made in any of the territory included under this Agreement by anyone of the licensed technical "KNOW-HOW" or of any unauthorized use or infringement of any patent included in Licensor's "PATENT RIGHTS" or unauthorized use or infringement of any Licensor's "TRADEMARK," and Licensor shall have the sole right to negotiate for settlement with any offending party and to institute and prosecute suit for such use or infringement. Licensee shall cooperate fully with Licensor in investigating the same and on request from Licensor shall assist and participate in all reasonable ways in preparing for, bringing and prosecuting appropriate legal action to enjoin such unauthorized use or infringement and to obtain full legal redress therefor, joining with Licensor as a party to any such litigation if appropriate and Licensor so desires. All expenses of such suit shall be borne by Licensor and all recovery therefrom shall become and remain the property of Licensor.

VI–6

(*Infringements*). (a) The Licensee shall use its best efforts to discover any unauthorized use of any of the patents or trademarks covered by this Agreement, and shall watch all applications for registration of patents and trademarks in the Manufacturing Territory to the end that patents or trademarks that may infringe upon the Licensor's existing or future industrial property rights may not be registered by third parties without the Licensor's knowledge.

(b) If at any time during the term of this Agreement the Licensor and the Licensee agree in writing that suit shall be brought for claims or damages resulting from the infringement of the Licensor's patents or trademarks in the Manufacturing Territory, such suit shall be brought by the Licensee in the name of and on behalf of the Licensor, and any costs and expenses relating to such action shall be borne in equal proportions by the parties hereto. Any sum or sums of money which may be collected pursuant to such suit, by judgment or settlement, shall be divided equally between them.

(c) If either of the parties desires to bring suit for the infringement of such patents or trademarks, it shall notify the other party thereof by registered letter, and if within thirty (30) days from the receipt of such notification the other party fails to communicate its willingness to participate in the said action, the party desiring to bring the suit may institute such legal proceeding and do everything it deems necessary for the effective protection of the infringed patents or trademarks, at its own cost and expense. Any sum or sums of money which may be collected pursuant to such suit, by judgment or settlement, shall belong entirely to the suing party, provided it holds the other party harmless from any and all counterclaims that may result from such action.

(d) In the case of any legal action under this Section, the Licensee shall make status reports to the Licensor at reasonable intervals, and the Licensor shall, at its own expense, furnish any information which it may have with relation to infringed patents or trademarks.

VI–7

Section 5. In the event that any infringement action, proceeding or claim of any kind or nature is instituted against any grantee because of the grantee's operations under any said grants, the grantee shall take timely steps (but in any event without liability to the grantor) at the grantee's own expense to defend or meet the same and promptly notify the grantor in writing, in reasonable detail, of the date and nature of such action, proceeding or claim and, from time to time, of the progress thereof. At the request of the grantor, the grantee shall permit the grantor to join or otherwise appear in or in connection with any such action, proceeding or claim, personally or through counsel selected by the grantor, but at the sole expense of the grantor.

Section 6. (a) In any infringement action, proceeding or claim in the Exclusive Grant Area of any kind or nature involving either party in connection with any Patent with respect to which a grant is made hereunder, the party having knowledge of such infringement shall promptly notify the other party, and the respective owner of any such infringed patent shall have the sole right to determine if any such action, proceeding or claim should be instituted.

(b) If the owner of the infringed Patent determines that an action, proceeding or claim should be instituted as provided for in Paragraph

(a) above, ALPHA and BETA (i) upon agreement to collaborate in such action, proceeding or claim against the infringer shall divide the expenses and recovery in the proportions agreed upon; (ii) where ALPHA and BETA cannot agree upon the division of any expenses in any case in which they have agreed to collaborate, in such case, the parties hereto shall allocate sixty percent (60%) of the expenses to the owner of the infringed patent and forty percent (40%) to the grantee and any recovery shall be paid to the parties in the same proportion; (iii) where the parties hereto decline to collaborate in any such action, proceeding or claim the other party shall have the right, at its own expense, to proceed against the infringer and to retain any recovery, provided, however, section (iii) hereof shall not apply to any of the Patents listed in Paragraph (1) of Schedule A wherein ALPHA has determined to institute such action, proceeding, or claim and BETA has declined to collaborate after being formally requested to do so by ALPHA; in such event the parties hereto shall allocate fifty percent (50%) of the expenses to ALPHA and fifty percent (50%) to BETA and any recovery shall be paid to the parties in the same proportion.

VI–8

(*Infringement Notices*). Licensee shall give notice in writing to Licensor of any infringement of said trademarks or names or misappropriation of any other rights of Licensor which shall come to its knowledge at any time within its licensed territory and, when requested, shall cooperate with Licensor in stopping such infringements. Licensor, with the advice of Licensee, shall decide as to the need for instituting legal action with respect to any infringement which may occur, and the cost of any such litigation or the policing of rights granted by Licensor hereunder shall be paid by Licensor. No legal action for infringement or unfair competition relative to any proprietary rights of Licensor may be taken by Licensee without the consent of Licensor. Licensor agrees to hold and save Licensee harmless from all damages, costs and expenses arising out of any patent infringement suit which may be instituted by any third party against Licensee for use of subject matter licensed hereunder, provided that Licensee shall give Licensor prompt notice in writing of the institution of any such suit and shall permit Licensor to conduct the defense if it wishes to do so. However, it is understood that neither Licensor nor Licensee is at present aware of any existing Japanese patents owned by third parties which cover the Licensed subject matter.

VI–9

(d) a warranty or representation that any manufacture, sale, lease or use hereunder will be free from infringement of patents other than those under which and to the extent to which licenses are in force hereunder; or

(e) an agreement to bring or prosecute actions or suits against third parties for infringement;

VII. Miscellaneous Provisions

A. Patent Marking

VII–A–1

On products manufactured by licensee, his sublicensee, his subsidiary company or his affiliated company under the license given in this agreement, a patent marking of licensed patents used in its manufacturing shall be affixed.

VII–A–2

On products manufactured by licensor and licensee under the license given by this agreement, a patent marking regarding patents used in its manufacturing shall be affixed.

VII–A–3

In case a patent for the abovementioned invention, or for its modification or improvement is granted, licensee and sublicensee shall affix an appropriate patent marking regarding each patent on products manufactured and to be sold by licensee and sublicensee during the effective term of each patent.

VII–A–4

A nameplate shall be attached to each product manufactured by the licensee in accordance with instructions from the licensor, appropriately marked with data concerning the Patent, if any, applicable thereto. The licensee shall also attach a nameplate to each product under this agreement.

B. Warranty

VII–B–1

It is understood and agreed that Licensor does not warrant that any Patent, Trademark, Technical Assistance, Technical information, or other information or data, which is furnished, or with respect to which rights are granted or disclosures made hereunder or under any Related Trademark Agreement to Licensee, is valid or can be so furnished, or can be used or otherwise disposed of without loss of, damage to, or loss of use of the property or business of Licensee or without liability by or injunction against Licensee or any of the officers, directors, or employees of Licensee. Licensee hereby waives any claim against Licensor, its officers, directors or employees, for any such loss of or damage to Licensee's property or business or for any reimbursement or other satisfaction for any said liability or said injunction which may be imposed upon the grantee.

Licensee agrees to assume all financial and service obligations for Covered Products manufactured and sold by it hereunder, and Licensor shall be absolved of all liability to Licensee and to others for any failure in production, design, operation or otherwise of any Covered Products manufactured and/or sold by Licensee.

VII–B–2

2.03. Each party warrants that it has the right to grant licenses of the scope, duration, and effect of the licenses granted herein with respect to all patents of which such party or any of its subsidiaries is the owner of record on the date specified in paragraph 2.02 or which may issue on any application for patent of which such party or any of its subsidiaries is the owner of record on the date specified in paragraph 2.02.

VII–B–3

Section 3. Except as otherwise expressly provided in this Article VI, all filing expenses and all taxes and charges to maintain in force each of the Patents under which any said grant is required under this Agreement shall be paid by the party hereto which is the owner of the Patent. Either party shall be relieved of its obligations to bear the maintenance expenses for any Patent from the time that it advises the other party of its intentions not to maintain any longer the protection of such Patent. From that time on, the other party may maintain in force each such Patent at its own expense.

VII–B–4

Licensee shall not contest, or assist others to contest, the validity of any patent of licensor within the scope and duration of the licenses granted to Licensee herein, but this paragraph shall not preclude participation in any contest of priority in the U.S. Patent Office.

VII–B–5

6.04. Each of the parties hereto agrees that it shall not contest, or assist others to contest, the validity of any patent with respect to which it is granted a license in this agreement, but the obligation of this paragraph 6.04 shall apply only so long as the party in question has a license under such patent by virtue of this agreement, shall apply only to contesting the validity of such patent within the scope of such license, and shall not preclude participation in any contest of priority in the U.S. Patent Office.

VII–B–6

Nothing contained in this agreement shall be construed as: restricting the right of Licensee or any of its subsidiaries to make, have made, use, sell, lease or otherwise dispose of any particular product or products not herein licensed.

VII–B–7

Nothing contained in this agreement shall be construed as: an admission by Licensee of, or a warranty or representation by as to, the validity and/or scope of any Licensed Patent, and Licensee is free to contest in any proceeding the validity and/or scope thereof.

VII–B–8

4.03. Nothing contained in this agreement shall be construed as (b) an admission by any guarantee of the validity of any patent except within the scope and period of the licenses thereunder; or

VII–B–9

4.01. BAKU shall pay to ALPHA, within ninety (90) days after ALPHA has declared in writing to BAKU that its delivery of information pursuant to paragraph 2.91 above is substantially complete, the sum of ______, as compensation for the cost of gathering and reproducing such technical information.

VII–B–10

A hereby warrants to B that the A DATA to be licensed, disclosed and furnished to B-A by A under the Technical Assistance Agreement shall be sufficient to permit competent persons utilizing the appropriate materials, equipment, and skills to obtain substantially the same results as are obtained by A in the manufacture of A PRODUCTS.

VII–B–11

1. The licensor makes guaranty that 100 parts by weight of the raw material A is converted to 90 parts or more by weight of product B, quality of which is as specified in the attached schedule. [Schedule is omitted here.]

2. The guaranty of the preceding clause shall be effective only when both of the following conditions are fulfilled:

(a) Licensee performs design and construction of the plant in accordance with the documents, drawings, and instruction supplied by the licensor.

(b) Licensee performs start-up operation of the plant in accordance with the operation specifications and instructions supplied by the licensor.

3. If the abovementioned warranty is fulfilled within the period of start-up operation of the plant provided in Article X hereof, all of licensor's warranty as to technical effect shall be deemed fulfilled.

4. Should the above guaranty's figure not be fulfilled within the start-up operation under the conditions of the above-clauses, the following provisions shall apply:

(a) In case the production capacity exceeds 97% of the guaranteed figure, the warranty shall be deemed to have been fulfilled.

(b) In case the production capacity is more than 95% but not more than 97% of the guaranteed figure, the running royalty of 5% provided in Article X shall be reduced to 45%. [remaining clause omitted.]

VII–B–12

(a) Licensor shall not be liable to Licensee or any other party for any injury, loss, damage or other liability incurred by Licensee or any other party in connection with (i) the manufacture, use, sale or servicing of any Product, (ii) the use of any Technical Data or Know-How made available by Licensor to Licensee, or (iii) any labeling packaging, advertising, or promotional activities with respect to any of the foregoing.

(b) Licensee shall carry adequate product and other liability insurance at its own expense.

VII–B–13

Licensor does not warrant that any licensed products to be manufactured, used or sold hereunder by the licensee will not infringe patents owned by a third party.

VII–B–14

Licensor shall indemnify licensee within the sum of down payment provided in Article X hereof against all actions claims, demands and costs arising from or incurred by reason of any infringement of a patent owned by a party.

In the event of any claim being made or action being brought against licensee arising from the matters referred to in this article, licensor shall be promptly notified thereof by the licensee and may at his own expense conduct all negotiations for the settlement of the same, and any litigation that may arise therefrom.

VII–B–15

(a) Licensor does not believe that the Products manufactured hereunder will infringe any existing patents, but Licensor does not represent or warrant that such is a fact, and it is understood and agreed that Licensor assumes no liability for damages of any kind by reason of any possible infringement, or claim of infringement. Licensor may, but shall not be obligated to, defend or save harmless Licensee against any suit, damage, claim, or demand based on actual or alleged patent infringement resulting from rights or licenses granted hereunder.

(b) In the event that any suit, action, or other proceeding shall be brought against Licensee involving any claim of patent infringement resulting from the exercise or use of any rights or licenses granted hereunder, Licensor shall have the right at its expense to take exclusive charge of the defense of any such claim, and of any negotiations for the settlement thereof, through counsel of its own choice. Licensee will notify Licensor promptly at any such proceeding against Licensee and shall send to Licensor copies of all papers served or delivered to Licensee. Licensee will cooperate fully with Licensor in the defense of such proceeding, its employees, officers, directors, managers, and other representatives shall testify when requested by Licensor, and it shall make available to Licensor all relevant records, papers, information, samples, specimens, and the like.

C. Most-Favored Licensee Clause

VII–C–1

When the licensor hereafter grants any other person or firm a license on the patent with a royalty of lower rate than that charged to the licensee under this agreement, the licensor shall give the licensee that benefit on and after the license with the above royalty of lower rate becomes effective. When the licensor grants such a license, the licensor shall immediately give notice of such agreement to the licensee and of the change of royalty rate under this agreement. However, this agreement shall effectively continue without any change other than the change regarding the royalty rate.

VII–C–2

Licensor agrees that if it hereafter concludes an agreement granting a license to use the licensed inventions or any of them, which license is more favorable as to royalties payable thereunder in connection with products _____ than the license here granted, Licensor will immediately notify Licensee of the granting of such a license and will give Licensee the benefit of such more favorable royalty rate payable thereunder in connection with such products, and Licensee shall have the benefit of such more favorable royalty rate in connection with such products sold and shipped or set aside for fabrication by it and any of its subsidiaries after the granting of such more favorable license but only so long as such more favorable royalty rate is enjoyed by another licensee in connection with the general sale and shipment or fabrication of such products.

D. Trademarks–Trade Names

VII–D–1

The licensor grants the licensee the nonexclusive right to use the trademark under registration No. _____ in connection with sales and manufacture of the licensed products.

VII–D–2

Licensee agrees that all the products manufactured hereunder shall bear the trademark _____ . Licensor will register _____ as a trademark in any country unless difficulties shall arise from the viewpoint of Trademark Law.

VII–D–3

In the event that Licensor creates a trademark or trademarks, Licensor does further grant to Licensee a nonexclusive right and license to use Licensor's "Trademarks" on or in connection with the Licensor's methods and procedures and the products produced by such methods and procedures; Licensee shall have no right to employ the same or any word or words similar to Licensor's "Trademarks" in its trade or corporate name or names and shall not use the Licensor's "Trademarks" in connection with any material or product other than that produced by the Licensor's methods and procedures under Licensor's "Know-how."

VII–D–4

(a) The Licensor grants the Licensee for the duration of this Agreement, with respect to the Licensed Products, the exclusive right to use in the Manufacturing and Sales Territories all trade names and all trademarks now owned by the Licensor that are registered in the Manufacturing Territory (listed in the Appendix).

(b) The Licensee agrees to attach, use, or display any such trademarks and trade names in substantially the same manner used by the Licensor on the Licensed Products, any deviation from such use requiring the prior approval of the Licensor under Section ___ of this Agreement. The Licensee shall remove all such trademarks, and the Licensor shall have the right to cancel this grant to use the Licensor's trademarks, unless the Licensee promptly meets the standards set by the Licensor for the Licensed Products.

(c) The Licensee agrees to refrain from using such trademarks or trade names, with respect to products not covered by this Agreement, and to cease and desist from any such trademarks or trade names at all times after the termination of this Agreement for any reason whatsoever.

VII–D–5

The licensee shall sell the licensed products under its own trademark. The licensee hereby admits the validity of the trademark _____ and the licensor's ownership thereof, and specifically agrees not to make any use, directly or indirectly, of the trademark _____ and/or any other trademarks of the licensor.

VII–D–6

Licensor agrees that Licensee and Sublicensees may have the right to use the trademark _____ and trademarks similar thereto, and further agrees to grant to Licensee and Sub-Licensees the right to use any trademarks which may be owned by Licensor or on which Licensor may have the right to grant such right of use. In case Licensor does not want to register "_____", it agrees that Licensee registers the same.

VII–D–7

The Licensor grants to the Licensee the sole and exclusive right and license to sell such _____ in Japan and to use the Licensor's trademark for "_____" in Japan, but in connection only with those products on which royalty is paid or payable as provided herein.

VII–D–8

Licensee shall have the right to apply to material and products manufactured under this Agreement, as well as to containers, invoices, letterheads, tags, labels and all advertising articles the indicated "Trademark" and such appropriate marks as Licensor may direct, including notice of registration and indication of license relationship.

VII–D–9

Licensor reserves the right to establish manufacturing standards of the products, and the trademarks provided for in this agreement shall not be used on any products which do not conform to the standards established by Licensor.

VII–D–10

B shall set up an adequate system for a continuous quality control of products. C and A shall use their best efforts to conform to the formulas and processes to be supplied by B, follow B's manufacturing methods, and maintain B's quality standards in the manufacture of products at all times.

VII–D–11

Licensee shall submit to Licensor at such intervals or upon such occasions as Licensor or his representatives may reasonably require specimens of products made in accordance with Licensor's "Patent Rights" and "Know-how" and to which any Licensor's "Trademark" is applied or is proposed to be applied.

VII–D–12

If the Licensed products manufactured by the licensee do not meet the quality standards given by the licensor or are remarkably different from products of the same kind manufactured by the licensor in quality, the licensor may cancel the license given to the licensee to use the trademark.

VII–D–13

All use of and reference to the "Trademarks" by Licensee shall conform with proper trademark practice and with such instructions as Licensor from time to time may issue or approve and in no event shall use of or reference to the "Trademark" be inconsistent in form or content with ownership of any "Trademark" by Licensor. Licensee shall instruct its vendees in conformity therewith and take all reasonable steps to secure their full compliance.

VII–D–14

Licensee shall submit to Licensor at such intervals or upon such occasions as Licensor or his representatives may reasonably require representative samples of advertisings, containers, displays, invoices, labels, letterheads, markings, tags, and the like used or planned to be used by Licensee and employing or referring to any of Licensor's "Trademarks."

VII–D–15

The licensee has to use the licensed trademark without adding anything to or amending the trademark.

VII–D–16

C recognizes the validity of B trademarks either registered or to be registered in Japan and shall neither question their ownership and validity, nor become a party, direct or indirect, to an attack on the validity of the B trademarks.

VII–D–17

Licensee hereby acknowledges and admits the exclusive right and title of the Licensor in and to all Licensor's "Trademarks" and the validity of all Licensor's registrations therefor and Licensee shall not contest any such right, title or validity directly or indirectly or aid others in doing so or in infringing the same, nor shall Licensee at any time infringe the "Trademarks" in any way or make use thereof other than in strict compliance with the provisions and limitations hereof or use any trademark similar thereto.

VII–D–18

Upon termination of this Agreement, Licensee shall immediately cease all use of the licensed inventions and licensed "Know-how" and use of licensed "Trademark" and shall promptly deliver to Licensor all drawings, writings and other records or reproductions or licensed "Know-how" and the licensed inventions, whether or not received from Licensor, and licensee shall delete from its production apparatus and processes all adaptation thereof to or utilization therein of licensed "Know-how" and the licensed inventions and use of the licensed "Trademark." All recognition of Licensee as licensed or registered user of the "Trademark" shall be cancelled forthwith, Licensee hereby expressly consenting thereto, and Licensee shall promptly furnish the Licensor an express consent to such cancellation for filing with the appropriate authority.

VII–D–19

The licensee shall not use the licensed trademark after the termination of this agreement, provided, however, that the licensee may use the licensed trademark only on the licensed products which were manufactured before the termination of this agreement and meet the quality standards given by the licensor.

VII–D–20

B shall have the right to sell and deliver any of the Articles which have been already manufactured and/or are in the course of manufacturing, but without using the licensed trademarks. B shall forthwith after termination return all the tags and labels supplied by A.

Notwithstanding the preceding paragraph, in the case of termination due to the expiration of the term of this Agreement B shall be allowed to use the licensed trademarks, provided that B complies with the following conditions and terms, that is, B is required to report to A immediately after the termination the quantity and other details which identify the Articles which B has the right to sell and distribute under the above paragraph, and required to restrict the sale and distribution of the Articles and restrict the period of such sale and distribution to within sixty days from the termination of the Agreement.

E. Confidential Obligation

VII–E–1

The licensor shall supply to the licensee, immediately after the conclusion of this agreement, technical information and data necessary for the licensee's study and examination of the invention relating to _____ , and shall cooperate with, assist, give advice to and direct the licensee free of charge at the licensee's request in connection with the above study and examination, provided however that the licensee shall reimburse the licensor for his expenses in connection with the above request by the licensee and that the licensor and the licensee shall mutually do their best effort to keep the above technical information and data secret from any person or firm who is not granted the license.

VII–E–2

The licensee and its employees shall not publish or let anyone publish, directly or indirectly, articles including or stating the content of the invention or patent application relating to _____ , without the prior written consent of the licensor, before the grant of the patent on this invention.

VII–E–3

The Licensee agrees to manage drawings, plans, etc., supplied by the Licensor under this agreement so as to keep them strictly secret and to make no use of them except for the purpose of facilitating manufacture of the licensed products by the Licensee.

VII–E–4

Licensee and Sublicensee shall do their best so that the know-how supplied by Licensor under this agreement shall not be disseminated to unlicensed persons, firms and corporations.

VII–E–5

Both Licensee and Licensor agree to treat as confidential all technical information relative to _____ furnished to Licensee or to Licensor and Licensee or Licensor shall not disclose any such information, to any person or corporation except employees and contractors of Licensee or Licensor and then only to the extent required by the nature of the work to be performed by such employee or contractor. Licensee and Licensor agree that they will not employ any contractor to render services in connection with any patent of Licensee or Licensor unless such contractor enters a binding, written agreement to treat as confidential all technical information disclosed to or acquired by contractor in the course of said employment.

Each party shall exercise the same degree of care for the secrecy of the other's information as he exercises with respect to his own important technical information.

VII–E–6

The Licensee promises not to allow a competitor of the Licensor to participate in the Licensee's business directly or indirectly without the prior written consent of the Licensor. The Licensee promises to keep secret from and not to disclose to a third person know-how or technical information furnished by the Licensor under this agreement. Moreover, the Licensee agrees not to allow its employee to use or disclose said know-how or technical information until said know-how or technical information has become publicly known by an announcement of the Licensor.

VII–E–7

All information and data given by the Licensor shall be considered absolutely confidential and shall not be disclosed to anyone by the Licensee without the prior written consent of the Licensor, and the Licensee shall require its employees and Sublicensees to treat such matters as confidential, and in the event of cancellation for cause, all right to further use of such information and data by the Licensee shall cease and the Licensee shall turn over all records regarding same to the Licensor.

VII–E–8

The Licensee is obliged not to divulge to anyone any know-how, technical information and data supplied by the Licensor under this agreement during the term of this agreement and three years after termination thereof. Provided, however, that the Licensee may disclose said know-how, technical information and data to a contractor or an engineer for the working thereof when the disclosure is made under an appropriate agreement including confidential obligation to which the Licensor has given his prior consent.

VII–E–9

Licensee shall receive and maintain each item of licensed know-how in trust and confidence until released by Licensor in writing from doing so or unless and until the same and its utilization in commercial practice have become generally known in the trade in the territory in which Licensee is operating without fault or negligence of Licensee or any of its directors, officers or employees.

Licensee shall limit the disclosure of each item of licensed Know-How to those of its directors, officers and supervisory employees to whom knowledge thereby is essential to performance of their duties and shall promptly secure from every such person a written undertaking in form and content acceptable to Licensor, to maintain the same in trust and confidence in the same manner as Licensee is obliged to do.

VII–E–10

C and A agree that each will at all times hereafter take all reasonable steps to keep all formulas, processes, and other information received or to be received in connection herewith secret and confidential and will not divulge any of the information to any person or persons. C and A further agree to exercise due diligence to ensure that their officers and employees adhere to the above obligation.

VII–E–11

C and A agree that the obligation stipulated in Article 34 shall remain valid for five (5) years after termination of this agreement.

VII–E–12

All information supplied to or acquired by Licensee hereunder, other than information available to the general public, shall be supplied or acquired in confidence solely for the use of Licensee under this agreement, and Licensee shall keep such information confidential and shall not disclose the same to any other person at any time during the life of this agreement, or after its termination.

VII–E–13

B-A shall not disclose to any third party or parties any of the A DATA, or any other data or information, acquired by B-A and/or its personnel, from A and/or its personnel except as necessary in the normal course of its business or as agreed to by A in writing. B-A shall use its best efforts to prevent its employees and contract manufacturers from making the disclosures prohibited above.

VII–E–14

The Licensee shall keep secret the said methods, processes and techniques and all information, knowledge, know-how, trade practices and secrets divulged, disclosed or in any way communicated by the Licensor to the Licensee pertaining thereto. The Licensor shall have the right, however, to communicate the same to its employees for the purposes of and to the extent necessary for manufacturing, distributing and selling the Licensed Products as herein provided, but each employee to whom such information is communicated shall correspondingly be bound to secrecy.

The parties agree that during the term of this Agreement and for ten (10) years after the termination of this Agreement the Licensee will hold confidential and will not disclose to any third party any of the methods, techniques, or other information furnished by the Licensor under this Agreement.

VII–E–15

1. B agrees that all technical data and information, processing tech-

niques, plant and equipment design, and other know-how disclosed to it or the New Company by A, pursuant to this agreement or any of the Exhibits hereto, shall be received and accepted in confidence and, except as permitted by Section 3, paragraph 2 of this agreement or Exhibit "No. 2", Section 5, paragraph 1, will not be disclosed by B to any person, firm, corporation or authority for a period of 20 years from the effective date of this agreement.

2. The information described above and received from A shall not be disclosed to any of the officers, directors or employees of B without receiving prior written assurance satisfactory to A that the information so disclosed will be held in confidence by them for the 20 year period, referred to in this Section 3, paragraph 1.

VII–E–16

New Company agrees that for a period of twenty years from the effective date of this agreement, New Company shall maintain in strict confidence the technical information relating to the design, construction and operation of a plant for the production of _____ furnished to it by A pursuant to Sections 2 and 4 hereof, and shall not disclose the same for use outside Japan to any person, firm, corporation or authority so long as and to the extent such technical information remains unpublished by A. New Company may disclose such technical information to contractors to the extent necessary for the construction of its plant or to third parties in connection with the license or sale of such information for use only in Japan, but in the event of such disclosure or disclosures New Company shall obtain an agreement in writing satisfactory to A from such contractors or such third parties agreeing to be bound by a similar obligation of nondisclosure. New Company shall require that every director, managing director or other officer of New Company and every agent, employee or other representative of New Company having access to such technical information shall be bound to a similar obligation of nondisclosure.

VII–E–17

The parties agree that B-A will not sell A PRODUCTS directly or indirectly in or to any country where A itself could not sell because of the prohibitions of the United States Trading with the Enemy Act or any similar law or regulation imposing restrictions on United States trade with foreign countries. A hereby represents that none of the countries included in the COMMERCIAL TERRITORY as defined in Section 1.05 above, come within the scope of the United States Trading With the Enemy Act. A will keep B-A informed of any change in the foregoing.

VII–E–18

No patent, Technical Information or other information or data, disclosed or with respect to which rights are granted to BETA pursuant to this Agreement shall, directly or indirectly, without the prior written consent of ALPHA, be permitted by BETA to be used, disclosed, sold or in any way transferred to or otherwise disposed of in or taken into any country or destination in Section 371.3 of the Comprehensive Export Schedule of the U.S. Department of Commerce or to which General License GTDU, as amended from time to time, of the U.S. Department of Commerce, is made inapplicable in any respect. Nor shall BETA disclose, sell or otherwise transfer such Patent, Technical Information or other information or data to any person or organization which BETA has reason to believe may in turn grant rights under or in connection with, disclose, sell or in any way transfer any of said items to anyone in such prescribed area.

VII–E–19

No right is granted to BAKU to transmit, directly or indirectly, such technical information or any product of such technical information, without the prior written consent of ALPHA, to Albania, Bulgaria, China, including Manchuria, Inner Mongolia, the provinces of Tsinghai and Sikang, Sinkiang, Tibet, the former Kwantung Leased Territory, the present Port Arthur Naval Base Area and Liaoning Province, but excluding Taiwan (Formosa), Communist-controlled areas of Vietnam, Czechoslovakia, East Germany, including the Soviet Zone of Germany and the Soviet Sector of Berlin, Estonia, Hungary, Latvia, Lithuania, North Korea, outer Mongolia, Rumania, Union of Soviet Socialist Republics, Poland, including Danzig, and Cuba. As used herein, the term "product" means the immediate product (including processes and services) produced directly by the use of such technical information or any commodity produced by such immediate product.

F. Technical Assistance

VII–F–1

The Licensor grants to the Licensee the right to manufacture in Japan and to sell in Japan and in _____ all articles listed in Schedule I attached hereto, and further agrees to furnish the Licensee with copies of the Licensor's technical data, manufacturing drawings, and other necessary information relating to the manufacture of articles listed in Schedules I and II.

The Licensor grants to the Licensee the license to manufacture in Japan and sell in Japan and in _____ the articles under the patents and patent applications listed in Schedule II and under any patent applications to be filed for said articles by the Licensor in Japan and in _____ .

VII–F–2

From the time this agreement takes effect the Licensor will supply the Licensee the complete set of drawings and full technical information and advice, including manufacturing data, specifications and all details and also the detailed standard specifications of the materials connected with the design and manufacture of _____ . If necessary, the drawings are supplied on paper suitable for reproduction. Furthermore, the Licensor will pass on to the Licensee the benefit of all knowledge gained by them as the result of their long standing experience in the design and manufacture of _____ specified in this agreement.

VII–F–3

The Licensee shall erect a suitable plant with the required machinery and equipment necessary to enter upon the manufacture of _____ . The Licensor shall have no obligation or responsibility as respects the building of the plant or equipment, but, if its services shall be requested by the Licensee and are voluntarily furnished by the Licensor, the Licensee shall pay the necessary traveling and living expenses and the salaries of the Licensor's personnel in connection therewith. The Licensee shall arrange within a reasonable time for suitable laboratory facilities for the testing of _____ made under this agreement and the Licensee shall furnish suitable samples to the Licensor at the latter's request. For the purpose of assuring that the quality shall be equal to the Licensor's standards, the Licensor shall test a reasonable number of samples of each new product made under this agreement without charge. The Licensor shall also render advice in connection with the performance of, as well as information about, competitive products until such time as the Licensee shall have arranged for suitable laboratories in Japan. If requested by the Licensee, the Licensor shall train in _______ technical service and operational personnel, and shall make available to the Licensee upon request the pertinent technical knowledge and assistance in possession of the Licensor. All expenses and costs for subsistence and travel in connection with this advisory and training service shall be borne by the Licensee.

VII–F–4

Should any of the required material be unobtainable in Japan, the Licensor undertakes to use every endeavour to procure such material for export to Japan, if so desired by the Licensee.

The Licensee will buy the more difficult parts for some series of prototypes of _____ from the Licensor. The number of such parts and their price will be settled on later.

VII–F–5 (*cf*., Example VII–E–1)

VII–F–6

(a) Licensor agrees to supply to Licensee soon after the effective date of this agreement all "know-how" including secret technical specifications, drawings, designs, research and development information relating to ____ which may be in Licensor's possession or under Licensor's control at the said effective date. Licensor further agrees to supply to Licensee all "know-how" relating to ____ which may subsequently be acquired by Licensor during the term of this Agreement, from time to time when the same shall be acquired. Such "know-how" shall be furnished in English.

(b) Upon request made by Licensee, Licensor agrees to cooperate with, aid, advise, and instruct Licensee with respect to "know-how," either by accepting technicians sent by Licensor's factories or by sending its technicians or independent technicians selected by it to ______, without charge, provided that Licensee will bear any expenses necessary for sending Licensee's technicians and will bear any direct expenses including travel and living expenses incurred by Licensor in sending the technicians to ______. If independent technicians are furnished by Licensor, the payment of direct expenses provided for in this paragraph (b) will be made directly to them, with notification of the licensor. The number of such technicians and the period of time during which such technicians will be sent or received will be agreed upon by Licensor and Licensee case by case.

(c) In case where LICENSEE grants a sublicense to C under Art. ___, LICENSEE may supply all or any parts of "know-how" acquired from LICENSOR under Art. ___, and SUBLICENSEE shall have the same right as the LICENSEE provided in Art. ___.

VII–F–7

B shall submit C such technical assistance as may be required by C to plan, organize and set up C's working divisions with a view of making C fully operative. Such technical assistance to include the following services:

(a) assistance in selecting sites of plant(s), warehouse(s), branch office(s), etc.;

(b) suggesting floor plans and placing machinery;

(c) reviewing building designs for proper utilization, process flow, etc.;

(d) assistance in selecting, purchasing appropriate machinery, equipment;

(e) assistance in designing and building special equipment;

(f) outlining specifications for ingredients, raw materials and packaging supplies;

(g) making available quality manuals;

(h) assistance in organizing market research;

(i) assistance in setting up sales analysis;

(j) organizing distribution;

(k) assistance in organizing sales promotions;

(l) setting up management and control for advertising;

(m) assistance in developing institutional and home economic services;

(n) assistance in setting up a direct mail department;

(o) assistance in selecting, training salesmen;

(p) setting up sales manpower utilization controls;

(q) setting up product management;

(r) setting up profit management.

VII–F–8

Licensor or his representatives shall disclose the methods and procedures covered by Licensor's "Patent Rights" and shall also disclose the existing licensed "Know-How" to Licensee promptly after execution of this Agreement, to whatever extent Licensor or his representatives have not already done so; Licensor or his representatives shall further disclose any future acquired licensed "Know-How" to Licensee promptly after Licensor utilizes the same in commercial practice.

VII–F–9

(Transfer of Know-How and Technical Assistance). (a) The Licensor shall within ninety (90) days after the effective date of this Agreement commence, and continue from time to time during the Term of this Agreement, to furnish the Licensee information pertaining to the License Products or the manufacture or adaptation thereof consisting of: (1) calculation and design sheets; (2) basic design data, including design drawings; (3) drawings; (4) process specifications; (5) material specifications; (6) performance specifications; (7) purchasing specifications; (8) test data; and (9) operating instructions and similar data generally known as engineering and manufacturing information and, at the option of the Licensor, designs and specifications relating to manufacturing equipment, tools, dies, jigs, fixtures, but shall include only such information as is available in the records of the Licensor or its affiliated companies and applicable to the Licensed Products.

(b) For the better fulfillment of the provisions of subsection (a) of this Section, the Licensor shall, at its expense, except as otherwise provided in subparagraph (4) hereof, during the term of this Agreement:

(1) generally assist the Licensee in an advisory capacity and explain the Licensor's know-how in the manufacture, use, and adaptation of the Licensed Products, including but not limited to, the preliminary stages of production, and the solution to such production or adaptation problems as may subsequently arise;

(2) render such other assistance as the Licensee may from time to time reasonably request;

(3) allow personnel of the Licensee to visit the plants of the Licensor or its affiliated companies for the study of systems, procedures, practices, methods, and know-how used by the Licensor or its affiliated companies in the manufacture and adaptation of the Licensed Products. The Licensor or its affiliated companies shall permit such personnel free access to these portions of their respective plants where the Licensed Products are being manufactured and where work is in process in connection with the improvements and developments specified in Section ___ , and shall furnish such personnel all reasonable assistance in fulfillment of their functions. Such personnel shall be required to abide by all the plant rules and regulations of the Licensor or its affiliated companies.

(4) The Licensor shall, at the specific request of the Licensee, provide technical specialists to direct and supervise the beginning of production at the plant of the Licensee, for which the Licensee will pay the Licensor a reasonable remuneration on a cost-plus basis to be agreed upon by the parties when the services are rendered.

VII–F–10

"A DATA" shall mean standards and specifications, drawings, designs, photographs, layouts, flow sheets and similar technological data necessary for the manufacture of A PRODUCTS, information relating to their application, installation and use, and similar technological data and information of a tangible written form, which is of a kind ordinarily used and prepared by A in its own operations.

VII–F–11

A shall render technical assistance to B-A and B and follows:

a. A shall, promptly upon the organization of B-A, prepare and ship to B-A, or to B if B-A so requests, a reasonable number of copies of data and information necessary for the manufacture and sale of A PRODUCTS. Changes made by A shall be binding on B-A and B.

b. A shall, within a reasonable time after B-A or B makes a request therefor, dispatch a person or persons trained in the manufacture and engineering of A PRODUCTS to B's plant or plants to consult with and instruct B's employees in the techniques of engineering and manufacturing A PRODUCTS, for a period or periods not to exceed thirty (30) man-days per year. B-A shall reimburse A for the travel expenses of any such personnel to and from their ordinary place of employment to B's plant, and for reasonable living expenses actually incurred by any such personnel while they are away from home. A shall not be required to dispatch any such personnel to B's plant for a period or periods exceeding thirty (30) man-days per year, unless A consents thereto in writing, and unless B-A agrees to reimburse A for their regular salaries.

c. A shall, within a reasonable time after B-A makes a request therefor, permit B's personnel to visit A's plant or plants for the purpose of studying and observing and receiving instruction in the techniques of engineering and manufacturing A PRODUCTS. A shall not be required to permit B's personnel to visit A's plant or plants for such purposes for periods in excess of thirty (30) man-days per year, except for good cause shown by B-A. All travel and living expenses and the regular salary of such personnel shall be the responsibility of B-A.

VII–F–12

1. A agrees that for a period of two years immediately following the date of this agreement and at the request of New Company, it will permit four teams from New Company, each of not more than five technicians and engineers, to visit A's plant at ______, U.S.A., for the purpose of studying the plant and processes for the manufacture of _____ currently being practiced at ______ by A.

2. The period for the visit of each team shall not exceed twenty working days, and the timing of the visit shall be mutually agreed between the parties and shall be arranged so as to avoid undue interference with A's manufacturing activities. During the visits contemplated under the provisions of this Section, the discussions will be in the English language, and, where necessary, New Company will provide competent interpreters or translators.

3. All representatives of New Company who may visit A's plant shall do so at the expense of New Company and shall observe all of the rules and regulations of the plant while on the premises and, in any event, A shall not be responsible for personal injuries or property damage which may be sustained by any such representatives while on A's premises, and New Company agrees to indemnify and hold A harmless from and against any and all liability to such representatives, their heirs and legal representatives.

G. Transferability, Assignability of Licenses, Licensor's Rights and Interests

VII–G–1

This agreement shall be binding upon and shall inure for the benefit of the Licensee and its successors, but shall not be assigned apart from the portion of its business relating to the manufacture of the said licensed subject matter, and shall be binding upon and shall inure for the benefit of the Licensor and its successors.

VII–G–2

This license agreement and the license granted in this agreement shall not be assigned to any person except the successor of either party or a person who took over from either party the business working the license under this agreement.

VII–G–3

The Licensee shall not assign this agreement and the license thereunder without the prior written consent of the Licensor.

VII–G–4

This agreement shall be binding upon and shall inure to the benefit of the successors and assignees of the parties.

VII–G–5

The Licensee may assign anyone the whole or a part of the license granted under this agreement, or grant a sublicense concerning all or part of the license under this agreement.

VII–G–6

This agreement shall be binding on and shall inure to the benefit of Licensor, its assignees and successors in interest, and shall be binding upon and shall inure to the benefit of Licensee and its assignees and successors in interest, but in no event shall Licensee assign this agreement without the prior written consent of Licensor.

VII–G–7

When a party to this agreement assigns all or part of his rights and/or obligations under this agreement to any other person, he shall, except in the case of transfer by merger, obtain the consent of the other party.

The approval of the Japanese Government shall be obtained regarding the transfer and assignment in the preceding paragraph.

VII–G–8

This agreement shall inure to the benefit of and be binding upon the successors and assigns of Licensor, and shall inure to the benefit of and be binding upon the successors and assigns of Licensee, but only upon the prior written consent of Licensor and prior validation by the Japanese Government.

VII–G–9

This agreement is nontransferable and nonassignable by Licensee except with the prior written consent of Licensor.

VII–G–10

This agreement shall be binding upon and shall inure to the benefit of the successors of the parties hereto, but shall not be otherwise assignable by any of the parties without the prior written consent of the others.

VII–G–11

Licensor shall grant Licensee nontransferable exclusive rights to manufacture the products in Japan and sell in Japan and such other countries as may from time to time be decided upon jointly by the parties. Licensee shall not sublicense and Licensor agrees not to license others to manufacture the products in Japan as long as this agreement shall remain in force except as is necessary to effectuate the provisions of Article 4. It is understood that Licensor and its affiliated companies reserve the right to import products into Japan for sale and distribution through Licensee and other distributors jointly appointed by Licensor and Licensee.

VIII. Termination of Agreement

A. Termination due to Default or Breach

VIII–A–1 (*Breach Subsequent to the Closing*)

In the event of any breach of this Agreement by either party hereto subsequent to the closing, B and A hereby unconditionally waive any right which they otherwise may be entitled to exercise under applicable provisions of law to terminate this Agreement and hereby recognize and accept as full and complete compensation and satisfaction in respect of any such breach by the other party hereto all remedies provided by applicable provisions of law, excluding the right to terminate this Agreement.

VIII–A–2

In the event of any termination of this agreement, all future rights and obligations hereunder shall cease and terminate, except the licenses granted by Licensee to Licensor for improvement inventions, the obligation to keep all information supplied by Licensor confidential, and the obligation to make reports and pay all sums accrued under this agreement. Licensee shall have the right during the ensuing year subsequent to the termination of this agreement to dispose of any stock of licensed products and parts therefor, provided that with respect to the sale of such stock Licensee shall pay to Licensor the royalty provided above. Such stock of licensed products and parts shall be identified in any reasonable manner which the Licensor may prescribe.

VIII–A–3

(a) Cancellation or termination of this Agreement in any manner will not relieve Licensee of the payment of royalty *due* at the date of such cancellation or termination.

(b) Upon termination of this Agreement, Licensee shall immediately cease all use of the licensed inventions and licensed "Know-How" and use of licensed "Trademark" or "Trademarks" and shall promptly deliver to Licensor all drawings, writings, and other records or reproductions of licensed "Know-how" and the licensed inventions, whether or not received from Licensor, and Licensee shall delete from its production, apparatus, and processes all adaptation thereof to or utilization therein of licensed "Know-how" and the licensed inventions and use of the licensed "Trademark" or "Trademarks." All recognition of Licensee as licensed or registered user of the "Trademark" shall be cancelled forthwith, Licensee hereby expressly consenting thereto, and Licensee shall promptly furnish to licensor an express consent to such cancellation for filing with the appropriate authority.

VIII–A–4

Upon the failure of either party hereto to fulfill any of its obligations under this agreement, the party injured by such default may give to the other written notice, by registered mail, of such default (such notice to refer specifically to the injured party's intention to terminate this agreement in the event of continued default), and, if after sixty (60) days from the date of such notice the defaulting party has failed or refuses to remedy such default, if capable of being remedied, or has failed or refuses to pay reasonable compensation in the case of a default not capable of being remedied, this agreement may be terminated forthwith by written notice given to the defaulting party, by registered mail, not later than ninety (90) days after the date of notice of such default, and such termination shall be without prejudice to any other rights or claims the injured party may have against the defaulting party.

VIII–A–5

This agreement may be terminated by written notice of either party upon default by the other party in the performance of any of the terms and conditions of this Agreement, unless such default is cured within sixty (60) days after written notice of such default; provided, however, that if the question of the existence of such default shall have been submitted to arbitration under the provisions of Section ___, the running of the sixty (60) day period shall be suspended during the pendency of such arbitration or any appeal therefrom.

C. Expiration

VIII–C–1

This agreement shall continue in effect for a period of ten (10) years from the date when it is finally accepted by both parties, which shall be the effective date of this agreement, subject to early termination as provided in Section ___. It shall be automatically renewed for subsequent terms of ten (10) years, unless either party within twelve (12) months before the expiration of a term of this Agreement notifies the other party of its desire to cancel this Agreement.

E. Insolvency or Bankruptcy of a Party

VIII–E–1

In the event that Licensee shall be adjudged insolvent or bankrupt or shall make an assignment for the benefit of its creditors or have a receiver appointed for it, Licensee shall promptly notify Licensor, stating the particulars thereof, and licensor shall have the right to terminate this agreement forthwith by notice to that effect.

VIII–E–2

This agreement shall automatically terminate: (a) In case of bankruptcy or insolvency of a party; (b) Upon the appointment of a receiver for any of the assets of a party; (c) Upon the making of an assignment for the benefit of the creditors of a party, or the taking of any similar action, such as requesting a creditor's agreement, which under Japanese law constitutes an act of insolvency or bankruptcy; (d) Upon the voluntary or involuntary dissolution of a party.

VIII–E–3

This agreement shall terminate upon the Licensee's being adjudged bankrupt or insolvent or upon the Licensee's filing voluntary bankruptcy or insolvency proceedings, if the Licensor so desires.

VIII–E–4

If Licensee shall go into liquidation (except for the purpose of reorganization, consolidation or merger), insolvency or composition then Licensor shall be at liberty by two months' notice in writing to determine this Agreement.

F. Acts of God, War, Strike, etc.

VIII–F–1

Neither party shall be liable for failure to perform its part of this Agreement (except payment by Licensee hereunder) when such failure is due to fire, flood, strikes, labour troubles or other industrial disturbances, inevitable accidents, war (declared or undeclared), embargoes, blockades, legal restrictions, riots, insurrections, or any cause beyond the control of the parties.

VIII–F–2

The royalty payment provided for herein shall be suspended while and to the extent that the plants of the Licensee are rendered inoperative by strikes, fire, pestilence, riots, war, acts of God, or other such causes beyond their control, and this agreement is hereby automatically extended for the time equivalent to the periods during which the plants are thus rendered inoperative.

G. Corporate Dissolution

VIII–G–1

(b) if the Licensee shall go into liquidation (other than for the purpose of amalgamation or reconstruction), or

(c) if the Licensee shall undergo any substantial change in management or control,

Licensor shall be at liberty to terminate this Agreement.

VIII–G–2 (*Liquidation, Bankruptcy*).

Except in the cases provided for in paragraph 15.01 below, either party may terminate this Agreement by written notice to the other party hereto in the event that such other party shall be dissolved or liquidated (other than in connection with a merger, consolidation or amalgamation with a solvent successor that assumes all obligations of this Agreement) or be declared insolvent or bankrupt.

H. Cross Licenses and Sublicenses

VIII–H–1

If ABLE shall fail to fulfill one or more of its obligations under this agreement, BAKU may, upon election and in addition to any other remedies that it may have, at any time terminate (subject to the provisions of paragraph 5.01 above) all licenses and rights granted to ABLE hereunder, by not less than six (6) months' written notice to ABLE specifying any such breach, unless within the period of such notice all breaches specified therein shall have been remedied.

If BAKU shall fail to fulfill one or more of its obligations under this agreement, ABLE may, upon election and in addition to any other remedies that it may have, at any time terminate (subject to the provisions of paragraph 5.05 below) all licenses and rights granted to BAKU hereunder, by not less than six (6) months' written notice to BAKU specifying any such breach, unless within the period of such notice all breaches specified therein shall have been remedied.

VIII–H–2

Any termination under the provisions of this Section 5 by one party of licenses and rights of the other party shall not affect the licenses and rights of the terminating party and its sublicensees, nor the obligations of BAKU under the provisions of Section 3, if it is the terminating party.

VIII–H–3

Except for termination by BAKU under the provisions of paragraph 5.02 above, all licenses and rights granted hereunder to ABLE shall continue for the entire terms that the respective patents under which they are granted are in force, notwithstanding any other termination hereof or hereunder or expiration of this agreement.

VIII–H–4

When a subsidiary's relationship to a party hereto changes so that such company is no longer a subsidiary of such party, any sublicenses granted hereunder to such subsidiary shall terminate, but licenses and rights acquired under the patents and patent rights of such subsidiary for inventions made prior to the date when such relationship changed shall not be affected by such change. Each equipment and each maintenance part, made hereunder by or for a subsidiary of BAKU, and on which royalty has accrued hereunder but which remains not sold, leased or put into use at the time such subsidiary ceases to be a subsidiary of BAKU, shall be deemed to have been put into use by such subsidiary immediately prior to such time at the place said equipment or part is then located.

IX. Settlement of Disputes

IX–1

Any question or dispute with respect to the construction, meaning, operation or effect of this Agreement or arising out of it involving two or more parties hereto shall be settled by arbitration under the Rules of Conciliation and Arbitration of the International Chamber of Commerce by three arbitrators appointed in accordance with the Rules. Any of the parties hereto may intervene in, and become a party to any such arbitration proceedings. The effect of this arbitral contract and the arbitral award which shall be rendered in accordance with the provision of the preceding sentence shall be governed and construed by the law of England. The arbitration proceedings shall be held at London, England, unless the parties to the proceedings otherwise agree. The expenses of arbitration proceedings shall be borne by the losing party. The arbitral award shall be final and binding upon the parties hereto and they shall comply in good faith with the decision. An application may be made to any court having jurisdiction for a judicial acceptance of the award and/or an order of enforcement as the case may be.

IX–2

Any controversy arising between the parties as to the performance of this Agreement, which cannot be amicably settled by the parties, shall be referred to arbitration in accordance with the Rules of the International Chamber of Commerce, and the decision of such arbitration proceedings shall be binding and conclusive upon the parties hereto.

IX–3

Unless otherwise settled by the parties, all disputes, controversies, or differences which may arise between the parties out of or in relation to or in connection with this Agreement, or for breach thereof, shall be finally settled by arbitration pursuant to the Japan-American Trade Arbitration agreement of 16 September, 1952, by which each party hereto is bound.

X. Governing Law

X–1

This Agreement shall be construed, interpreted and applied in accordance with the laws of Japan.

X–2

The construction and performance of this Agreement shall be governed by the law of the State of New York.

XI. Notices

XI–1

Any notice to be given under this Agreement shall be deemed sufficiently served when reduced to writing and deposited in the United States or Japanese mails, as the case may be, in a sealed envelope with sufficient postage affixed, registered, with return receipt requested, and addressed to A, ______ U.S.A., or to B ______, Japan, as the case may be. Either party may change its address for the purpose of this paragraph by giving written notice to the other party of such change in the manner hereinabove provided.

XI–2

All notices required or authorized to be given hereunder shall be in writing and shall be directed to the addresses set forth below or to such other address as either of the parties may, from time to time, designate by notice in writing to the other. All notices so addressed, if sent by registered airmail, shall be deemed to have been received on the seventh (7th) day next after the date on which such notices were posted.

XI–3

All notices to be given under this Agreement shall be made in the form of registered airmail and shall be addressed to A, ______ U.S.A., or to B ______ Japan, as the case may be, or to such other address as either of the parties may, from time to time, designate by notice in the manner hereinabove provided. All notices so made shall become effective when duly delivered to the addresses.

Remedies for Breach of License Agreements

EUGENE LEE AND YUTAKA KUBOTA

I. Introduction

This chapter is concerned with remedies for breach of a license agreement and is intended to be introductory rather than definitive. It begins with a description of the pertinent court systems and the basic concepts of jurisdiction, and it goes on to discuss contractural alternatives to judicial adjudication, such as arbitration and conciliation. Then, "choice of court" and "choice of law" clauses, which directly affect the judicial process, are considered. Finally, judicial remedies under contract and patent law are discussed.

II. Courts and Procedure

A. Courts

1. Japan. Japan does not have a federal system and therefore has only one set of courts.[1] The court of first instance is the district court.[2] Appeals from district court decisions are made to the high court.[3] At the highest level is the Supreme Court,[4] which has the final power to

1. There are special family courts that handle delinquency of minors and family matters at the prelitigation stage (*Saibanshohō*, Law of courts) art. 31–3 (Law No. 59, 1947), in 2 EHS No. 2010, and there are summary courts which handle petty cases (*Id.* art. 33). Such courts are not relevant to this article.

2. *Id.* art. 24. Each of the forty-seven prefectures of Japan has one district court, except Hokkaido which has four, and there are fifty district courts in all. *Id.* art. 2(2); *Kakyū saibansho no setsuritsu oyobi kankatsu kuiki ni kansuru hōritsu* (Law concerning establishment and area of jurisdiction of lower courts) Attached Schedule II (Law No. 63, 1947)

3. *Saibanshohō* art. 16(i). There are eight high courts that have several branches. *Kakyū saibansho no setsuritsu oyobi kankatsu kuiki ni kansuru hōritsu* Attached Schedule I; *saibanshohō* art. 22; *Kōtō saibansho shibu setchi kisoku* (Rule concerning establishment of branches of high courts) Attached Schedule (Supreme Court Rule No. 1, 1948)

4. The Constitution of Japan, art. 81 reads, "The Supreme Court is the court of last resort with power to determine the constitutionality of any law, order, regulation or official act."

decide the constitutionality of laws and decrees, and at the same time is the highest interpretive authority of law for civil and criminal cases.[5] Further, the Supreme Court has no power to screen cases (certiorari) and it is not uncommon in important cases to appeal to the Supreme Court.[6]

A suit for patent infringement committed in Japan or for breach of a license agreement where a Japanese national is the licensee can be originally instituted in a Japanese district court.[7]

2. *United States.* In the United States there are two independent judicial systems of original jurisdiction. In the federal court system the district court is for most civil litigation the court of original jurisdiction. From it a losing party can go to a circuit court of appeals. In a license-breach case he will usually be able to reach the United States Supreme Court only on a writ of certiorari. Each of the fifty states has its own independent judicial system consisting of *nisi prius* courts, a tier of intermediate appellate courts (in some states), and a court of highest authority. A case is filed in one system, and appeals are taken within that system. A case litigated fully in the state system may be subject to a limited review by the United States Supreme Court if it involves a federal statute or the federal constitution, but decisions of federal courts are never appealed to a state court.

A licensor can sue a licensee in either the state system or the federal system, but must select a court that has jurisdiction over both the subject matter and the defendant. Subject matter will be no problem in a state court of original jurisdiction. Service problems significant in obtaining personal jurisdiction will be discussed later. Federal district courts must assume jurisdiction where the adverse parties are residents of different states or one of the parties is an alien (in other words, where there is diversity of citizenship) and the amount in

5. *Saibanshohō* art. 7; CODE OF CIVIL PROCEDURE arts. 393, 394, 395; CODE OF CRIMINAL PROCEDURE arts. 405, 406.

6. The percentage of cases appealed to the Supreme Court from the civil judgments of nationwide high courts was 42.6 in 1958, 41.7 in 1959, 43.2 in 1960, 41.7 in 1961, 42.7 in 1962, 41.4 in 1963, 42.6 in 1964, 41.6 in 1965, 42.5 in 1966, 41.4 in 1967, 40.2 in 1968, 38.5 in 1969, 37.7 in 1970, 48.3 in 1971, 35.9 in 1972, and 26.2 in 1973. 21 Hōsō Jihō (Lawyers Association Journal) (1969) and 27 Hōsō Jih 738, 743 (1975).

7. It might be mentioned that one result of not having a jury system [For only crimanal cases, the jury system was once adopted by virtue of *Baishinhō* (Law of jury) (Law No. 50, 1923), but the enforcement of *Baishinhō* has since been suspended by *Baishinhō teishi ni kansuru hōritsu* (Law concerning suspension of the law of juwy) (Law No. 88, 1943).] is that appeal trials are not expensive and the party who loses in the court of first instance usually appeals to the high court. The percentage of cases appealed from the first instance civil judgments of nationwide district courts was 31.6 in 1958, 32.3 in 1959, 33.9 in 1960, 33.2 in 1961, 33.1 in 1962, 33.4 in 1963, 29.6 in 1964, 29.6 in 1965, 31.0 in 1966, 29.3 in 1967, 26.3 in 1968, 26.5 in 1969, 27.0 in 1970, 30.1 in 1971, 29.3 in 1972, and 29.4 in 1973. 21 HŌSŌ JIHŌ (Lawyers Association Journal) 569 (1969) and 27 Hōsō Jihō 738, 745 (1975).

controversy exceeds $10,000.[8] An action brought in a state court can, if the requirements of diversity of citizenship and jurisdictional amount in controversy are met, be removed to a federal court.[9] Neither diversity of citizenship nor the $10,000 requisite can be waived by the parties.[10] There are, of course, few lawsuits involving international technological contracts that do not involve more than $10,000 exclusive of interest and costs,[11] and that do not satisfy the diversity of citizenship requirement.

Jurisdiction has been specifically conferred on the federal courts in certain matters regardless of diversity or amount in controversy (subject matter jurisdiction). One such area is patent infringement suits. A state court that otherwise has jurisdiction is not deprived of jurisdiction by the fact that a federal court also has jurisdiction.[12]

B. Procedure

1. Japan. The Japanese Code of Civil Procedure, first adopted in 1891, was almost a literal translation of the German Code.[13] In 1929

8. 28 U.S.C. §1332 (1964).
9. 28 U.S.C. §1441 (1964).
10. Mitchell v. Maurer, 293 U.S. 237, 244 (1934); Blount v. Peerless Chems. (P.R.) Inc. 316 F.2d 695, 697 (2d Cir. 1963).
11. This means that the amount claimed in the suit must be $10,000 or more. If the suit were for damages incurred through an infringement of the plaintiff's patent, for example, the amount of the plaintiff's lost profits or the undue reward of the defendant which the plaintiff seeks to recover through the lawsuit must constitute the minimum amount. Interest on the amount claimed or the costs of the litigation which the plaintiff also may seek to recover are not considered for purposes of calculating the $10,000 amount in controversy.
12. "Exclusive jurisdiction" is given the federal courts but it is "exclusive" only for suits that may be brought in the federal courts. In other words, exclusiveness results from having jurisdiction to the exclusion of state courts. This was settled long ago in Pratt v. Paris Gas Light & Coke Co., 168 U.S. 255, 259 (1897), which involved a grant of exclusive jurisdiction to the federal courts in cases arising under the patent laws. There, suit was brought in a state court on a common-law contract claim. The complaint contained no mention of a patent, but the invalidity of certain patents was set up in defense. In response to the argument that this deprived the state courts of jurisdiction, the Court said:

> Section 711 [the jurisdictional provision] does not deprive the state courts of the power to determine *questions* arising under the patent laws, but only of assuming jurisdiction of "*Cases*" arising under those laws. There is a clear distinction between a case and a question arising under the patent laws. The former arises when the plaintiff in his opening pleading—be it a bill, complaint or declaration—sets up a right under the patent laws as ground for a recovery. Of such the state courts have no jurisdiction. The latter may appear in the plea or answer or in the testimony. The determination of such questions is not beyond the competency of the state tribunals. (Emphasis in the original.)

13. Court procedure is governed by the Code of Civil Procedure (hereinafter cited as CCP). There are special procedural rules which apply to certain types of cases such as administrative suits [*Gyōsei jiken soshōh* (Law concerning procedure of administrative suits) (Law No. 139, 1962, in 2 EHS No. 2391] and divorce suits [*Jinji soshō tetsuzukih* (Law concerning procedure of personal status suits) (Law No. 13, 1898, in 2 EHS No. 2330]. Those are outside the scope of this topic.

the articles governing trial procedure were amended,[14] and after World War II several amendments based on the Anglo-American pattern were made in conjunction with the adoption of the new Constitution. Prior to World War II, witnesses were directly examined by the court,[15] but now counsel may conduct the examination and cross-examination.[16] Basically, the Code of Civil Procedure still follows the German pattern.

Japan has no jury system and all cases are tried before either one or three judges (three judges usually try large cases).[17] Japanese court procedure is quite different from the American system. There are, for instance, neither pretrial nor discovery procedures. The first "hearing" is held within about two months after filing the complaint,[18] and subsequent "hearings" are held at one- or two-month intervals depending upon the schedule of the particular court. At each hearing the parties may present briefs, produce evidence, and examine witnesses.[19]

Sometimes there is a special "preliminary procedure" for complicated cases. One judge from the three-judge panel is specially assigned to clarify the issues before referring the case to formal trial.[20]

14. For further details of the history of CCP, *see* H. KANEKO, MINJI SOSHŌHO TAIKEI (System of the code of civil procedure) 58 *et seq.* (1956).

15. The old art. 299 of CCP provided that the parties may request the presiding judge to ask necessary questions or with his approval may ask questions (directly).

16. The current CCP art. 294 provides: "(1) A witness shall first be examined by the party who applied for the examination of the witness, and after the examination has been concluded by such party, the other party may examine him. (2) The presiding judge may examine a witness after the examination by the party has been concluded." [To supplement art. 294 of CCP, the Supreme Court included detailed provisions (arts. 33, 34, 35 and 36) in *Minji soshō kisoku* (Rule concerning civil procedure) (Supreme Court Rule No. 2, 1956), which has been enacted by virtue of the power granted to the Supreme Court under art. 77 of the Constitution.]

17. *Saibanshohō* art. 26.

18. CCP art. 230. *Minji soshō kisoku* art. 15(2) provides that such date shall be within thirty days from the day on which the suit has been instituted, except where there exist some unavoidable circumstances.

19. CCP art. 137: "Except as otherwise provided for, the means of attack or defense may be produced up to the closing of oral argument." In some extreme cases, however, the court may reject the production of such means. CCP art. 139.

20. CCP arts. 249, 250; *Minji sosho kisoku* art. 16 *et seq.* As in other countries, court trials are time consuming. It usually takes between one and three years for a decision to be issued by the court of first instance. In complicated cases, proceedings lasting at least two years are anticipated. According to the recent statistics in 21 HŌSŌ JIHŌ (Lawyer's Association Journal) (1969), as far as ordinary first instance suits (as distinguished from administrative suits, appellate cases, and bills and notes suits) are concerned, there were 30,655 cases decided, for which judgment was rendered in 1967. For 852 of these cases, judgments were rendered within one month from the time the suit was instituted; for 10,136 cases, within three months; for 5,883 cases, within six months; for 4,603 cases, within one year; for 4,619 cases, within two years; for 2,076 cases, within three years; for 1,056 cases, within four years; for 557 cases, within five years; and for 873 within more than five years. The average trial period in 1967 was 11.1 months; in 1973 it was 17.4 months, 27 HŌS˘JIHŌ 738, 756.

Hearings are, of course, conducted in Japanese, and a document written in a foreign language must be translated into Japanese.[21] Under the Constitution hearings must be open to the public save where the subject matter is related to morality.[22]

2. United States. Actions brought in a federal court in the United States are conducted under the Federal Rules of Civil Procedure,[23] and actions brought in a state court are governed by the rules of civil procedure enacted in that particular state. Many states have adopted rules of procedure similar to the federal rules.

As in Japan the litigation process can be time-consuming, but for a different reason. In the United States the delay between the time the action is filed and the hearing is caused by congested courts and dilatory tactics by counsel. Once the trial is actually begun, it will normally run continuously until judgment. This is significantly different from the Japanese system, where a series of hearings are conducted over a period of months or even years.

In the United States pretrial procedures[24] aimed at clarifying the issues in an informal setting are widely used. The judge has an opportunity to eliminate insubstantial issues before the formal hearing[25] and to encourage settlement.

Discovery procedures,[26] which permit depositions[27] to be taken from the opposing parties and their witnesses and provide access to relevant documents,[28] are an important part of an American trial. Use of these techniques tends to prevent surprise in the trial and to make a trial a search for truth rather than a contest between gladiators.

III. Jurisdiction

The Japanese legal system derives from the civil law as it developed in certain parts of Europe, while the American legal system is rooted in the English common law. The diversity in origins explains a basic difference in the concept of jurisdiction. Under the civil-law system one or more explicit contacts between the defendant and the forum confers jurisdiction. Service of process relates to notice and not to jurisdiction. A predicate of the common-law system is the assumption that the defendant is physically within the geographical limits of the forum. It was once necessary to physically capture the defendant;

21. *Saibanshōhō* art. 74, CCP art. 248.
22. Japanese Const. art. 82(1) (2); *Saibanshōhō* art. 70. This practice could present problems, for instance, for a licensor seeking to litigate a trade secret case.
23. *See* 28 U.S.C. §2072 (1964).
24. *See* Fed. R. Civ. P. 16.
25. *Id.* 16(1).
26. *Id.* 26–37.
27. *Id.* 26–31..24–31.
28. *Id.* 34.

however, now the act of "capture" is performed symbolically through service of process, which consequently has a jurisdictional significance as well as a notice function.

Both systems of jurisdiction have developed ramifications far beyond these fundamental ideas, as will be seen below.

1. Japan. Before 1950 international transactions were not as important in Japan as they now are, and little need was felt for a rule of international jurisdiction.[29] Even today Japan has no statute for jurisdiction in a Japanese court over a case involving foreign elements.[30] A significant body of case law has gradually developed in the field of family matters,[31] but in the fields of law related to business there are still many problems to be resolved. Therefore, the following comments merely represent the writers' views based on treaties and decisions which are concerned with foreign elements.

Service of process is important in Japan even though it is not necessary for jurisdiction.[32] After the complaint is accepted by the court it sends a copy to the defendant (usually by special-delivery mail).[33] This satisfies the notice requirements of Japanese law. If a copy of the complaint does not reach the defendant, the complaint should be rejected.[34] Under certain circumstances service can be made by public notice,[35] or, in the case of a nonresident alien, through government channels.[36] Japan is now a party to the "Convention relative a la Pro-

29. The scarcity of court decisions and theses on this subject shows that they were not even conscious of such problems.

30. S. IKEHARA, KOKUSAI SHIHŌ (International private law) 384, in 20(4) KEIEI HOGAKU ZENSHŪ (1967).

31. *Id.* at 388; Tei v. Tei, 18 Minshū 486 (Sup. Ct., G.B., March 25, 1964).

32. Service of process is made on the premise that the court has jurisdiction over the person to be served. *See* H. KANEKO, MINJI SOSHŌHŌ TAIKEI, *supra* note 14, at 187 *et seq.*

33. CCP art. 229(1); CCP art. 162: "(1) Service shall be effected by a bailiff or by mail. (2) In regard to service by mail, a postman shall be an official effecting service." CCP art. 177: "The official who has effected service shall draw up a document, enter therein the matters relating to the service and submit it to the court." *See also, Yubiukō* (Mail law), art. 66.

34. CCP art. 229(2): "The provisions of the preceding Article shall apply to a case where the service of the complaint has been impossible." CCP art. 228: "(1) In case a complaint has been drawn up contrary to the provisions of Article 224 paragraph 1, the presiding judge shall, fixing an appropriate period, order to supplement the defects within the period so fixed by him. . . . (2) In case the plaintiff does not supplement the defects, the presiding judge shall dismiss the complaint. . . ."

35. CCP art. 178:

> (1) In the event that the domicile, residence of a party or any other place at which service is to be effected in a foreign country, it is impossible to do so in accordance with the provisions of Article 175, or even if made thereby, it is deemed of no effect, service by public notice may be effected upon motion by obtaining the permission from the presiding judge. (2) The court may, if it deems in the case of the preceding paragraph necessary for avoiding delay in the litigation, order to effect service by public notice even without motion. . . .

36. CCP art. 175: "Service to be effected in a foreign country shall be made upon entrustment thereof by the presiding judge to the competent government authorities of that country or to the Japanese ambassador, minister or consul stationed therein."

cedure Civile" and the "Convention on the Service Abroad of Judicial and Extrajudicial Documents in Civil or Commercial Matters" (which came into force with respect to Japan on 26 July and 27 July, 1970, respectively), and the United States is a party to the latter convention. Under the two conventions, the means of serving process have been facilitated and service may be made by mail.

A Japanese court has jurisdiction (or authority to exercise judicial power over all Japanese nationals, whether resident in Japan or not and over foreigners who have a residence (*jūsho*) in Japan.[37] The nationality or residence of the plaintiff does not matter since he is deemed to have submitted to the jurisdiction of the Japanese court voluntarily.[38] Therefore, if the defendant is either a Japanese national or a resident of Japan, the court will accept the case unless the subject matter of the suit is considered to be within the exclusive jurisdiction of another country (for example real property located abroad).[39]

Venue is treated in detail in the Code of Civil Procedure (hereafter CCP). Article 1 provides that the court which is within the general forum of the defendant shall have venue. Articles 2 to 4 provide that the general forum of an individual is determined by his residence (*jūsho*) and that of a corporation by its principal place of business. Articles 5 through 20 provide for overlapping venues under certain specific circumstances, and articles 21 through 34 provide for various matters regarding venue, such as venue by consent (art. 25), by appearance (art. 26), or upon transfer of a case to avoid damage or delay (*forum non conveniens*) (art. 31).

The basic jurisdictional principles stated above imperfectly provide for the situation where the defendant is neither a Japanese national nor a resident of Japan.[40] It can be argued that the venue provisions are relevant, and that if there is venue there must be jurisdiction.[41] It can also be argued that the courts of Japan should through decisions develop reasonable jurisdictional rules for this situation on the basis of contacts between the subject matter and Japan.[42]

Since the general forum of an individual is determined by his *jūsho* and a court in the general forum of the defendant has venue,[43] it

37. H. KANEKO, *supra* note 14, at 65.

38. Rosterott v. Admiral Sales Co., 10 Kakyū minshū 1204, 1212 (Tokyo Dist. Ct., June 11, 1959).

39. H. KANEKO, *supra* note 14, at 66–67.

40. Rosterott v. Admiral Sales Co., 10 Kakyū minshū 1204; S. IKEHARA, *supra* note 30, at 384–86. *See also*, comment by Kubota in JURISURO SHŌGAIHANREI HYAKUSEN (Selected 100 cases involving foreign relations) 170 (1967).

41. H. KANEKO, *supra* note 14, at 66; Egawa, *Kokusai shihō ni okeru saiban kankatsuken* (Jurisdiction in international private law), in 60 HŌGAKU KYŌKAI ZASSHI (The Journal of the Jurisprudence Association) 369, 374 (1942).

42. S. IKEHARA, *supra* note 30, at 384–86.

43. CCP arts. 1 and 2.

follows that jurisdiction exists in some Japanese court when the defendant has a *jūsho* in Japan. The Japanese word *jūsho* is usually translated as "residence," and in a way is similar to the American concept of domicile. It may be defined as "the base of life."[44]

If there is no *jūsho* in Japan, or if the *jūsho* is not known, the general forum is determined by *kyosho* ("temporary residence")[45] in the case of a Japanese national who has no *jūsho* in Japan, but this principle is not automatically applied to a non-Japanese who has a *jūsho* outside Japan and a *kyosho* in Japan. Unless there is some contact other than *kyosho*, a foreigner probably will not be subject to the jurisdiction of the Japanese court merely because he has a *kyosho* in Japan.

The general forum for a foreign corporation or association is determined by the location of its office or place of business in Japan.[46] If there is no office or place of business, but there is a resident individual in charge of the operation, then the general forum of the corporation or association is determined by the place of that person's *jūsho* in Japan. Additionally, a foreign corporation may be subject to the general jurisdiction of a Japanese court if it has an office or a place of business in Japan.[47]

A foreign company doing business continually in Japan must register its office and representative.[48] Failure to comply with this regula-

44. CIVIL CODE art. 21: "The principal base of living of each person shall be his permanent residence." The concept of *jūsho* used in CCP is considered to be the same as the one provided in the Civil Code. Yamada v. Watarimura Senkyo Kanri Iinkai Iinchō, 8 Minshū 1907 (Sup. Ct., G.B., 1954). The former interpretation was that presence and intent to remain were necessary for there to be a *jūsho*. Recently, since intent to remain is a volatile idea, most scholars say that intent is not necessary but that a close connection between the person and the place is sufficient. 1 S. WAGATSUMA, MIMPŌ KŌGI (Lectures on the Civil Code) 95 (1965); 1 CHUSHAKU MIMPŌ (Civil Code annotated) 245, 246 (T. Taneguchi ed. 19). As a result of eliminating intent as a requirement, the present interpretation is that a person can have two or more *jūsho* (S. WAGATSUMA, *supra*, at 95; 1 CHŪSHAKU MIMPŌ, *supra*, at 246–48) and a husband and wife may have different *jūsho*. In addition there is the concept of *honseki*, which is one's official residence registered with the family register [*Kosekihō* (Family register law) art. 6 (Law No. 224, 1947), in 2 EHS No. 2150.] This concept is legally only for the sake of convenience to determine where the family register is kept and may be changed at any time, but is not changed in a lifetime. Residence, as distinguished from *honseki*, is more easily established in Japan than domicile is in the United States.

45. CCP art. 2(2). *Kyosho* is a place with which one has a rather continuous relationship, but not as close as a *jūsho*. 1 S. WAGATSUMA, *supra* note 44 at 97. Formerly, when intent to remain was a requirement for a *jūsho*, it was easy to distinguish the two concepts. 1 CHUSHAKU MIMPO, *supra* note 44, at 253.

46. CCP art. 4(3).

47. Egawa, *supra* note 41, at 376.

48. COMMERCIAL CODE art. 479:

> (1) If a foreign company intends to engage in commercial transactions as a continuing business in Japan, it shall appoint a representative in Japan and establish an office of business at the residence of such representative or at any other place designated by him. (2) In the case mentioned in the preceding paragraph, such foreign company shall, in respect of its office of business, make a registration and give a public notice. . . . (3) A foreign company shall,

tion, however, does not deprive a Japanese court of jurisdiction if the realities of the commercial activity show that the requisite contacts are present.[49]

It is generally agreed that a Japanese court has jurisdiction over a wrongful act committed in Japan and over a case concerning real property located in Japan. Indeed, jurisdiction in the latter instance is considered to be exclusively in Japanese courts. As to a delict, jurisdiction is nonexclusive. Under special circumstances, such as where the action is between two foreigners residing abroad and involves a wrongful act committed while the parties were temporarily present in Japan, a Japanese court might refuse to accept jurisdiction.[50]

Art. 8 of CCP provides that an action may be brought against a person who has no residence in Japan but has property there which is the object of the claim or which is attachable. This is the only article which specifically provides for an action against a nonresident and, as in the case of art. 23, German Code of Civil Procedure, it is generally thought that this article applies to foreigners. However, a district court has denied jurisdiction on the ground that the contact with Japan was not sufficient under the circumstances.[51]

An action for relief which is "monetarily measurable" may be brought in a court located where the obligation is to be performed.[52] In 1908 the Supreme Court recognized jurisdiction over a nonresident foreigner under this provision.[53] However, it is doubtful whether a court will find jurisdiction exists if the only contact is a promise performable in Japan.[54] For example, if an alien, because of some event that occurred outside of Japan, is obligated to pay money to a Japanese national at a Japanese bank, a Japanese court might not take jurisdiction over an action brought by the Japanese against the alien.

Under some legal systems a court of the place where a contract is

simultaneously with the registration mentioned in the preceding paragraph, also make registration of the proper law on which it had been incorporated, as well as the full name and permanent residence of its representative in Japan. . . .

49. *Cf.* COMMERCIAL CODE art. 481(2), "Any person who has engaged in commercial transactions in contravention of the provisions of the preceding paragraph [a foreign company does business without having the required registration completed] shall jointly and severally be liable with the company for any commercial transactions handled by him."; 8(2) CHŪSHAKU KAISHAHŌ (Corporation law annotated 362) T. Ōmori & A. Yazawa eds. (1969).

50. We have no precedent for their solution.

51. Clinton G. Rosterott (phonetic) v. Admiral Sales Co., Inc. 10 Kakyū minshū 1204 (Tokyo Dist. Ct., June 11, 1959).

52. CCP art. 5.

53. Vacuum Oil Co. v. Dampsipsrederai Union A.G. (phonetic), 14 Minroku 786 (Gr. Ct. Cass., G.B., June 26, 1908).

54. But some authorities believe that the result of the old Supreme Court decision would be followed even at present. See 1 H. KANEKO, HANREI MINJI SOSHŌHŌ (Judicial precedents on CCP) 50 (1962).

made has jurisdiction over the parties to that contract if a dispute occurs.[55] This result does not necessarily follow in Japan. For domestic contracts in Japan there is no venue provision relating to the place where the contract was made, and jurisdiction probably would not be recognized in an international dispute if the only contact Japan has with the dispute is the fact that the contract was made in Japan.[56]

Jurisdiction can be conferred on a court by the consent of the parties[57] or by appearance.[58] However, an appearance solely to raise an objection to the court's jurisdiction over the case on the merits does not of itself create jurisdiction.[59]

2. *United States.* Under American law there are three types of jurisdiction: *in personam, in rem,* and *quasi in rem*. The key element in acquiring personal jurisdiction (which is the most important type for the purposes of this discussion) is service of process. Process, a notice which informs the defendant of the action,[60] is generally accomplished by serving the defendant personally within the boundaries of the state[61] and confers personal jurisdiction. In the United States there can be jurisdiction over a transient who has none of the contacts

55. England, for example. *See* Egawa, *supra* note 41, at 72.

56. *But see* Rosterott v. Admiral Sales Co., 10 Kakyū minshū, at 1214.

57. CCP art. 25; however, there may be exceptions in certain situations such as divorce.

58. CCP art. 26.

59. Jurisdiction may be challenged in Japan by a plea to that effect made before responding to the plaintiff's contentions which constitute the merits of the case. When such a plea is made, the court may restrict debate to the question of jurisdiction. If the court is persuaded that it has no jurisdiction, CCP provides that the court will order the case to be transferred to a proper court. In the case of an international dispute, if the court thinks that there is no court having jurisdiction in Japan, it dismisses the case, even though there is no such provision in CCP. If the court thinks it has jurisdiction, it will enter an intermediate judgment dismissing the defendant's challenge to jurisdiction. Even when a plea challenging jurisdiction is made and is still pending, the court may request the defendant to answer the plaintiff's contentions on the merits of the case. In that event, the defendant challenging jurisdiction is expected to respond to such assertions, but may expressly retain the challenge to jurisdiction. Failure to submit an answer is treated as an admission of the plaintiff's contentions. The court in its final judgment may still dismiss the case on jurisdictional grounds.

60. In the formal sense there are many types of process. This reference is solely to the documents delivered to the defendant to apprise him of the suit that has been filed against him. The method of issuing and serving process is provided by statute in each jurisdiction. In some jurisdictions this is issued by the court and then transmitted to the proper person to deliver it personally to the defendant. In other jurisdictions it may be issued by the plaintiff or plaintiff's lawyer.

61. The requirement that the defendant be personally served with process has been alleviated by statute. For instance, "substituted" personal service, whereby the process is left at the defendant's usual abode with a person of suitable age and discretion, is usually allowed. If a defendant is domiciled in the forum state, but is absent from that state, service is sufficient if it is "reasonably calculated to give him actual notice." (Milliken v. Meyer, 311 U.S. 457) (1940).

with the forum that would be necessary to jurisdiction in the Japanese sense.

Where authorized by statute there can also be "constructive" service, a type of service completed by publication, by personal service outside the state, or by mail. The details vary in different states.

Consent to jurisdiction and a general appearance in the action are also ways of conferring personal jurisdiction in certain situations.[62]

State statutes have extended jurisdiction in a variety of circumstances felt to justify control by the state. One example is a statute that allows constructive service on a nonresident motorist who causes an accident in the forum state.[63] Other statutes give like effect to such conduct as the commission of tortious acts within the state[64] and doing business within the state.[65] These statutes are subject to the test enunciated by the United States Supreme Court in *International Shoe Co.* v. *Washington*.[66] The jurisdiction conferred must not violate traditional notions of fair play and substantial justice. Recently the concept of "doing business" has been extended by statutes (so-called "long-arm statutes") and court decisions. It is now difficult for a foreign corporation to avoid the jurisdiction of United States courts if the dispute arises out of transactions having some connection with the United States market (such as liability for products exported to the United States).

A judgment *in rem* (in contrast to a judgment *in personam*) not only settles the rights of the parties, but settles the interests in a certain thing (*res*) as against everyone in the world.[67] In an *in rem* action, jurisdiction over nonresidents can be obtained through constructive service using the method prescribed by local statute. In general, the property in question is attached and service is then made by publishing notice of the suit in the newspaper. Constructive service is rationalized on the ground that property is always in the possession of the owner, and thus, when the property is attached, the owner will be aware of it.[68] In the case of intangibles, notice by publication alone is

62. Most states have a procedure known as a "special appearance." Through this a party may appear in court for the sole purpose of questioning the court's jurisdiction. If he argues the merits of the case, general jurisdiction is imposed regardless of whether the defendant claimed he was making a special appearance.

63. Hess v. Pawloski, 247 U.S. 352 (1927).

64. Gray v. American Radiator Standard Sanitary Corp., 222 Ill.2d 432, 176 N.E.2d 761 (1961).

65. Henry L. Doherty & Co. v. Goodman, 294 U.S. 623 (1935).

66. 326 U.S. 310 (1945).

67. This is most important in actions concerning land, but is used in admiralty, in determining the ownership to stock certificates and even in divorce proceedings.

68. Pennoyer v. Neff, 95 U.S. 714, 727 (1877).

not adequate if the nonresident parties are known and reachable.[69]

Jurisdiction *quasi in rem* is jurisdiction over a nonresident, nonpresent defendant to the extent of property attached in the state. This type of jurisdiction was recognized in *Harris* v. *Balk*,[70] in which jurisdiction was obtained over a nonpresent defendant by service on the defendant's debtor who was temporarily present in the forum state. The judgment was effective, of course, only to the extent of the amount of the attached debt.

It should be pointed out that in all three types of American jurisdiction, as in the Japanese system, once jurisdiction has been acquired it will continue for the duration of the proceedings.

IV. Choice of Forum and Arbitration

A. Choice of Forum

In general, jurisdiction can be effected by an agreement between the parties. Agreements that designate a court or area in which litigation shall be prosecuted are known as "choice of court" or "prorogation" clauses. These can be drawn to cover either existing or future causes of action.[71]

The comparative speed of the trial process is a factor to be considered in determining the better forum. In Japan, since the parties must appear in court several times before a decision is reached, a trial can take a very long time. In the United States once a trial is started it usually runs continuously until completion, and the primary waiting period is caused by the backlog of cases that must be worked through before a given case's turn is reached. The period of delay varies from court to court. It is difficult to say which judicial system provides the speedier justice.

Securing a judgment and collecting a judgment can raise quite different problems. If enforcement procedures must be used, collection is easier and quicker if the judgment was rendered in the country where enforcement is sought.

The convenience of the parties is also important in choosing a forum. Litigation in another country, when most of the witnesses and parties are in Japan, is obviously inconvenient.

The efficiency of the two systems can be compared in certain respects. Japanese courts do not have a contempt-of-court procedure for the enforcement of judgments, and in certain situations, such as injunctions or orders to allow inspections, this makes a Japanese judgment worthless. On the other hand, American procedures for

69. Mullane v. Central Hanover Bank & Trust Co., 339 U.S. 306 (1950).

70. 198 U.S. 215 (1905).

71. Because of the preference of judges to apply the law of the forum, prorogation clauses sometimes may be an effective tool for determining the governing law as well.

such details as pleading, proof of foreign law, and the use of expert witnesses are more cumbersome than in Japan. It is likely that a Japanese judgment in a damage suit will be smaller than in the United States.

1. *Prorogation in the United States.* For existing causes of action the majority view in the United States is that prorogation clauses are proper and enforceable. However, in a small minority of jurisdictions, such a provision will be considered to be a violation of public policy.[72] In planning and negotiation the concern is with a prorogation clause covering causes of action that might subsequently arise out of the contemplated transaction. As to this type of agreement, the view adopted by the Supreme Court in *M/S Bremen* v. *Zapata Off-Shore Company*[73] is that forum-selection clauses are *prima facie* valid and will be enforced, unless enforcement is shown by the resisting party to be unreasonable under the circumstances.[74] The factors to be considered resemble those used in *forum non conveniens* analysis and include the possible use of overweening bargaining power in the selection of a forum, the availability of parties and witnesses, and the ability of the stipulated court to handle the matter. Formerly, the view was that a provision that limits actions to certain courts is void as against public policy and would not bar litigation in a jurisdiction not authorized by the clause.[75] Agreements to arbitrate, discussed below, have been met with increasing favor by the courts. The prorogation clause is in many ways analogous, and there is no good reason why a court should approve one and disapprove the other.

2. *Prorogation in Japan.* Japanese courts will enforce a prorogation clause and require litigation in the specified foreign court if certain conditions are met. The first is that courts of the named jurisdiction take the suit.[76] This condition makes it important to ascertain the law in the contemplated place before specifying it in the contract. The matter must not be one that belongs exclusively to Japanese jurisdiction.[77] Scholarly opinions vary on the question of whether it

72. Kylar v. United States Trotting Ass'n, 210 N.Y.S.2d 25 (4th Dept. 1961); Huntley v. Alehandre, 139 so.2d 911 (D. Ct. App. Fla. 1962); Arsenis v. Atlantic Tankers, Ltd., 39 Misc. 2d 124, 240 N.Y.S. 2d 69 (Civil Ct. N.Y. 1963).

73. 407 U.S. 1, 92 S.Ct. 1907, 32 L.Ed. 2 (1972).

74. *Ibid.* 92 S.Ct., at 1913. *See also* Wm. H. Muller & Co. v. Swedish Am. Line, 224 F.2d 806 (2d Cir. 1955); Takemura & Co. v. S. S. Tsuneshima Maru, 197 F.Supp. 909 (S.D.N.Y. 1961).

75. Nute v. Hamillton Mut. Ins. Co., 72 Mass. (6 Gray) 174 (1856); Huntley v. Alejandre, 139 So.2d 911 (1962).

76. Glegoe (phonetic) v. Ubantoff (phonetic), 22 Minroku 1909, 1922 (Gr. Ct. Cass., G.B., Oct. 18, 1916); Tokyo Kaijō-Kasai Hoken K. K. v. Royal Interocean Lines, Hanrei Jihō (no. 799) 13 (Sup. Ct. 1975).

77. *Supra* note 76, Tokyo Kaijō-Kasai Hoken K.K. v. Royal Interocean Lines.

is necessary that the judgment of the selected court satisfy the requirements for recognition of foreign judgments in Japan stated in art. 200 of CCP.[78] The most important of the requirements in art. 200 is reciprocity. The reason for applying art. 200 is that otherwise the plaintiff is not adequately protected, since it is uncertain which matters belong exclusively to Japanese jurisdiction. However, a recent Supreme Court decision denied the applicability of art. 200.[79]

B. Arbitration

"Arbitration is a procedure whereby the parties involved submit a dispute to private individuals for decision, rather than to a court."[80] In the United States the validity of an arbitration clause is now assured by statute in many jurisdictions. Arbitration is permitted by statute in Japan and its effectiveness there has never been doubted. License agreements between Japanese and American parties commonly provide for arbitration.

In Japan, the Japanese law of arbitration is in Book VIII of the Code of Civil Procedure, the provisions of which are almost literal translations of the corresponding articles of the German Code of Civil

78. T. Kikui & T. Muramatsu, Minji Soshōhō (Code of Civil Procedure) 86, in 11(1) Hōritsugaku Taikei Conmentāru (1957). H. Kaneko, Jokai Minji Soshōhō, Vol. I, p. 66. CCP art. 200:

> A foreign judgment which has become final and conclusive shall be valid only upon the fulfillment of the following conditions:
> (1) That the jurisdiction of the foreign court is not denied in laws and orders or treaty;
> (2) That the defendant defeated, being a Japanese, has received service of summons or any other necessary orders to commence procedure otherwise by a public notice or has appeared without receiving service thereof;
> (3) That the judgment of a foreign court is not contrary to the public order or good morals in Japan;
> (4) That there is mutual guarantee.

CCP art. 514:

> (1) Execution based on the judgment of a foreign court may be carried out only when its lawfulness is pronounced by a judgment of execution by the Japanese court.
> (2) In regard to a suit demanding a judgment of execution, the district court of the place where the general forum of a debtor exists shall have the jurisdiction and in case no general forum exists, the court having the jurisdiction over the suit against the debtor shall have the jurisdiction.

CCP art. 515:

> A judgment of execution shall be rendered without inquiring into justifiableness of the decision.
> 2. A suit demanding a judgment of execution shall be turned down in the following cases:
> (1) When it is not certified that the judgment of a foreign court has become final and conclusive;
> (2) When the foreign judgment does not fulfil the requirements as prescribed in Article 200.

79. *Supra* note 76, Tokyo Kaijō-Kasai Hoken K.K. v. Royal Interocean Lines.

80. Davis, *Arbitration in Patent Disputes*, in The Encyclopedia of Patent Practice and Invention Management 72 (R. Calvert ed. 1964).

Procedure of 1877.[81] The coverage is unfortunately general, rather than detailed, and the procedures are by no means clear.

Under the code, a matter can be arbitrated only when the subject matter is such that it could be decided by a court. For instance, arbitration could not be used to settle a deadlock in a closely held corporation because re-solution of such matters of business policy is not a function of the courts. Appraisal of the value of disputed property (e.g., shares of a company) is not arbitrable for the same reason. However, an agreement to refer the determination of value to a third party will give the parties contractual rights and obligations that can constitute a cause of action. Since the arbitration must have the power to settle the matter that is the subject of the arbitration,[82] it is not possible to arbitrate such matters as divorce actions or administrative disputes.[83]

A promise to arbitrate a future dispute is enforceable, provided the dispute arises from a specific legal relationship.[84] Therefore, future disputes arising out of a license agreement can be the subject of an arbitration.

An arbitration agreement can be set up as a defense to a lawsuit, the bringing of which violates the agreement. Thus, if there is an arbitration clause in a license agreement, the court properly should reject a complaint predicated on a cause of action covered by that clause and not merely stay or suspend the action.[85]

If one party fails to appoint an arbitrator as required by his agreement, the other party may petition the court to make the appointment.[86] The request may ask the court to order the defaulting party to

81. This is one of the parts of the Code of Civil Procedure which has not undergone revision since it was enacted in 1891. H. KANEKO, MINJI SOSHOHO TAIKEI, *supra* note 14, at 58 *et seq*.

82. CCP art. 786: "An agreement for submission of a controversy to one or more arbitrators shall be valid insofar as the parties are entitled to effect a compromise regarding the subject matter in dispute."

83. N. KOYAMA, CHŪSAIHŌ (Arbitration law) 58, in 38 HŌRITSUGAKU ZENSHŪ (1958).

84. CCP art. 787.

85. Although this has not been specifically provided in the Code of Civil Procedure, it has become the established interpretation and practice. *See* Compania de Transportes del Mar, S.A. v. Mataichi, 4 Kakyū minshū 502 (Tokyo Dist. Ct., April 10, 1953); Hinode Kagaku Kōgyō K.K. v. Sankō Kisen K.K., 10 Kakyū minshū 970 (Osaka Dist. Ct., May 11, 1959); Tōwa Kōgyō K.K. v. Mitsui Sempaku K.K., 1 Kakyū minshū 1913 (Yokohama Dist. Ct., Nov. 1950); Continental Inn Co. v. Fuji Shōkai, 2 Kokusai shihō kankei jiken saiban reishū 1728 (Tokyo App. Ch., Aug. 5, 1935); Yamada v. Bellini, 6 Minroku 142 (Gr. Ct. Cass, Nov. 27, 1900).)

86. CCP art. 789:

> If both parties are entitled to nominate arbitrators the first proceeding party shall make a pressing notice to the other party in writing of the arbitrator nominated by him and call upon the other party to do so on his side within a period of seven days.
>
> 2. Upon expiration of the foregoing period, the jurisdictional court shall, upon motion of the first proceeding party, nominate arbitrators.

appoint an arbitrator, but this relief is inadequate because the power of a Japanese court to compel a defendant to do a certain act is very limited. A better course of action is to request that the court appoint the arbitrator itself.

If the arbitrators render an award, it can be defeated by judicial action only if there is a specified procedural defect.[87] If the losing party does not comply with the award, the other party may bring an action for an execution judgment[88] and this relief will be granted.[89] An execution judgment has the same effect as an ordinary judgment.

In the United States, the common-law idea that an agreement to arbitrate is an attempt to "oust the court of its jurisdiction" produced differences from state to state[90] before statutes authorizing arbitration were enacted at both the federal and state levels.[91]

The Federal Arbitration Act[92] incorporates many of the features of the various state arbitration statutes. Section 4 states:[93]

> A party aggrieved by the alleged failure, neglect, or refusal of another to arbitrate under a written agreement for arbitration may petition any court of the United States which, save for such agreement, would have jurisdiction under the judicial code at law . . . for an order directing that such arbitration proceed in the manner provided for in such agreement. . . . Service thereof shall be made in the manner provided by law for the service of summons in the jurisdiction in which the proceeding is brought. The court shall hear the parties, and upon being satisfied that the making of the agreement for arbitration or the failure to

87. CCP art. 801:

> Motion for cancellation of an award shall be made in the following cases:
> (1) In case an arbitration procedure should not be allowed;
> (2) In case an award condemns a party to perform an act the performance of which is prohibited by law;
> (3) In case the parties were not represented in accordance with the provisions of law;
> (4) In case the parties were not examined in the arbitration procedure;
> (5) In case the award is not accompanied by reasons;
> (6) In the case of Article 420 items (4) to (8) inclusive, there exist conditions allowing a suit for retrial.
> 2. Cancellation of an award shall not be made of the reasons as mentioned in items (4) and (5) of this Article in case parties have otherwise agreed.

88. CCP art. 802(1).

89. CCP art. 802(2), "The foregoing judgment shall not be rendered in case there exists a reason under which cancellation of award may be moved."

90. Restatement of Contracts 550 (1932) reflects the traditional approach:

> *Bargain for arbitration.*
> Except as stated in sec. 558, a bargain to arbitrate either an existing or a possible future dispute is not illegal, unless the agreed terms of arbitration are unfair, but will not be specifically enforced, and only nominal damages are recoverable for its breach. Nor is any bargain to arbitrate a bar to an action on the claim to which the bargain relates.

91. For citation to the arbitration statutes enacted in the various states of the United States see M. Domke, Commercial Arbitration 108–10 (1965).

92. 9 U.S.C. §1–14 (1964).

93. 9 U.S.C. §4 (1964).

> comply therewith is not in issue, the court shall make an order directing the parties to proceed to arbitration in accordance with the terms of the agreement. . . . If the making of the arbitration agreement or the failure, neglect or refusal to perform the same be in issue, the court shall proceed summarily to the trial thereof.

The act "envisages exertion by the court of equitable checks and balances; supervision of the arbitration by the court is expected."[94] Because of its statutory basis an arbitration clause is less susceptible to challenge than is a prorogation clause.[95] The twenty-seven states that have arbitration statutes include those most important in Japanese/American commercial practice.[96] The essential features of a typical statute are as follows:[97]

1. The irrevocability of any agreement to submit future disputes to arbitration;
2. The power of a party, pursuant to a court directive, to compel a recalcitrant party to proceed to arbitration;
3. The provision that any court action instituted in violation of an arbitration agreement may be stayed until arbitration in the agreed manner has taken place;
4. The authority of the court to appoint arbitrators and fill vacancies when the parties do not make the designation, or when arbitrators withdraw or become unable to serve during the arbitration;
5. The restrictions on the court's freedom to review the findings of facts by the arbitrator and his application of the law; and
6. The specification of the grounds on which awards may be attacked for procedural defects and of time limits for such challenges.

Modern statutes put teeth in the machinery for enforcing arbitration clauses, making them effective as dispute-resolving devices. Even without statutes, there are a few states that maintain the traditional view that an agreement to arbitrate future disputes is unenforceable (*United Association of Journalism, 2 App. of Plumbing, etc.* v. *Stine* 351 P. 3d 965 [1960]; *Park Court Co.* v. *Independent School Dist. No. 32*, 296 N.W. 475 [1941]).

In international transactions additional support for the enforceability of arbitration clauses is provided by the Treaty of Friendship, Commerce, and Navigation between the United States and Japan.[98] It

94. Leesona v. Cotwool, 315 F.2d 538, 542 (1963).

95. Kawakami & Henderson, *Arbitration in U.S./Japanese Sales Disputes*, 42 WASH.L.REV. 541, 558 (1967).

96. HENDERSON, FOREIGN ENTERPRISE IN JAPAN 483, n. 35 (1973).

97. M. DOMKE, COMMERCIAL ARBITRATION 18 (1965).

98. Treaty with Japan on Friendship, Commerce and Navigation, April 12, 1953 [1953] 4 U.S.T. 2063, T.I.A.S. No. 2863 [hereinafter cited as FCN Treaty.]

is helpful,[99] although limited to the enforcement of foreign awards and contract provisions calling for arbitration abroad or by foreign arbitrators. It was relied upon as one basis for decision in *Oregon Pacific Forest Products Corp.* v. *Welsh Panel Co.*[100] The Japanese defendant sought to stay an action pending arbitration as required by the parties' contract, and prevailed. The court reiterated the established concept that a treaty is the supreme law of the land and added that "state law must yield when it is inconsistent with or impairs the policy or provisions of a treaty inasmuch as a state has no power to refuse enforcement of rights based on a federal policy which is evidenced by an international compact or agreement."[101] Recently, the United States acceded to the "Convention on the Recognition and Enforcement of Foreign Arbitral Awards" sponsored by the United Nations (to which Japan has been a party since 1961), and at the same time amended the Federal Arbitration Act by adding a new Chapter II consisting of eight sections. The accession as well as the amendment of the act came into force on 29 December, 1970. The new Chapter II appears to have solved most questions relating to recognition and enforcement of agreements to arbitrate foreign arbitral awards in foreign countries.

In the United States the separability of arbitration and contract elements is a problem.[102] In earlier practice, if fraud in the inducement were alleged, that issue was one for judicial decision. The weakness of this approach was that by alleging fraud, a party could move a dispute into court, frustrating the time-saving purpose of the arbitration clause. Under the developing "separability" approach, the arbitration clause is considered separately from the rest of the contract. It is reasoned that although there may have been fraud in the inducement to enter into the contract, the parties still clearly indicated that

99. *Id.* art. IV(2):

> Contracts entered into between nationals and companies of the other Party, that provide for the settlement by arbitration of controversies, shall not be deemed unenforceable within the territories of such other party merely on the grounds that the place designated for the arbitration proceedings is outside such territories or that the nationality of one or more of the arbitrators is not that of such other Party. Awards duly rendered pursuant to any such contracts, which are finally unforceable under the laws of the place where rendered, shall be deemed conclusive in enforcement proceedings brought before the courts of competent jurisdiction of either Party, and shall be entitled to be declared enforceable by such courts, except where found contrary to public policy. When so declared, such awards shall be entitled to privileges and measures of enforcement appertaining to awards rendered locally. It is understood, however, that awards rendered outside the United States of America shall be entitled in any court in any State thereof only to the same measure of recognition as awards rendered in other States thereof.

100. 248 F.Supp. 903 (D. Ore. 1965).

101. *Id.* at 910.

102. *See generally* M. DOMKE, COMMERCIAL ARBITRATION 49 (1965); Kawakami & Henderson, *supra* note 95, at 567.

disputes were to be settled by arbitration. Thus, so long as there is no fraud relative to the arbitration clause itself, the issue of fraud in the principal contract is a matter for the arbitrators to decide.[103] Another problem in enforcing arbitration agreements is that United States courts have, in several decisions, stated that if an issue of antitrust is involved the dispute must be decided by a judicial court in spite of the arbitration clause in the parties' agreement (*American Safety Equip. Corp.* v. *J. P. Maguire Corp.*, 391 F. 2d 821 [1968]; *Cobb* v. *Lewis*, 488 F. 2d 41 [1974]; *Overseas Motors, Inc.* v. *Import Motors Ltd., Inc.* 375 F. Supp. 499 [1974]). A recent United States Supreme Court decision, however, states that disputes should be arbitrated according to the agreement even though an issue of federal securities law is involved. (*Shork* v. *Alberto-Culver Co.*, 94 S.Ct. 2449 [1974]). It is still unclear whether the Supreme Court will decide the same way where an antitrust issue is involved.

An arbitration award rendered in Japan can be enforced in the United States in one of two forms of procedures. The award can be reduced to judgment in Japan, and then execution of that judgment can be sought in the United States; or the award can be reduced to a judgment in the United States and then executed. Under the FCN Treaty, an arbitration award rendered in either country can be enforced in the other country if it is shown that the award is valid.[104]

Arbitration is now a mature and well-established institution. The International Chamber of Commerce provides widely used arbitration services under its Rules of Conciliation and Arbitration. According to the rules, the parties must exchange their arguments through the headquarters of the International Chamber of Commerce located in Paris.[105]

Also helpful are the American Arbitration Association (AAA) and the Japan Commercial Arbitration Association. The rules of the two are almost identical, and each can provide a panel of arbitrators if the parties wish this service. The two associations have entered into an agreement with respect to the use of arbitration by parties from the two countries and suggest use of the following contract clause:[106]

103. Prima Paint v. Flood & Conklin Mfg. Co., 388 U.S. 395, 403–04 (1967), *aff'g* 360 F.2d 315 (2d Cir. 1966); Arbitration Clauses and Fraudulent Inducement, 42 Wash.L.Rev. 621 (1967).

104. *See* note 99 *supra*.

105. International Chamber of Commerce, Rules of Conciliation and Arbitration Arts. 3–5.

106. Agreement Between The Japan Commercial Arbitration Association and the American Arbitration Association to Facilitate the Use of Commercial Arbitration in Trade Between Japan and the United States of America, Sept. 16, 1952, in Kawakami & Henderson, *supra* note 95, at 586.

> All disputes, controversies, or differences which may arise between the parties, out of or in relation to or in connection with this contract, or for the breach thereof shall be finally settled by arbitration pursuant to the Japan-American Trade Arbitration Agreement, of 16 September, 1952 by which each party hereto is bound.

In technology-licensing transactions between American and Japanese companies arbitration is useful and this clause merits consideration. It does not fix the place of arbitration. This is a detail which should be added to the basic clause.

Since feudal times litigation has been avoided, wherever possible, in Japan, and this tradition is reflected even today in Japanese court statistics, although the situation is gradually changing.[107] Traditional Japanese alternatives to litigation are still used. The effectiveness of dispute-resolving techniques other than litigation and the Japanese tendency to avoid lawsuits explain the fact that in the ten years between the mid-1950s and the mid-1960s Japanese were parties in only approximately twenty-five commercial cases in the United States (most of which were in admiralty), despite burgeoning Japanese-American commercial contacts.[108]

Although arbitration is widely used in international commercial contracts in Japan, a very useful alternative which has some of the commonly enumerated advantages of arbitration is available. This technique is conciliation,[109] a voluntary procedure from which either party can withdraw at any time, and which is much used in intra-Japan matters.

Conciliation proceedings are conducted in the courthouse by a judge and two outsiders assigned from a list of conciliators who are usually practicing lawyers.[110] The petitioner must first file a petition in writing,[111] but thereafter the parties jointly or alternately explain their positions to the two nonjudge conciliators. Then the conciliators express their opinions to the parties. If this is not mutually acceptable, the conciliators propose what they consider to be the best solution based on their understanding of the facts and law and their own common sense, while trying to "save face" for both parties. The parties are free to agree to the conciliation decision, to reject it, or to make counter proposals. If the parties agree, the nonjudge con-

107. D. HENDERSON, CONCILIATION AND JAPANESE LAW 214 (1965).

108. Kawakami & Henderson, *supra* note 95, at 547 n. 24.

109. *Minji chōteihō* (Civil Conciliation Law) (Law No. 222, 1951), in 2 EHS No. 2360.

110. *Id.* arts. 6, 7. In the case of conciliation of family matters, this is usually a lawyer and a reputable layman.

111. Although practically unused, under *Minji Chōtei Kisoku* (Civil Conciliation Rule) art. 3 (Sup. Ct. Rule No. 9, 1951), oral petition is permitted.

112. N. KOYAMA, CHŌTEHŌ, *supra* note 83, at 44 *et seq.*

ciliators show the solution to the judge who examines the legality of the terms, obtains a statement by the parties that they really want the settlement under the terms specified, and issues a final proposal.[112] The settlement, once agreed on by the parties, is in effect a court judgment and can be executed. In that sense it differs from the arbitration award.[113]

Conciliation cannot effectively be agreed upon in advance by the parties, but once its use is invoked, its scope is limitless. The negotiations are secret[114] and usually carried out in a small closed chamber.[115] Since the settlement is made by the parties' own agreement, it does not leave the harmful aftermath that can follow a forced decision. In terms of tactics, listening to the opponent's story and seeing the lawyer-conciliators' reaction may better enable the parties to evaluate what they might get through a court action. Conciliation as a dispute-settlement method is not widely known and consequently is little used by foreigners. It merits consideration.

V. Governing Law

A. Introduction

Parties to international contracts often express strong and natural preferences for the law of their home countries. As is suggested below, at times there can be practical advantages in the acceptance of provisions which apply the law of the other party's home country and no real disadvantages in preagreed use of a foreign court. Each transaction must be individually evaluated to determine the better course. The parties can exercise a certain amount of autonomy in selecting the law which will govern their transaction, but future problems can cover such a wide range that it is virtually impossible to predetermine the most beneficial law. There are, however, some common factors that counsel, in an effort to determine which law or legal system might be preferable, may consider.

One of the primary functions of law, to provide predictability in societal and commercial relations, may not be accomplished if a court in one country is called upon to apply the law of another country. An American judge will not know Japanese law or how a Japanese court would apply Japanese law, cannot effectively research that law, and may find it impossible to understand either the Japanese legal system or the society in which Japanese courts operate. A Japanese judge has

113. *Minji chōteihō* art. 16.

114. *Minji chōtei kisoku* art. 10.

115. E.g., speed, informality, reduced expense, diminished risk of an aftermath of ill-will.

116. Van Hecke, *Choice-of-Law Problems in European Contracts*, in International Contracts Choice of Law and Language 44 (W. Reese ed. 1962).

the same problems with American law. Therefore, it is sometimes desirable for the forum court to apply its own law to problems that develop in an international transaction in order to maximize predictability. For this reason it is often best to designate as the chosen law that of the forum in which litigation is most likely to occur.

Due to difficulty in trying to determine which legal system would be the most desirable, or to oversight, sometimes no selection of governing law is made by contracting parties. A transaction thus left to the vagaries of future events can come to litigation in either country, and the choice of law rules of the forum will be of paramount importance. Concerning these rules, there is a notable lack of uniformity in the many jurisdictions in the United States. There is no certainty in this approach. It can lead to bizarre results. For instance, an American jury can determine Japanese law on the basis of questions asked of an expert witness by counsel. If the result of the suit resembles that to be expected were a Japanese judge to try the case, the similarity could only be fortuitous. To avoid the risk of a gross miscarriage of justice, and to achieve the maximum amount of predictability, specification both of the court and of the governing law by the parties is advisable.

Selection of the governing law is routine in the negotiation of international contracts in Japan. Each party is apt to prefer his own law and the issue is often resolved by the relative stubbornness or bargaining positions of the parties, although there is a tendency to use the law of the place that has the highest degree of involvement with those elements of the transaction which have legal ramifications. For example, simple licenses of Japanese patents normally provide for Japanese governing law because of a common-sense acceptance by foreign licensors of the fact that Japanese law really ought to determine the primary relationships in this kind of an agreement. However, in many situations there are no clearly discernible criteria as to the national law that must or properly should govern.

1. The Law in Japan. Freedom to select a governing law ultimately depends on the legal rules prevailing in the forum where a suit is brought. Most countries, including Japan, allow a substantial degree of party autonomy as to this detail in international contracts.

The basic Japanese choice-of-law statute permits contracting parties to choose the governing law.[117] Some Japanese scholars take the view that the scope of this choice must be limited to countries that have a

117. *Hōrei* (Law concerning the application of law) art. 7 (Law No. 10, 1898), in 1 EHS No. 1001: "The intention of the parties shall determine what law will govern the creation and effect of a juristic act.

(2) If the intention of the parties is uncertain, the law of the place of acting shall govern."

reasonable relation to the contract (such as the nationality of the contracting party, the place of performance, or the place of contracting) and that a choice of governing law which has no real contact with the agreement should not be permitted or accepted by a Japanese court.[118] The preponderance of Japanese scholarly opinion is to the contrary.[119]

In theory, the selection of a particular body of law must not conflict with Japanese public policy.[120] This principle has frequently been applied in the area of family law,[121] but has not been extended to other areas.[122]

Writers agree, however, that the parties can select the law of only one legal system to govern the contract, since formation (*seiritsu*) and effect (*kōryoku*) are inseparably combined with each other.[123]

An additional problem that can arise is whether a choice of governing law refers to the whole law of the designated country, including its conflicts principles, or only to its internal law. This detail should be clarified in the contract. If no designation is made, *Hōrei*, art. 7 may refer only to the internal substantive law of the designated country.[124] This approach does, of course, prevent *renvoi* problems. This gives the impression that there is no *renvoi* problem in Japan. In contract this is true, but in family and capacity matters art. 29 of *Hōrei* provides for *renvoi*.

2. The Law in the United States. In this area the answers must be found in decisions that have an unfortunate tendency to vary in language and outcome with the facts, the time when the case was decided, and the jurisdiction. There are courts in which a properly prepared governing-law clause will be sustained, and this is the really

118. Y. Orimo, Kokusai Shihō (International private law) 92, in 60 Hōritsusgaku Zenshū (1959).

119. S. Ikehara, supra note 30, at 374.

120. *Hōrei* art. 30: "Where the law of a foreign country is applicable (according to the preceding article 7), it will not be applied if its provisions are contrary to public order and good morals."

121. Arakawa v. Santos, 9 Kakyū minshū 1261 (Tokyo Dist. Ct., July 10, 1958); Ōtani v. Crain, 8 Kakyū minshū 340 (Tokyo Dist. Ct., Feb. 20, 1957).

122. *But see* George v. International Air Service, 16 Rōdō reishū 308, Hanrei jihō (No. 408) 14 (Tokyo Dist. Ct., April 24, 1965). In this case, Japanese labor law was applied in the face of an employment-contract term calling for the application of California law. The court held that the international common nature of most areas of private law does not exist in the labor field. Consequently, public policy was used to restrict the application of *hōrei* art. 7.

123. H. Egawa, Kokusai Shihō (International private law) 219 (1963). This view would prevent naming the laws of Japan to govern aspects where those laws are desirable and naming the laws of another country to govern other aspects.

124. Statements in Hasegawa, *Gaikokuhō no tekiyō to saibansho* (Application of foreign laws and the courts), in 1 Kokusai Shihō Kōza 215, 233–34 (1953), seem to support this position.

important fact. To insure effectiveness, select the right jurisdiction.

In general, the approach to be expected in earlier cases was a conflicts approach. Every problem was classified, and then, depending upon the classification, the appropriate conflict of laws rule was applied. For instance, in determining the law that governed a contract, the law of the country or state where the contract was made controlled, and that law governed the validity of the contract as well as its effectiveness and interpretation. Moreover, in choice of law problems, the autonomy of the parties was limited. The courts maintained the view that parties to a contract could not do a legislative act and therefore could not specify law in a contract. The courts seemed jealous of their area of control and seemed to view substitution of foreign law as an attempt to subvert the power of the courts.[125] These decisions are useful both as a background for the development of more sensible rules in recent cases and because this approach is still used to a certain extent.

The modern trend is to avoid automatic use of rules based on an initial formal classification and to choose the law in relation to the substance of the particular transaction. An example is the "grouping of contacts" or "center of gravity" theory. Under this approach the place of contracting is but one factor to be considered in determining which law should be applied. All other contacts relevant to the transaction, such as the actualities of the transaction and the intent of the parties, are also considered. Choice by the parties of the law that is to govern is viewed more as a contracting function than as a legislative or court-ousting one. This view and the trend toward attaching more weight to the intent of the parties greatly increases party autonomy. Fortunately, the more modern and flexible approach is being taken in most of the states having greater commercial importance.

However, there are still, in the United States as a whole, numerous limitations on party autonomy. In some jurisdictions, the traditional classification approach, already mentioned, operates to limit autonomy. Procedure versus substance is still a widely used classification, and courts will apply the law of the forum to matters felt to be procedural, ignoring a contrary choice of law clause. There is an obvious limitation on autonomy if a statute or treaty invalidates a governing-law clause. Public policy, a concept used to avoid enforcing a foreign law repugnant to the forum country, is another limitation sometimes invoked to defeat such a clause. The public-policy doctrine is sometimes used to justify a court's application of a local law it prefers.

125. A. Ehrenzweig, Conflicts in a Nutshell 134 (1965); E. Gerli & Co. v. Cunard S.S. Co., 48 F.2d 115, 117 (1931).

The most often observed limitation is the requirement that there be a reasonable contact between the transaction and the chosen law. For this approach there is a plausible theory. The parties may choose the law of a particular place only if there is a logical and good faith reason for choosing that law.[126]

The difficulty in proving foreign law[127] that has already been observed makes it important to select not only a governing law but also a particular forum. In other words, it is not enough to designate the law, for example, of New York. It is also desirable to limit jurisdiction to the courts of New York.

VI. Remedies in Japan

A. Laws

1. Law of Contract. The Civil Code came into force in 1898. Chapter II of Book III deals with contracts; formation, effect, and cancellation of contracts and special provisions for several types of contracts are mentioned therein. Book III deals with obligations in general, including contract, and the general provisions of Chapter I are also relevant. The Civil Code was originally drafted by a French lawyer,[128] and naturally his model was the French Civil Code. While this draft was being debated, the first draft of the German Civil Code was published in 1888, and, because of its logical clarity, the Japanese Civil Code was redrafted incorporating the structure of the German Civil Code, while still keeping some of the elements of the original draft.[129] Contract law has basically remained the same since the first code enactment;[130] thus its basic concepts are from the continental legal system (and especially German law) rather than from the Anglo-American legal system.

126. Siegelman v. Cunard White Star, Ltd., 221 F.2d 179 (1959); Tsakomtes v. Transpacific Carriers Corp., 368 F.2d 426 (1966); Lauritzen v. Larsen, 345 U.S. 571 (1953). Uniform Commercial Code §1–105 also requries a reasonable contact.

127. *See* Chinchilla v. Foreign Tankship Corp., 91 N.Y.S. 2d 213 (1949), where Panamanian law, which was specified in the employment contract, was not applied in a suit for damages for breach of employment, because that law was not adequately proved.

128. "Gustave Boissonade, who came to Japan in November 1873 and began to teach French law in 1874, was an outstanding figure. He was interested in natural law and lectured on that subject as well as on more technical subjects. In his days the *école d'exégèse* was still dominant in France in the field of private law; the 'revival of natural law' in France, which took place at the close of the century, was not yet underway. Boissonade may have read Ahrens' *Cours de droit naturel*, which was first published in 1837 and ran through many editions; and, as is shown by his *Le nouveau code civil italien comparé au doce Napoleon*, published in 1868, he had some interest in *législation comparée* before he came to Japan. However, his other works from this period indicate that his main interest lay in the historical aspects of various private law institutions. Judging from his previous publications, one would suppose that he was a positivist interested in history. . . ." A. von Mehren, Law in Japan 27–28 (1964).

129. For further details, *see* 1 Chūshaku Mimpō, *supra* note 44, at 15–21.

130. In contrast, Books IV and V of the Civil Code, which deal with family relationship and succession, have been completely amended since World War II.

Under Japanese law, a license agreement is a contract. The features of Japanese contract law pertinent to the present discussion are these:

1. In general, the parties are free to make any contract not in conflict with public order or good morals.[131] In the case of international license agreements, this principle may be ameliorated by the provisions of the Foreign Investment Law,[132] the Foreign Exchange and Foreign Trade Control Law, and the administrative conditions for approval imposed by the governmental agencies that examine agreements. Formerly, the Ministry of International Trade and Industry (MITI) intervened in virtually every aspect of international licenses. For example, it would decree that royalty rates of 10 percent were too high and should be reduced to a stated rate, or that a fifteen-year term of agreement was too long and should be shortened to ten or seven years. However, because of the campaign for "liberalization," true freedom of contract is now possible in this type of agreement, although administrative guidance is occasionally issued in exceptional circumstances. The Fair Trade Commission especially has become more active in reviewing and requesting revision of international license agreements.

2. Neither consideration nor cause is required for the formation of a contract under Japanese law.[133]

3. Save for exceptions[134] that do not include license agreements, a writing is not required for the formation of a contract. An oral license contract is as effective as a written one. Moreover, lawsuits are tried by career judges without juries,[135] and there are no rules of evidence, such as the parol evidence rule, to restrict the admissibility of evidence in court.[136]

131. CIVIL CODE art. 90: "A juristic act which has for its object such matters as are contrary to public policy or good morals is null and void."

132. *Gaishi ni kansuru hōritsu* (Foreign investment law) (Law No. 163, 1950), in 5 EHS No. 5410. The Foreign Investment Law is a special law in relation to *Gaikoku Kawase oyobi gaikoku bōeki kanrihō* (Law concerning foreign exchange and foreign trade control) (Law No. 228, 1949), in 5 EHS No. 5010.

133. This is a startling concept for common-law lawyers, who cannot conceive of a contract without consideration. However, it is just as startling to Japanese lawyers to find that consideration is an essential element for the existence of a contract under common law, since in Japan offer and acceptance is all that is needed to form a valid contract. Thus, in Japan there can be contracts that have only a unilateral obligation or are gratuitous. 5(1) S. WAGATSUMA, MIMPO KOGI, *supra* note 44, at 49–50 (1954).

134. For instance, a lease agreement concerning farm land (*Nōchihō*) (Agricultural land law) art. 25 (Law No. 229, 1952) and a building construction agreement (*kensetsugyōhō*) (Construction business law) art. 19 (Law No. 100, 1949) must be in writing.

135. One rationale for this approach is that since the judge must try both fact and law and in addition to his legal training should be skilled in perceiving such things as hearsay, there is not the same need for strict rules of evidence as there may be in countries where a jury composed of laymen is used.

136. *See* H. KANEKO, MINJI SOSHOHO TAIKEI, *supra* note 14, at 275–76.

A license agreement between a foreign licensor and a Japanese licensee must, however, be in written form for submission to the government in order to obtain approval of the license.[137] Japanese courts may nevertheless find additional terms in such agreements on the basis of verbal discussions conducted either before or after the execution of the license agreement.

4. Even if there is a breach by nonperformance or anticipatory repudiation, a contract will continue to be effective and binding on both parties during the specified term of the contract, unless it is rescinded by a party who has proper grounds.

5. The primary remedy for breach is "specific performance,"[138] but this remedy is not known by that name in the United States because the court's order will not be enforced by contempt proceedings and the claimant will often end up with only a money award.[139] The details are discussed below.

2. *Patent Law.* In patent licenses, as opposed to know-how licenses, remedies are also available to the licensor under the patent law. After termination of the license, the former licensor as a patentee has recourse against the former licensee whose use of the patent during the time of the license agreement exceeded the scope of the license. Theoretically, he may bring a patent infringement action.[140] The details are discussed below.

B. Remedies

1. Specific performance. One of the remedies for a breach of contract is specific performance,[141] a proceeding in which the injured party will obtain a judgment ordering the defaulting party to perform as he promised. There is no special requirement (such as inadequacy of damages) for a court action seeking this remedy. In a license transaction it is sufficient for the licensor to prove the license and the breach. A negative covenant, that is, a promise not to do something—for example, not to reveal secret technology—will be specifically enforced as readily as will an affirmative one.[142]

The enforcement procedures for a judgment for specific performance are not adequate. Disobedience is not punishable by contempt proceedings. The court can either allow the judgment-obligee to do

137. *Gaishi ni kansuru hōritsu shikō kisoku* (Enforcement regulation for the foreign investment law) art. 3(2) (Gaishi Iinkai Regulation No. 2, 1950), in 5 EHS No. 5430.

138. Civil Code art. 414(1).

139. Civil Code art. 545.

140. *Tokkyohō* (Patent law) art. 100(1) (Law No. 121, 1959), in 6 EHS No. 6850A.

141. Note 138 *supra*.

142. Forseco Japan Ltd. v. Okuno et al., Hanrei-Jihō (No. 624) 78 (Nara Dist. Ct. Oct. 23, 1970).

the act himself and require the judgment-obligor to reimburse the expenses,[143] or order the judgment-obligor to pay damages for his nonobservance.[144] The former course is often not practical because the obligee is not able to do the act.

There have been very few recorded cases involving specific performance and none in which the breach was of a license agreement. Thus, the amount of evidence required to prove noncompliance with the judgment and the standard for determining the amount of damages are not clear.[145] If the licensee's damages-exposure is only moderate, he has little incentive to obey a specific performance judgment. This remedy is unsatisfactory for another reason. Complicated procedures are necessary in order to recover a money award for expenses or penalties from the defendant's property through execution procedures.[146]

Specific performance is also a remedy for a breach of license involving infringement of a patent and has in that area the same drawbacks. Injunction against an infringer is also possible and is more often sought than are damages,[147] since damages are difficult to prove.[148] An injunction is not easily enforced if the defendant decides to resist, but normally the order will be observed voluntarily.

Additional remedies against infringement are provided under the patent law, and these are more particularly discussed below under "Infringement of Patent." Of particular interest is an order directing the destruction of infringing products or facilities used in infringement.[149] The impression of the authors is that a court tends to be more willing to issue such orders for patent infringement than for breach of contractual obligations. Products or facilities can be destroyed by the judgment-obligee without waiting for the judgment-

143. CCP art. 733.

144. CCP art. 734.

145. If strict evidence must be presented, it would amount to a retrial.

146. Fortunately, ordinary people are not daring enough to defy judgments, and usually the plaintiff expects the defendant to voluntarily obey the court order once the judgment is given. In the case of a breach of a license agreement, since licensees are usually big corporations in Japan, they are expected to obey the court's decision to avoid injuring their reputation.

147. M. Miyake & H. Takura, Kōgyō shoyūkenhō gairon (Outline of industrial property right law) 436 (1968).

148. *Id.* at 444–45.

149. *Tokkyohō* art. 100(2):

> A patentee or an exclusive licensee may, at the time of making the demand under the provisions of the preceding paragraph, demand any act necessary for the prevention of infringement such as the destruction of things constituting the act of infringement (including any thing created from the act of infringement in the case of a patented invention of process to produce things) and removal of facilities used for the act of infringement.

obligor's action.[150] Patent infringement is also a criminal offense,[151] and, although the police and the public procurator's office are usually reluctant to treat patent infringement as a criminal case because of its intricacy, the risk of criminal punishment could provide an effective deterrent against infringement after injunction.

2. *Damages.* The principle followed in Japan as to claims for damages is little different from the common law rule laid down in *Hadley* v. *Baxendale*.[152] The injured party can request the monetary value that would have been realized if there had been no breach or infringement. However, there must be a reasonable relationship between the cause (breach, infringement) and the effect (damage), and claims for disproportionate damages the defaulting party could not have foreseen are generally not granted.[153] The defendant is liable for damages only if his default or infringement was intentional or negligent.[154] The theoretical burden of proof, as to the absence of intention or negligence, is in practice gradually being shifted to the defendant by court decisions.[155] In patent infringement, negligence is presumed by statute (art. 103 of the patent law).

The types of damages to which a licensor is entitled are actual loss, lost profits, and incidental expenses.[156]

150. CCP art. 733.

151. *Tokkyohō* art. 196:

(1) Any person who has infringed a patent right or an exclusive license shall be punished by penal servitude for not more than five years or by a fine of not more than five hundred thousand yen.

(2) Any person who has infringed the right under Article 52 paragraph 1 shall, in case the establishment of said patent right has been registered, be punished by penal servitude for not more than five years or by a fine of not more than five hundred thousand yen. (3) The offense under the preceding two paragraphs shall be considered upon accusation.

152. 9 Exch. 341, 96 Rev. Rep. 742 (Exch. 1854).

153. CIVIL CODE art. 416: "(1) A demand for damages has for its object the reparation by the obligor of such damage as would ordinarily arise from the non-performance of an obligation. (2) The obligee may demand compensation also for damage which has arisen through special circumstances, if the parties have foreseen or could have foreseen such circumstances." *See* S. WAGATSUMA, MIMPO KOGI, supra note 44, at 118, 147.

154. CIVIL CODE art. 415; S. WAGATSUMA, MIMPŌ KŌGI, *supra* note 44, at 105, 145.

155. 4 S. WAGATSUMA, MIMPŌ KŌGI, supra note 44, at 105, 146.

156. In connection with item (c), it should be pointed out that the court does not consider lawyer's fees a reimbursable cost of the action. H. KANEKO, MINJI SOSHOHO TAIKEI, *supra* note 14, at 360; however, 4 S. WAGATSUMA, MIMPŌ KŌGI, supra note 44, at 126 maintains that lawyer's fees should be claimed as a part of the damages. In Lin v. Uchiyama, HANREI JIHŌ (No. 548) 19 (Sup. Ct., P.B., Feb. 27, 1969), the Supreme Court for the first time held that the lawyer's fees which the injured party in a wrongful act incurred in bringing an action against the wrongdoer for the protection of his, the injured party's, interests may be claimed as damages and that there is a reasonable relationship betewen the wrong and such damages. The case involved a public auction of immovables which the defendant initiated on the basis of an already invalidated mortgage registration. The court did not find that the defendant knew that the

In addition to the fact that lost profits of a licensor present difficult problems of calculation, a damage action in Japan is probably more difficult than one in the United States. First, there are no punitive damages for breach of contract or patent infringement. Only actual damages are compensated.[157] Secondly, the plaintiff must specify the exact amount of damages in the complaint and must prove them during the course of the trial by satisfactory evidence.[158] Although the plaintiff may amend the amount of damages after filing the complaint,[159] he must explain the basis for his estimate in the complaint and prepare minimum evidence that must be filed at the initial stage of the trial, thus making damage actions very difficult.[160]

There are procedures in the course of the trial whereby the defendant may be required to produce his books. These statutory procedures overlap those of the Commercial Code,[161] the Code of Civil Procedure,[162] and the patent law.[163] However, in practice, the court is reluctant to order a defendant to produce his books for fear that he may have to disclose unrelated trade secrets. Since a civil court does not usually pursue a defendant's perjury or forgery, there can be no assurance that the defendant will actually produce original, true, and correct records.

The plaintiff may find it necessary to disclose his production costs

mortgage registration was without substance, but he had initiated the public auction procedure. The court said that the defendant was at least negligent in not knowing that the mortgage registration was an empty one and held that initiating such public auction under the circumstances constituted a wrongful act and that there is a reasonable relationship between the disbursement of lawyer's fees (damages) which was required for bringing an action against the defendant for cancellation of the mortgage registration and the initiation of the public auction. In automobile injury cases and pollution cases, it is now common for the injured plaintiff to include lawyer's fees in his claim, but such practice is not seen in patent infringement cases, although the damage claim is based on the same tort theory. Probably it is due to the plaintiff's selfrestraint. Some day it may become common to ask for lawyer's fees in patent cases too. An action for breach of a license agreement is a contractual claim and lawyer's fees will not be allowed, at least at the present time.

157. 4 S. Wagatsuma, Mimpō Kōgi, *supra* note 44, at 117–18.

158. H. Kaneko, Minji soshōhō taikei, *supra* note 14, at 170. The court cannot render a judgment which leaves the amount of damages open and orders the defendant to submit his books and records for the court master to calculate the amount of damages after the judgment.

159. CCP art. 232.

160. For example, the plaintiff may need to state the quantity of sales by the defendant.

161. Commercial Code art. 35.

162. CCP art. 311; CCP art. 313, "A motion applying for production of a document shall clearly indicate the following matters: (i) Indication of the document; (ii) Gist of the document; (iii) The holder of the document; (iv) The fact to be proved; (v) The ground of obligation for production of the document."

163. Tokkyohō art. 105.

and sales expenses in order to prove his lost profits and might prefer to withdraw the action rather than disclose such information to the defendant and to the public through open hearings. Under such circumstances, determination of the amount of damages depends very much on the attitudes of the particular court and the particular defendant. Recognizing such difficulties, the patent law offers, in addition to the ordinary damages of the patentee, the two other alternative measures of the profits of the infringer and a reasonable royalty (art. 103, I and II). Although these additional measures are helpful, the above-mentioned difficulties have not been completely solved. Measurement and proof of damages or the alternative bases for payment must be carefully handled in each case.

Still more difficulties arise in Japan after a judgment is obtained. The Japanese law on execution of judgments is probably the most liberal in the world, from the perspective of the debtor. Civil procedures and criminal procedures are clearly distinguished and a civil court will not put the judgment-debtor into prison even if he disobeys an order of the court. If the judgment is for money, the judgment-creditor may attach the defendant's property and recover by selling the property through public auction. Fortunately, however, judgments in patent infringement cases have been voluntarily observed, as mentioned before, probably because the defendants are big companies and consider their reputation more than legal techniques.

3. Cancellation of license. One of the remedies available for breach of contract, cancellation of the license,[164] is often the only realistic solution for its breach. The license ends when the act of cancellation has been completed.[165] The injured party will demand performance and set a reasonable time within which the defaulter can cure. Cancellation occurs upon noncompliance. A license agreement, if well drafted, will provide for termination by the injured party in the event of breach.

Cancellation is not a condition to a suit for damages,[166] but it is common practice to cancel the contract if the injured party intends to seek damages in order to avoid an argument that in bad faith, he permitted the contract to continue.

164. CIVIL CODE art. 541, "If one of the parties does not perform his obligation, the other party may fix a reasonable period and give a peremptory notice demanding its performance, and may rescind the contract, if no performance is effected within such period."; CIVIL CODE art. 543, "If performance becomes impossible in whole or in part by any cause for which the obligor is responsible, the obligee may rescind the contract."

165. CIVIL CODE art. 541–545.

166. 4 S. WĀGATSUMA, MIMPŌ KŌGI, *supra* note 44, at 112.

C. Details according to the Types of Breach

1. Nonpayment of royalties. Procedurally, this is the easiest type of action, since a license agreement always expressly states the standard by which royalties will be computed. Monetary judgments are comparatively easy to enforce. If royalties are based on sales, the licensor must, of course, prove the sales figures.[167] To do this he will usually have to inspect the licensee's records. A right to inspect should be provided in the license agreement. If the licensee refuses to allow inspection, the licensor can ask a court to order the defendant not to resist inspection, or make a rough estimate and request the production of records in the course of the damage action.[168]

2. Manufacture of Competitive Products. Whether a licensor can prohibit the licensee from handling competitive products is a delicate problem under the Japanese antimonopoly law.[169] Here we are assuming cases in which such a provision can be lawfully included. "Competitive products" means products having a use or application so similar to the products to be produced under the license that the two products compete with each other in the consumer market. If competitive products are manufactured by a licensee, he is not apt to market the licensed products as vigorously as he otherwise would, and thus may ultimately strengthen a competitor, all to the serious injury of the licensor.

If the licensed product is covered by a patent, competitive products may infringe it. If so, the remedies provided by the patent act for

167. This is simple if the licensee's products are a type registered with some government agency or trade association such as pharmaceuticals. *See Yakujihō* (Pharmaceutical law) Ch. 4 (Law No. 145, 1960).

168. In the writers' opinion, the licensor must first consider the possibility of resorting to the procedure called "preservation of evidence," discussed in notes 206–11 and accompanying text *infra*.

169. [Whether a license shall forbid the handling by the licensee of competitive products is a problem to be carefully examined in light of the anti-monopoly law. For instance,] the Fair Trade Commission's guidelines provide that "Among the restrictions which are liable to come under unfair business practices in international licensing agreements" is "(3) To restrict the licensee from manufacturing, using or selling goods, or employing technology which are in competition with the licensed subject." *Kokusaiteki gijitsu donyu keiyaku ni kansuru nintei kijun* (Antimonopoly act guidelines for international licensing agreements) art. I(3) (Kosei Torihiki Iinkai, May 24, 1968), in Kosei Torihiki Iinkai, Nintei kijun no kaisetsu (Commentary on Guidelines) 130 (1968) [hereinafter cited as Licensing Guidelines]. The guidelines provide for the exception as follows: "However, such cases are excluded where the licensor grants an exclusive license and imposes no restriction on goods already being manufactured, used or sold, or technology already being utilized by the licensee." So far, the authors' impression is that the Fair Trade Commission has been literally sticking to the criterion and the exception in reviewing international license agreements ex post facto. However, the commission has become accustomed to the exercise of power and may adopt a more severe attitude toward restrictions on competitive activities.

ordinary patent infringement are available. However, if the licensor has no patent and wants to restrict the licensee's manufacture of competitive products, the draftsman faces a severe test of his skill. Serious basic problems are description of the conduct that will violate the covenant and drafting to take into consideration remedy problems that can develop. If the licensor sues for breach, specific enforcement is available, though it is not an effective weapon in Japan.[170] Destruction of competitive products currently in the licensee's hands is a useful remedy,[171] but this remedy, like remedies in general in this type of situation, requires that the covenant on which the licensor must rely impair freedom of enterprise, and thus he must expect a court to interpret it narrowly.

For breach of a covenant not to manufacture competitive products, damages will probably be claimed on the theory that the licensee should pay royalty on the products wrongfully sold, at the rate set in the license for licensed products. Whether he will succeed in persuading a court that this is a proper damage measure is uncertain. There may be difficulty in establishing the necessary causal relationship. The licensee can argue that he sold the competitive products because of their superior quality, or that the licensed products could not for any of a variety of reasons have been sold even had the competitive products not been sold.

3. Sales Outside the Agreed Territory. If a licensee wrongfully sells outside the licensed territory[172] and in a country where the licensor has a patent, the licensor will be protected by his patent,[173] as well as

170. There is one district court temporary injunction decision, in which one of the writers was involved, prohibiting retired employee's competition based on his covenant not to compete within two years after the retirement. (Y. K. Foseco Japan Limited v. Okuno et al, Nara Dist. Ct. October 23, 1970 624 HANREI JIHŌ 78).

171. *See* notes 147–50 and accompanying text *supra*.

172. This is another kind of license term which involves the anti-monopoly law. *Shiteki doknsen no kinshi oyobi kōsei torihiki no kaknho ni kansuru hōritsu* (Law relating to the Prohibition of Private Monopoly and Methods of Preserving Fair Trade) [hereinafter cited as Anti-Monopoly Law] art. 6 (Law No. 54, 1947), in 2 EHS No. 2284.

173. Licensing Guidelines, *supra* note 169, at art. I(1). "To restrict the area to which the licensee may export the goods covered by patent rights, etc. (hereinafter referred to as patented goods). However, cases coming under a, b, or c listed below are excluded: (a) In case the licensor has patent rights, etc. which have been registered in the area to which the licensee's export is restricted (hereinafter referred to as the restricted area); (b) In case the licensor is selling patented goods in the restricted area in his normal business; (c) In case the licensor has granted to a third party an exclusive license to sell in the restricted area." Art. II says that the aforementioned guidelines shall apply to international know-how licensing agreements. Accordingly, even though the licensor has no patents in other countries, sales of the licensed product by the licensee may still be restricted if the licensor is selling the licensed product in such area or if there is an exclusive licensee there. So far, the Fair Trade Commission's policy does not seem to have changed, but we cannot predict its future attitude.

by the license. In the absence of a patent, the licensor will have to find his remedy in the law governing the license or in the enforcement of the terms of the license. None of the legal remedies is apt to be satisfactory, and the best protection will probably be found in a well-drafted termination clause.

Injunction against infringement by unlicensed sales is complicated by various problems compounded by the geographic complexities. Subterfuge and evasive tactics can be expected of a licensee determined to continue his wrongful conduct. Mustering the evidence of violations of the injunction will often be difficult. At best, injunction is not a very forceful weapon in Japan.

Damage claims will turn on the quantity of goods sold outside the licensed territory, and the necessary data may be hard to assemble. If the licensor does not sell in the restricted area or have a licensee there, he may find that he cannot prove he actually lost anything.

4. *Unauthorized disclosure of confidential information*. Japan has no statute protecting unpatented technical information, and so no statutory remedies such as are available for patent infringement exist.[174] The license must be drafted so as to provide the necessary protection for the licensor.

The threshold clause will recite a carefully worded covenant by the licensee not to divulge the information save as authorized by the license. For violation of this covenant the usual contract remedies will be available, the most useful perhaps being cancellation. Damages will usually be difficult to prove, and the right to damages will accordingly be more theoretical than practical. On the theory that sales by the competitor to whom the information was wrongfully divulged have replaced sales of the licensed products, the licensor may assert a claim to royalties measured by such sales. If the competitor committed a tort in obtaining the information the licensor can also sue him for this wrongful act.[175]

5. *Use of know-how after termination of agreement*. It was for some years the policy of the Japanese Ministry of International Trade and Industry (MITI) to require the deletion of provisions denying to a licensee a right to use know-how after expiration of the license. In MITI's view, the purpose of the license agreement was to buy the know-how, and, unless the technique was covered by patents, provisions that required the licensee to cease using the know-how after the expiration of the

174. The legal nature of know-how or confidential information is discussed in text accompanying notes 212–18 *infra*.

175. However, he may not demand the discontinuance of manufacture by the competitor because of the limitation of remedies available to the wrongful act (*see* notes 212–18 and accompanying text *infra*).

agreement were not permissible.[176] However, there have been changes in governmental policy since the liberalization of technological assistance agreements announced by the government in 1968 and the content of such provisions is now left to the parties.

Know-how problems in the post-termination period may be divided into several categories in Japan. A general improvement in the technical skill of the licensee's employees during the license period cannot be prohibited by any other means. However, exact copying of the licensor's product is another matter. Although it is doubtful whether an act of product-simulation can be enjoined under the Unfair Competition Prevention Law,[177] it seems certain that appropriate provisions can effectively be incorporated into the license.[178] Between these two extremes, the obviously improper and obviously proper conduct, there are all manner of subtle nuances. For example, the former licensee may continue to use the licensor's techniques and yet not make identical or even nearly identical products.

This difficult area is more fully discussed in the chapter on license drafting.[179] One obvious solution is to permit the continued use of know-how after termination,[180] with appropriate safeguards. At the other pole is a flat prohibition against use, with the anticipation that the threat of injunction or damages will insure compliance, an expectation that may or may not be justified.

In the gray area between employee-skill-improvement and outright copying, there is also room for drafting calculated to obviate the risk of dispute. The parties can agree that particular kinds of conduct are or are not to be deemed use of the technical information received by the licensee during the license period.

6. *Bankruptcy of the licensee.* If a Japanese licensee becomes bankrupt, the licensor must present his royalty claim to the bankruptcy court.[181] His more serious problems are recovery of documents evidencing his

176. *See* K. Osumi, Gijutsu Teikei (Technical cooperation) 161 *et seq*, in 11 Keiei Hōgaku Zenshū (1967).

177. *Fusei kyōsō bōshihō* (Unfair competition prevention law) (Law No. 14, 1934), in 6 EHS No. 6895.

178. K. Ōsumi, Gijutsu Teikei, *supra* note 175, at 162. *see also* D. Nagata, Gijutsu Enjo Keiyaku (Technical assistance agreements) 268 (1962); Nagai & Noguchi, Gijutsu enjo keiyaku no jissai (Practice in technical assistance agreement) 241 (1967).

179. Woodward and Matsuo, *supra*. I.

180. It will be interesting and beneficial to the bar to see the decision, if a licensee's attempt to keep his business going after termination of the license, by making similar products but not identical ones, is litigated. The court probably will sustain a covenant against continued use of know how, but in determining whether the licensor's know how is in fact incorporated in the product sold by the licensee after the agreement there is much room for discretion. The court will be hesitant to order a shut-down of the Japanese licensee's plant to enforce the contract.

181. *Hasanhō* (Bankruptcy law) art. 228 (Law No. 71, 1922), in 2 EHS No. 2340.

technology and disposition of licensed products in the bankrupt's inventory. These are details for which the law makes inadequate provision. Detailed drafting solutions should be attempted. Termination of the license in the event of the licensee's bankruptcy is a minimum license-agreement provision and is routinely used. A right to protect the licensor's interest in licensed products is more difficult. The licensor will want to avoid distress sales that might disrupt the market and sales of goods not up to standard. Insolvency problems are more fully discussed in the chapter on license drafting.[182]

7. *Merger.* Merger is an increasingly common phenomenon in Japan, yet the relation between merger and licenses continues to be chaotic under Japanese law. If a Japanese licensee wants to merge, it may find that the prospective merger partner is in the same business field and already has a license from a competitor of the licensor, or that it has its own techniques for making similar products. In theory, the surviving company acquires all of the rights and obligations of the merging companies, since there is no break in the legal-personality continuity.[183] In practice, when a license agreement is involved, the licensor may unexpectedly become the licensor of a bitter competitor or of a competitor's licensee, an embarrassing and difficult position. This problem is also considered in the chapter on license drafting, referred to above.

The legal situation apart from preagreed solutions is unsatisfactory. According to the Commercial Code, a "creditor" may object to a merger within a period fixed by the merging company. If there is an objection, the merging company pays or deposits collateral or places its assets in trust.[184] A law meant to protect creditors with existing monetary claims is quite inadequate in a license transaction. Even where the statute does apply, no one can predict what the court will regard as proper payment or collateral.[185] Just how a licensor can

182. Ordinarily, bilateral contracts are not automatically terminated, but the trustee has the option to cancel or to perform the duty on the part of the bankrupt. *Hasanhō* art. 59. This undoubtedly assumes an ordinary spot transaction, such as the sale of a particular product. In addition, the Civil Code makes the lessee's bankruptcy a cause for termination. Civil Code art. 621. Since a license is similar to a lease, this article of the Civil Code may be applicable; however, this is not certain, because a license agreement is also a bilateral contract. A bankrupt licensee will default on the contract because of nonpayment of royalty, but payment is usually made periodically, so the licensor must wait to confirm the default. Also, if the licensee files a petition for company reorganization, (similar to Chapter X of the Bankruptcy Act) the licensor's right to terminate may be restricted to the extent that the court thinks the licensed business is vital to the licensee's reorganization.

183. 1 T. Ishii, Shōhō (Commercial code) 492–93 (1956).

184. Commercial Code arts. 416, 100.

185. For such difficulties, see Shōji Hōmu Kenkyūkai (Commercial Law Center), Kaisha no Gappei to Bunkatsu (Merger and splitting of corporations) 112–13 (1966).

invoke the Commercial Code for his protection is exceedingly obscure.

D. INFRINGEMENT OF PATENT

After termination of a license and of the licensee's right to use a patent, continued use will be an infringement. So will use, during the license period, that goes beyond the use authorized in the license. Third parties in various relationships with the licensee may infringe. There are serious problems for which the legal remedies are those provided by the patent act or, if the license was properly drafted, by the license. An infringement action may or may not be a satisfactory way in which to attack the licensor's need for relief.[186]

As was indicated above, one remedy for infringement is injunction, with or without additional demands for the destruction of infringing products and of the facilities used in the infringement.[187] A claim for damages can be, but often is not, joined, as such a claim delays getting to a final judgment. Calculation of damages is always difficult, and evidence is often insufficient. The patentee is probably more concerned about stopping the infringement.

In addition to the damages recognized under the general principles of the Civil Code,[188] the patent law provides two measures of substitute damages: the profits of the infringer, and a reasonable royalty.[189]

Procedurally, in addition to the usual letter of warning and out-of-court negotiation, a patentee may take any or all of the following actions: ordinary lawsuit; preliminary injunction; preservation of evidence.

1. Ordinary lawsuit. In order to enjoin an infringer from permanently utilizing a patent, or to demand damages, the patentee must institute a lawsuit in a competent district court.[190] In Japan, the roles

186. Contrary to the breach of a license agreement, there are many court decisions on patent infringements; only characteristic points are dealt with here, leaving detailed discussions to other articles specifically dealing with this problem.

187. *Tokkyohō* art. 100.

188. CIVIL CODE art. 709 *et. seq.*

189. Tokkyohō art. 102:

> (1) If a patentee or an exclusive licensee demands of any person who has intentionally or by negligence infringed his patent right or exclusive license indemnification for damages incurred by such infringement, and such person has gained a profit by the act of infringement, the amount of such profit shall be presumed to be the amount of damages sustained by the patentee or exclusive licensee. (2) A patentee or an exclusive licensee may demand of any person who has intentionally or by negligence infringed his patent right or exclusive license indemnification for an amount corresponding to the amount of money normally obtainable for the working of such patented invention, as the amount of damages sustained by him. (3) The foregoing provisions shall not preclude a demand for damages exceeding such amount as is therein prescribed. In this case if there is no intention or gross negligence on the part of the person who has infringed a patent right or an exclusive license, the court may take it into account with respect to the fixing the amount of damages.

190. These suits differ from like suits in the United States in that the defendant cannot attack the validity of the patent. Yoshida v. Oi, 10 Keiroku 1679 (Gr. Ct. Cass., Sept. 15, 1904).

of the court and the patent office are differentiated; the patent office has the power to grant or to invalidate a patent,[191] and the judicial court has the power to decide the question of infringement.[192] If invalidity is an issue, the proper forum is the patent office. Therefore, the defendant interested in invalidating the patent must try to delay the court action until the invalidation proceeding in the patent office is concluded.[193] However, this tactic usually is not successful where a mere petition for invalidation is filed with the patent office.

In a patent infringement action, the techniques concerned are explained to the judges, sometimes at informal meetings, and impartial expert witnesses may be appointed by the court to give an opinion on the technical issues.[194]

2. *Preliminary Injunction.* One way to stop an infringer's manufacture, use, or sale is to sue, either for damages, an injunction, or both, but this is a lengthy process. It will take two or three or more years to obtain a judgment at the trial-court level on patent infringement. Therefore, it is not uncommon in patent cases to apply for a preliminary (temporary) injunction, a remedy that is one aspect of the so-called "Provisional Disposition Procedures" (*kari-shobun*), by which the court takes protective measures during the pendency of the suit.[195] A preliminary injunction is the strongest of the "provisional dispositions"; it rectifies temporarily the alleged wrong where the petitioner might be irreparably damaged by delay.[196] A lawsuit is always a theoretical prelude to a preliminary injunction, but in practice, a preliminary injunction can be obtained without the actual institution of a supporting lawsuit. Quite often, the dispute is settled by such an order without bringing suit at all.[197]

A temporary injunction not made permanent will have been injurious to the defendant who prevails in the final judgment, and a money

191. Tokkyohō arts. 66, 28, 123(1), 157.

192. JAPANESE CONST. art. 76; *Saibanshohō* art. 3; *Tokkyohō* arts. 105–06.

193. Tokkyohō art. 168(2).

194. M. MIYAKE & TAKURA, *supra* note 147, at 422–24; CCP art. 131. The Tokyo and Osaka District Courts have special sections for patent cases, but other courts have no such special section and the judges have practically no experience in patent cases. M. DOHIHARA, TOKKYO JITSUYŌSHINAN NI KANSURU KARISHOBUN NO KENKYŪ (Study on the provisional disposition involving patents and utility models) 1, in 20 SHIHŌ KENKYŪ HŌKOKUSHO (1968). Y. KUBOTA, *Tokkyo shingai to Karishobun* (Patent infringements and preliminary injunctions), 24 TOKKYO KAURI 1171 (1974). Even in the Tokyo and Osaka courts, one cannot expect a judge to have sufficient knowledge of the particular technical field concerned. Therefore, in patent suits, it is imperative for the plaintiff first to explain the nature of the case so that the judge may clearly understand the issue. This requires additional effort by the plaintiff patentee.

195. CCP art. 758.

196. CCP art. 760.

197. *See* M. DOHIHARA, *supra* note 193, at 10.

deposit is therefore required to compensate him for his losses.[198] The amount of the deposit is fixed by the court. There is no definite standard.[199] In theory, the deposit will be appropriated to cover the defendant's losses,[200] but in practice, once the order is entered, the infringer usually approaches the patentee for settlement, and the deposit is refunded with the infringer's consent.

A temporary injunction is granted on *prima facie* evidence (*somei*),[201] and in ordinary civil cases can be had in two or three days *ex parte*, that is, without a hearing at which the defendant can present his argument. In patent cases, however, it usually takes from three months to more than a year to get the order because of the inherent complexity of the situation, and in a very difficult case, the applicant may be asked by the court to institute an ordinary suit.[202]

The judgment in an ordinary suit will become operative only when the period for appeal has passed or when an appeal is rejected by the Supreme Court, but a preliminary injunction immediately stops the infringing activities.[203] The infringer can, of course, try to attack the order by arguing that no proper basis for it exists.[204] Or, if there are special circumstances that may cause him disproportionate losses, he may ask for its cancellation.[205]

Since a preliminary injunction is a temporary remedy for situations in which relief is urgently needed, an important part of the petitioner's case is a showing that the infringement will cause him irrecoverable losses if relief is delayed.[206]

3. Preservation of Evidence. The burden of proving that the infringer is manufacturing the infringing product or is using the infringing equipment or process rests with the patentee.[207] Therefore, the first

198. CCP arts. 756, 741.

199. *See* M. Dohihara, *supra* note 19, at 54.

200. CCP arts. 756, 741, 513, 113. Art. 113 reads, "The defendant has the same right as a pledgee in respect of court costs over the security so deposited in accordance with the preceding Article."

201. CCP arts. 756, 741.

202. *See* M. Dohihara, *supra* note 193, at 20. However, the manner in which court conducts temporary injunction cases varies from judge to judge. *See* Kubota.

203. CCP art. 749.

204. CCP art. 744.

205. CCP art. 759.

206. CCP art. 760. *See* note 195 *supra*.

207. CCP art. 343: "The court may, if it considers that there exist such circumstances as make the use of the evidence in question difficult unless examination thereof is made beforehand, conduct an examination of evidence, on motion, in accordance with the provisions of this Chapter."; CCP art. 345: "(1) The following matters shall be made clear in a motion for preservation of evidence: (i) Identification of parties; (ii) Facts to be proved; (iii) Evidence; (iv) Reason for preservation of evidence. (2) The reason for preservation of this evidence shall be explained."

thing the patentee must do is to ascertain what process or apparatus is being used by the infringer.[208] There is in Japan nothing like the discovery procedures used in the United States. The only comparable tactic is "preservation of evidence," and this is often resorted to by a patentee.[209] This procedure was originally designed to preserve evidence that might be lost, such as the testimony of a dying witness or inspection of perishable goods.[210] To get a court order that will enable him to cause an inspection to be made of the equipment being used by the suspected infringer, the patentee will state a plausible reason for preserving this evidence. Advance service on the opponent is not required, but some courts do serve notice shortly before the actual inspection.[211] The inspection is made by a judge and a court clerk accompanied by plaintiff's lawyers, and, occasionally, impartial experts. Since the procedure is conducted by the court, quite often the opponent will disclose its process or equipment, but in fact, this is not compulsory, and the patentee can do nothing if the opponent refuses.[212] In that case, the patentee must resort either to an ordinary suit or to a petition for a preliminary injunction based on his best guess about the opponent's equipment. Quite often it takes several days of hearings to ascertain the facts concerning the infringer's equipment or process.

E. Unauthorized Use of Know-How by a Third Party

"Know-how" traditionally has had no status in Japanese law.[213] However, many know-how license agreements have been made by Japanese in the last twenty-five years, and the area has finally become the subject of scholarly discussion. Still, so far as the authors are aware, there has been only one court decision dealing with the nature of know-how.[214] In the opinion of the court, although know-how has

208. This is often very difficult, because the process is exercised and the apparatus is situated in the infringer's factory, which is not open to the patentee.

209. M. Miyake & H. Takura, *supra* note 147, at 464.

210. H. Kaneko, Minji Soshō Takei, *supra* note 14, at 267.

211. M. Miyake & H. Takura, *supra* note 147, at 466.

212. *Id.* at 465. If the opponent is a small-scale company which has no retained lawyer, disclosure is likely, but if it is a major corporation which consults a lawyer specialized in patent cases, it usually refuses to allow the inspection.

213. K. Ōsumi, Gijutsu Teikei, *supra* note 175, at 31 *et seq.*

214. Deutsche Werft Aktiengesellschaft v. Chūetsu Waukesha Yūgen Kaisha, 17 Kakyū minshū 769 (Tokyo High Ct., Sept. 5, 1966). The Tokyo High Court rejected an appeal from the decision of the Tokyo District Court which rejected a petition for a preliminary injunction from respondent's manufacturing and selling a certain product. The grounds for the petition are not clear from the reports but it appears that the petitioner, a German corporation, had a know-how license agreement with an American company, whereby the licensee presumably was obligated not to manufacture and sell the licensed product in Japan. In spite of this promise, the American licensee

proprietary value, Japanese law does not provide a remedy for its protection as against third parties. Apparently, the owner of this kind of asset must protect himself by security measures.

This very conservative rule leaves open to the licensor only an action for breach of a promise not to disclose the know-how. The prevailing scholarly view seems to be that it the manner by which a third party acquires know-how is unlawful in itself, he should also be liable in tort for damages to the owner of the know-how.[215] The difficult point is that under Japanese law injunctions are not available for this situation.[216] Therefore, the licensor cannot ask the court to forbid the act of the wrong-doer and, even if the third party's act of acquiring the know-how was unlawful, it is unlikely that the court will enjoin the third party from using the know-how.[217]

Moreover, the court procedures are in principle open to the public and the owner will not want to disclose his know-how to the public. However, in order to win his case he must disclose it.[218]

Therefore, under present Japanese law, other than by termination of an agreement for breach, the owner of know-how will find it very difficult to obtain effective remedies from civil courts. The practical

incorporated a joint-venture company in Japan with a Japanese partner and had the joint-venture company manufacture and sell the product. According to the petitioner's contention, although the licensee owned only 45 percent of the joint-venture company, it had the controlling position in the company by virtue of the provisions in the joint-venture agreement. The Tokyo High Court stated that know-how undoubtedly has certain proprietary value but is not recognized as a legal right, that the licensee naturally had the obligation not to disclose the know-how acquired by the license agreement beyond the scope permitted by the agreement, that such obligation is a contractual obligation, and that the licensee who disclosed such know-how to third parties in violation of the agreement was responsible for damages under the contract law, but that the licensor cannot prohibit the use of know-how by a third party who has acquired the know-how from the licensee or otherwise. Concerning this case, see T. Doi, Kokusai Torihikihō Hanrei Kenkyū (The law of international transactions: comments on selected cases 137 (1967). *See also*, Foseco v. Okuno, *supra* note 170.

215. *See* 19 Chūshaku Mimpō 33 *et seq.* (I. Kato ed. 1965).

216. This theory may sound strange, but the remedies available to an injured person because of another's wrongful act are limited to damages. *See Id.* at 346 *et seq.*

217. That there is no injunction for a wrongful act is an established principle which would be a hard obstacle for lawyers to overcome. To grant an injunctive remedy for disclosure of know-how, we have to adopt a different approach; namely, to treat know-how as a "thing" comparable to ordinary real and personal property and to treat the right to know-how as "ownership." However, the fact that there can hardly be exclusive control over know-how because of its nature would cause Japanese lawyers to hesitate to adopt such an idea at present. K. Osumi, Gijutsu Teikei, *supra* note 175, at 31; M. Ono, Eigyō himitsu no hogo (Protection of trade secrets) 503–07 (1968).

218. M. Ono, *supra* note 216, at 453 *et seq.* Especially, know-how must be related to complicated techniques, and must be explained in detail to the judges for them to understand the case. If one resorts to a temporary injunction, the procedure is kept confidential. However, as the method of proof is limited in an injunction procedure, it is doubtful whether the court will grant a temporary injunction in matters concerning complicated techniques.

remedy probably is to file a complaint with the police or the public procurator's (district attorney's) office and have the wrongdoer criminally prosecuted.[219]

VII. Remedies in the United States

A. Laws

In a nation that has a federal system, there are two distinct bodies of law, state law and national law, and either can theoretically be relevant in a particular lawsuit. The Constitution of the United States empowers Congress to enact legislation for the protection of inventions,[220] and the First Congress enacted a patent act in accordance with this power.[221] Out of these beginnings grew the present federal patent legislation[222] under which the federal district courts have original and

219. Unlawful acquisition of another party's know-how usually involves physical transfer of samples, materials, products, or papers describing a secret formula, and such acts are considered to be theft or embezzlement and governed by the Criminal Code. CRIMINAL CODE art. 235, 252, 253. Recently, to the writers' knowledge, there have been three cases in which company employees sold a company's secrets to competitors. The employees and the persons who bought the information were arrested and indicted in the criminal court. Although the monetary value of the materials or papers themselves was small, the penalties were far higher than for ordinary thefts of things of similar value.

In Japan v. Teenchef, 7 Kakyū keishū 1319 (Tokyo Dist. Ct., June 26, 1965, the Tokyo District Court punished, among others, an employee of a printing company who copied secret records of the company using the company's copying machine and sold the copies to a competitor through an industrial spy. The court considered the crime as theft and not embezzlement, because the employee was not in a position to take custody of the records. The court also said that the object of the theft was not the copied papers but the copied records (a little unclear). The person who bought the records was punished for purchase of stolen property.

In another case, the Osaka District Court punished on the ground of embezzlement a former employee of a chemical company who at the time of his voluntary resignation took away a handful of products and a file of copies of research reports as souvenirs and later sold them to the company's competitor. In this case, the accused was a researcher and was in a position to take custody of the materials. HANREI JIHŌ (No. 494) 74 (Osaka Dist. Ct., May 31, 1967), name of the accused unreported.

In 1967, there was a famous industrial espionage scandal. A big synthetic fibre company bought secret drawings of a competitor's employees. Several persons including an officer of the company were arrested, and they are now being criminally prosecuted on the ground of theft, embezzlement, and purchase of stolen property. Under social pressure, this company has also given up the project of starting a new type of synthetic fibre, which was the purpose of buying the drawings. (Newspaper article in re Nihon Rayon). The official draft revision of the Criminal Code, which was finalized in 1974 by a special committee at the request of the Minister of Legal Affairs, contains a provision making unauthorized disclosure of trade secrets per se a punishable crime. However, in view of the revision's unpopularity, it is doubtful if it will be codified in its present form.

220. U.S. CONST. art. I, ¶9, cl. 8 reads as follows: "The Congress shall have the power . . . to promote the progress of science and useful arts, by securing for limited times to authors and inventors the exclusive right to the respective writings and discoveries."

221. *See* B. BUGBEE, THE GENESIS OF AMERICAN PATENT AND COPYRIGHT LAW (1967).

222. *See* WALKER ON PATENTS 72 *et seq.* (2d ed. A. Deller ed. 1964).

exclusive jurisdiction over the subject matter of suits testing the validity of patents.[223]

In a controversy arising out of a patent license, contract law rather than patent law governs. The applicable law may be that of a foreign country. Otherwise, it will be state rather than national law to which the court must look for answers. Such a controversy would not fall within federal subject-matter jurisdiction. The action is transitory rather than *in rem* and can be brought wherever service can be had, including a federal court, if diversity of citizenship between the parties exists and if at least $10,000 is in controversy. Even if the case is tried in the federal courts on the basis of diversity of citizenship, the law which will govern the substantive (versus the procedural) issues will be that of the state in which the contract law is applicable.[224]

B. Infringement Actions

Since the federal district courts have original and exclusive subject-matter jurisdiction over patent infringement claims,[225] infringement actions must be brought in the federal district court either (1) where the defendant resides, or (2) where the defendant has committed acts of infringement and has an established place of business.[226]

Trial in a damages case can be by either judge or jury,[227] but a jury is not available in an injunction procedure. Because of the technical nature of the subject matter, a jury trial will rarely merit serious consideration.

Remedies for patent infringement are statutory and include both damages[228] and an injunction against further infringement.[229] Damages will not be less than a reasonable royalty.[230]

Additional remedies are available in design patent cases,[231] where a reasonable royalty may be either an already established royalty or a judicial determination of what would be reasonable.[232] Additionally, it may be possible to use a percentage of the infringer's profits as a measure of damages[233] or, in a proper case, the plaintiff's lost busi-

223. 28 U.S.C. 1338 (1964).
224. Erie R.R. Co. v. Tompkins, 304 U.S. 64 (1938).
225. 28 U.S.C. §1338 (1964).
226. Free, *Infringement Suits*, Encyclopedia of Patent Practice and Invention Management 451 (R. Calvert ed. 1964); 28 U.S.C. 1400(b) (1964).
227. *See supra* note 225, at 456.
228. 35 U.S.C. §281 (1964).
229. *Id.* §283.
230. *Id.* §284.
231. *See* Craig, *Accounting After Infringement Suits—Damages*, Encyclopaedia of Patent Practice and Invention Management 7 (1964).
232. *Id.*
233. Ric-Wil Co. v. E.B. Kaiser Co., 179 F.2d 401 (1950).

ness.[234] Recent cases have denied claims that the infringer's profit should be the basis for damages and have instead asserted that the proper measure is the difference between the patentee's actual profit and what that profit would have been had the infringement not occurred.[235]

If infringement is conscious, deliberate, and willful, a court can treble the amount of damages. Interest will also be allowed under proper circumstances, and, if the patentee can show an established royalty, the interest runs from the time the royalty should have been paid. If the amount must be judicially determined, interest does not begin to run until payment on the judgment is in default.[236] The costs of the litigation will be charged to the losing party,[237] and attorney's fees can be awarded to the prevailing party.[238] One view, however, is that attorney's fees should be awarded only where there is evidence of unfairness or bad faith on the part of the losing party.[239]

If the infringement continues after a restraining order, the infringing party will be in contempt and subject to both civil and criminal penalties. Such an order can issue before the trial on the merits.[240]

This is in striking contrast to the Japanese practice. In Japan, there is no contempt procedure, since confinement of a defendant in a civil matter is thought to impair his fundamental personal rights. As a result of this principle, violation of a court order to perform a certain act can be enforced only by a monetary award.

Injunctive relief is also available in proper situations and is governed by the general principles of equity under which injunctive relief occurs within the discretion of the court.[241] Injunctions are difficult to obtain where there has not yet been infringement and the likelihood of future infringement is not clear.[242] Courts also generally insist that

234. 35 U.S.C. §284 (1964); Kreiger v. Colby, 106 F.Supp. 124 (1952).

235. Marvel Speciality Co. v. Bell Hosiery Mills, Inc., 386 F.2d 287, 155 (4th Cir. 1967), *cert denied*, 390 U.S. 1030 (1968); Georgia Pac. Corp. v. United States Plywood Corp., 243 F.Supp. 5003 (S.D.N.Y. 1965).

236. Swan Carburetor Co. v. Nash Motors Co., 133 F.2d 562 (1943).

237. FED. R. CIV. P. 54(d).

238. 35 U.S.C. §285 (1964).

239. Park-In Theatres v. Perkins, 190 F.2d 137 (1951); In Maxon Premix Burner Co. v. Mid-Continent Metal Prods. Co., 279 F.Supp. 164 (N.D. Ill. 1967), bad faith was presumed where the defendant knew of the plaintiff's patented device and manufactured and sold his copy without advice of counsel.

240. Chas. Pfizer & Co. v. Davis-Edwards Pharmaceutical Corp., 385 F.2d 533 (2nd Cir. 1967); Radiant Color Co. v. Switzer Bros., Inc., 261 F.Supp. 582 (N.D. Cal. 1966).

241. *See* Bagley, *Injunctions in Patent Cases*, in ENCYCLOPAEDIA OF PATENT PRACTICE AND INVENTION MANAGEMENT 464 (1964).

242. Gambrell & Kayton, *Patent Law in Perspective* (1967), 36 GEO. WASH. L. REV. 545, 579 (1968).

the validity of the patent be clearly established before a preliminary injunction will be issued.[243]

Another alternative is to petition for a declaratory judgment. This is a procedure whereby a party threatened with an infringement suit by a patentee can obtain advance relief in the form of an adjudication of their respective rights. There is statutory support for this remedy in the Federal Declaratory Judgment Act.[244] The petitioner must show a "justiciable controversy"[245] and must sue in a federal court inasmuch as the action arises under the patent laws of the United States.[246] It can be difficult to determine whether a justiciable controversy exists. The necessary elements are: "(1) actual or potential manufacture, use or sale by the plaintiff, coupled with (2) threats or charges of infringement, direct or indirect, by the patent owner or his successor in interest."[247] In the patent field, relevant evidence can be found in correspondence and advertising.[248] If a right to trial by jury would otherwise be available, that right is not affected by the fact that the controversy first came to issue in a declaratory judgment action.[249]

Where there is no genuine issue as to any material fact, a motion for a summary judgment can be made under Rule 56 of the Rules of Civil Procedure.[250] Whether issues of material fact actually exist is a difficult question and one which courts approach with caution.

Since a patent infringement suit must be commenced in a federal district court,[251] appeal will be to the court of appeals in the circuit in

243. *Id.*; H.J. Ashe, Co. v. Bridgeport Metal Good Mfg. Co., 273 F.Supp. 196 (S.D.N.Y. 1967).

244. 28 U.S.C. §§2201–02 (1964):

2201. Creation of remedy.
In the case of an actual controversy within its jurisdiction, except with respect to Federal taxes, any court of the United States, upon the filing of an appropriate pleading, may declare the rights and other legal relations of any interested party seeking such declaration, whether or not further relief is or could be sought. Any such declaration shall have the force and effect of a final judgment or decree and shall be reviewable as such.

2202. Further relief.
Further necessary or proper relief based on a declaratory judgment or decree may be granted, after reasonable notice and hearing, against any adverse party whose rights have been determined by such judgment.

245. Aetna Life Ins. Co. v. Haworth, 300 U.S. 227 (1937).

246. 28 U.S.C. §1338 (1964).

247. Whinston, *Declaratory Judgment Actions*, in THE ENCYCLOPAEDIA OF PATENT PRACTICE AND INVENTION MANAGEMENT 188 (R. Calvert ed. 1964).

248. *Id.*

249. FED. R. CIV. P. 57.

250. Allen Bradley Co. v. Air Reduction Co., 273 F.Supp. 390, (W.D. Pa. 1967), *aff'd*, 391 F.2d 282 (3d Civ. 1968); C-Thru Prods., Inc. v. Uniflex, Inc., 262 F.Supp. 213 (E.D.N.Y. 1966).

251. *See generally* Free, *supra* note 225, at 451, 459 (1968).

which the judgment was rendered.[252] The action is a civil one, governed by the appropriate federal rules.[253]

Direct appeal to the Supreme Court from a circuit court is not available as a matter of right. A writ of certiorari can be filed with the Supreme Court,[254] but it is rarely granted unless there is a conflict between circuit courts of appeal.[255] A circuit court can certify questions of law on which instructions are desired to the Supreme Court; the latter may give the requested instructions or may ask that the entire case be sent to it for decision.[256]

C. Exclusion of Infringing Goods

Infringement by manufacture in a foreign country by an infringer who cannot be sued in the United States raises difficult problems. The patentee can sue a person who possesses or sells the infringing goods in the United States, but this method of control may be ineffective because of the many suits necessary. This problem in the enforcement of patent rights was carefully considered by the Congress, and a partial solution was formulated in Section 337 of the Tariff Act.[257] Entry into the United States of goods infringing a United States patent can be prevented by resort to the procedure available under the Tariff Act.[258] The statute empowers the Tariff Commission to exclude goods when it finds that any of the following unlawful activities occur:[259] "Unfair methods of competition and unfair acts in the importation of articles into the United States, or in their sale . . . the effect or tendency of which is to destroy or substantially injure an industry, efficiently and economically operated, in the United States. . . ."

Investigations are initiated either in response to a complaint or upon the commission's own initiative.[260] All hearings are required to

252. 28 U.S.C. §1291 (1964).

253. *See* especially Federal Rules of Civil Procedure.

254. 28 U.S.C. §1254 (1964).

255. General Talking Pictures Corp. v. Western Elec. Co. 304 U.S. 175 (1938).

256. 28 U.S.C. §1254 (1964).

257. Tariff Act of 1930, ¶337, 19 U.S.C. ¶1337 (1970). This historical development has been frequently mentioned by U.S. courts in deciding cases brought under Section 337 of the Tariff Act. *See, e.g.*, In re Amtorg Trading Corp., 75 F.2d 826, 828–29 n.3 (C.C.P.A.) *cert. denied*, 296 U.S. 576 (1935); In re Orion Co., 71 F.2d 458, 466–67 (C.C.P.A. 1934).

258. Tariff Act of 1930, ch. 497, 46 stat. 590 (codified in 19 U.S.C.).

259. 19 U.S.C. §1337(a) (1970).

260. 19 U.S.C. §1337(b)(1) (1974); *see* Callman, *Unfair Competition with Imported Trademarked Goods*, 43 VA. L. REV. 323, 327 1957):

> In construing section 337 (Tariff Act), the courts made the following fundamental observations:
>
> (1) The Tariff Commission is an administrative, fact-finding agency with no judicial powers. Issues with respect to the validity of a patent are reserved to the courts and the Commission must therefore accept all issued patents as prima facie

be made "on the record after notice and opportunity for a hearing"[261] in conformity with sections 551 to 559 of the Administrative Procedure Act.[262] Once begun, an investigation must be concluded within twelve months unless it is designated by the commission as a "more complicated investigation,"[263] in which case the time limit is eighteen months.[264]

Section 337 of the Tariff Act outlines the facts the commission must find. It must first determine what unfair methods of competition and unfair acts are; then it must determine whether, if committed, they have the effect or tendency . . . to destroy or substantially injure an industry, efficiently and economically operated . . . to restrain or monopolize trade and commerce. Facts to support a holding that patent infringement is an unfair method of competition involve "[P]roblems of substitution of equivalents, change of materials, omission of elements, and scope and construction of claims in view of the prior art. . . . These are clearly questions of law peculiar to patents."[265] The Tariff Commission has the necessary power, but the practical difficulties are pervasive and reminiscent of the problems that have long plagued the Fair Trade Commission in implementing the Sherman and Clayton Anti-trust acts.[266]

If it finds a violation of Section 337, the commission is empowered to order that the infringing articles be barred from entry (permanent exclusion). The determination must be published in the *Federal Register*[267] and transmitted to the president. The president can, within sixty days, disapprove the determination for reasons of policy and thereby

valid. The Commission can go no further than determine (a) the patent had issued, (b) it had not expired, and (c) it had not been held invalid by a court of competent jurisdiction. (Frischer & Co. v. Bakelite Corp. 17 C.C.P.A. (Customs) 494, 509–10, 39 F.2d 247, 258, *cert. denied*, 282 U.S. 852 (1930) (dictum).

(2) The Commission acts in the public interest. The language of the statute ("unfair methods of competition and unfair acts in the importation of articles . . . or in their sale . . . the effect or tendency of which is to destroy or substantially injure an industry, efficiently and economically operated. . . .") and the appearance of section 337 in the same act with provisions for duties, warehouses, revenues, and tariff provisions indicates section 337 was not intended to confer power upon the Commission to determine conflicting property rights. It was designed solely to assist the President in regulating foreign commerce consistently with national economic policy. (In re Orion Co., 22 C.C.P.A. (Customs) 149, 160–61, 71 F.2d 458. 465 (1934) (dictum).

261. 19 U.S.C. §1337(c) (1974).

262. 5 U.S.C. §§551–59 (1966).

263. 19 U.S.C. §1337(b)(1) (1974).

264. The Tariff Commission is required to publish in the Federal Register its reasons for so designating a particular case. §1337(b)(1).

265. Callmann, *supra* note 259, at 335 (emphasis in original).

266. *Id.* at 336 *et seq.*

267. 19 U.S.C. §1337(g)(1) (A) (1974).

prevent effectuation.[268] If he does not do so, the commission determination becomes final[269] and will be enforced by the secretary of the treasury.[270] Exclusion will be effective so long as the conditions that prompted the commission to act still exist.[271] The offender may appeal the Tariff Commission determination to the United States Court of Customs and Patent Appeals.[272]

Permanent exclusion is not the only weapon available to the commission, however. Temporary exclusion may be ordered when the commission "has reason to believe that there is a violation,"[273] but is not certain. The commission may also issue a cease-and-desist order, directed to the violating party, that is more circumscribed in its effect than an exclusion order.[274] Moreover, importation is conditioned upon the posting of bond where a temporary exclusion order has been issued, or during the sixty-day, presidential intervention period.[275]

Importation by or for the United States is not subject to exclusion, but the patent owner affected may, upon a commission finding of violation, sue in the Court of Claims for reasonable and entire compensation.[276]

One of the most important interpretations of the pre-amendment Section 337 was enunciated in the case of *In re Von Clemm*.[277] The plaintiff in that case held a patent covering a process for making synthetic star sapphires and star rubies and sought exclusion of similar stones imported by the defendant. The defendant admitted that the stones he was importing met the product claim, but claimed there was no unfair competition, as is necessary under Section 337 of the Tariff Act, since there was no "palming off." The Tariff Commission recommended an exclusion order, finding that since the imported products met the description of the process and product claims in plaintiff's patent, the importation was unfair and consequently was an "unfair method of competition." The defendant appealed to the

268. *Id.* §1337(g)(1)(B)(2).
269. *Id.* §1337(g)(1)(B)(4).
270. *Id.* §1337(d).
271. *Id.* §1337(h).
272. *Id.* §1337(c).
273. *Id.* §1337(e).
274. *Id.* §1337(f).
275. *Id.* §1337(e).
276. *Id.* §1337(i). The exclusion remedy operates *in rem*, and can have the unfortunate effect of barring importation even when the violation in question has ceased to exist. A cease-and-desist order, on the other hand, operates *in personam* against the violator, and may be modified or terminated at any time. 19 U.S.C. 337(f). By providing a less drastic alternative to exclusion, the cease-and-desist order provision gives the commission greater flexibility.
277. 229 F.2d 441 (C.C.P.A. 1955).

Court of Customs and Patent Appeals and lost there too. The court recognized that the "unfair methods of competition standard" in Section 337 is not limited to the standards applicable to internal commerce, and thus a finding of "unfair methods of competition and unfair acts in importation" was issued.

The holding of the *Von Clemm* case is a significant advance in the protection of United States patent rights against imported goods. Under the "readability test," the traditional concepts of unfair competition and infringement need not be satisfied. A patent holder has even greater leverage than he would have against a domestic infringer of his patent. Furthermore, since the validity of a patent cannot be questioned by the Tariff Commission or the Court of Customs and Patent Appeals,[278] the defenses available to an importer in a proceeding for an exclusion order are restricted.

The scope of an exclusion order can be surprisingly broad, applying to all importers of goods falling within the description of the excluded goods.[279] This, in effect, constitutes an additional "readability test." Exceptions to the exclusion order will be made for goods covered by a license or by an authorization order.

The Tariff Act is thus a potent weapon in the arsenal of remedies for holders of United States patents to protect their patent rights against infringing products produced abroad and imported into the United States.

D. Breach of Patent License

A patent license is a contract, and, if it is breached, the usual remedies—damages, rescission, and specific enforcement—are available.

Various kinds of breach produce varying losses for which damages are recoverable. Breach of a confidentiality covenant, for example, can open up a wide range of potential losses. Damages are often measured by royalty due and unpaid and royalty to be later paid.[280]

Rescission is, in effect, termination for a material breach. An injured party can both declare his freedom from further obligation under the contract (rescind) and recover damages.

Specific enforcement is practicable only as an injunction against certain kinds of actual or threatened harm, such as violation of a confidentiality covenant.[281]

278. *Id.* at 444.

279. 19 U.S.C. §1337(e) (1970).

280. *See* Walker on Patents 524 *et seq.* (A. Deller ed. 1956).

281. *See* Brumley Metals, Inv. v. Bargen, 275 F.2d 46 (7th Cir. 1960), where the licensor was preliminarily enjoined from disposing of molds which had been used to manufacture for licensee's competitors in violation of the license agreement.

The parties to a license agreement will usually feel that these remedies are too crude to meet their needs and that drafting refinement of them is desirable. Material breach, a concept that underlies several remedial techniques—discharge of the injured party, recovery of damages measured both by past defaults and future obligations, and rescission—is to be determined by criteria the application of which often cannot be known until a court has resolved the fact issues involved. The parties need to know with particularity what events will justify termination of the agreement, and what the legal situation will be after termination. These problems are considered in Chapter V.

If a party to a license agreement claims that he was induced to enter into the transaction by fraudulent representations made by the other party, he can elect either to disaffirm the contract or to affirm it and seek damages for deceit. Allegations of fraud have produced an arbitration problem on which the decisions are divided. The question is whether the fraud issue can be resolved by the arbitrators or whether it must be resolved by litigation before arbitration can proceed.[282]

Until quite recently, a licensee, sued for breach of a license agreement, could not defend himself on the ground that the licensed patent was invalid,[283] save where an antitrust issue was raised.[284] This estoppel doctrine was overturned by the United States Supreme Court in *Lear* v. *Adkins*.[285] The ramifications of this change in the law will be fully known only through the development of additional litigation.

E. Know-How and Trade Secrets

A trade secret has been defined as "any formula, pattern, device, or compilation of information which is used in one's business and which gives an opportunity to obtain an advantage over competitors who do not know or use it."[286] Although know-how as a term seems to stress techniques, methods, skills and the like, the dividing line between trade secrets and know-how is a tenuous one.[287] Either interest can be licensed, and for breach of such contract the remedies discussed above are available.[288] Both damages, including accounting for profits derived by the wrongdoer through his breach and injunction against

282. T. Kawakami and D. Henderson, 42 Wash. L. Rev. 621 (1967).

283. United States v. Harvey Steel Co., 196 U.S. 310 (1905); Automatic Radio Mfg. Co. v. Haseltine Research Inc., 339 U.S. 827 (1950); Westinghouse Elec. & Mfg. Co. v. Formica Insulation Co., 226 U.S. 342 (1927).

284. Sola Elec. Co. v. Jefferson Elec. & Mfg. Co., 317 U.S. 173 (1942).

285. 395 U.S. 653 (1969).

286. Restatement of Torts 757, comment *b* at 5 (1939).

287. Ladas, *Legal Protection of Know-How*, 54 Trademark Rep. 160, 161 (1964).

288. *Id.* at 162.

wrongful use or disclosure of the subject matter are of routine interest in these transactions.[289]

As in a patent licensing, drafting concerning the consequences of default is desirable in trade-secret and know-how licenses and is typically used.

Particularly pressing are the problems a licensor faces if third persons come into wrongful possession of the licensed trade secrets or know-how. For these problems, there is no specific statutory solution, in either country, other than criminal statutes of limited utility.[290] The injunction is the only preventive remedy open to the injured party.[291] Tort principles must supply both the theory and the damage measure for recovery from the wrongdoer for the losses sustained.[292]

The risk of wrongful disclosure by an employee of the licensee requires especially careful analysis by the parties and their counsel. Remedies are afforded by basic legal principles, but these are hardly adequate. A recovery in tort against the employee is not likely to be a satisfactory solution. More effective is injunction against wrongful disclosure,[293] but an injunction does not cure the consequences of previous disclosure. Wrongful disclosure has been made a crime in a number of states,[294] but there is no reason to think prosecutors can easily be moved to prosecute for this type of offense.

This is an area which should engage the further close attention of all concerned—the business community, the legal profession, and legislators. The increasing importance of technology and the accelerating incidence of industrial espionage combine to focus attention on the problems.

What is the appropriate balance between the interests of owners of secret technology, some of which represents years of effort and the expenditure of many millions of dollars,[295] and the interests of employees in maximum utilization of their skills? This is one aspect of the basic problem. Certainly the employee's right to change employers and to continue working in the area of his particular expertise must be considered when devising means for the protection of secret technology. The general rule so far applied is that skilled

289. *See* S. Turner, The Law of Trade Secrets 430 (1962).

290. Ladas, *supra* note 178, at 167.

291. *Id.* at 171.

292. *See* Restatement of Torts 757 (1939).

293. Bagley, *supra* note 240, at 464; In re Bettinger Corp., 197 F.Supp. 273 (1961).

294. *See generally* McTiernan, *Employees' Responsibilities As To Trade Secrets*, in Encyclopaedia of Patent Practice and Invention Management 242 (R. Calvert ed. 1964).

295. *See Developments in the Law—Competitive Torts*, 77 Harv. L. Rev. 888, 954–55 (1964).

employees may take with them to another employer their own "faculties, skill, and experience" but not "confidential information secured solely through their employment."[296] Since this type of protection relies upon the finding that a certain act was inequitable, "courts have not protected trade secrets as property, but have instead focused upon the wrongfulness of the means by which the secret was obtained."[297] The requirements imposed by the courts have been that the information was in fact kept secret and that there was an improper taking.[298]

The remedies are relatively simple as against a licensee who violates a duty of confidentiality if the secrecy still exists at the time of the trial. The plaintiff will be interested in damages, both in terms of his lost profits and the profit derived by the defendant through the wrongful disclosure, and an injunction to prevent the defendant from further wrongdoing.

Procedurally, in his pursuit of a judicial remedy, the plaintiff-licensor may have to reveal his secret to the court before the court can decide whether or not the defendant committed the alleged wrong. The judge may allow this testimony to be taken in an *in camera* proceeding[299] so that the secret will not come into the public domain through a court hearing open to the public.

After an injunction against use of secret technology has been granted against a particular defendant, that information may become known to the public through no fault of the defendant. In that case, there is a split of authority as to whether the defendant can use the information.[300] Under the *Shellmar* rule,[301] which is followed in the Sixth and Seventh Circuits, use of improperly acquired knowledge may be enjoined, even after the general public is free to use such information due to an unauthorized disclosure. Thus, use of the knowledge by the wrongdoer is enjoined in perpetuity.

The alternative rule was stated in *Conmar Products* v. *Universal Slide Fastener Co.*[302] Under the approach taken in that case and in the cases that have followed its pattern, knowledge improperly gained may be used after public disclosure.[303] The rationale is that after public dis-

296. Aronson v. Orlov, 228 Mass. 1, 116 N.E. 951, *cert. denied*, 245 U.S. 662 (1917); *see also* Restatement of Contracts 515 (1932).

297. *Developments in the Law—Competitive Torts*, 77 Harv. L. Rev. 888, 948 (1964).

298. *Id.* at 949.

299. This is a hearing held in closed chambers which only authorized parties can attend.

300. *See* A. Turner, The Law of Trade Secrets 427 *et seq.* (1962).

301. Shellmar Prods. Co. v. Allen-Qualley, 87 F.2d 104 (7th Cir. 1936).

302. 172 F.2d 150 (2nd Cir. 1949).

303. *See* Gambrell & Kayton, *supra* note 240, at 607.

closure, through no fault of the defendant, there is nothing that requires the protection of an injunction.

Know-how and trade secrets transferred with patents are always important and are sometimes more important than the patents, the exploitation of which is not possible without the technology. Security precautions should routinely engage the full attention of the parties and their counsel.

Since the law concerning the protection of know-how and trade secrets is in a developing stage, special care must be taken in drafting confidentiality clauses. These too are considered in Chapter IV.

VII. Conclusion

In an ideal international license transaction, careful drafting and smooth working relations between the parties will so reduce the incidence of disagreements that legal remedies should not become a factor. Both drafting and smooth relations are especially important where the parties are from countries where business customs and legal systems differ as widely as do those of Japan and the United States. It will usually take more time properly to finalize the details of the transaction than is necessary in an entirely domestic transaction, but the extra effort is very worthwhile. The effort expended by each party during the negotiation stage in getting a full understanding of the other's ideas and position can do much to reduce the risk of later dispute. It is certainly better to avoid controversies than to need the remedies with which this chapter has been primarily concerned. If a dispute does develop, sound working relations will foster an amicable solution.

The importance of sound drafting in the first instance as a foundation for an international license transaction can hardly be overstated. If the documentation tells the parties exactly what they are to do and not to do and spells out the consequences of nonperformance, and if the parties are fully advised when the agreement is executed, the range of potential disagreements serious enough to pose threats of litigation or arbitration should be narrowed to factual issues. These are especially amenable to resolution in ways that make it possible for the parties to continue to do business together.

Regulation of International Licensing Agreements under the Japanese Antimonopoly Law

MICHIKO ARIGA

I. Introduction: The General Picture of the Japanese Antimonopoly Act

A. General

The act[1] concerning Prohibition of Private Monopoly and Maintenance of Fair Trade (Law No. 54 of 1947, hereinafter referred to as the Antimonopoly Act, or the act),[2] enacted on 31 March, 1947 and put into force on 20 July of the same year, is the first permanent law in Japanese history for the promotion of free and fair competition of enterprises in Japan. The act was patterned after the antitrust laws of the United States, adopting ideas from the Sherman Act, the Clayton Act, the Federal Trade Commission Act, and the Robinson-Patman Act into a single statute.

The act announces its purpose in Section 1 as follows:

> *Section 1.* This Act, by prohibiting private monopolization, unreasonable restraint of trade and unfair business practices, by preventing the excessive concentration of power over enterprises and by excluding undue restriction of production, sale, price, and technology through combina-

1. For a general detail study of the Antimonopoly Act, *see* Yoshio Kanazawa, *Regulation of Corporate Enterprise: the Law of Unfair Competition and the Control of Monopoly Power*, Law in Japan 484–490 (A.T. von Mehren ed. 1966); *Hiroshi Iyori*, Antimonopoly Legislation in Japan, (1969); Guide to Legislation on Restrictive Business Practices, OECD Vol. 3; Michiko Ariga and L.V. Rieke, *The Antimonopoly Law of Japan and Its Enforcement*, Wash. L. Rev. 437 (1964); Kazushige Imamura, *Dokusen Kinshī Ho* (Antimonopoly Law) 52 Horitsu-gaku Zenshu (Complete Collection on the Law) ed. 1961); Akira Shoda, Dokusen Kinshi Ho (Antimonopoly Law) (1966).

2. *Shitekidokusen no Kinshi oyobi Kosei Torihiki no kakuho ni kansuru Horitsu*; here the term "act" is used instead of "law," and each provision of the act is called "section" instead of "article" in accordance with the agreed rules of translation in the Organization of Economic Cooperation and Development (OECD).

tion or agreement, and all other unreasonable restraint of business activities, aims to promote free and fair competition, to stimulate the initiative of entrepreneurs, to encourage business activities of enterprises, to heighten the level of employment and people's income, and thereby to promote the democratic and wholesome development of the national economy as well as to assure the interest of the general consumer.

As is seen from the above provision, the immediate purpose of the Antimonopoly Act is to promote free and fair competition by prohibiting private monopolization, unreasonable restraint of trade, unfair business practices, holding companies, and such combinations of enterprises through merger, stockholding, or interlocking directorates as may result in a substantial restraint of competition in a particular field of trade.

The act controls business activities of entrepreneurs. Trade associations, whether incorporated or not are also under the control of the act. Private individuals who are not engaged in an entrepreneurial business are outside of the control of the act.

The original act of 1947 was stricter than the American antitrust laws. In order to make the act meet the actual economic situation of Japan, it was amended several times.[3] The first major amendment, made in 1949, eased the control on intercorporate stockholding and interlocking directorates among noncompetitive companies. The second major amendment of 1953, made one year after Japan recovered her independence from the occupation, relaxed the act further with the plausible purpose of making it more suitable to the realities of the Japanese economy. "Substantial restraint of competition in a particular field of trade," a concept which had been the substantive criterion of illegality of a private monpolization or an unreasonable restraint of trade (a cartel agreement), was extended to cases involving stockholding, interlocking directorates, and mergers.[4]

Exemption was provided for cartel agreements of producers formed to cope with certain economic difficulties defined in the act—"depression cartels,"[5] and cartel agreements formed by producers for the rationalization of enterprises, including, among other things, technical development, quality improvement, cost reduction, and efficiency promotion—"rationalization cartels."[6] The prohibition against establishing a holding company or operating a company as a holding company has been maintained without any change.

The act also contains provisions exempting enterprises (such as

3. For detailed description of the amendments to the act, see Yoshio Kanazawa, and Kazushige Imamura, *supra* note 1.

4. §§10(1), 13, 14, 15(1), 16(1).

5. §24–3.

6. §24–4.

railroads, and producers and distributors of gas or electricity) that constitute a monopoly by the very nature of the business, and the acts of firms or trade associations done in conformity with a special law or an order issued under a special law. Also exempted are acts of a cooperative of small-scale entrepreneurs or consumers for mutual aid, and lastly, acts in exercise of industrial property rights.[7]

B. The Fair Trade Commission

The act is administered and enforced by the Fair Trade Commission, a government agency established by the act.[8] The commission is an external organ of the prime minister's office, which exercises its power over the commission only in the appointment of the chairman and commissioners of the commission and in control over the budget of the commission.[9] The commission maintains complete independence in the performance of its duties.[10] This type of administrative agency was new to Japan at the time the act was enacted. During the period of the occupation, there were established many commission-type government agencies in various branches of administration, but for one reason or another they all, excluding only the Fair Trade Commission, have been dissolved and their powers transferred to the respective government ministry.

The Fair Trade Commission enforces, in addition to the Antimonopoly Act, two other laws closely related to the Antimonopoly Act. They are as follows: the Act against Delay in Payment to Subcontractors of 1956,[11] and the Act against Unjustifiable Premiums and Misleading Representations of 1962.[12] These laws control specific, unfair business practices for the protection of, in the former instance, small enterprises dependent on large contractors, and for the protection of, in the latter instance, the interest of consumers.

The Fair Trade Commission consists of five commissioners including the chairman.[13] They are appointed by the prime minister for a five-year term from among persons of above thirty-five years of age who have knowledge and experience in law and economics. Their appointment is subject to the consent of both houses of the National Diet.[14] Reappointment of the chairman or a commissioner is possible,

7. §§21 to 24.
8. §27(1).
9. §27(2).
10. §28.
11. *Futo Keihinrui oyobi Futo Hyoji Boshi Ho* (Law No. 120 of 1956), the latest amendment to this act was made in 1965.
12. *Shitauke Daikin Shiharai Chien Boshi Ho* (Law No. 134 of 1962).
13. §29(1).
14. §29(2), (3).

but the tenure of the chairman or a commissioner ends when he reaches the age of sixty-five.[15] The chairman represents the Fair Trade Commission, and his appointment is attested by the emperor.[16] The chairman and commissioners are fulltime public service officials. They enjoy independent status like that of judges of courts and are forbidden to engage in any business activities. They are forbidden to express, outside of the commission, their views on violation cases or to divulge trade secrets of entrepreneurs.[17]

A staff office is attached to the Fair Trade Commission for the discharge of its business. The number of personnel of the staff office for the fiscal year of 1973 was 369 including clerks, typists, and other workers, and the budget was approximately one billion yen.[18] The staff office has seven local branches: in Osaka, Nagoya, Fukuoka, and four other cities.[19] The staff office, headed by the secretary-general, has four divisions: secretariat, investigation division, economic division, and trade practices division. There are, at present, five hearing examiners in the secretariat who conduct hearings on violation cases initiated by the commission.[20]

The major functions of the commission are as follows:

1. Investigation of suspected violations of the act on its own authority or upon complaint from the public,[21] rendering decisions on those cases through recommendation procedure or formal hearing procedure,[22] and court litigation in appealed cases;[23]

2. Designation of unfair business practices to be curbed;[24]

3. Receiving various reports or notifications, including advance notifications of mergers from companies[25] and reports by trade associations,[26] conducting various economic researches,[27] giving advisory opinions to persons upon request, and coordinating draft legislation

15. §30.
16. §30(3), 33.
17. §§29(4), 31, 38, 39.
18. KOSEI TORIHIKI IINKAI NENJI HOKOKU (FTC Annual Report) 1973, 305, 307. *See also* Act §35.
19. §§35–6.
20. §35(2), (3).
21. §§45, 46, 47.
22. §§48, 49, 50 to 61.
23. §§77, 80 to 83, 85.
24. §§2(7), 71, 72. Under sec. 2(7), FTC Notification No. 11 of 1953, concerning Unfair Business Practices applicable to entrepreneurs generally, was issued (hereinafter Unfair Business Practices). Under §71 notifications designating unfair business practices applicable to entrepreneurs in specific industries *e.g.*, newspaper, shipping, soy sauce, margarine and shortening, rubber footwear, and match industry have been issued.
25. §§10(2), 13(3), 14(2), 15(2), 16.
26. §8(a), (3), (4).
27. §§27, 35–4(i), 40, 41.

or policies of other government ministries with the antimonopoly policy;[28] and

4. Granting approval to depression or rationalization cartels,[29] and giving consent to other government agencies that have primary jurisdiction over certain cartels of enterprises.[30]

C. Prohibited Acts

1. Private monopolization. The act prohibits private monopolization and not monopoly itself. If an entrepreneur, independently or by combination or conspiracy with other entrepreneurs, or in any other manner, excludes or controls the business activities of other entrepreneurs, whether they are its competitors or not, and thereby causes a substantial restraint of competition in any particular field of trade, it violates the first part of Section 3.[31]

2. Unreasonable restraint of trade. An unreasonable restraint of trade refers to a horizontal agreement of entrepreneurs, that is, an agreement of competitors, whereby a substantial restraint of competition in a particular field of trade is effected. Under this category falls an agreement to limit the amount of production or shipment; an agreement to fix, enhance, or maintain prices; an agreement to restrict technology, product, or facilities; or an agreement to allocate territory, customers, or suppliers.[32]

A vertical agreement wherein entrepreneurs of different levels of business function participate does not constitute by definition an unreasonable restraint of trade prohibited by the latter part of Section 3.[33]

3. Unfair business practices. Unfair business practices are business activities of an entrepreneur that impede fair competition and that have been designated as unfair business practices by the Fair Trade Commission.[34] Employment of unfair business practices is prohibited by Section 19. In the General Designation of Unfair Business Practices, twelve types of unfair business practices are specified. Boycot-

28. §35–4(iii).
29. §§24–3, 24–4.
30. *E.g.*, §34 of the Export and Import Trading Act, (*Yushutsu Nyu Torihiki Ho*) Law No. 299 of 1952.
31. Definition of a private monopoly is given in §2(5).
32. Definition of an unreasonable restraint of trade is given in 2(6).
33. *Asahi Shimbun Sha hoka 26 mei ni taisuru ken* (Asahi Newspaper Company and 26 Others) FTC April 7, 1951, 2 Kosei *torihiki iinkai shinketsu shu* (hereinafter referred as FTC Decision Report) 4, Tokyo High Court, Ghyo (na) 10 and 11 of 1951, 4 FTC Decision Report 145; *Toho Kabushiki Kaisha hoka ichimei ni taisuru ken* (Toho and Shintoho Companies case), FTC April 23, 1951, 3 FTC Decision Report 52, Tokyo High Court, Gyo (na) 10, December 7, 1953, 5 FTC Decision Report 118.
34. §2(7) see note 24 *supra*.

ting, discrimination, dumping, predatory practices affecting customers, undue exclusive dealing, tie-ins, imposition of undue restrictions, undue business interference, and unwarranted use of dominant position are typical practices specified.[35] In contrast to the limitation of controls over unreasonable restraints of trade to horizontal agreements, a vertical agreement—a contract or agreement between entrepreneurs of different business function, e.g., between supplier and customer, by which fair competition in any level of business is impeded, is banned by Section 19 if it falls under any one of the designated unfair business practices. Therefore, a patent licensing contract involving licensor-supplier and licensee-customer is primarily subject to the control of Section 19.

D. Procedures

The act provides two types of procedure against violation: administrative procedure and criminal procedure.

1. Administrative procedure. Administrative procedure is conducted by the Fair Trade Commission. Upon completion of investigation of a case initiated upon complaint from the public or on its own authority, the commission issues to the alleged violator either a recommendation or a formal notice of hearing.[36] It has become a customary practice of the commission to initiate the administrative procedure by issuing a recommendation to the alleged violator. He will be advised to take measures, recommended by the commission, to remedy the alleged violation, and if the recommendation is rejected, which has rarely been the case, then the commission resorts to the formal hearing procedure. If the recommendation is accepted by the respondent, the commission renders a decision with an order in line with the recommendation.

A formal hearing procedure is usually conducted by a hearing examiner in a manner similar to a court proceeding.[37] Except for a big case, it is very seldom that the commission itself conducts a hearing.[38]

Upon the completion of hearings, the hearing examiner writes an initial decision and transmits it to the commission. A copy of the initial decision is also sent to the respondent. The respondent may file an objection to the initial decision with the commission. The commission, after reviewing the initial decision and any objection filed, renders its

35. Appendix 1.
36. §§48, 49.
37. §§35(2), 51–2, 51–3 to 53–2.
38. The formal hearing of the case of merger of Yawata Steel Company and Fuji Steel Company was conducted by the commission itself after a recommendation to stop the merger had been rejected by the merging companies.

decision with an order setting forth the measures to be taken to eliminate the acts in violation.[39] A consent decision may be applied for at any time after hearing procedure has been started up to the time of the entry of a formal decision by the FTC.[40]

The corrective measures to be ordered statutorily vary depending on the type of violation. In an instance of private monopolization or unreasonable restraint of trade, the violator may be ordered to report on certain matters, to cease and desist from the acts in violation, to divest a part of the business or to perform other acts deemed necessary to eliminate the violation. Against the employment of unfair business practices, an order to cease and desist from the acts in violation is the only remedy. In the case of violation by a trade association, dissolution of the trade association may be ordered, in addition to other remedies, such as an order to report or an order to cease and desist from the violation.[41]

An appeal against the decision of the commission may be made to the Tokyo High Court, which has the exclusive appellate jurisdiction.[42]

2. Criminal procedure. Private monopolization and unreasonable restraint of trade are subject to criminal penalties by imprisonment for not more than three years or fine of not more than 50,000 yen. Nonobservance of an order stated in an FTC decision is also subject to criminal penalties. For unfair business practices, no criminal penalty is provided. Criminal procedure can only be initiated upon an accusation of the Fair Trade Commission.[43] There were three accusations in the very early days of the commission, but then followed a hiatus of more than twenty years, until the accusations against a cartel of oil companies and a petroleum trade association were brought in February 1974.

II. The Antimonopoly Act and the Exercise of Patent Rights

A. General

The exercise of industrial property rights is exempted from the application of the Antimonopoly Act by Section 23, which reads as follows: "*Sec. 23*. The provisions of this Act shall not apply to acts recognizable as the exercise of rights under the Copyright Act, the Patent Act, the Utility Model Act, the Design Act, and the Trademark

39. §54.
40. §53–3.
41. §§7, 8–2, 20.
42. §85.
43. §96.

Act." For the purposes of this paper, only patent rights will be discussed.

Section 100 of the act provides for revocation of a patent right which has been misused in violation of the act. It is accordingly important to know just what conduct is and is not protected by the words "recognizable as the exercise of rights under . . . the Patent Act." The Section 23 mandate is abstract and requires specification. The Fair Trade Commission must be prepared with the preliminary demarcation in this field in order that it will enforce the act against matters involving patent rights.[44]

B. Development by Periods

Historically, there have been three stages in the development of demarcation by the Fair Trade Commission with respect to the scope of the exemption for a patent right.

With respect to international contracts or international agreements including international patent licenses, Section 6 of the original act of 1947 provided that prior approval of the Fair Trade Commission was necessary. This prior approval system was, however, changed to post reporting system by the amendment of 1949 to meet the strong desire of business for expediting the introduction of foreign technology.

In 1949 those wartime-suspended patent license contracts under which Japanese nationals had been licensees were revived and filed with the Fair Trade Commission for scrutiny under Section 6.[45]

The first stage is seen in the occupation period, when the Fair Trade Commission was strongly guided by GHQ in the enforcement of the act. The Fair Trade Commission was led to take action against

44. §100 of the act reads:

(1) The court may make in a case coming under Section 89 or 90, according to circumstances, the following declaration at the time of pronouncing penalty: Provided that the declaration under paragraph (i) hereunder shall be made only when the said patent right, or exclusive or non-exclusive licensed right on a patented invention belongs to the offender.

i) That the patent which is the basis of the patent right, or the exclusive or non-exclusive licensed right on a patented invention, to which the offence relates shall be revoked;

ii) That the offender shall be barred from becoming a party to a contract with the government for a period of not less than six months and not more than three years after the date when the decision became final and conclusive.

(2) When a decision accompanying the declaration as provided for paragraph (i) of the preceding subsection becomes final and conclusive, the court shall transmit a certified copy thereof to the Director-General of the Patent Office.

(3) The Director-General of the Patent Office shall, upon receipt of the certified copy of the decision under the provisions of the preceding subsection, revoke the patent concerned, or annul the exclusive or non-exclusive licensed right on a patented invention.

45. *Kogyo Shoyuken Senji Ho* (Industrial Property Rights Wartime Act) of 1917 was evoked in 1942, *Tokkyo Hakusho* (Patent White Paper) (1968) 208; *Rengokokujin Kogyo Shoyuken Sengo Sochirei* (Cabinet Order concerning the Post War Measures on Industrial Property Rights of the Allied Nationals) of September 1, 1949, Patent White Paper, *id.* 16, 208–09.

certain license contracts on the ground that restrictions imposed upon Japanese licensees were illegal under the act.

In this period the Fair Trade Commission attacked twenty international licensing contracts[46] and gained rudimentary knowledge about the licensee restrictions which may run afoul of the act.

The following restrictions in the above licenses were found in violation of the act:

1. Restriction on getting license of competing technology or use of new technology .... 16 licenses
2. Restriction on products to be handled .... 11 licenses
3. Restriction on export .... 9 licenses
4. Requiring the licensee to notify its newly conceived inventions to the licensor before filing patent application .... 1 license
5. Demanding royalty on the working of licensee's patented invention .... 1 license

The second stage in the development of demarcation was the occasion when the Fair Trade Commission was assigned the task of formulating a reply to the questionnaire sent by the secretary-general of the United Nations to the Japanese government in 1963.[47] Although the reply was an informal one, it is significant in that it forced the Fair Trade Commission to consider by itself for the first time the relationship between the Antimonopoly Act and the exercise of patent rights. The Fair Trade Commission's only knowledge and experience in the matter, at that time, was the knowledge and experience gained in the international license cases mentioned above. There were no domestic cases, and Japanese literature on the subject was almost nonexistent.[48]

46. Of the twenty cases, fourteen clearly concerned patent license contracts, but as to the remaining six cases, although FTC's decisions do not indicate the case concerned an international contract involving a patent license, it is assumed that at least they involved transfers of technology or know-how.

47. *The Role of Patents in the Transfer of Technology to Undeveloped Countries, United Nations, Economic and Social Council* (Thirty-seventh session Provisional agenda Item 13) Report by the Secretary-General.

48. There was one article on the subject, MICHIKO ARIGA, *Tokyo to Dokusenkinshi Ho* (Patent and Antimonopoly Law) in I GENDAI SHOHO NO SHOMONDAI (Problems under Contemporary Laws), 559–99, (ed. 1959). Later, several books or articles discussing this matter appeared. They are: MICHIKO ARIGA, *Shiteki Dokusen Kinshi Ho* (Antimonopoly Act), in KOGYO SHOYUKEN BENRAN (Industrial Properties Cycropedia, 1965) at 387–407; ARIGA, *Dokkinho to Tokkyoho tono Sesshoku ni tsuiteno Kokunaiteki Kokusaiteki Shomondai* (Domestic and International Problems relating to the interaction of the Antimonopoly Act and the Patent Law), in KOGYO SHOYUKEN NO KIHONTEKI KADAI (The Basic Problems of Industrial Properties) (1971); ARIGA, *Gijitsu Enjo Keiyaku to Dikkinho no Kankei* (The Antimonopoly Act and Technical Assistance Contract) in GIJITSU ENJO KEIYAKU (Technical Assistance Contract) 271–328 (Daijiro Nagata, ed. 1962); DAIJIRO NAGATA, JISSHI KEIYAKU (Licensing Contracts) (1966).

The questions of the United Nations and the gist of the replies to them are set out in the following numbered paragraphs. The questions were about restriction-validity, were mainly concerned with restrictions in patent license contracts, and appear in the paragraph headings. The reply is given under each question.

1. Restriction on amount of production? A licensor may restrict the amount of production of the licensee in either an exclusive licensing or a nonexclusive licensing contract. This restriction imposed by the patentee or the exclusive licensor is considered as being within the legitimate scope of acts in the exercise of the patent right. In the case of nonexclusive license, however, one must be aware of the following principle. If there are several nonexclusive licensees, and the restriction on amount of production of each licensee is made in observance of an agreement among such licensees, this is a cartel agreement of licensees and may constitute, as far as the licensees are concerned, an unreasonable restraint of trade prohibited under Section 3 of the act.

2. Restriction on minimum price of commodities produced by the licensed invention? A patentee or an exclusive licensor may set a minimum price or fix the price at which the patented goods are to be sold by a licensee. This restriction is considered lawful under the Antimonopoly Act, although the Patent Act does not specifically provide that such restrictive act is within the patent right. However, a price agreement among licensees of the same patented good may fall under unreasonable restraint of trade.

The reply of the Fair Trade Commission did not answer the question of whether a licensor may fix prices of a product produced by licensees where not only his patented invention but another patented invention not belonging to him are involved, or where a part of the product involves no patent.

3. Restriction on resale price? Once a patented commodity leaves the hands of the licensee-producer by sale, his patent right is exhausted, and he can no longer claim his patent privilege on such commodity. Therefore, neither the licensor or the licensee shall fix the resale price of the licensee's products in the wholesale level or the retail level. Resale price maintenance is prohibited. This is an unfair business practice as it falls under item 8 of the General Unfair Business Practices.

However, from the general prohibition of resale price maintenance there are exemptions for certain classes of goods, e.g., cosmetics and drugs designated by the Fair Trade Commission.

4. Restriction on field of use? Restriction on field of use is considered lawful as being an act in exercise of the patent right.

A patentee has the right to exclude others from manufacturing, selling, handling, or importing the product that is covered by his patented invention. As he can limit this exclusiveness by granting a license to others, he can put a restriction on the field of use within which the licensee may practice the licensed invention.

5. Restriction on market—export restriction? The patent right based on the Patent Act of Japan is, of course, effective only within the territory of Japan and not outside of Japan. Export restriction is not recognized as an exercise of a patent right. On this basis the Fair Trade Commission attacked export restrictions in nine of the twenty international licensing cases mentioned above.

However, the reply on this point did not accurately reflect actual Fair Trade Commission practice at the time (1963), because many licensing contracts having export restrictions had survived commission attack. This was due to the fact that in the screening of international licenses under the Foreign Investment Act[49] during that pre–1963 period the government, feeling that Japanese technology was considerably behind foreign technologies and that the introduction of foreign technology was of paramount importance, took a rather lenient attitude on export restrictions. Furthermore, Japanese manufacturing companies had been busy meeting strong domestic demand and the export restriction imposed on them did not affect them because they did not have enough production for export.

According to the survey reported in the *Present Condition of Foreign Technology Introduction and Its Problems* by the Ministry of International Trade and Industry, issued in 1962, 53 percent of the international licensing contracts by which foreign technology was introduced into Japan contained restrictions on market, e.g., on export.[50]

6. Tying arrangement? If the tied product is indispensable to the working of the patented invention and there is no way to get a supply of it except from the licensor, then such a restriction is not regarded as an unfair business practice. However, if the raw materials for the production of patented goods or parts to be used in the production of the patented goods are avilable from other sources within the country or abroad, then, such tying arrangement falls under unfair business practice.

7. Cross-licensing and patent pooling? Cross-licensing and patent pooling are not per se illegal. The reply notes, however, that if these

49. *Gaishi ni kansuru Horitsu* (Law No. 163) 1950, Article 10; *Gaikoku Kawase oyobi Gaikoku Boeki Kanri Ho* (Foreign Exchange and Foreign Trade Control Law) (Law No. 228 of 1949) §27.

50. *Gaikoku gijitsu donyu no genjo to mondai ten* (The Present Condition of Introduction of Foreign Technology and Its Problems) MITI (1962).

arrangements are abused, they may be unreasonable restraints of trade or private monopolizations prohibited by Section 3.

The principles enunciated in the reply to the United Nations and the precedents provided by the twenty cases from which those principles were derived were the basis on which the Fair Trade Commission during this period formulate decisions concerning the application of Section 23 of the act to patent rights. An important part of the commission's work was consultation with the Foreign Investment Council. The council advised the minister of finance, who was charged by the Foreign Investment Act with responsibility for advance approval of every contract or license that required a Japanese national to make payment abroad. The screening committee of the council admitted a staff member of the commission for the purpose of advice concerning conformity of restrictive clauses with the Antimonopoly Act. The objective was to assure deletion or modification of violative clauses, before the license was approved and the license transaction became operative.

Although this participation by the commission in the procedures of the council was informal and not legally binding on the commission, in no instance was a complaint issued by the Fair Trade Commission against an international patent license approved by the finance minister.

The third stage of the demarcation development came in 1968 when the Fair Trade Commission issued its Guidelines on International Licensing Contracts,[51] which were made desirable by highly significant developments on the economic front.

Japan became in 1964 a Section 8 country under the International Monetary Fund Treaty (IMF) and joined the Organization of Economic Cooperation and Development (OECD). In its effort to meet its obligations under the above treaties, the government announced in 1968 that the introduction of foreign technology would be liberalized to a great extent and that the screening procedure and approval system which had been practiced for almost twenty years in accordance with the Foreign Investment Act of 1950 would be abolished. Those procedures were designed to restrict the import of foreign technology to those deemed necessary for the development of Japanese industries and also to guarantee the availability of foreign exchange for license payments. Meanwhile, the industrial and economic situation of Japan had changed to such an extent that strict control with respect to licenses for introduction of foreign technologies was no longer necessary. With the control under the

51. Full text of the Guidelines is given in Appendix 2.

Foreign Investment Act removed, most international licensing contracts became subject to review only under the Antimonopoly Act. That act specifically regulates international agreements or contracts. Section 6 of the act as amended in 1953 reads:

> (1) No entrepreneur shall enter into an international agreement or an international contract which contains such matters as constitute unreasonable restraint of trade or unfair business practices.
>
> (2) An entrepreneur who has entered into an international agreement or an international contract shall file, in accordance with the Regulations of the Fair Trade Commission, a report thereof with the said Commission, accompanied by a copy of the said agreement or contract, a document describing the contents thereof, within thirty days as from the execution of such act.
>
> (3) [Omitted.]

Recognizing that the filing was to be made after the contract had been executed and also that the interest of a foreign party—the licensor—would be affected indirectly by an order of the commission addressed to a Japanese party—the licensee—to eliminate or modify the violating provision, the commission issued the Guidelines in July 1968. These are reprinted, in English translation, as Appendix 2 to this chapter. It is the purpose of the Guidelines to help both the Japanese and the foreign parties, during the negotiation stage of their transaction, to understand and anticipate the probable extent of applicability of the Antimonopoly Act to a patent license. Discussion of the restrictions the Guidelines enumerate will be undertaken in the following section.

What is relevant in this section on the problem of demarcation is item 3 of the Guidelines, which formally states the Fair Trade Commission's position on "act recognizable, as the exercise of rights under the Patent Act." Although the Guidelines relate to international licensing contracts, the same principles will be applicable to domestic licenses. Item 3 of the Guidelines says that the following acts shall be regarded as the exercise of rights under the Patent Act or the Utility Model Act:

1. To grant license to manufacture, use, sell, etc., separately;
2. To grant license for a limited period within the life of patent rights, etc., or for a limited area within the whole area covered by patent rights, etc.;
3. To restrict the manufacture of patented goods to a limited field of technology or to restrict the sale thereof to a limited field of sales;
4. To restrict the use of patented processes to a limited field of technology;
5. To restrict the amount of output or the amount of sales of

patented goods or to restrict the frequency of the use of patented process.

This part of the Guidelines was formulated after discussions with the patent office and several judges who were experts on the Patent Act,[52] since the scope of exemption from the Antimonopoly Act for the exercise of patent rights is mainly determinable by the Patent Act.

Section 68 of the Patent Act provides that "a patentee is exclusively entitled to work his patented invention in business." Section 2(3) of the Patent Act gives a definition of the working mentioned in Section 68 for each of the three types of invention, namely, product invention, process invention, and process invention for manufacturing a product. For a product invention, the working includes manufacturing, using, transferring, leasing, exhibiting for transfer or lease, and importing the patented article; for a process patent, use of the patented process; and for a process patent for manufacturing a product, in addition to use of the patented process, the use, transfer, lease, exhibition for transfer or lease, or importation of the product manufactured by the patented process. The Patent Act grants a patentee the above exclusive right for the period of fifteen years from the day of the publication of the application or for twenty years from the day of filing the patent application.[53]

A patentee not only is entitled exclusively to work his patented invention in business as stated above, but he also may grant a license to another person either exclusively or nonexclusively.[54] A person who has been granted a license is entitled to work the licensed patented invention only to the extent permitted by the terms of the license.[55] A license contract can grant less than the full scope of the right to work the invention and such a limitation is of a patented invention by a license contract a lawful restriction on the business activities of a licensee in connection with the licensed patent. If such limitation is violated by the licensee, he is liable for infringement of the patent right of the licensor. And, since the licensor's right to effect such limitation is based on the Patent Act, the limitation is an exercise of the licensor's patent right.

It goes without saying that the Patent Act of Japan is effective and enforceable only within the territory of Japan. A right to restrict export is not included in the patent right.

52. *Tokkyoho* (Law No. 122 of 1960 as amended several times).
53. §67 of the Patent Act.
54. §§77(1) and 78(1) of the Patent Act.
55. *Id.* §77(2).

Part III of the Guidelines in enumerating the above five kinds of restriction is intended to state all the restrictions that may with assurance of lawfulness be imposed in granting a license on a patent. The act of imposing an indicated restriction is exempted from the application of the Antimonopoly Act. Any other type of restriction may be vulnerable to attack.

What about a price restriction on a licensee? There is no mention of this point either in the Patent Act or in part III of the Guidelines. The Fair Trade Commission, although taking the position of the GE doctrine of 1926, seems to have decided not to legitimatize price restriction in the Guidelines since there may be circumstances in which price restriction will be considered not safe, from the perspective of the Antimonopoly Act. On the other hand, as a practical matter, a license to manufacture a patented good may not be readily granted by a patentee who also manufactures the patented good if the licensor is not permitted to impose price restriction on the licensee. If one admits that the patent system, which promotes competition in the development of technology by granting a patent monopoly, does not contradict the Antimonopoly Act, which controls restraint of competition, price restriction has to be considered in the context of the broader question—Will it contribute to enhance the benefit attained by technical development and therefore be reasonable from the antimonopoly standpoint? The Fair Trade Commission does not take the position that price restriction as such is exempted. It may consider it reasonable or not, according to circumstance.

III. The Guidelines on International Patent Licensing[56]

That part of the Guidelines which is particularly concerned with exemptions based on the Patent Act, was discussed in the preceding Section. The concern here is with the general provisions, which are stated in the Guidelines as Item I. The text of each Guideline statement concerning a restriction appears in Appendix 2 to this chapter.

A. Guideline on Restrictions Likely to Violate the Act

The Guidelines enumerate only certain of the restrictions that may be used in an international contract licensing patent rights or utility

56. This chapter is based on Gijutsu Enjo Keiyaku Nintei Kijun no Kaisetsu (Explanation of the Guidelines on Technology Instroduction Contracts), (Yuichi Nakamura, ed. 46–100, 1968). The contributors to this book are persons who were or are staff members of the International Section of the FTC.

model rights and which may be liable to attack as unfair business practices. Therefore, it is dangerous to assume that a restriction not mentioned in the Guidelines would not violate the Antimonopoly Act. As the Guidelines is concerned only with unfair business practices, other violations of the act such as monopolization or unreasonable restraint of trade, involving a patent right, are possibilities. For such violations revocation of the patent right or exclusive licensed or nonexclusive licensed right on patent is possible under Section 100.[57] The risk of violation must be avoided by careful study of the relevant substantive provisions and Section 23 of the Antimonopoly Act.

The Fair Trade Commission has thought that the enumerated restrictions are those of major concern, in the light of its experience in scrutinizing of international patent licensing contracts, and upon considering the vast case law of the United States as well as the provisions of the Act against Restraint of Competition of Germany.[58]

1. Restriction on export area. This provision aims to ensure the licensee's freedom of exportation and is based on a court decision. In a case involving an application for a preliminary injunction to stop the exportation of the licensee's goods, the Tokyo District Court stated that even though the plaintiff, who granted a license to the defendant to manufacture and sell goods by using his patented invention "in the whole area of Japan," intended thereby to preclude the defendant from exporting the licensed goods, the defendant should not be deprived of his freedom to export the licensed goods unless he is under the positive obligation not to export.[59]

The exceptions stated in subparts a, b, and c of Item I (1), however, show a lenient attitude of the Fair Trade Commission with respect to restriction on export area. It is assumed that the commission had recognized the strong interest of Japanese enterprises in getting licenses from foreign patentees. There would be difficulties on the part of a licensee as well as the commission in finding out whether the export-area restriction is admissible due to the circumstance mentioned in a) to c) of the proviso.

Examples of license-contracts containing export-area restrictions are diversified. Export restriction is a rather common practice in license-contracts concluded in almost all industries except the camera,

57. N. 42, 44; Text of Section 23 is given in Section II 1 above.

58. §20 of the Act against Restraint of Competition of 27 July 1957 as amended. English text of the legislation is given in 1 *Guide to Legislation on Restrictive Business Practices*, OECD.

59. *Tokkyoken karishobun shinsei jiken* (The case applying for a preliminary injunction on the basis of a patent right) No. 2397 (yo) 1962, Tokyo Dist. Ct. May 18, 1963, 14 Lower Minshu No. 5, 979.

light, electric, and fiber-processing industries. Three types of export restriction are used: (1) overall restriction, (2) partial restriction, and (3) restriction with condition.

Partial restriction is the limitation of export to certain areas. By this limitation licensees are usually permitted to export only to Asian countries. This type of limitation can produce disputes. A licensee who, when the contract was made, had no broader geographic interests may as his business grows develop a strong desire to enter another territory—to export to Europe, for instance.

A restriction with condition is a provision under which the licensor demands payment on export in addition to the agreed royalty, or which permits export upon consent of the licensor.

If an export restriction is in a license contract there is an antimonopoly question even though the licensee lacked at that time the intention or ability to export. A small enterprise eager to get an exclusive license on a lower royalty is apt to accept an export restriction which it may later regret.

Certain provisions of the Fair Trade Commission Notification No. 11 of 1953, which is set out in Appendix 1 to this chapter, are relevant to licenses which restrict export areas. The second item under Unfair Business Practices, which bans discrimination among customers, applies where a licensor imposes an export restriction on one licensee and not on other licensees, with respect to the same patent. Items 8 and 10 are also of interest in this connection.

2. Restriction on export price or export volume. "Export price" includes, in addition to F.O.B. price or C.I.F. price, the wholesale or retail price in the country to which export is made. "Export volume" means direct or indirect exportation by the licensee. This restriction is used where export by the licensee is permitted.

However, Guideline (2) is not applicable where the licensee is permitted to export to special areas falling under any of a), b), or c) of the proviso to the Guideline (1) above, if the restriction is of reasonable scope. The reasonableness of the restriction on export price or export volume in a license which allows export to an area falling under the proviso will depend on the circumstances of the licensor and the licensee.

Cases in which restriction on export price or export volume has been made are rare. However, cases where a licensee was permitted to export to a special area but was required to make such export through the licensor or person designated by the licensor are often found. Sometimes such a restriction will be advantageous to the licensee, therefore, the reasonableness of the restriction has to be considered.

The applicable provisions of the General Unfair Business Practices stated in Fair Trade Commission Notification No. 11 of 1953 (see Appendix 1) are Items 8, 10 and 2.

3. Restriction on competing products or technology. This restriction is often seen in a license contract. "Competing product" means any product similar to or a substitute for the product to be produced under the licensed patent, whether it is manufactured by using the licensee's technology or that of someone else.

Where an exclusive license is granted, it is usually expected that the licensee will not handle a competing product or manufacture a competing product using a different technology. The guideline, however, prohibits the licensor from requiring the licensee to discontinue practices already established. As to these, the licensee must be free to decide for himself. Initiating later a competitive practice is another matter, not covered by the prohibition. The second paragraph of Guideline 3 accordingly approves the restriction, where the license is exclusive and the licensee undertakes to refrain from thereafter beginning the manufacture of competitive products or the use of a competitive technology.

A restriction otherwise bad is probably not saved by a recital that it will be inoperative if the licensor consents or if the licensee will pay a sum in addition to the agreed royalty. Also questionable is a restriction, in a nonexclusive license, which purports to cover only goods both manufactured and sold by the licensee. Nor is success likely for a restriction that does not directly forbid handling or manufacture of competing products but seeks to gain some of the same advantages by forbidding the licensee from holding stock in a competing company or having interlocking directorates with a competing company.

The applicable provisions of the General Unfair Business Practices will be Items 2, 7, 8, 10.

4. Restriction on source of raw material or parts. A restriction of this type is safe from Section 19 when the raw material or parts supplied by the licensor are essential to the manufacturing of the patented goods and are not readily available in Japan. However, except in this situation, the freedom of the licensee to get raw material or parts from any source he chooses has to be protected not only for the sake of the licensee himself but also in aid of potential suppliers.

This restriction is frequently attempted and is often phrased in sophisticated ways. For instance: (1) "if the licensee cannot get raw material or parts within Japan, then he should get them from the licensor or a person designated by the licensor"; (2) "if the raw material or parts are unavailable in Japan, the licensee should get them from the licensor or a person designated by him, but in this case the price will be the internationally competing price"; or (3) "the licensee should get raw material from the licensor as far as it is possible"; (4) "the licensee should get raw material from the licensor. The royalty is made free"; or (5) "the licensee is expected to make efforts to get raw material from the licensor. For each yearly purchase of 1,000 tons, the royalty will be reduced by 10 percent."

The provision applicable where the supplying source of raw material or parts is limited to the licensor himself is Item 6 of the Unfair Business Practices, because the licensor compels the licensee to do business with him on raw material by tying the raw material with the licensing.

To the case in which the licensee is obliged to get raw material from the person designated by the licensor, the first part of Item 8 of the Unfair Business Practices is applied.

Items 10 or 2 of the Unfair Business Practices will be applicable to both of above cases.

5. *Restriction on distribution channels.* Manufacturers have a primary freedom to sell their products to whomsoever they choose. The Unfair Business Practices provisions applicable to this type of restriction are Items 8, 10 and 2, according to the circumstance.

6. *Restriction on resale price.* This restriction is applied to prices at two distribution levels in Japan, wholesale and retail. The price at which the licensee sells is not deemed a resale price.

Resale price restriction is statutorily prohibited. It falls under the middle part of Item 8 of the Unfair Business Practices. However, as to certain drugs and cosmetics, an exemption to the above provision has been recognized in accordance with Section 24–2 of the Antimonopoly Act.

7. *Restriction on improvement or invention.* This restriction is concerned with a so-called "grant-back clause" in a patent license. "Grant-back" includes: (1) supplying information to the licensor concerning knowledge or experience obtained by the licensee with respect to the licensed technology; (2) assignment to the licensor of the right to apply for a patent on, or assignment to the licensor of a patent granted to the licensee on, an the improvement made by the licensee on the licensed technology; and (3) granting a license to the licensor on licensee's improvement patent.

The proviso to Guideline 7 says that if the supplying of information is on a reciprocal basis between the licensor and the licensee and is balanced between the two, the antimonopoly question will not arise. Reciprocal exclusive licensing is not included in this proviso because there is a problem of concentration of technologies in the hands of the two parties and a division of market is likely to result. To be balanced, the terms of restriction such as period, royalty, and area have to be considered.

A restriction on making any improvement on the licensed technology is the worst type used because the licensor wishes to maintain his prestige in the relevant technology or feels a danger to his business in raw material or parts that he manufactures and sells. This restriction falls under Item 10 of the Unfair Business Practices and also Item 2 according to the circumstance.

8. Demand of royalty on product for which the licensed technology is not used. It is clear that a licensor is not entitled to demand payment of royalty on a product which has nothing to do with the licensed technology. A case wherein the licensor demands royalty on a product similar to the product covered by the license, or one deemed similar to the licensed product, falls under Guideline I 8.

However, in the cases wherein it is not determinable whether the licensed technology has been used or not, and royalty has been decided at reasonable price, then such royalty demand will not fall under this guideline.

Package-licensing royalty, minimum royalty in a case other than an exclusive licensing, demand of royalty on exports made to areas where the licensor does not have a relevant patent and a royalty-payment period which does not end until the expiration of the last patent among the several relevant patents in several countries, are all likely to fall under this guideline. Items 10 and 2 of the Unfair Business Practices are applicable to this restriction.

9. Restriction on quality of raw material or parts. A restriction flowing from a specification in the patent itself is, of course, valid. The proviso to this Guideline takes into consideration reasonable circumstances such as the necessity to ensure the good-faith of a registered trademark or the necessity to secure the effectiveness of the licensed technology. If the restriction goes beyond what is reasonable, it will fall under the middle part of Items 8 and 2, Unfair Business Practices.

Besides the commonly used restrictions enumerated in the Guidelines, there may be other practices which are vulnerable to attack. As: (1) the maintenance of a restriction for several years after the license contract expired; (2) compelling the use of the licensor's trademark; (3) tying of goods manufactured by the licensor or any other person which are not the raw material or parts to be used for manufacture of licensed products; and (4) a provision for unilateral cancellation of the contract by the licensor. The first of these will likely fall under Unfair Business Practices Items 7, 8, 10, and 2. The second comes under Item 10. The third comes within the middle part of Item 8. The fourth falls under Item 10.

As to restrictions in know-how licensing, the above Guidelines are applied *mutatis mutandis*. Since know-how is technology secretly held by the owner, the rule of reason mentioned in the Guidelines is applicable as long as this secrecy is maintained. But, if the know-how comes into the public domain during the period of license, it can no longer be restricted. If the secrecy is still maintained after the contract has expired, the licensee is not free to disclose the know-how to the public.

B. Form of Reporting

In accordance with Section 6 of the Antimonopoly Act, Regulation No. 1 of 1953 was issued. It is concerned with the form of reporting required by Section 6, as well as other matters. The latest amendment to the regulation was made in 1970. Because the reporting form under the regulation is too general (see Appendix 4), the International Section of the FTC advises a reporting company to submit a more detailed report, in order to save time and energy in scrutiny of the contract reported. An example given in Appendix 5 will give reporting companies an idea about the points the FTC is interested in developing.

IV. Antimonopoly Enforcement of International Patent Licenses

Japan's Antimonopoly Act, enforcement of which has a history of but twenty-seven years, has not established a good deal of precedent with respect to patent practices. No FTC decision concerned with a case involving patent practices has been litigated in court. Therefore, there is no court-case law.

There are two reasons for this dearth of Fair Trade Commission precedent. First, the cases involving patent right on which the commission initially took action were international cases which came early, in a two year period, 1949 and 1950. All were disposed of by consent decision without any hearing, except for one case which will be discussed later.

Second, in contrast to the enforcement of the United States antitrust laws, domestic cases involving patent rights which would contribute to more sophisticated applications of the law in this field, are very few in number. This is due to the facts that (1) Japanese entrepreneurs are not statutorily required to file their domestic patent license contracts as they are in the case of international patent license contracts and; (2) they have rarely brought complaints to the FTC urging investigation,[60] because they do not realize that their interests may have been unreasonably affected by illegal restrictions in a patent license contract whether they are parties to the contract or not; and furthermore (3) the interest of Japanese entrepreneurs in the Antimonopoly Act enforcement is low as the act does not provide treble or double damages but only ordinary damages and even then only after the Fair Trade Commission's decision adjudicating violation has become final and conclusive.[61]

Therefore, in a discussion of Antimonopoly Act enforcement and specific patent practices, international cases have to be dealt with first. Domestic cases will be discussed later in this chapter.

1. Early cases. The Fair Trade Commission rendered twenty consent decisions up to 1953, against domestic companies that were parties to international patent license contracts. In all these cases, although the restrictions shown in IIB above were found to be illegal under the act as amended in 1949 and the companies were ordered to modify or delete the relevant provisions. Nothing, however, was said in the decisions about the relation of the restriction and Section 23 of the Antimonopoly Act, which exempts acts recognizable as in the exercise of a patent right. The decisions simply said that the concerned restrictions violated Sections 4, 6(1), 19 and sometimes the first part of Section 3.[62] The application of the law by the FTC in these cases was not only diversified but also was unbalanced, but this is not important today.

What is relevant today is the application of Section 19 and the first part of Section 3 to a patent license contract wherein only a licensor and a licensee are involved. In a court decision which was rendered later, it was held that Section 19 is concerned only with a vertical arrangement and that the first part of Section 3 is concerned with a horizontal agreement; and that the latter section cannot be applied to a contract wherein the parties are not competitors as far as the license is concerned.[63]

This interpretation of the law by the court has been respected and followed by the FTC in subsequent cases, including patent-license

60. §45.

61. §§25 and 26.

62. §4 of the original Act of 1947, which was deleted by a 1953 amendment, prohibited entrepreneurs from acting together: (1) to fix, maintain or enhance prices; (2) to restrict volume of production or sales; (3) to restrict technology, product, territory or customer, and (4) to restrict establishing newly or expansion of facilities, or adoption of new technology or new production system. §6(1) of the act as amended by 1949 prohibited entrepreneurs from concluding an international contract containing matters in Section 4 above which was not affected by 1949 amendment.

63. *See* note 33 *supra*, and the statement made in Item 1 of II of the Announcement of the Guidelines, Appendix 2.

contract cases, which have come under the Guidelines. The only concern of the Guidelines is with unfair business practices.[64]

The following discussion is of an illustrative international license case. It involved exaction of unwarranted royalty. Eleven hearings were held, and the hearing examiner was ready to render a decision, but the matter was finally ended in 1953 by a consent decision.

A Japanese shipbuilding company obtained a license from a Swiss company for manufacture of its patented combustion engines. The licensor required in the license contract, among other things, that the licensee should pay royalty on such types of combustion engines as the licensee might develop and patent even without use of the licensor's patented invention or any technical information supplied by the licensor. The Fair Trade Commission held that the demand for royalty on the use of the licensee's patented invention constituted an unfair method of competition falling under Section 2(6), and that it violated Section 19.[65]

B. Cases After the Guidelines was Issued

As mentioned above, the so-called liberalization which started in 1967 made unnecessary the procedure whereby antimonopoly problems in international licensing contracts were informally screened in the Foreign Investment Council, and produced a great increase in the number of license contracts filed with the Fair Trade Commission. To help cope with this situation the Antimonopoly Guidelines for International Licensing Agreements were issued on 24 May, 1968.

It goes without saying that the Guidelines is not a law passed by the National Diet, but rather is simply a formal announcement of the Fair Trade Commission's position in screening international technology licensing contracts. Nevertheless, since there is no published case law on the subject except for those twenty old cases mentioned above, the Guidelines may serve, at least, as a list of check points for both Japanese and foreign firms that contemplate entering into technology licensing arrangements.

The number of international licensing contracts filed with the Fair Trade Commission by which Japanese companies received patent licenses from foreign patentees has grown and, is still growing sharply according to the Fair Trade Commission statistics given in its annual

64. The term unfair "method of competition" used in the original Antimonopoly Act was changed by the 1953 amendment to "unfair business practices". The first part of Sec. 2(6) under the 1949 amendment is substantially similar to the provision of Item 8 of the Unfair Business Practices. Section 19 has not been changed since the original act of 1947.

65. *Mitsubishi Zosen Co., Ltd.* and *Sulzer Freres, Societe Anonyme* Case, April 23, 1953, 5 FTC Decision Report 1.

reports of 1961 to 1973.[66] Yet, there was not during this period a single instance of litigation involving FTC action on a patent matter. According to the Fair Trade Commission's annual report of 1971, the Fair Trade Commission Staff Office found restrictive clauses in violation of Section 19 in 83 out of 101 foreign technology licensing contracts, in light of the Guidelines.[67] The practice of the Fair Trade Commission, instead of taking any formal action, is first informally to advise the parties—generally the Japanese company concerned—to modify or delete the offending clause. Such advising is termed "administrative guidance." Usually such guidance is accepted and the contract is modified accordingly. This is the reason why there is no decision record with respect to international technology licensing contracts.

The Fair Trade Commission's annual reports disclose the data on restrictions in international contracts including patent licenses, sales agent licenses, and loan contracts as to which its administrative guidance has been given. Although the details of each restriction specifically found in licenses on technology are not separately given, a general idea may be obtained from the fact that in 1971, 82 percent of 101 international contracts were license contracts. The figures for that year also show that, of 101 contracts, 71 were concerned with restrictions on improved technology, 28 were concerned with restrictions on dealing in competitive products, 7 were concerned with restrictions on resale price, 4 were concerned with restrictions on the source of raw materials or parts, 1 was concerned with restrictions on customers, and 2 were miscellaneous. The figures for 1972 and 1973 show about the same proportions.

It is interesting to note that transfer of improved technology, commonly termed "grant-back," is by far the most frequently found restriction. It must be borne in mind that a grant-back restriction is not regarded as per se illegal. Thus, the Guidelines state a sort of rule of reason that no violation will exist where both sides, licensor and licensee, have similar grant-back obligations, which are balanced in substance as well as in form.

As an additional aid to would-be parties to international technology licensing arrangements, the Fair Trade Commission gives in its annual report of 1970 five examples of international contracts to which its guidance was given to eliminate violations.[68] One is concerned with a patent pool, which will be described separately later. The other four are listed below.

66. Appendix 3.
67. FTC Annual Report of 1971, 143.
68. FTC Annual Report of 1970, 132–33.

1. Grant-back (Guideline 1-7). The original contract between *A* Company (Japanese) (licensee) and *B* Company (Swiss) (licensor)—the names of the companies are not given in the Annual Report—prescribed that "with respect to patents on improvement made by the licensee on the product, the licensor has the right to submit patent applications in such countries as the licensor deems fit." This provision purports to make rights (including the right to apply for patent) on technology improved by the licensee belong to the licensor. The parties were advised to modify the provision as "the licensee primarily has the right to decide whether to apply for a patent on his improvements. Only if the licensee does not apply for patent will the licensor has the right to file such patent application."

In all these examples, the statement of the case indicates that the proposed agreement constitutes an unfair business practice and will be violative of Section 19 of the Antimonopoly Act, but does not indicate under what particular unfair business practice of the Unfair Business Practices the example falls. This first case would probably fall under Item 10—abuse of dominant position.

2. Restriction on competitive products (Guideline 1-3). In a contract between *A* Company (Japan) and *B* Company (U.S.) establishing a joint-venture company *A* Company was prohibited from dealing in any product in competition with the product of the joint-venture company "as long as either of *A* Company or *B* Company remains as stockholder, and for three years after either of the parties disposed of the stock held by it." Considering *A*'s liability to be too severe, the Fair Trade Commission advised the parties to reduce the restriction period to "(1) the period during which *B* Company remains as stockholder of or (2) the period of two years after *A* Company disposes of its entire stock in, the joint company."

This second case would probably fall under Item 7 of the Unfair Business Practices—unjustifiable exclusive dealing.

3. Restriction on purchasing source of raw material or parts (Guideline 1-4). A contract concluded between *A* Company (Japan) and *B* Company (Sweden) provided that *B* Company would license a patent right to *A* Company and that *A* Company would sublicense the patent to *C* Company, and that the sublicense would provide that *C* Company would purchase component parts only from *B* Company except where *C* Company could manufacture such parts or buy them from another source, at a price better than that of *B* Company.

The parties were advised to delete the provision calling for the purchase by *C* Company of component parts, from *B* Company.

This third case would fall under tie-in, or Item 8 of the Unfair Business Practices.

4. Charging excessive countervalue (Guideline 1-8). In the original patent licensing contract concluded between *A* Company (Japanese) (Licensee) and *B* Company (U.S.) (Licensor), it was stipulated that *A* Company should pay such and such a royalty on the "licensed products" manufactured by *A* Company. However, the term "licensed products" was defined to mean all machines or equipments substantially similar to products manufactured by *B* Company. By virtue of this definition, *A* Company was made liable to pay royalty on number of products other than the products licensed by *B* Company. Deletion of the relevant part of the definition was advised. This case would also probably fall under Item 10 of the Unfair Business Practices, abuse of dominant position.

V. Cross Licenses

Until recently, cross licensing has not been common in Japan since this is a practice to be seen where the technological standards of both parties are equal. In contrast to the introduction of foreign technologies into Japan, transfers of technologies by Japanese firms to foreign firms have so far been very few in number. Even in 1970 and 1971 the figures were 78 and 223 respectively, and it is believed that there are not many cross license contracts.[69] No violation case involving a cross license contract has so far been reported.

VI. Patent Pooling and Package Licensing

A patent pool, whether it is domestic or international, is not illegal as such. However, sometimes antimonopoly problems arise. The FTC's Annual Report of 1970 reports one international patent pool agreement.[70]

Two Japanese Companies, one English Company, one German Company, and one Swiss Company concluded a patent pool agreement. The agreement established a regime for the exchange of technology relating to machines they manufactured between the Japanese group and the European group. Among other things they agreed that (1) the Japanese group would not sell their machines in England, Germany, and Switzerland, and the European group would not sell in Japan (thereby mutually imposing a sales territory restraint); and (2) before any of the parties should grant a license on any of the patents included in the agreement, the prior consent of all the other parties was necessary.

The Fair Trade Commission advised the parties, with respect to (1) above, that the provision relating to sales territorial restraint should

69. FTC Annual Report of 1970, 126; FTC Annual Report of 1971, 141.
70. FTC Annual Report of 1970, 133.

be replaced with a provision stating that a party was entitled to obtain, if it wished, a nonexclusive license from the other party concerned; and that (2) be deleted. The ground for this advice was that, considering the market position of the five companies, the danger of substantial restraint of competition in the affected market was great, and such restraint could not be recognized as within the litigimate scope of the exercise of patent rights.

This is a cartel case involving five patent owners and violation of the first part of (1) of Section 6(1) of the Antimonopoly Act. The Guidelines does not cover a cartel agreement. In spite of Section 6(2), which requires filing of all international contracts or agreements with the Fair Trade Commission, a cartel agreement is rarely filed. The writer assumes that this is the first case in which FTC was informed of an illegal patent pool agreement.

With respect to package licensing, no case has been brought before the commission. This is a type of tying contract, and the writer believes that the applicable theory is the same as that used in a domestic case involving block-booking practices, in the motion picture industry.[71]

VII. Joint Venture

In establishing a joint-venture company in Japan by a Japanese firm and a foreign firm that owns a patent in Japan, the foreign partner will pay for its stock in the new company with a license or assignment of its patent together with such money, if any, as is necessary to complete its contribution to the corporate capital.

Regarding a joint-venture program, a Japanese firm is advised by MITI to have the majority share in the joint-venture company. If the foreign partner's patent is licensed to the joint-venture company, MITI advises that such license should be an exclusive one. However, if the foreign partner is prohibited from granting an exclusive license by a court decision grounded on its past foreign antitrust violation, then a nonexclusive license would be admitted.

Restrictions on the activities of a joint venture, whether made in the basic joint-venture agreement or in the license contract itself, are subject to the FTC's scrutiny in the light of the Guidelines.

VIII. Domestic Cases

In the United States, domestic antitrust cases involving patents are numerous, whereas in Japan there are only four domestic antimonopoly cases involving patents. One of the four was concerned

71. *Shochiku Company Ltd.* and 66 others, FTC February 27, 1959, FTC Decision Report 114.

with an unfair business practice, and another one concerned an illegal cartel agreement among competitors, involving patents. The remaining two cases related to merger, where patents were involved. A brief account of each of them follows.

Restriction on Customers and Retail Prices

Yakuruto Honsha Co., Ltd., the owner of a process patent for manufacturing a fermented milk drink called "Yakuruto," in granting licenses under its patent and trademark to persons wishing to manufacture and sell the product, required them to sell only to so-called "Class A" retailers. These were retailers who had separately entered into contracts with Yakuruto Honsha stipulating that they would observe the retail prices, areas, and sales volume prescribed by Yakuruto Honsha. The license agreement also required the licensees to keep watch over the "Class A" retailers to make sure that they observed these restrictions. The Fair Trade Commission held that the above acts of Yakuruto Honsha were acts not recognized as an exercise of patent rights under the Patent Act and that they violated Section 19 of the Antimonopoly Act.

This was a case of a recommendation procedure in which the Fair Trade Commission recommended that the company delete the offending provisions from the license contracts. Yakuruto Honsha accepted the recommendation, and a decision was rendered along the lines of the recommendation.[72]

Cartel agreement among patentee-producers

Nihon Konkuriito Kogyo and five other concrete-pile producers that supply in competition substantially all the requirements of this product in the major areas of Japan, held individual competing patent or utility model rights relating to the manufacture of concrete piles. They entered into an agreement for the purpose of stabilizing the market.

They stipulated in the agreement the market share and sales quota of each member. They also agreed that in case a member granted a license of his patent to a third party, such license should be approved in advance by all the members of the agreement, and such licensee's shipments should be deducted from the market share allotted to the licensor by the agreement. They further agreed that the license contract should include a provision that the licensee should observe the market stabilization scheme of the six members. After this arrangement had been in existence for some time, licensees gradually came to

72. *Yakuruto Honsha Co., Ltd.* Case, FTC September 13, 1965, 13 FTC Decision Report 14.

be allotted their shipment shares directly from the agreement, but they were still not admitted as full members of the group.

The Fair Trade Commission held that the above patentee-producers agreement substantially restricted competition in the sale of concrete piles and constituted an unreasonable restraint of trade in violation of Section 3 of the Antimonopoly Act. It ordered the parties to abandon the agreement.

This case was treated purely as an illegal cartel agreement among competing suppliers and nothing was mentioned with respect to the validity of the restrictions contained in the individual licenses.[73]

Corporate mergers

1. The merger of Mitsubishi Jyukogyo Co., Ltd. and two other companies. The merger, or rather, reunion of the three Mitsubishi Jyukogyo heavy industry companies, which had been made into three independent companies by virtue of the law concerning Elimination of Excessive Concentration of Economic Power of 1947, was effected in 1963. Two of the companies had licenses for paper-manufacturing machines, under separate patents from different foreign companies, one being a United States company and the other being a Swiss company. These patents were world famous and dominating. If the surviving company, after the merger, continued to use both patents, its 63 percent market share would give the company a monopoly position in the paper-manufacturing machine industry.

Under the Antimonopoly Act, a merger is not allowed (1) when the effect of a merger may be substantially to restrain competition in any particular field of trade, or (2) where an unfair business practice has been employed in the course of the merger. Every company that is desirous of becoming a party to a merger has to notify its intention to the Fair Trade Commission and have its plan screened by the commission. The prospective merger is not allowed to be consummated until after a period of thirty days from the date of filing (Section 15). If the Fair Trade Commission thinks that the prospective merger will be violative of the Antimonopoly Act, it has to issue a complaint or recommendation to stop the merger within the above waiting period.

In this merger case, the Fair Trade Commission was of the opinion that the holding of both of the two leading world famous licenses by the company after merger would substantially restrain competition. Having received the Fair Trade Commission's strong informal advice to this effect, the parties promised to cancel one of the licenses after the merger. The Fair Trade Commission, in reliance on this promise,

73. *Nihon Konkuriito Kogyo Co.*, Ltd. (Japan Cement Industry Co., Ltd.) Case, FTC August 5, 1970, 17 FTC Decision Report 86.

let the thirty day period pass without issuing a formal recommendation or complaint; the merger was then consummated; and one of the licenses was cancelled as promised.

Since the Fair Trade Commission did not issue either a recommendation or a complaint in this case, the case does not appear in the commission's Decision Report.[74]

2. *Yawata Steel Manufacturing Company and Fuji Steel Manufacturing Company merger.* In the merger case of Yawata Steel Manufacturing Company and Fuji Steel Manufacturing Company, the Fair Trade Commission issued a complaint to the parties alleging that the prospective merger would restrain substantially the competition in four items of their steel products, namely, foundry pig iron, plate for food cans, rails for railways, and sheet piles, and that the merger would violate Section 15 of the Antimonopoly Act. The parties applied for a consent decision by proposing to the commission various counter measures to eliminate the alleged violations, mainly by transferring important relevant physical assets to third parties so as to reduce the relevant market shares of the merged company. The Fair Trade Commission, deeming that the proposed transfers would create competitors having effective power to check the business behavior of the new company, rendered a consent decision along the line of the proposed counter measures. The decision also included the order to supply relevant technological know-how and to grant licenses under patents that the respondents had on manufacturing foundry pig iron, rails for railways and sheet piles, to the transferees of the physical assets concerned. The Fair Trade Commission further ordered that in granting patent and know-how licenses the new company should not impose the licensees any restrictions with respect to output, selling price, and sales area.[75]

IX. Claim of Damages

Section 25 of the Antimonopoly Act provides that one who has employed unfair business practices shall be liable to indemnify the person injured, not treble damages but only a single damage, and that "no entrepreneur may be exempted from liability by proving the non-existence of malice or negligence on his part." A suit claiming damages for loss sustained by an antimonopoly violation must be made to the Tokyo High Court, but this cannot be done until after a Fair Trade Commission decision adjudicating violation becomes final and conclusive. Such suit must be filed within three years from that

74. FTC Annual Report of 1963.

75. *Yawata Seitetsu Co., Ltd.* and *Fuji Seitetsu Co.*, Ltd. Case, FTC Decision October 30, 1969, 16 FTC Decision Report 46.

day.[76] There have been only a few cases of damage suits instituted under this provision, and none of them relates to licensing, either international or domestic.

Persons who have been injured by a violation of the Antimonopoly Act by an entrepreneur may theoretically file a suit as a tort case with a district court under Section 709 of the Civil Code. However, in such a private civil case, the plaintiff has to show that the defendant violated the Antimonopoly Act in addition to the fact that he has been injured by the violation. The burden of proof on the part of the plaintiff is too heavy to justify instituting a private single damage suit at district court. Therefore private antitrust enforcement as a remedy has been weak.

X. Extraterritorial-Application Problem and Section 6 of the Antimonopoly Act

Section 6 of the Antimonopoly Act is so constituted as to avoid the extraterritorial-application problem. The party liable for compliance with this provision is primarily the party resident in Japan; in most of the international licensing contract cases this is a Japanese firm or a foreign firm having a branch office in Japan. Section 6 prohibits primarily-Japanese parties from entering into an international contract or agreement containing an unreasonable restraint of trade or an unfair business practice, whether they are the initiators or the victims of such practice. In a purely domestic case where an unfair business practice is found to have been employed, the violator of the Antimonopoly Act is the one who employed the practice and not the person against whom such practice was employed, even if he agreed to have it employed against him.

In an international contract or agreement the foreign party is not usually to be found in the territory of Japan. To avoid jurisdictional problems and to eliminate violation, Section 6 is carefully phrased. However, the extraterritorial-application problem seems not to have been completely avoided by this provision. Novo Industry Co., Ltd., a Danish Company, concluded with Amano Pharmaceutical Company, a Japanese Company, a contract relating to continuous sale in Japan of Novo's product called "Alcalase," an enzyme-decomposing, alkaline bacterial protein. The contract provided, inter alia, that Amano should not produce or sell any alkaline bacterial protein decomposing enzyme for industrial use that might compete which Novo's Alcalase, for three years after termination of the contract.

The Fair Trade Commission issued a recommendation to Amano that it had concluded an international contract containing an unfair

76. Section 26(1) of the Antimonopoly Act.

business practice falling under Items 7 and 8 of the Unfair Business Practices. Upon acceptance of the FTC recommendation by Amano, the Fair Trade Commission rendered a decision in line with the recommendation.[77] Then in order to observe the order of the decision, Amano asked Novo to agree to change the offending provisions, but Novo at first refused. After the contract was eventually terminated by Novo, it appealed to the Tokyo High Court objecting to the Fair Trade Commission's decision, and asserting that Novo's interest was affected by the decision. The court rejected the appeal, because this FTC decision was an administrative order, directed to Amano and not to Novo. The only persons who have a right to appeal from such a decision are the recipient of the decision or one who has a legal interest to apply for its revocation. Therefore Novo did not have standing to appeal.[78]

XI. Organization of Economic Cooperation and Development (OECD)

In an international antimonopoly violation case wherein foreign companies are involved, jurisdictional disputes and conflicts of interest with the countries concerned have frequently occurred. To cope with this situation, the Committee of Experts on Restrictive Business Practices (RBP Committee) of the Organization of Economic Cooperation and Development (*OECD*) has been practicing the so-called Notification System following the Recommendation of the Council of the OECD made to the committee in October 1967. This is a system whereby a member of the RBP Committee notifies such other member country or countries of antitrust action that it has taken or is about to take against a company of another member country. This system aims to achieve an amicable solution to the jurisdictional problem.

Although this system is an entirely voluntary one, it has been operating satisfactorily. Japan has sent notifications to several member countries in two cases, one of which was the Novo case mentioned above, and has received notifications in cases where a Japanese firm was involved, from several countries including the United States.

77. *Amano Seiyaku Kabushiki Kaisha ni Taisuru Ken* (Case concerning Amano Pharmaceutical Co., Ltd.), FTC January 12, 1970, 16 FTC Decision Report 134.

78. Novo Industry Co., Ltd. v. FTC, Tokyo High Court May 19, 1971, Gyo (ke) No. 16, 1970; 17 FTC Decision Report 297.

Appendixes

1: Fair Trade Commission Notification
NO. 11 OF 1953

In accordance with the provisions of Section 2(7) of the Act concerning Prohibition of Private Monopoly and Maintenance of Fair Trade (Act No. 54 of 1947), unfair business practices, other than specific business practices in a particular field of trade to be designated in accordance with the procedure as provided for in Section 71 of the said Act, shall be designated as follows:

UNFAIR BUSINESS PRACTICES

1. Unduly refusing or limiting deliveries from certain entrepreneurs or to supply to certain other entrepreneurs, commodities, funds, or other kinds of economic benefit.

2. Affording, without good reason, substantially favourable or unfavourable treatment to certain entrepreneurs in regard to the terms or execution of transactions.

3. Excluding specific entrepreneurs from concerted activities or from a trade association, or unduly discriminating against specific entrepreneurs in the concerted activities or the trade association, thereby causing to such entrepreneurs undue disadvantage with respect to their business activities.

4. Supplying or receiving, without good cause, commodities, funds, or other kinds of economic benefit at prices which discriminate between customers in different places or between customers.

5. Supplying commodities, funds, or other kinds of economic benefit at unreasonably low prices or receiving them at unreasonably high prices.

6. Inducing or coercing, directly or indirectly, customers of a competitor to deal with oneself by offering undue advantages or threatening undue disadvantages in the light of normal business practices.

7. Dealing with customers on the condition that they shall, without good cause, not supply commodities, funds, or other kinds of economic benefit to, or not receive commodities, funds or other kinds of economic benefit from a competitor of oneself.

8. Dealing with customers on conditions, which, without good reason, restrict any transaction between the said customers and the

supplier of commodities, funds, or other kinds of economic benefit to them or between the said customers and any person receiving those from them, or any relationship between the said customers and their competitors.

9. Dealing with a company on the condition, without good reason, that the appointment of officers of that company [meaning those as defined by subsection (3) of Section 2 of the Act concerning Prohibition of Private Monopoly and Maintenance of Fair Trade] shall be subject to prior direction or approval by oneself.

10. Trading with customers on conditions which are unduly unfavourable in the light of normal business practices by making use of one's predominant position over the said customers.

11. Unjustly interfering with a transaction between other entrepreneurs who compete in Japan with oneself or with the company of which oneself is a stockholder or an officer and their party to such transaction by preventing the execution of a contract, or by inducing breach of contract, or by any other means whatsoever.

12. Unjustly inducing, abetting, or coercing a stockholder or an officer of a company which competes in Japan with oneself or a company of which oneself is a stockholder or an officer, to act against the interest of such company by the exercise of voting rights, transfer of stock, divulgence of secrets, or any other means whatsoever.

2: On the Announcement of "Antimonopoly Act Guidelines for International Licensing Agreements"

24 May, 1968
Fair Trade Commission

I. The Intention of the Commission

As liberalization measures for introduction of foreign technology are to be put into effect, the Fair Trade Commission prepared "Antimonopoly Act Guidelines for International Licensing Agreements" as attached herewith and decided to make it public.

In reference to international licensing agreements, subsection 1 of Section 6 of the Act concerning Prohibition of Private Monopoly and Maintenance of Fair Trade (Antimonopoly Act) prohibits an entrepreneur from entering into an international agreement which contains such matters as constituting unreasonable restraint of trade or unfair business practices. The Guidelines concern especially with restrictions which are liable to come under unfair business practices.

The Antimonopoly Act provides for post notification of international agreements (subsection 2 of Section 6) and measures for elimination of illegal agreements (Section 7). However, there has been almost no agreement filed with the commission which was found to violate the Antimonopoly Act due to the fact that undue restrictions originally contained in the agreements had so far been modified or removed in the process of screening under the Foreign Investment Act.

However, after the regulations for the introduction of technology are liberalized, the screening process will no longer be undertaken with respect to restrictions, and restrictions will be subject only to post scrutiny under Section 6 of the Antimonopoly Act.

It is the intention of the commission, on the basis of the Guidelines, to more closely scrutinize undue restrictions and strive to eliminate them. The commission expects that each contracting party will give due consideration to the Guidelines in advance and will not enter into such an agreement which will violate the provisions of the Antimonopoly Act. If there is any doubt as to the application of the

Antimonopoly Act concerning the provisions of an agreement, the commission is ready to respond when it is consulted.

II. Concerning the Guidelines

Item 1: This item enumerates restrictions which are liable to come under unfair business practices in international licensing agreements on patent rights or utility model rights. However, this item enumerates only certain outstanding restrictions; therefore, any other restrictions not mentioned herein should not be considered as not falling under the Antimonopoly Act.

Item 2: Restrictions in international know-how licensing agreements will be treated in the same manner as those in international licensing agreements on patent rights or utility model rights.

Item 3: Section 23 of the Antimonopoly Act exempts the acts which are regarded as exercise of rights under the Patent Act, etc. This item serves to clarify that the restrictive practices herein enumerated shall be regarded as the exercise of such rights.

Antimonopoly Act Guidelines for International Licensing Agreements

24 May, 1968
Fair Trade Commission

Item I. Among the restrictions which are liable to come under unfair business practices in international licensing agreements on patent rights or utility model rights (hereinafter referred to as "patent rights, etc.") the following are the outstanding:

1. To restrict the area to which the licensee may export the goods covered by patent rights, etc. (hereinafter referred to as "patented goods").

However, cases coming under a, b, or c listed below are excluded.

a. In case the licensor has patent rights, etc. which have been registered in the area to which the licensee's export is restricted (hereinafter referred to as the "restricted area");

b. In case the licensor is selling patented goods in the restricted area in his normal business;

c. In case the licensor has granted to a third party an exclusive license to sell in the restricted area.

2. To restrict the licensee's export prices or quantities of patented goods, or to make it obligatory for the licensee to export patented goods through the licensor or a person designated by the licensor.

However, such cases are excluded where the licensor grants license to export to the area coming under either of the preceding a, b, or c and said restrictions or obligations imposed are of reasonable scope.

3. To restrict the licensee from manufacturing, using or selling goods, or employing technology which are in competition with the licensed subject.

However, such cases are excluded where the licensor grants an exclusive license and imposes no restriction on goods already being manufactured, used or sold, or technology already being utilized by the licensee.

4. To make it obligatory for the licensee to purchase raw materials, parts, etc. from the licensor or a person designated by the licensor.

5. To make it obligatory for the licensee to sell patented goods through the licensor or a person designated by the licensor.

6. To restrict the resale prices of patented goods in Japan.

7. To make it obligatory for the licensee to inform the licensor of knowledge or experience newly obtained regarding the licensed technology, or to assign the right with respect to an improved or applied invention by the licensee to the licensor or to grant the licensor a license thereon.

However, such cases are excluded where the licensor bears similar obligations and the obligations of both parties are equally balanced in substance.

8. To charge royalties on goods which do not utilize licensed technology.

9. To restrict the quality of raw materials, parts, etc. or of patented goods.

However, such cases are excluded where such restrictions are necessary to maintain the creditability of the registered trademark or to insure the effectiveness of the licensed technology.

Item II. The aforementioned Guidelines shall apply to international know-how licensing agreements.

Item III. In international licensing agreements on patent rights, etc., the following acts shall be regarded as the exercise of rights under the Patent Act or the Utility Model Act:

1. To grant license to manufacture, use, sell, etc. separately;

2. To grant license for a limited period within the life of patent rights, etc. or for a limited area within the whole area covered by patent rights, etc.;

3. To restrict the manufacture of patented goods to a limited field of technology or to restrict the sale thereof to a limited field of sales;

4. To restrict the use of patented processes to a limited field of technology;

5. To restrict the amount of output or the amount of sales of patented goods or to restrict the frequency of the use of patented processes.

3: Introduction of Foreign Capital by Year

Year Contract	1961	1962	1963	1964	1965	1966	1967	1968	1969	1970	1971	1972	1973
Technical assistance	309	282	617	388	484	543	609	1.345	1.112	1.179	1.352	1.409	1.762
Loan	25	50	85	132	63	36	123	265	211	279	422	490	558
Purchase	2	2	4	3	21	12	11	44	37	41	484*	512	955
Joint venture	18	9	21	28	28	47	29	51	87	90	88	125	134
Others	6	28	39	62	5	1	8	9	23	34	1.514	230	659
Total	360	371	766	713	601	639	780	1.714	1.470	1.623	4.461	33.117	4.068

SOURCE: Dokusen Kinshi Seisaku Nijyu Nenshi (Antimonopoly Policy Twenty Years History) FTC Annual Reports for 1968 at 94; 1969 at 130; 1970 at 126; 1971 at 1 '0; 1972 at 108; and 1973 at 214.

*In the Annual Report of 1971 the type of contract termed as purchase is changed to import agency.

4: Regulation Concerning Reporting of International Contract, Stockholding, Interlocking Directorate, Merger, and Business Transfer

FTC REGULATION NO. 1 OF 1953

In accordance with the provisions of Section 6 . . . of the Antimonopoly Act the regulating on reporting . . . is hereby decided as follows.

Section 1. [Omitted]

Section 2. Any person who is going to file a report on the conclusion of an international agreement or international contract in accordance with the provisions of subsection 2 of Section 6 shall submit to the Fair Trade Commission two sets of reporting paper, one original and one copy thereof written in the Form No. 1.

(2) The preceding reporting paper shall be accompanied by a document of agreement or contract or a copy thereof showing the contents of the agreement or contract (if the agreement or contract is a verbal one, a paper describing the contents thereof).

[Omitted.]

Form No. 1 (paper size, B4 of Japan Standard Specification)
Report of Conclusion of International Agreement
(International Contract)

Date ________

To: The Fair Trade Commission

Name (Names of Company and
its representative)
Seal

I hereby submit in accordance with the provisions of subsection 2 of Section 6 of the Antimonopoly Act, the following report together with the document as prescribed in subsection 2 of Section 2 of the Fair Trade Regulation No. 1 of 1953.

1. Matters concerning the person who files report:
   (a) Address (if there is a business office or any contacting point in Tokyo, such address and telephone number)
   (b) Name or title of company
   (c) Date of establishment
   (d) Business history
   (e) Amount of capital and assets (as of month year)
   (f) Outline of the present business;
2. Matters concerning the other party:
   (a) Address
   (b) Name or title of company
   (c) Date of establishment and the law under which it was established
   (d) Amount of capital and assets (as of month year)

(e) Outline of the present business;

3. Relation heretofore between the parties to the agreement (contract);
4. Date of conclusion of the agreement (contract) and the its effective period;
5. Gist of the agreement (contract);

Remarks: In the accompanying document, a statement certifying that it is a true copy of the original, shall be made.

5: An Example of Report on Conclusion of International License Contract Prepared According to Form No. 1 of FTC's Regulation No. 1 of 1953

1.
2. [Omitted because these items will
3. not raise questions]
4.
5. Gist of the Contract

Licensing of technological information, trademark, and patent relating to the manufacture of synthetic resin projecting machine.

(a) Manufacture area
exclusive in Japan

(b) Sales area

(1) exclusive:
Japan, and East and South Asian Countries

(2) nonexclusive:
Japan, East and South Asian Countries, and any country in the world except the United States and Canada

(c) Patent registration
2 patents
Patent No. _____
Patent No. _____

(d) Trademark registration
1 trademark
Registered No. ßßßßß

(e) Sublicense
a prior approval of the licensor is required

(f) Consideration
a. running royalty 4% of sale price
b. initial payment 100,000 US dollars
c. minimum royalty none

6. Restrictions
   a. Sales of competing products are prohibited
      (Article 8 of the Contract)
   b. Source of supply of raw material is restricted
      (Article 12 of the Contract)
   c. Customers to whom the manufactured products are sold is restricted
      (Article 15 of the Contract)
   d. Others

*Antitrust-Patent Problems Under United States Law, with Particular Reference to International Aspects**

WILBUR L. FUGATE

I. General Principles of Antitrust and Patent Law

A. Antitrust Goals

The basic United States antitrust law, the Sherman Act,[1] termed a "Charter of Freedom" by Chief Justice Hughes of the Supreme Court,[2] was enacted in 1890 at a time when there was great concern in the United States over the monopoly threat of giant trusts. The idea of control of the market by a few individuals or companies was repugnant to the American concept of political and economic freedom. The Sherman Act expressed this fundamental principle of equality of business opportunity and competition.

The Sherman Act makes it a crime to restrain trade or monopolize a market. The terms of Section 1 refer to "every restraint of trade," but in the *Standard Oil* case of 1911[3] the Supreme Court announced the "rule of reason" under which only unreasonable restraints violate the Act. Chief Justice White in that case and in the later *American Tobacco* case,[4] referred to the Anglo-American common law that had held that those agreements and combinations were illegal "which operated to the prejudice of the public interests by unduly restricting competition or unduly obstructing the due course of trade or which, either because of their inherent nature or effect or because of the evident purpose of the acts, injuriously restrained trade. . . ."[5]

*Some of the material herein has been taken from Chap. 8 of the author's book, *Foreign Commerce and the Antitrust Laws* (2d ed., 1973), and grateful acknowledgment is made to Little, Brown, and Co., Boston, Mass. for its use.

1. 26 Stat. 209 (1890) as amended, 15 U.S.C. §1 (1970).
2. Appalachian Coals v. U.S., 288 U.S. 344, 359–60 (1933).
3. Standard Oil Co. v. U.S., 221 U.S. 1 (1911).
4. United States v. American Tobacco Co., 221 U.S. 106 (1911).
5. *Id.* at 179.

Some practices under the Sherman Act, however, have been considered to be unreasonable per se, including price-fixing and division of markets by competitors, group boycotts, agreements to control production, and "tying clauses" in patent licenses requiring the licensee to purchase unpatented goods from the patentee.

B. Patent System Goals

The patent laws in effect carve out an excepted area from the usual operation of the antitrust laws. Article I, Section 8 of the United States Constitution provides that the Congress shall have power "to promote the progress of science and useful arts, by securing for limited times to authors and inventors the exclusive right to their respective writings and discoveries." The patent laws enacted under this constitutional authority provide for a grant to inventors "for the term of seventeen years, of the right to exclude others from making, using or selling the invention throughout the United States."[6]

The patent system, as seen by the framers of the United States Constitution, was entirely consistent with the American free-enterprise system. For example, Thomas Jefferson, who was a great believer in a free economy, was also a chief proponent of the patent system. The patent system is intended to provide an incentive for the inventor to create new and useful inventions by offering him the reward of exclusivity for a limited time. New inventions foster new products and new technology, both of which advance our trade and commerce.

While patents give the patentee the right to exclude, the whole line of United States patent-antitrust cases indicates that patent rights, since they constitute an exception to the general rule of competition, will be strictly construed. In fact the Supreme Court has characterized the patent right as a "privilege which is conditioned by a public purpose."[7] The Court has also emphasized that the "progress of science and useful arts" is the primary purpose of the patent grant.[8]

Patents and copyrights, each of which has a constitutional basis and a lawful monopoly aspect, have been given similar treatment by the courts in the field of antitrust law. Technology, know-how, and secret processes have received a different treatment but usually with the patent-antitrust principles being in the background of the decisions;

6. 66 Stat. 804 (1952); 35 U.S.C. §154 (1964).

7. Mercoid Corp. v. Mid-Continent Inv. Co. 320 U.S. 661, 666 (1944). *See also* issue of APLA Quart. J. devoted to the patent-antitrust interface, 2 APLA Quart. J. 1 *et seq.* (Winter 1974); Joelson, *International Technology Transfers and the United States Antitrust Laws*, 8 J. of Int. Law and Economics 85 (1974).

8. *Id.* at 665. *See also* Blonder–Tongue Laboratories v. University of Illinois Foundation, 400 U.S. 313 (1971).

the fact that for these interests there is no legal monopoly is a distinguishing feature. Trademarks also do not have a statutory monopoly since the essential purpose of trademarks is to designate the source of origin of goods.[9] This is still true in a day when a trademark can be more valuable than the product it designates.

In international trade and licensing, perhaps the most significant characteristic of a patent is limitation of the legal monopoly granted by a country to rights within that country. The United States Supreme Court from an early date has held that foreign patents give no rights in the United States[10] and that United States patents give no rights outside of the United States.[11]

The Paris Convention for the Protection of Industrial Property[12] provides (after stating the principle of the independence of national patents) for obtaining protection in other countries. Under this convention a patentee can, without losing his claim to novelty, file an application for a patent within a year after first filing in the country of origin.[13] It also contains provisions under which a state may direct the licensing of a patent in its own territory if the owner of the patent does not exploit it there. However, a compulsory license may not be applied for on the ground of failure to work for at least three years after the granting of the patent.[14] Compulsory licensing of patents in the United States by court decree in antitrust cases will be referred to later. It is particularly important from an antitrust standpoint to remember that patent rights in different countries are not the same even though the patents cover the same invention.

C. Application of Antitrust to United States Foreign Trade

In the application of the antitrust laws to the foreign trade of the United States, questions of jurisdiction have frequently been raised. In *Continental Ore Co.* v. *Union Carbide & Carbon Corp.*,[15] the Supreme Court reiterated that "a conspiracy to monopolize or restrain the domestic or foreign commerce of the United States is not outside the

9. United Drug Co. v. Rectanus Co., 248 U.S. 90 (1918). In Timken Roller Bearing Co. v. United States, 341 U.S. 593, 598 (1951) the Supreme Court stated: "Nor can the restraints of trade be justified as reasonable steps taken to implement a valid trademark licensing system, even if we assume with appellant that it is the owner of the trademark 'Timken' in the trade areas allocated to the British and French corporations."

10. Boesch v. Graff, 133 U.S. 697 (1890).

11. Brown v. Duschesne, 19 How. 183 (U.S. 1856).

12. Paris Convention for the Protection of Industrial Property of March 20, 1883, *as last revised* at Stockholm on July 14, 1967. United International Bureaux for the Protection of Industrial Property (BIRPI), Geneva 1968.

13. *Id.*, Article 4.

14. *Id.*, Article 5.

15. 370 U.S. 690 (1962).

reach of the Sherman Act just because part of the conduct complained of occurs in foreign countries."[16] This decision follows a uniform line of antitrust cases in the foreign commerce area.[17]

Most of these cases were brought by the Department of Justice in attacks on international cartels among producers in different countries. Typically, the companies involved divided up the world into exclusive marketing areas and allocated or attempted to control world production. In practically all instances, the United States was one of the markets subject to the territorial division. A substantial effect upon United States foreign commerce is an essential jurisdictional requirement when acts outside of the United States are in question. Judge Learnėd Hand, in the *Alcoa* case,[18] indicated the rationale of these antitrust cases so far as international law is concerned: "Any state may impose liabilities . . . for conduct outside its borders that has consequences within its borders which the state reprehends."[19] Restrictions which have their essential effect only within other countries, without appreciable effects intended or felt in United States exports or imports, fall outside of the general ambit of matters of concern under the United States antitrust laws.

Another essential element for the imposition of liability in these foreign trade cases is personal jurisdiction by a United States court over at least some of the parties to the international arrangement brought into question under the antitrust laws. Such parties must be properly brought before the court and must be given an opportunity to defend the charges. A judgment is not binding upon a party not before the court, for example, a foreign party not doing business here.[20] It is not necessary, however, to have all of the parties before

16. *Id.* at 704.

17. Timken Roller Bearing Co. v. United States, 341 U.S. 593 (1951); United States v. National Lead Co., 332 U.S. 319 (1947); United States v. Sisal Sales Corp., 274 U.S. 268 (1927); Thomsen v. Cayser, 243 U.S. 66 (1917); United States v. Pacific & Arctic Ry. & Nav. Co., 228 U.S. 87 (1913); United States v. American Tobacco Co., 221 U.S. 106 (1911). The Court has also heard an antitrust case involving a joint venture in Latin America between Pan American Airways, Inc., and W.R. Grace & Co., operating the Panagra airline, but disposed of it on the issue of the jurisdiction of the Civil Aeronautics Board. Pan American World Airways, Inc. v. United States, 371 U.S. 296 (1963). In general, *see* BREWSTER, ANTITRUST AND AMERICAN BUSINESS ABROAD (1958); FUGATE, FOREIGN COMMERCE AND THE ANTITRUST LAWS (2d ed. 1973); *International Antitrust Law Symposium*, 8 J. OF INT. LAW AND ECONOMICS, Pt. I, 1 *et seq.* (1973) and Pt. II, 157 *et seq.* (1973).

18. United States v. Aluminum Co. of America, 148 F.2d 416 (2d Cir. 1945). *See also* RESTATEMENT OF THE FOREIGN RELATIONS LAW OF THE UNITED STATES, §18 (1965).

19. *Id.* at 443. *Cf.* Pacific Seafarers, Inc. v. Pacific Far East Line, Inc., 404 F.2d 804 (D.C. Cir. 1968), *cert. dėnied*, 393 U.S. 1093 (1969), upholding U.S. jurisdiction as to the transportation of U.S. aid financed cargos by U.S. vessels between foreign ports.

20. United States v. Bayer Co., Inc., 105 F.Supp. 955 (S.D.N.Y. 1952).

the court.[21] The absence of jurisdiction over foreign parties to arrangements that may adversely affect the commerce of the United States may, of course, hamper effective relief in antitrust cases in the area of foreign commerce. This and occasional friction over jurisdictional questions have been incentives to the United States for closer cooperation with other nations, including Japan, in antitrust enforcement.[22]

D. Procedural Aspects

The procedural aspects of patent infringement suits have been covered elsewhere in this book, and it will have been noted that a foreign patentee may sue in the United States federal courts for unauthorized manufacture, use, or sale of the patented product in the United States. In such a suit, antitrust issues can be raised. The patent-antitrust case law in the United States has been developed both in suits by the government to enforce the antitrust laws and in private suits, either actions for damages incurred by reason of antitrust violation, or in infringement suits where antitrust violation or patent misuse has been asserted as a defense. In the United States there has developed a sizable body of law on patent misuse. Indeed, patent misuse as a defense to an infringement action developed in connection with the patent tying clauses later described. In short, a patentee who has misused his patent by a tying clause, by package licensing, by price fixing, and like practices, may not enforce his patent against infringers, at least not until the effects of the misuse have been dissipated.[23]

Antitrust suits brought by the Department of Justice involving patents have only rarely asserted patent invalidity. In the main, in these cases the government has attacked certain restrictive practices alleged to violate the antitrust laws which were defended as being within the patent grant or ancillary to the patent grant. In some recent antitrust

21. United States v. National Lead Co., 332 U.S. 319, 342–43 (1947).

22. *See* OECD Council Recommendation on Co-operation between Member Countries on Restrictive Business Practices Affecting International Trade (Oct. 1967) (reprinted as an Appendix to Markert, *Recent Developments in International Cooperation*, XIII Antitrust Bulletin 355 (1968)), and the more recent Recommendation Concerning Action Against Restriction Practices Relating to the use of Patents and Licenses, Jan. 25, 1974 (C (73) 238 Final). This later recommendation followed a *Report by the OECD Committee on Restrictive Business Practices Relating to Patents and Licenses* (1972). For other actions affecting patents by international bodies, *see* Davidow, *Antitrust and International Patent Licensing, Remarks for Panel on Antitrust and International Business Transactions*, ABA Antitrust Section Meeting, 43 Antitrust L. J. 530 (1974). The Japanese Fair Trade Commission has issued "Antimonopoly Guidelines for International Licensing Agreements (*hereafter "Japanese Guidelines"*). *See* Chapter VII, Ariga, *supra*.

23. *See* Morton Salt Co. v. G.S. Suppiger Co., 314 U.S. 488 (1942); Mercoid Corp. v. Mid-Continent Investment Co., 320 U.S. 661 (1943).

suits, however, the government has asserted invalidity of patents and also fraud on the patent office in the procurement of a patent.[24]

II. Antitrust Aspects of Specific Patent Practices and Agreements

A. Acquisition of Patents; Grant-Backs

1. *Acquisition.* Antitrust problems do not generally arise, in the United States, in the acquisition of a patent, either by grant or by purchase. A company may usually acquire as many patents as it wishes, just as it may acquire other property. In the *Hazeltine* case,[25] the Supreme Court stated that the mere acquisition of patents was not illegal, and this was again indicated in the more recent *Singer* case,[26] which will be mentioned later.

An antitrust violation may result, however, from the enforcement of a patent obtained by intentional fraud on the patent office. The Supreme Court held that the enforcement of patents obtained by such fraud may constitute monopolization under Section 2 of the Sherman Act if other requisites of Section 2 are met.[27] Moreover, the use of fraudulently procured patents may constitute an unfair trade practice in violation of Section 5 of the Federal Trade Commission Act.[28]

It should also be pointed out that one or more companies can monopolize patents and can use patents for monopolization of an industry. For example, such monopolization was found to have taken place when a company acquired substantially all of the patents covering an important aspect of oil-well digging equipment with intent to monopolize and control the industry, and when a company acquired

24. The complaint in United States v. Glaxo Group Limited, et al., Civ. 558–68, D. D.C. 1968, stated: ". . . the Imperial patent, contrary to the requirements of 35 U.S.C. §112, fails to disclose to the public the manner to practice the method in return for which the statutory monopoly was granted; and such method claims are invalid." The government's right to challenge validity was upheld, 410 U.S. 52 (1973). (It may be noted that a licensee can now challenge the validity of patents under which he is licensed. Lear v. Adkins 395 U.S. 653 [1969]). In United States v. Union Camp Corp., 1969 Trade Cas. ¶¶72,689 and 72,843 (Consent degrees 1969), the government charged defendant with fraud on the courts in maintaining a patent infringement suit on a known invalid patent. *See* Walker Process Equipment Co. v. Food Machinery & Chemical Corp., 382 U.S. 172 (1965).

25. Automatic Radio Mfg. Co. v. Hazeltine Research, Inc., 339 U.S. 827 (1950).

26. United States v. Singer Mfg. Co., 374 U.S. 174 (1963).

27. Walker Process Equipment, Inc. v. Food Machinery & Chemical Corp., 382 U.S. 172 (1965). *See also* Corning Glass Works v. Anchor Hocking Glass Corp., 253 F.Supp. 461 (D. Del. 1966), *aff'd on this point*, 374 F.2d 473 (3d Cir. 1967).

28. American Cyanamid Co. v. Federal Trade Commission, 363 F.2d 757 (6th Cir. 1966).

the bulk of parking meter patents with a like intent.[29] In the G. E. *Incandescent Lamp* case,[30] the court held that General Electric Company (G.E.) had monopolized the patents in the incandescent lamp field, and in the RCA case[31] settled by consent decree, the government charged that Radio Corporation of America (RCA) had monopolized patents in the communications field. G. E., Philips (N.V. Philips' Gloeilampenfabrieken, the Dutch company), and the other defendants in the *Incandescent Lamp* case were required to "dedicate to the public any and all existing patents on lamps and lamp parts."[32] In the RCA judgment, that company was required to license domestic patents at reasonable royalties and grant immunity under corresponding foreign patents.[33]

It should also be noted that the Celler-Kefauver Antimerger Act (the Amended Section 7 of the Clayton Act)[34] applies to the acquisition of patents, copyrights, and trademarks. That act forbids the acquisition by one corporation of the stock or assets of another corporation (both must be engaged in United States interstate or foreign commerce) where the effect may be substantially to lessen competition or tend to create a monopoly in any line of commerce in any section of the country.

In the so-called *Screen Gems* case (*U. S.* v. *Columbia Pictures*),[35] the government attacked the transfer of exclusive rights in a group of valuable copyrighted motion picture films for use in television. While the district court held in that case that there was no violation of the statute, it did say that the grant of the exclusive rights in the copyrighted films could be a violation of the Antimerger Act.

In *U.S.* v. *Lever Brothers*,[36] the Court had to consider whether the acquisition of the trademarked detergent product All, together with

29. Kobe Inc. v. Dempsey Pump Co., 97 F.Supp. 342 (N.D. Okla. 1951), *aff'd* 198 F.2d 416 (10th Cir. 1952), *cert. den.* 344 U.S. 837 (1952); United States v. Vehicular Parking, Ltd., 54 F.Supp. 828 (D. Del. 1944), mod., 61 F.Supp. 656 (D. Del. 1945). *See also* United States v. General Electric Co. (Carboloy case), 80 F.Supp. 989 (S.D.N.Y. 1948). *Cf.* United States v. United Shoe Machinery Co., 110 F.Supp. 295 (D. Mass. 1953), *aff'd per curiam*, 347 U.S. 521 (1954), *further hearing on relief*, 266 F.Supp. 328 (D. Mass. 1967), *rev'd*, 391 U.S. 244 (1968).

30. United States v. General Electric Co., 82 F.Supp. 753 (D. N.J. 1949).

31. United States v. Radio Corp. of America., 1958 Trade Cas. ¶69, 164, (S.D. N.Y. 1958).

32. United States v. General Electric Co., *Opinion on relief*, 115 F.Supp. 835, 843 *et seq.* (D. N.J. 1953).

33. Note 31 *supra*.

34. 38 Stat. 731 (1914), as amended; 15 U.S.C. §§18, 21 (1970).

35. United States v. Columbia Pictures, Inc. 189 F.Supp. 153 (S.D. N.Y. 1960).

36. United States v. Lever Bros., 216 F.Supp. 887 (S.D. N.Y. 1963).

37. *See* Ariga, *supra* note 22.

the patents, goodwill, and business of making this product, was within this statute. After a trial, the government again was not successful, but the Court held that the patents and trademarks connected with the product could be within the Celler-Kefauver Act.

It may be noted that in Japan, patent licenses may also play a part in determining the antitrust effect of a merger.[37]

2. *Grant-Backs.* A grant-back is a provision in a patent license that requires the licensee to assign or license all improvement patents to his licensor. In *Transparent-Wrap Machine Corp.* v. *Stokes & Smith Co.*[38] (known as the "*Transwrap*" case), the Supreme Court of the United States held that grant-backs were not "illegal *per se* and unenforceable." This rule has been followed in subsequent cases,[39] but grant-backs have been held to be unlawful when used as part of a scheme to monopolize or restrain trade.[40]

The validity of a grant-back of an assignment or of an exclusive license, however, has been questioned by Department of Justice officials as being more restrictive than necessary to protect the legitimate interest of the licensor to have access to improvements upon his invention.[41] This can be accomplished by the grant-back on a nonexclusive license. The American Bar Association Supplement to the Attorney General's Antitrust Committee Report states that "grant-back by assignment or exclusive license should be subject to closer scrutiny . . . since they are more restrictive and have a greater propensity to dull the licensee's incentive to invent."[42] In assessing the legality of grant-backs, the very limited scope of the *Transwrap* case should be emphasized. While in that case there was a formal assignment, the facts of the case indicate that the net result of the arrangement was a grant-back of much less than a normal assignment inas-

38. 329 U.S. 637 (1947); *on remand*; Stokes & Smith Co. v. Transparent Wrap Corp., 161 F.2d 565 (2d Cir. 1947), *cert. denied*, 332 U.S. 787 (1947).

39. *See e.g.*, Binks Mfg. Co. v. Ransberg Electro-Coating Corp., 281 F.2d 252, 259 (7th Cir. 1960), *cert. denied*, 364 U.S. 926 (1961); International Nickel v. Ford Motor Co., 166 F.Supp. 551, 565 (S.D. N.Y. 1958); Zajicek v. Koolvent Metal Awning Corp., 283 F.2d 127, 131–32 (9th Cir. 1960); Sperry Products, Inc. v. Aluminum Co. of America, 171 F.Supp. 901, 936–38 (N.D. Ohio 1959) *mod. and aff'd*, 285 F.2d 911 (6th Cir. 1960), *cert. den.* 368 U.S. 890 (1961).

40. United States v. General Electric Co. (Incandescent Lamp case), 82 F.Supp. 753, 815–816 (D. N.J. 1949); United States v. General Electric Co. (Carboloy), 80 F.Supp. 989, 1005–1006 (S.D. N.Y. 1948); United States v. Associated Patents, Inc., 134 F.Supp. 74 (E.D. Mich. 1955).

41. *See* McLaren, speech before PTC Institute, 1969, 5 CCH Trade Reg. Rep ¶50,246 (1969); Turner, *Antitrust Enforcement Policy*, 29 ABA Antitrust J. 187, 192 (1967). In Japan the licensing obligations as to improvements must be mutual. *See* Ariga, *supra* note 22, referring to Japanese Guidelines par. (7).

42. ABA Antitrust Developments, 1955–1968, 170 (1968); ABA Antitrust Law Developments, 336–337 (1975).

much as the licensee had the right to continue its exclusive license until all the patents had expired.[43]

B. NON-USE; EXCESSIVE ROYALTIES

1. *Non-Use.* Many countries have "working provisions," and as noted, the Paris Convention specifically covers this point. In another part of this book, the provisions of the Japanese patent statutes relative to working are described.[44] The United States patent laws do not contain such working provisions, and in fact, the matter of patent non-use has seldom been raised. The United States Supreme Court in the old *Paper Bag* case (the only one which directly concerns the subject of non-use)[45] held that reasonable non-use of patents by a single patentee was not ground for refusing to enjoin infringement of the patent. The Court relied on the fact that there were sound business reasons for the patentee's failure to work the invention. For example, it would have been expensive to make the necessary changes in machinery. Moreover, there was no question, the Court said, of a diminished supply or of an increase in prices.[46] This is to be contrasted with non-use as part of a plan to suppress technology. Combinations or conspiracies for the use of patented inventions to "fence in" or block competing technology have been held illegal.[47] In the *Incandescent Lamp* case, the Court in condemning sales limitations imposed by G.E., the licensor, upon its licensees, referred to the adverse effects of the restrictions upon the licensees' research. (The government's claim that G.E. had actually attempted to suppress research and development activities by its licensees was held not to have been proved.[48])

2. *Royalties.* It is not illegal in the United States for a patentee to charge as much royalty as he can exact, absent elements of monopolization or a conspiracy to restrain trade.[49] However, the Federal Trade Commission (FTC) has held that discriminatory royalty rates may constitute a violation of Sec. 5 of the Federal Trade Commission Act

43. Transparent Wrap Machine Corp. v. Stokes & Smith Co., note 37 *supra* at 646. *See* Chevigny, *The Validity of Grant-Back Agreements Under The Antitrust Laws*, 34 FORDHAM L. REV. 569, 576 (1967). *See also* Chapter V, Woodward and Matsuo, *supra*.

44. *See* Someno and Someno, *supra*.

45. Continental Paper Bag Co. v. Eastern Paper Bag Co., 210 U.S. 405 (1908).

46. *Id.* at 429.

47. Hartford Empire Co. v. U.S., 323 U.S. 386, 431 (1945); Blount Mfg. Co. v. Yale & Towne Mfg. Co., 166 Fed. 555 (C.C.D. Mass. 1909); *See also* Vitamin Technologists, Inc. v. Wisconsin Alumni Research Foundation, 146 F.2d 941, 944–6 (9th Cir. 1944), *cert. den.*, 325 U.S. 876 (1945); Foster v. American Machine & Foundry Co., 492 F.2d 1317, 182 U.S.P.Q. 1 (2d Cir. 1974).

48. United States v. General Electric Co. (Incandescent Lamps), 82 F.Supp. 753, 856–58, (D. N.J. 1949). *See also* the discussion of Grant-Backs, text *supra* at notes 38–43.

49. Brulotte v. Thys Co., 379 U.S. 29, 33 (1964).

(declaring unlawful unfair methods of competition), if used improperly by a patentee to protect himself against competition. In affirming the FTC's decision, the Court of Appeals stated that the gist of the violation was "the utilization of monopoly power in one market resulting in discrimination and curtailment of competition in another."[50]

In *American Photocopy Equipment Co.* v. *Rovico*,[51] the Court, in a preliminary proceeding, referred to the "exorbitant, oppressive royalty" exacted by the patentee (6 percent on the retail price of machines manufactured and sold under the patent). The Court questioned the legality of such a royalty. The Supreme Court has held that a patentee cannot collect royalties beyond the expiration of a licensed patent.[52] Furthermore, an attempt to collect royalties on unpatented as well as patented products goes beyond the patent grant where it is part of a conspiracy to restrain trade in the unpatented article.[53] However, the gross sales of a plant have been allowed as a reasonable measure of royalties where a large number of patents are licensed, and there is no coercion of such an agreement by the patentee.[54]

C. Patent Licensing

A general rule as to licensing or assignment practices is that a patentee cannot agree that he will not compete with his licensee or assignee. Restrictions upon the patentee are outside of the patent grant, gain no justification from being included in a patent license, and will be judged under the general antitrust law as to legality.[55] It is true that an exclusive license automatically excludes the patentee, and that this is permissible. Quite different is a contract accompanying such a license, obligating the patentee not to enter the field of the patent, not to enter any other field, or (in the case of licensing a foreign patent) not to export to the country where foreign rights are granted.[56] Even in the case of a product patent—for example, product patents in the United States and Japan, with a license only under the Japanese patent—such language of exclusion (say from the United States, in a license under the Japanese product patent) may be more than merely

50. La Peyre v. F.T.C. 366 F.2d 117, 121 (5th Cir. 1966). *See also* Note, *Antitrust-Patents-Licenses-Regulation of Patent License Royalty Rates under the Antitrust Laws*, 65 Michigan L. Rev. 1631 (1967).

51. 359 F.2d 745 (7th Cir. 1966), *on remand*, 257 F.Supp. 192 (N.D. Ill., 1966).

52. Brulotte, et al. v. Thys Co., 379 U.S. 29 (1964).

53. United States v. U.S. Gypsum Co., 333 U.S. 364, 397 (1948).

54. Automatic Radio Co. v. Hazeltine Research, 339 U.S. 827, 832–33 (1950); Zenith Radio Co. v. Hazeltine Research, Inc., 395 U.S. 100, 140 (1969. *Cf.* Ariga, *supra* note 22, discussing the Japanese Licensing Guidelines which mention as a restrictive practice the charging of a royalty on goods which do not utilize licensed technology.

55. *See e.g.*, Pfotzer v. Aqua Systems, 162 F.2d 779, 784 (2d Cir. 1947).

56. *See e.g.*, McCullough v. Kammerer Corp., 166 F.2d 759 (9th Cir. 1948); U.S. v. General Electric Co., 82 F.Supp. 753, 846 (D. N.J. 1949).

"gilding the lily." The licensor may now have additional remedies such as cancellation of the license for its breach, and a suit in Japan (where the agreement might not be illegal) for an injunction or damages.

The main question in judging restrictions in patent licenses under United States law is whether such restrictions are within the scope of the patent monopoly. United States courts have had to consider a great variety of licensing provisions, and consequently there is a large body of law on the subject. United States law applies both to American and foreign owners of United States patents, and some of the important patent licensing cases have concerned foreign patent owners. It may also be noted that rights under foreign patents have often been involved in United States cases. Here, we are considering the licensing of technology, including that covered by patents (both United States and foreign), and some that may be unpatented. As to the latter, some may be in the nature of secret process and some merely know-how. It is important to distinguish the protection afforded under each of these (i.e., under patents, secret processes and nonsecret know-how) when antitrust law is in question.

1. Pricing. The question of the legality of pricing provisions in patent licenses has concerned the courts in a number of cases. The rule of the 1926 *General Electric* case[57] that a patentee may legally stipulate the licensee's resale price barely survived, in a 1967 Supreme Court case, by a split decision,[58] and has been greatly narrowed by later cases. It is not applicable to a combination of patentees nor to multiple licensees.[59] Nor does it cover pricing in connection with licensing a process patent[60] or patents on parts for an assembled product.[61] In *Simpson* v. *Union Oil Co.*,[62] the Supreme Court denied the validity of resale price maintenance in "consignment" selling to independent dealers but distinguished the 1926 G.E. case also relating to consignment selling as involving the sale of patented products. Subsequently, the Department of Justice specifically raised the resale issue, in a case against G.E. and directed again to G.E.'s consignment selling. When the defendant conceded that its patents were not "controlling," as they were in 1926 as applied to large lamps, the Court held the 1926

57. United States v. General Electric Co., 272 U.S. 476 (1926).

58. United States v. Huck Mfg. Co., 382 U.S. 197 (1965). *Cf.* discussion of such price stipulations in Japan, Ariga, *supra* note 22.

59. Newburgh Moire Co. v. Superior Moire Co. 237 F.2d 283 (3rd Cir. 1956); Tinnerman Prods., Inc. v. George K. Garrett, 185 F.Supp. 156 (E.D. Pa. 1960), *aff'd*, 292 F.2d 137 (3rd Cir. 1961), *cert. den.*, 368 U.S. 833 (1961).

60. United States v. Line Material Co., 333 U.S. 287 (1948); Interstate Circuit, Inc. v. U.S., 306 U.S. 208 (1939).

61. United States v. General Electric Co., 82 F.Supp. 753 (D. N.J. 1949).

62. 377 U.S. 13 (1964).

G.E. case to be inapplicable and found G.E.'s agency consignment system as of this time to be illegal.[63]

The same rules have been applied in foreign trade to the extent that the situations are analogous. For example, in the *Carboloy* case,[64] an American company obtained rights to United States patents held by a German company. There was an agreement on prices for sales in the United States by either company, and the German company was not to manufacture here. Such restrictions were held to go beyond the narrow G.E. doctrine. In the *Incandescent Lamp* case,[65] it was held that the G.E. doctrine would not support price and other restrictions on domestic licensees including a qualified prohibition against selling abroad.

2. *Territorial Restrictions*. In domestic situations, the patent statute expressly provides, despite the usual rule against divisions of markets in the United States,[66] that a patentee may grant an exclusive right for a patent "to the whole or any specified part of the United States."[67] This provision is practically limited, however, by the fact that a purchaser of a patented article in one part of the United States may resell it anywhere in the United States.[68]

Many of the antitrust cases relating to divisions of world markets have involved patents, but this does not mean that a patentee may not use his patents legitimately in foreign licensing situations. A patentee may grant a license under his foreign patents and then enforce his United States patents to prevent imports. The international patent antitrust cases have involved arrangements going far beyond these rights. The cases, which will be discussed under cross licensing, contain a good part of the law on territorial restrictions.

In addition to his infringement remedy, a patentee may invoke Sections 337 and 337(a) of the Tariff Act.[69] These sections provide for stopping, at customs, goods imported by unfair acts of competition, and cover imports protected by a United States patent or made abroad by a United States patented process. The statute specifies that

63. United States v. General Electric Co., 303 F.Supp. 1121 (S.D. N.Y. 1969), 358 F.Supp. 731 (S.D. N.Y. 1973), 1974 Trade Cas. 74, 942 (S.D. N.Y. 1974 consent decrees). *Cf.* Ariga, *supra* note 22, referring to Japanese Guidelines making it a restrictive practice to restrict the resale prices of patented goods in Japan.

64. United States v. General Electric Co., 80 F.Supp. 989 (S.D. N.Y. 1948).

65. Note 61 supra.

66. This was laid down at an early time by the Supreme Court. Addyston Pipe & Steel Co. v. United States, 175 U.S. 211 (1899).

67. 35 U.S.C. §261 (1970). *But see* Baxter, *Legal Restrictions on Exploitation of the Patent Monopoly: An Economic Analysis*, 76 Yale L.J. (1966).

68. Keeler v. Standard Folding Bed Co., 157 U.S. 659 (1895); Adams v. Burke, 17 Wall 453 (U.S. 1873).

69. 19 U.S.C. §1337, 1337(a) (1970).

there be a threat of injury to an American industry. While the language of the statute has been held to be broad and inclusive, complainants in the past had a difficult time persuading the Tariff Commission of their injury.[70] In recent years, however, the Tariff Commission has entered exclusion orders in a number of cases despite Justice Department intervention stressing the value of foreign competition, particularly where domestic industries are concentrated.[71]

3. Field of Use. "Field of use" restriction is one of the areas of patent-antitrust law which is undergoing new scrutiny and analysis. It has been consistently held that field of use restrictions in patent licenses to manufacturing licensees do not offend the antitrust laws, at least where licenses are available for the other fields, since the old Supreme Court case of *General Talking Pictures* v. *Western Electric Co.*[72] In that case, the Western Electric Company licensed the manufacture and sale of patented vacuum tube amplifiers for use in the noncommercial field. A licensee made these amplifiers for commercial use and sold them to a purchaser who knew that they were made and sold in violation of the license. This was held to be an unauthorized manufacture and sale, and an infringement. The Court did not decide what the result would have been as to a sale in the ordinary channels of trade to an unknowing purchaser.

Despite *General Talking Pictures*, the current trend of analysis indicates that some field of use restrictions may be subject to challenge.[73] In the case of *Baldwin-Lima-Hamilton* v. *Tatnall*,[74] the patentee attempted to restrict the use of his patented article to incorporation into specified types of machinery sold by his licensees. The Court held that this practice was contrary to the settled rule that the sale of a patented

70. The "broad and inclusive" interpretation is contained in In re Von Clemm, 229 F.2d 441, 443–44 (C.C.P.A. 1955). Tariff Commission findings of "no injury" include: In-The-Ear Hearing Aids, Inv. No. 337–20, T.C. Publ. 182, July 1966; Self-Closing Containers, Inv. No. 337–18, T.C. Publ. 55, April 1962.

71. *See* Large Power Transformers from France, Italy, Japan, Switzerland and the United Kingdom, 37 Fed. Reg. 8136 (Tariff Comm. 1972); Elemental Sulphur from Mexico, 37 Fed. Reg. 9417 (Tariff Comm. 1972); Furazalidone (Tariff Comm. 1968).

72. 304 U.S. 175; 305 U.S. 124 (1938). *See also* Automatic Radio Mfg. Co. v. Hazeltine Research, Inc., 339 U.S. 827 (1950); U.S. v. Birdsboro Steel Co., 139 F.Supp. 244 (W.D. Pa. 1956).

73. *See e.g.*, McLaren, *Patent Licenses and Antitrust Considerations*, Speech before PTC Research Inst., George Washington U., Washington, D.C. June 5, 1969; Austern, *Fish Traps, Indians, and Patents: The Antitrust Validity of Patent License Restrictions on Sales Price, Field Use, Quantity, and Territory*, 28 U. PITT. L. REV. 181 (1967); Kestenbaum, *Antitrust Aspects of Effective Use of Patents–Field of Use Restrictions in Patent Licensing*, Speech before New York Patent Law Assn., Mar. 2, 1967; Turner, *Patent, Antitrust and Innovation*, 28 U. PITT. L. REV. 151 (1967). *Cf.* discussion of use restrictions in Japan in Ariga, *supra* note 22.

74. 136 F.Supp. (E.D. Pa. 1958) *aff'd per curiam*, 268 F.2d 395 (5th Cir. 1959), *cert. den.*, 361 U.S. 894 (1959).

article exhausts the legal monopoly and thus that restrictive covenants running with the article are unlawful.

The same doctrine was invoked in the *Glaxo/ICI*[75] case in which the district court, affirmed by the Supreme Court held illegal per se restrictions in licenses of drug patents that limited the purchaser-licensees to resale of the drug in dosage rather than bulk form. The stipulation in the basic contract between the two defendant British companies, Glaxo and ICI, that ICI should place these restrictions upon vendees to whom it licensed and sold the product was also held to be illegal per se insofar as it applied to United States vendees of ICI.

In another drug case, the Department of Justice in *United States* v. *Farbenfabriken Bayer, A. G. and Chemagro Corp.*,[76] challenged an arrangement under which Bayer licensed its insecticide patent to the Chemagro Corp. (which sold the insecticide to manufacturers for admixture with fertilizers, pesticides, and other products) on condition the Chemagro's vendees use the insecticide only in products designed for home and garden, or commercial purposes. The case was settled by a consent decree. The same license and its restriction had previously been upheld by a lower court in a matter involving other parties.[77]

4. Tying Clauses. Commonly designated as a per se violation of the antitrust laws is an agreement that requires unpatented goods to be purchased from the patentee or a source he has designated. Such an arrangement is also a misuse of patent under the patent laws.[78] The condition need not be expressly stated in the license but may consist

75. U.S. v. Glaxo Group, Ltd., 328 F.Supp. 709 (D.D.C. 1971), *rev'd on grounds of inadequate relief and on issue of right to challenge patent validity*, 410 U.S. 52 (1973).

76. 1969 Trade Cas. ¶72,918. The complaint in this case, as in some other Department of Justice cases, used as a basis of jurisdiction the patent statute conferring jurisdiction over foreign holders of U.S. patents as to matters connected with the patent, 35 U.S.C. §293 (1970). On challenge the jurisdiction was sustained. 1968 Trade Cas. ¶72,569 (D.D.C. 1968), *application for appeal denied*, 1968 Trade Cas. ¶72,570 (D.C. Cir. 1968), *Appeal dismissed*, 393 U.S. 216 (1968).

77. Chemagro Corp. v. Universal Chemical Co., 244 F.Supp. 486 (E.D. Tex. 1965). As to the validity and logic of the department's position see Fugate, *Restrictions on Fields of Use*, 2 APLA QUART. J. 44 (1974); Wilson, *Patent and Know-How License Agreements: Fields of Use, Territorial, Price and Quantity Restrictions*, Remarks at Antitrust Section Meeting, Washington, D.C., August 1973 (excerpts Reprinted in 2 APLA QUART. J. 87 (1974). Mr. Bruce Wilson, then Deputy Assistant Attorney General in the Antitrust Division, in the above-cited speech, differentiated the situation of the patentee reserving for himself well defined manufacturing fields out of several uses of his invention and that where field of use licenses divide fields among licensee-competitors.

78. International Salt Co., Inc., v. United States, 332 U.S. 392 (1947); Leitch Mfg., Co. v. Barber, 302 U.S. 458 (1938); Morton Salt Co. v. G.S. Suppiger Co., 314 U.S. 488 (1942); Mercoid Corp. v. Mid-Continent Investment Co., 320 U.S. 661 (1944). Tying clauses are also illegal in Japan. *See* Ariga, *supra* note 22.

merely of a practice of granting licenses only to those who purchase such unpatented goods or articles from the patentee.[79] Section 1 of the Sherman Act and Section 3 of the Clayton Act may also be violated by tying demands. In the leading case of *United States* v. *International Salt Co.*,[80] the offense alleged consisted of leasing patented, salt-tablet dispensing machines for use only with salt tablets purchased from the lessor. The Court there stated that it was illegal per se to foreclose any substantial market to competitors.[81]

As has been noted by the American Bar Association, tying clauses may constitute a misuse of patents even though there is no showing of the anticompetitive effects ordinarily required to establish an antitrust violation.[82] The antitrust rationale in tying situations is amplified in the following discussion of package licensing.

5. *Package Licensing*. On the same theory as appertains in the tying clause cases, it is generally held that it is illegal to license patents or copyrights in a group, refusing to license each individually or exacting an unreasonable royalty for the individual patents composing the package.

The leading case on package licensing is *United States* v. *Loew's Inc.*[83] in which defendants, not acting in concert, had "conditioned the license or sale of one or more feature films upon acceptance by the [television] station of a package containing one or more unwanted or inferior films." The Supreme Court, relying on the *Northern Pacific*[84] and *International Salt* cases, which involved tying arrangements, held that package licensing violated Section 1 of the Sherman Act. It adopted a similar rule, to wit: the tying product must have sufficient economic power so as to "appreciably restrain free competition in the market for the tied product." As it did in the tie-in cases, the Court did not limit its definition of economic power to market dominance, but also inferred economic power from a product's desirability or uniqueness. It held that "the requisite economic power is presumed when the tying product is patented or copyrighted." The theory is that each patented product is unique since it is the function of the patent laws to reward inventiveness by the grant of a seventeen year monopoly. Thus, by virtue of his monopoly, the patentee is presumed to have sufficient power to restrain trade in the tied product.

Although the Supreme Court has stated that package licenses

79. *See* the cases cited in note 78 *supra*.

80. International Salt Co., Inc. v. United States, 332 U.S. 392 (1947).

81. *Id.* at 396.

82. ABA ANTITRUST SECTION, ANTITRUST DEVELOPMENTS 1955–68, 174 (1968). *See e.g.*, Berlenbach v. Anderson & Thompson Ski Co., 329 F.2d 782 (9th Cir. 1964).

83. 189 F.Supp. 373 (S.D. N.Y. 1960), *aff'd and modified*, 371 U.S. 38 (1963).

84. Northern Pacific Ry. Co. v. United States, 356 U.S. 1 (1958).

"serve hardly any purpose beyond the suppression of competition,"[85] there are two possible exceptions to the general rule enunciated by the *Loew's* case. The first is referred to as the "Single Product" doctrine. In *International Mfg. Co.* v. *Landon, Inc.*,[86] the defendant in a patent infringement case argued that the plaintiff had violated the Sherman Act, and misused his patent, by refusing to individually license the two patents in question. The Court of Appeals rejected this argument on the basis that one patent was useless without the other since both were necessary for the sole article for which they were applicable, and thus the package was justified. The second possible justification is where the package is necessary for quality control.[87]

D. Cross-Licensing and Patent Pools

The danger in cross-licensing and patent pooling in foreign commerce situations was emphasized in the *Singer* case.[88] The complaint charged Singer, the sole American manufacturer of household zigzag sewing machines, with combining with two European manufacturers to use their United States patents to keep out the competition of Japanese importers. Singer entered into cross-licensing agreements first with an Italian company and later with a Swiss company concerning patents upon a new improved household sewing machine. Both foreign companies were selling sewing machines in the United States. Ostensibly, the latter agreement was to settle a patent contest in the United States Patent Office. Each party, however, agreed to facilitate the allowance in any country of patent claims as broad as possible on the conflicting patents, and Singer was given the right to enforce the Swiss company's United States patent. The Supreme Court held that the arrangement was illegal as a concerted effort by competitors to protect the parties against competing Japanese importers.

A number of earlier foreign-trade cases involved cross-licensing of patents and technology between American and foreign competitors, with mutual territorial restrictions. The participants in these cartel cases were usually major firms and the agreements went beyond the actual patent, trademark, or technological rights possessed by the parties. Commonly, each licensed the other for all of the patents and

85. United States v. Loew's Inc., 371 U.S. 38 (1962) p. 44, citing Standard Oil Co. of California v. United States, 337 U.S. 293, 305–306 (1948).

86. 336 F.2d 723 (9th Cir. 1964). *But cf.*, American Security Co. v. Shatterproof Glass Corp., 268 F.2d 769 (3d Cir. 1959), *cert. denied*, 361 U.S. 902 (1959).

87. United States v. Jerrold Electronics Corp., 187 F.Supp. 545 (E.D. Pa. 1960) *aff'd per curiam*, 365 U.S. 567 (1961), *rehearing denied*, 365 U.S. 890 (1961). It should be noted that this matter involved a special situation inasmuch as a necessary service, rather than an unpatented article, was the tied item.

88. U.S. v. Singer Mfg. Co., 374 U.S. 174 (1963).

technology owned or controlled in a broad field, and future patents and inventions were also included.

The *National Lead* case,[89] for example, involved a network of patent license agreements between American and foreign competitors. National Lead Company, owning United States titanium patents, through a subsidiary entered into an agreement with a Norwegian company owning foreign titanium patents. Each gave to the other an exclusive license as to titanium patents and technology for respective territories, and each appointed the other its sole agent in the other's territory for all products in the licensed field. This agreement specifically prohibited each party from exporting products in the licensed field into the other's territory. Subsequently, similar agreements were made with major companies in the field in other countries, and National Lead and E. I. duPont de Nemours & Company exchanged nonexclusive licenses in the United States. The district court in that case had little difficulty in declaring the arrangement illegal, saying, "Agreements creating a world-wide patent pool of all present and future patents of the parties, covering an entire industry, and embracing a division of the world into exclusive territories within which each of the parties is to confine its business activities, with respect to patent protected commodities, as well as unpatented, for the purpose and with the effect of suppressing imports into and exports from the United States, are unlawful under the Sherman Act; they constitute an unreasonable restraint of trade."[90]

In the *National Lead* case, it was indicated that where companies are dominant in an industry, a patent exchange, even on a nonexclusive basis, may be illegal. The Supreme Court quoted the district court that ". . . this exchange between two corporations, who between them controlled the entire market, becomes an instrument of restraint . . . to continue the mastery of the market . . . achieved by means of the illegal international agreements."[91]

In the *ICI* case,[92] the United States company, Dupont, and the British company, ICI, had mutual patent licenses whereby DuPont licensed ICI under its British patents and ICI licensed DuPont under its United States patents. The result was that each could only use its own patents in its own territory. It could, however, also use its com-

89. U.S. v. National Lead Co., 63 F.Supp. 513 (S.D. N.Y. 1945), *mod. and aff'd.*, 332 U.S. 319 (1947). *See also* pending case, United States v. Westinghouse Electric Corp., Civ. No. C. 70–852, N.D. Calif. Filed 1970, attacking cross licenses between Westinghouse and two Japanese Mitsubishi companies.

90. *Id.* at 527.

91. U.S. v. National Lead Co., 332 U.S. 319, 328 (1497).

92. United States v. Imperial Chemical Industries, Ltd., 100 F.Supp. 504 (S.D. N.Y. 1951).

petitors' patents in its own territory. The Court held that the parties used this cross-licensing for the purpose of dividing territories, being no doubt influenced by the fact that the parties had had older agreements which specifically spelled this out. The Court held the cross-licensing arrangement illegal and directed compulsory licensing of the patents of both parties (ICI being before the United States court).

In ICI and other foreign trade cases, the courts did not have to determine the legality per se of the exchange of patent rights on a territorial basis, since they found a primary purpose to divide markets and also found that the territorial limitations were not confined to patent rights.

The *Singer* case indicates the dangers of combining patents as part of a conspiracy among competitors to exclude other competitors. It should be noted that Justice White thought that the agreement to settle the patent office interference, and the resulting broad claims, was contrary to the public interest.[93] It is also noteworthy that the majority opinion cited Singer's proceeding under Section 337 of the Tariff Act (mentioned above) as one of the acts taken to effectuate the conspiracy.

The *Timken* case[94] stands for the proposition that neither patents nor trademarks will support agreements to divide world markets. Originally, American Timken had licensed a subsidiary of the British Vickers company, later British Timken, under both patents and trademarks with territorial restrictions. At the time the case was brought, the patents had expired, but it was argued by analogy that the division of markets was justified by the licensing of the trademark Timken. The Supreme Court noted that the agreements went far beyond protection of this trademark since they dealt with control of the manufacture and sale of bearings whether or not bearing the name. In any event, the Court held that "a trademark cannot legally be used as a device for Sherman Act violation."[95]

In *Zenith Radio Corp.* v. *Hazeltine Research Inc.*[96] the district court found that a United States company participated in patent pools in Canada, the United Kingdom and Australia for the purpose of preventing United States exports to those countries, with consequent injury to Zenith. The Supreme Court, as had the Court of Appeals, reversed as to injury from the United Kingdom and Australian pools,

93. United States v. Singer Mfg. Co., 374 U.S. 174 (1963), (Concurring Opinion).
94. Timken Roller Bearing Co. v. U.S., 341 U.S. 593 (1951).
95. *Id.* at 599.
96. 239 F.Supp. 51 (N.D. Ill. 1965), *aff'd in part, rev'd in part* 388 F.2d 25 (7th Cir. 1967), *aff'd in part, rev'd in part and remanded* 401 U.S. 321 (1971).

holding that government restrictions and embargoes were responsible for Zenith's inability to export to those countries. The Supreme Court affirmed the district court's holding as to injury from the Canadian pool. The Department of Justice had earlier attacked this practice, as to participation by other United States companies in a Canadian patent pool.[97]

In *U. S.* v. *Joseph A. Krasnov*,[98] the dominating companies in an industry formed a patent interchange and agreed to refrain from licensing others. This was held to be illegal. The old "*Oil Cracking*" case[99] which is still a precedent, although sometimes questioned, held that a patent pool by members of the industry was not necessarily illegal if membership in the pool was available on equal terms to all who wished to join.[100]

III. Remedies

Judgments in the foreign-trade cases as well as in the domestic cases have often provided for compulsory licensing of patents, as in the *Singer* case which has been mentioned.[101] The Supreme Court in the *Hartford Empire* case[102] affirmed the propriety of compulsory licensing at reasonable royalties to restore competition, but indicated that the compulsory royalty-free licensing there ordered by the district court amounted to forfeiture and was not a favored form of relief. Later, in the *National Lead* case,[103] the Court reserved the question as to the constitutionality of such licensing.[104] However, in the *Incandescent Lamp* case,[105] the district court considered dedication to the public by G.E. of existing patents on lamps and lamp parts to be "an essential remedy as a preventive against a continuance of monopoly in this industry."[106] In the more recent *Glaxo/ICI* case,[107] the Supreme Court held that compulsory licensing at reasonable royalties and mandatory

97. United States v. General Electric Co., *et al.*, Civ. 140–57, (S.D. N.Y. 1958), 1962 Trade Cases. ¶'s 70,342, 70,428, 70.546.

98. 143 F.Supp. 184 (E.D. Pa., 1956), *aff'd per curiam*, 335 U.S. 5 (1959).

99. Standard Oil Co. (Indiana) v. U.S., 283 U.S. 163 (1931).

100. *See also* Consent judgments, U.S. v. Automobile Mfgs. Ass'n., Inc., 1969 Trade Cas. ¶72.907 (C.D. Calif. 1969), and 1976–1 Trade Cas. ¶'s 60, 810 (S.D. N.Y. 1967). U.S. v. Manufacturers Aircraft Ass'n., Inc., 72 Civ. 1307 (S.D. N.Y. 1972).

101. United States v. Singer Mfg. Co., 231 F.Supp. 240 (S.D.N.Y. 1944) (On remand).

102. Hartford Empire Co. v. United States, 323 U.S. 386 (1945).

103. United States v. National Lead Co., 332 U.S. 319 (1947).

104. *Id.* at 349.

105. United States v. General Electric Co., 115 F.Supp. 835 (D. N.J. 1953). (Opinion on Relief).

106. *Id.* at 844.

107. U.S. v. Glaxo Group Ltd., 410 U.S. 52 (1973).

selling on specified terms were recognized remedies and should have been ordered by the district court, which had found antitrust violations in license restrictions confining licensees to dosage-form drug sales. As indicated, royalty free licensing or immunity under foreign patents to allow United States exports has often been decreed.

IV. Technology and Know-How

As stated by the American Bar Association in its Supplement to the Attorney General's Committee Report: "Although there is relatively little law on the subject, know-how licensing is in wide use and it appears to be generally accepted that licenses of substantial, valuable and secret know-how may contain restrictions which are reasonably necessary and commensurate with the know-how licensed."[108]

Several antitrust cases have indicated that unpatented know-how will not support as ancillary restraints any restrictions which would be invalid under a patent license, such as division of markets or price fixing.[109] In the *Timken* case, the district court stated that "one who possesses greater knowledge or superior skill in the manufacture of a product is entitled to be fairly and adequately compensated. . . . He is not entitled, however, to exact as a price for such contribution complete freedom from competition."[110] And in the *Incandescent Lamp* case, the Court stated that "even in the secret processes cases . . . restraints accorded the owner of the secret are limited to what is reasonably necessary. . . ."[111] There the Court distinguished secret processes from the "vague" term, "know-how," saying it was difficult to tell to what extent the parties actually used the know-how there involved.[112]

Other courts have made the same distinction, and even international divisions of market territories (which likely would have been illegal if based on a patented process) have been upheld by two lower courts in recent years on the basis of old precedents in antitrust cases

108. ABA Antitrust Section, Antitrust Developments, 1955–68 186 (1968); ABA, Antitrust Law Developments 351–353 (1975). *See* MacDonald, *Know-How, Licensing and the Antitrust Laws*, 62 Mich. L. Rev. 351 (1964); Barton, *Limitations on Territory, Field of Use, Quantity and Price in Know-How Agreements with Foreign Companies*, XII Antitrust Bull. 243 (1967).

109. United States v. General Electric Co., 80 F.Supp. 989 (S.D. N.Y. 1948), Carboloy case; United States v. General Electric Co. 82 F.Supp. 753 (D. N.J. 1949) (Incandescent Lamp case); United States v. Timken Roller Bearing Co., 83 F.Supp. 284 (N.D. Ohio 1949), *aff'd*, 341 U.S. 593 (1951); United States v. Imperial Chemical Industries, 100 F.Supp. 504 (S.D. N.Y. 1951).

110. United States v. Timken Roller Bearing Co., 83 F.Supp. 284, 313 (N.D. Ohio 1949), *aff'd* 341 U.S. 593 (1951).

111. United States v. General Electric Co., 82 F.Supp. 753, 815 (S.D. N.Y. 1949).

112. *Id.* at 846.

involving secret process: the *Benelux*[113] and *Cellophane*[114] cases. However, the *Benelux* case was reversed on other grounds, and the issue was not actually raised in the *Cellophane* Supreme Court opinion.[115]

The Ninth Circuit in *A. & E. Plastik Pak Co., Inc.* v. *Monsanto Co.*,[116] emphasized the nature of the technology involved. There the Court refused to consider as a *prima facie* restraint of trade a "know-how" license providing that the licensor, the Monsanto Co., would purchase from the licensee five million pounds of a new product to be made by the know-how, "apparently," according to the Court, "for the purpose of allowing [the licensee] the economies of large-scale production while refraining from competition with Monsanto. . . ."[117] The Court wished to ascertain whether, as in *Timken, ICI* and *Incandescent Lamp*, there was "a lack of any true trade secrets or that what secrets existed were not sufficient to support restraints of such magnitude."[118] The Court did not rule on a claim that the technology was the same as that in an expired patent. The Supreme Court in *Kewanee Oil Co.* v. *Bicron Corp.*[119] has reversed an opinion of the Sixth Circuit, setting at rest an attack upon the whole theory of protecting patentable trade secrets under state law. The Court held that the federal patent system and state trade-secret law could exist side by side.

The general direction of the law in this area would seem to be that the know-how and technology will have to be of substantial nature and in the category of a secret process or trade secret to support any ancillary restraints. In any event, restraints which have been held unreasonable in patent licenses will doubtless be held unreasonable in know-how licenses.[120] Since a patentee obtains his legal monopoly by making a disclosure to the public whereas a licensor of know-how only makes it available to one or more licensees, it would be anomalous if he were allowed to impose greater restrictions than a patentee.

On the whole question of territorial division, two cases decided in 1967 should be mentioned. The Supreme Court in the *Sealy* case[121]

113. Foundry Services Inc. v. Benelux Corp., 110 F.Supp. 857 (S.D.N.Y. 1953), *rev'd*, 206 F.2d 214 (2d Cir. 1953).

114. United States v. E.I. DuPont de Nemours & Co., 118 F.Supp. 41 (D. Del. 1954), *aff'd*, 351 U.S. 377 (1956).

115. Even so, three justices made the worldwide territorial division between DuPont and La Cellophane a point in their dissent. *Id.* at 419. *See* Chapter V, Woodward and Matsuo, *supra.* note 43.

116. 396 F.2d 710 (9th Cir. 1968).

117. *Id.*

118. *Id.*

119. 478 F.2d 1074 (6th Cir. 1973), *rev'd*, 94 S.Ct. 1879, 416 U.S. 470 (1974).

120. *See* ABA Antitrust Section, Antitrust Developments, 1955–68, 187, especially the cases cited in notes, 5, 6, and 7; Davidow, *Antitrust and International Patent-Licensing*, note 22 *supra*; Chapter II, Lyon and Doi, *supra*.

invalidated a territorial allocation among a group of relatively small independent bedding manufacturers located in different parts of the United States who collectively advertised and sold the bedding under the trademark Sealy. The arrangement itself was not attacked. In the *Schwinn* case[122] the Court held it per se unlawful for a bicycle manufacturer to impose territorial restrictions on its distributors and dealers in the United States where the latter actually purchased the bicycles from the manufacturer.

V. Conclusion

The discussion above has pointed out the many antitrust aspects that may be involved in the exploitation of a patent grant in the United States. In the field of international licensing, both the United States companies and the foreign companies involved must take account of the application of the United States antitrust laws to activities affecting United States commerce even though these activities may be carried on outside of United States borders. As indicated by the chapter in this book prepared by Michiko Ariga, the Japanese antitrust laws also apply to international licensing, and the Japanese Fair Trade Commission Guidelines on the subject also deserve close attention.

121. United States v. Sealy, Inc., 388 U.S. 350 (1967).
122. United States v. Arnold, Schwinn & Co., 388 U.S. 366 (1967).

United States Taxation of Patent and Know-how Licensing

JOHN J. COOPER

I. Taxation of Foreign Corporations

A. The Foreign Investors' Tax Act of 1966

United States jurisdiction over taxation is predicated on citizenship, residence, and source of income. Following the unitary system of taxation of most industrial nations, citizens and residents of the United States and domestic corporations pay income tax on all their income from whatever source derived.[1] The jurisdictional nexus is the citizenship or residence of the taxpayer.

Prior to the enactment of The Foreign Investors' Tax Act of 1966 (hereinafter referred to as the 1966 Act), source of income provided the jurisdictional connection for taxation of nonresident corporations. The rate of taxation of a foreign corporation with United States source income, however, turned on whether it was engaged in a trade or business in the United States. A foreign corporation engaged in a trade or business in the United States was taxable on all its United States source income at regular corporate rates, while a foreign corporation not engaged in a United States trade or business was taxed only on its "fixed or determinable" income from United States sources at the reduced rate of 30 percent.[2] Correspondingly, the latter corporations were restricted in their deductions to those items allocable to United States income.[3] The concept that a foreign corporation engaged in business in the United States should pay full United States tax on all income from United States sources regardless of its character and irrespective of whether derived from a United States business was known as the "force-of-attraction" rule.

1. Treas. Regs. §§1.1–1(b) (1956) and 1.11–1(a) (1956).
2. Int. Rev. Code of 1954 (hereinafter cited as I.R.C.) Ch. I, §§881–82, 68A Stat. 282 (1954) prior to amendment by the 1966 Act.
3. I.R.C. Ch. 1, §882, 68A Stat. 282 (1954) prior to amendment by the 1966 Act.

Royalties from patent and know-how licensing were included within the "fixed or determinable" income category. Thus foreign corporations without a trade or business in the United States were taxed on their licensing income from the United States at the flat rate of 30 percent, whereas such licensing income of foreign corporations with a United States trade or business was taxable at the full United States rates.

Substantial changes in the scheme of taxation of foreign corporations were made in the United States tax laws as a result of the 1966 Act. As the Senate Finance Committee Report states:[4] "This bill represents a substantial revision of the tax treatment of foreign corporations and nonresident aliens, an area which has not been revised for some 30 years." The objectives, as announced by President Kennedy,[5] and stated by the Fowler Task Force on "Promoting Foreign Investment in the United States and Increased Foreign Financing for United States Corporations Operating Abroad" were directed toward the simplification of United States taxation of foreign investors and the elimination of tax inequities. An inequity existed under the "force-of-attraction" rule because of the differing tax treatment of the investment income of foreign corporations depending on whether the foreign corporation was engaged in a trade or business in the United States. As noted, under prior law, this income was taxed at the reduced rate of 30 percent if the foreign corporation was not engaged in a United States trade or business. On the other hand, if the foreign corporation was engaged in a United States trade or business, under this rule, all its United States source fixed or determinable income was fully taxable in the United States at corporate rates. Congress believed that this was not only inequitable but also deterred foreign corporations from investing in the United States and the corporations that had invested here from commencing a business in the United States.

Following enactment of the 1966 Act, all fixed or determinable United States source income of foreign corporations effectively connected with a United States trade or business became taxable in the same manner as like income of a United States corporation; but all such income not effectively connected with a trade or business became taxable at 30 percent.[6] Income tax conventions can lower the rate even more.[7] The 1966 Act thus repealed the "force-of-attraction" rule

4. S. Rep. No. 1707, 89th Cong., 2d Sess. 9 (1966).

5. 109 Cong. Rec. 12249 (1963).

6. I.R.C. §§881–82.

7. This rate is 10 percent under Article 14 of the Convention between Japan and the United States for the Avoidance of Double Taxation and the Prevention of Fiscal Evasion with respect to Taxes on Income, March 8, 1971, 23 U.S.T. 967 (hereinafter cited as Double Taxation Treaty).

whereby a foreign investor was taxed at ordinary rates on investment income if he happened to be engaged in trade or business even though the income was not related to the business.[8]

If the changes in the United States tax laws had stopped here, the objective of simplification would have been achieved. However, the scope of the proposed legislation was changed to reach foreign source income of a foreign corporation. H.R. 11297 in 1965 would have taxed all foreign source income where effectively connected with a United States trade or business. Subsequently, the bill was modified to limit to three the categories of such income to be taxed by the United States.[9] One such category was rents or royalties for the use of intangible property. This provision was enacted into law, and royalty income derived by a foreign corporation from outside the United States is subject to United States taxation just the same as the royalty income of a United States corporation if effectively connected with the conduct of a United States trade or business.[10] (Royalties for the use of intangible property that are not so connected, but which have a United States source, continue to be subject to tax at the 30 percent rate.)[11]

The purpose of this change was to preclude the use of the United States as a "tax haven" by foreign corporations. The reasoning of Congress is indicated in the following statement:[12]

> The interplay between the tax rules of certain foreign countries and the United States has in some cases permitted the use of the United States as a tax haven. The tax avoidance in such a case can be illustrated by a foreign corporation which is organized in a country which does not tax its domestic corporations on income derived from the conduct of a business outside the country. If such a corporation desires to sell products into countries, other than the United States or the country of its incorporation, it can, in many instances, avoid all or most taxation on the income from these sales by establishing a sales office in the United States. The income from the sales in such cases is not taxed in the United States because (under the title passage rule) it is not derived from sources within the United States. The income may not be taxed by countries where the products are sold because the corporation does not have a permanent establishment there, and the income is not taxed by the country of incorporation because the business is not conducted there. . . . In addition, U. S. tax may be avoided in the case of rents and royalties from a licensing business. . . .

8. For an historical analysis of this development, *see* Jones, *Foreign Investors Tax Act: The "Effectively Connected Concept and Taxation of Domestic Source Income,"* N.Y.U. 26th INST. ON FED. TAX. 389 (1968).

9. H.R. 13103, 89th Cong., 2d Sess. (1966).

10. I.R.C. §§864(c)(4) and 882(a),(b).

11. I.R.C. §881.

12. S. REP. No. 1707, 89th Cong., 2d Sess. 18 (1966).

As noted, the early House bill would have reached all foreign source income effectively connected with a United States trade or business. The 1966 Act, however, limited United States taxation of foreign source income of foreign corporations to rents or royalties for the use of intangible property; dividends, interest, or gains or losses from the sale of securities or debt obligations; and the sale of inventory.[13] The thrust of this legislation was to amend the jurisdictional rules of taxation. It specifically affects the licensing income received by a foreign corporation and alters the rules of United States taxation of this income.

B. "Effectively Connected" Licensing

Foreign corporations licensing intangible property in the United States for use in the United States or abroad must now consider whether this income is effectively connected with a United States trade or business. Licensing income effectively connected to a United States trade or business is now fully taxed by the United States regardless of its source. Even though it has a foreign source, such licensing income will be taxed to the foreign corporation at United States corporate tax rates. This is particularly important to a Japanese corporation that conducts licensing in or through the United States. Under the Japanese Special Investment Law, a Japanese corporation receives favorable tax treatment in connection with royalties derived abroad.[14] The tax advantage provided by this concession will be lost if this income becomes subject to full United States tax. It is important, therefore, to determine the circumstances under which licensing income of a foreign corporation will be effectively connected with a United States trade or business. If not effectively connected, the licensing income of the foreign corporation will not be taxed at all unless it has a United States source, and if it does, this income will be taxed as fixed or determinable income.

Two sets of rules exist for making this "effectively connected" determination. If the licensing income has a United States source, section 864(c)(2) of the United States Internal Revenue Code (hereinafter referred to as the Code) provides that the factors to be taken into account include (1) whether the income is derived from property used in the conduct of a United States trade or business, and (2) whether the activities of the United States trade or business were a material factor in realizing the income.

According to the House Report and applicable Treasury Regula-

13. *See* I.R.C. §864(c)(4).
14. Chapter X, Nakamura, Toyama, and Dodge, *infra*.

tions,[15] whereas the first factor (the asset-use test) is important in determining whether passive investment income is effectively connected because business activities are not likely to be a material factor in producing this income, the business activities test is important in determining whether income from the licensing activity is effectively connected. Examples contained in the House Report and Treasury Regulations illustrate the result where a foreign corporation with a United States sales office through which patented products are sold also licenses the patents.[16] In this situation the royalties will not be effectively connected income provided the business in which the patents are used has no "direct relationship" to the business carried on in the foreign corporation's United States office and provided the licensing negotiations are handled by employees of the foreign corporation not connected with the United States branch.

In those cases where the royalty income has a foreign source, section 864(c)(4) and (5) of the Code sets forth the following five requirements that must be met to establish that the royalty income is effectively connected with a United States trade or business:

1. The foreign corporation must have an office or other fixed place of business in the United States,
2. The royalty income must be derived in the active conduct of a trade or business carried on by that United States office,
3. The royalty income must be attributable to that office,
4. The United States office must be a material factor in the production of the royalty income, and
5. The United States office's activities must be of the type that produce this income.

What constitutes an office or other fixed place of business is detailed in Treasury Regulations. The concept is similar to many treaty provisions pertaining to permanent establishments. The Code, like the treaty rules, provides that an agent's office is to be disregarded unless the agent is other than an independent agent acting in the ordinary course of business, and either has authority (regularly exercised) to conclude contracts or has a stock of merchandise from which he regularly fills orders on behalf of the foreign corporation.[17] The Code does not expressly provide that a subsidiary is to be disregarded in ascertaining whether the foreign corporation has an office. The normal treaty provision, including the income tax treaty between

15. H.R. Rep. No. 1450, 89th Cong., 2d Sess. 58 (1966); Treas. Reg. §1.864–4(c), 34 Fed. Reg. 1032 (1969).

16. H.R. Rep. No. 1450, 89th Cong., 2d Sess. 61, Example 6 (1966); Treas. Reg. §1.864–4(c)(3)(ii), Example 2, 34 Fed. Reg. 1033 (1969).

17. I.R.C. §864(c)(5)(A); Treas. Reg. §1.864–7(d), 34 Fed. Reg. 1039 (1969).

Japan and the United States, does so provide in determining whether the foreign corporation has a local permanent establishment. It appears, however, from the Senate Report[18] that such a result was intended. Treasury Regulations, section 1.864–7(d)(1)(i), confirms this result as follows:

> In determining whether a nonresident alien individual or a foreign corporation has an office or other fixed place of business, the office or other fixed place of business of an agent who is not an independent agent, as defined in subparagraph (3) of this paragraph, shall be disregarded unless such agent (a) has the authority to negotiate and conclude contracts in the name of the nonresident alien individual or foreign corporation, and regularly exercises that authority, or (b) has a stock of merchandise belonging to the nonresident alien individual or foreign corporation from which orders he obtains are regularly filled on behalf of such alien individual or foreign corporation. A person who purchases goods from a nonresident alien individual or a foreign corporation shall not be considered to be an agent for such alien individual or foreign corporation for purposes of this paragraph where such person is carrying on such purchasing activities in the ordinary course of its own business, even though such person is related in some manner to the nonresident alien individual or foreign corporation. For example, a wholly owned domestic subsidiary corporation of a foreign corporation shall not be treated as an agent of the foreign parent corporation merely because the subsidiary corporation purchases goods from the foreign parent corporation and resells them in its own name. However, if the domestic subsidiary corporation regularly negotiates and concludes contracts in the name of its foreign parent corporation or maintains a stock of merchandise from which it regularly fills orders on behalf of the foreign parent corporation, the office or other fixed place of business of the domestic subsidiary corporation shall be treated as the office or other fixed place of business of the foreign parent corporation unless the domestic subsidiary corporation is an independent agent within the meaning of subparagraph (3) of this paragraph.

To be effectively connected, royalty income must be derived from an active conduct of a trade or business, and the activities of such trade or business must be a material factor in producing the royalties. If the United States office of a Japanese corporation is engaged primarily in sales activities and does not participate in the licensing activity, it is not a material factor in producing the royalty income. Treasury Regulation, section 1.864–6(b)(2)(i), which deals with rents, royalties, or gains on sales of intangible property specifically provides that the United States office is a material factor in producing

> rents, royalties, or gains or losses, from intangible personal property . . . if the office or other fixed place of business either actively participates in soliciting, negotiating, or performing other activities required

18. S. Rep. No. 1707, 89th Cong., 2d Sess. 19–21 (1966).

to arrange the lease, license, sale or exchange from which such income, gain, or loss is derived or performs significant services incident to such lease, license, sale, or exchange. An office or other fixed place of business in the United States shall not be considered to be a material factor in the realization of income, gain, or loss for purposes of this subdivision merely because the office or other fixed place of business conducts one or more of the following activities: (a) develops, creates, produces, or acquires and adds substantial value to, the property which is lease, licensed, or sold, or exchanged, (b) collects or accounts for the rents, royalties, gains, or losses, (c) exercises general supervision over the activities of the persons directly responsible for carrying on the activities or services described in the immediately preceding sentence, (d) performs merely clerical functions incident to the lease, license, sale, or exchange, or (e) exercises final approval over the execution of the lease, license, sale, or exchange. The application of this subdivision may be illustrated by the following example(s):

(*Example 1*). *F*, a foreign corporation, is engaged in the active conduct of the business of licensing patents which it has either purchased or developed in the United States. *F* has a business office in the United States. Licenses for the use of such patents outside the United States are negotiated by offices of *F* located outside the United States, subject to approval by an officer of such corporation located in the United States office. All services which are rendered to *F*'s foreign licensees are performed by employees of *F*'s offices located outside the United States. None of the income, gain, or loss resulting from the foreign licenses so negotiated by *F* is attributable to its business office in the United States.

Another requirement in the case of *foreign source* royalties is that the United States office must regularly carry on activities of the type from which such income is derived. In its commentary, the House Report states that generally, royalty will not be attributable to the United States office unless the license is made by or through that office.[19] The House Report goes on to state that whether the license is made by or through the United States office turns on whether that office actively participates in soliciting, negotiating, or performing other activities to arrange the license or performs significant services incident to the license. It concludes with the statement that no income will be attributable to the United States office simply because that office developed or acquired the intangible property, or exercised general supervision over the persons carrying out the licensing activities. The Senate Report specifies that the United States office's activities must contribute significantly to the production of the royalty income to be material, though they need not be the major factor.[20]

If the license is only incidental to the United States trade or business or the United States office normally does not engage in licensing

19. H.R. Rep. No. 1450, 89th Cong., 2d Sess. 64 (1966).
20. S. Rep. No. 1707, 89th Cong., 2d Sess. 20–21 (1966).

activities, it is clear that the royalties are not effectively connected. Thus, if a foreign corporation is engaged in the business of exporting and selling its products through a local office, royalty income from the United States licensing of intangible property will not be effectively connected to that office unless the office also is actively engaged in licensing this property and participates in the particular licensing activity.[21]

Royalty income with a foreign source also must be attributable and allocable to the United States office to be effectively connected to that office. How such attribution and allocation is to be made was left open by the statute.[22] The bases for allocation and attribution between the United States and the foreign office could include which office developed and maintained the property, which office was responsible for instituting, negotiating, and deciding on licensing terms, which office is to provide the technical assistance, and which office is to be responsible for supervision of the license. The House Report suggests that little weight should be given to the development of the property and that the licensing activities are critical in the determination of whether royalty income is to be attributable to the United States office. The Treasury Regulations adopt this view.[23]

Another important change made by the 1966 Act pertinent to the licensing activities of the foreign corporation concerns the treatment of gains from the sale of intangible property.[24] Under prior law a foreign corporation not engaged in a United States trade or business was taxable only on its fixed or determinable income from United States sources.[25] This class of income included royalties, but it did not include capital gains,[26] with the result that gains from the sale of intangible property were not subject to United States taxation.[27] This rule also was altered by the 1966 Act.[28] Now capital-gain payments to foreign corporations contingent on the production, use or disposition of intangible property are classed as royalty income and made subject to the 30 percent tax. To insure taxation of these royalties as ordinary

21. H.R. REP. No. 1450, 89th Cong., 2d Sess. 61, Example 6 (1966).

22. Brudno & Hawkins, *The Foreign Investors' Tax Act—The "Effectively Connected" Concept and Taxation of "Foreign Source" Income*, N.Y.U. 26th INST. ON FED. TAX. 417 (1968).

23. Treas. Reg. §1.864–6(b), 34 Fed. Reg. 1036 (1969).

24. I.R.C. §§871(a)(1)(D) and 881(a)(4).

25. I.R.C. Ch. 1 §881, 68 Stat. 282 (1954) prior to amendment by the 1966 Act.

26. Treas. Reg. §1.1441–2(a)(3) (1956). *Cf.* Gordy, *Foreign Investors Tax Act, Problems of Nonresident Alien Individuals: Income, Estate, and Gift Tax*, N.Y.U. 26th INST. ON FED. TAX. 451 at 470 (1968).

27. Commissioner v. Celanese Corp., 140 F.2d 339 (D.C. Cir. 1954); Kimble Glass Co., 9 T.C. 183 (1947).

28. I.R.C. §881(a)(4).

income, the 1966 Act provides that if more than 50 percent of the gain for any taxable year derives from such contingent payments, all the gain is to be treated as contingent.[29] If, however, this income is effectively connected to a United States trade or business, this change in the tax law is not applicable, and in this event the income will be taxed on a capital gains basis.

This new rule generally will not impose any significant additional tax burden on the Japanese licensor because of the treaty protection. If the Japanese corporation is licensing on a capital gains basis, and this income is effectively connected to a United States trade or business, it will be taxed on a capital gains basis exactly as before the 1966 Act. If this income is not effectively connected, although it is now subject to taxation by the United States, it will be taxed only at the lower 10 percent treaty rate.[30]

C. Foreign Tax Credit

Prior to the 1966 Act, foreign tax credits against any United States tax were not available to the foreign taxpayer. The basis for this denial was that it was the responsibility of the foreign country to protect its nationals from double taxation through foreign tax credits. With the changed jurisdictional rules allowing taxation of foreign source income, changes in the foreign tax credit rules were required.

Under the revised rules, the foreign tax credit is available to a foreign corporation taxed by the United States on foreign source income effectively connected with its United States office.[31] Only the income taxed as "effectively connected" is taken into account in calculating the limitation on the tax credit, however.[32]

No credit is allowed for foreign taxes paid on royalties and other fixed or determinable income with a United States source.[33] In most jurisdictions, the source rules for royalty income will be the same as the United States rules, and this is so for Japan.[34] Thus royalty income with a United States source will not be taxable elsewhere except in the licensor's country of incorporation. In most such jurisdictions, however, including Japan, the tax credit rules will allow full credit for United States taxes paid on United States source income.[35]

No United States tax credit is available if the income is United States source income which would not be taxed by the foreign country but

29. I.R.C. §871(e).
30. Double Taxation Treaty, *supra* note 7.
31. I.R.C. §§901(b)(4) and 906.
32. I.R.C. §906(b)(2).
33. I.R.C. §906(b)(3).
34. Nakamura, *infra* note 10.
35. *Id.*

for the fact that such corporation was organized or is domiciled there.[36] This is a continuation of existing tax credit rules.

D. Effect of the Income Tax Treaty Between Japan and the United States

In the past, tax treaties provided for an exemption from tax or a reduction in tax rates on "industrial or commercial profits" for the foreign corporation that did not maintain a United States "permanent establishment," but permitted these profits to be fully taxed where the foreign corporation was engaged in business in the United States through a permanent establishment. Royalties from intangible property were treated specially under income tax treaties, and taxation by the source country was at reduced rates unless the foreign corporation had a "permanent establishment" in the source country. Thus the rate of tax on royalties turned on whether the foreign corporation had a permanent establishment in the source country.

This was modified slightly by Article VII of the prior treaty between Japan and the United States. Under that article the lower 10 percent rate applied if either the licensor did not have a permanent establishment or the permanent establishment constituted only a "special type of business"[37] and the royalties were not related to that business. In the ordinary situation before the 1966 Act, however, the reduced rate of tax on royalty income under this treaty was dependent upon the absence of a permanent establishment.

The treaty rule was changed by the 1966 Act. The objective of the 1966 Act was to lower the tax on investment income not effectively connected with a United States trade or business, irrespective of whether the foreign corporation happens to possess a United States permanent establishment. Section 894(b) of the Code was added by the 1966 Act to achieve this end. Thus the 1966 Act eliminated the tax inequities that existed between foreign corporations with United States permanent establishments and those without such establishments so long as the royalties are not effectively connected with a United States trade or business.

In 1971 the income tax treaty between Japan and the United States was revised. A major change in the new treaty was the elimination of the "force-of-attraction" principle to conform the treaty to the provisions of the 1966 Act, as well as to other recent income tax treaties entered into by the United States. Under the revised treaty, royalties are taxable at a reduced rate of 10 percent unless the intangible prop-

36. I.R.C. §906(b)(1)(B).
37. *See* Nakamura, *infra* note 83 for the definition of this term.

erty is effectively connected to a permanent establishment.[38] (As in the 1966 Act, the term "royalty" includes periodic payments for the use of the intangible property even though such payments are gains from the sale of the property.) Thus under this recent treaty the Japanese corporation will obtain the benefit of the reduced treaty tax rate unless it maintains a permanent establishment in the United States and the intangible property which is the basis for the royalty is effectively connected to that establishment.

The treaty carefully defines the term "permanent establishment," specifically providing that the fact that the United States resident is related to the Japanese corporation shall not be taken into account in determining whether it constitutes a permanent establishment of the Japanese corporation. Thus a subsidiary of a Japanese corporation engaged in business in the United States will not constitute its permanent establishment.[39]

Tax planning under the 1966 Act and this treaty requires a Japanese corporation doing business in the United States, that desires also to conduct licensing here, to incorporate its business and to conduct its licensing activities directly rather than through the subsidiary. This approach should insure that the royalty will be taxed at the reduced rate. As we have seen, under the 1966 Act royalty income not effectively connected with a business conducted in the United States by the Japanese corporation will be relieved from full United States taxation. Under the treaty the royalty qualifies for the reduced treaty rate if the Japanese corporation has no permanent United States establishment to which the intangible property can be effectively connected. On the other hand, if a branch is used for the conduct of its United States business, it will constitute a United States permanent establishment of the Japanese corporation, and under the 1966 Act, if it can be shown that the royalty income is effectively connected with that branch, regular corporate rates will apply to the royalty.

E. Source of Licensing Income

Source rules for royalty income continue to be important under the 1966 Act. Under this statutory change if the royalty income is effectively connected with a United States trade or business, it will be taxed at full United States corporate rates irrespective of its source. However, if the royalty income is not so connected with a United States trade or business, source rules continue to be important. If the source is foreign there will be no United States tax. Where the royalty income

38. Double Taxation Treaty, *supra* note 7, Articles 8 and 14.

39. Thus the Double Taxation Treaty functions with Treas. Reg. §1.864–7(d)(1)(i) (quoted in text following n. 18 *supra*).

has a United States source, it will be subject to tax at the 30 percent rate specified in section 881. Furthermore, since the treaty specifically exempts the Japanese corporation from United States taxation on royalties that have a non–United States source, source rules continue to be very important to it.[40]

The source of income for royalty payments on the use of patents turns on the place of use. Royalty payments for the use of patents outside the United States is foreign source income.[41] Payments for the use of patents in the United States are United States source income.[42] In the event the license covers both United States and foreign patents, the royalties allocable to the foreign rights are foreign source income.[43] In the case of mixed rights, the parties should allocate the basis of royalty calculations, since the taxpayer must carry the burden of proof in this regard.[44]

The source of income for royalty payments for the use of secret processes and other know-how likewise turns on the place of use of the know-how. Where the know-how is used abroad, the royalty payments are foreign source income.[45] To the extent the know-how agreement involves the performance of personal services, the place where the services are rendered determines the source of income.[46] Revenue Ruling 55–17[47] involved a nonresident foreign corporation not engaged in trade or business within the United States. The foreign corporation licensed a United States corporation to use its technical know-how for the recovery and purification of certain chemicals and agreed to provide instruction to employees of the domestic corporation. It was ruled that since the contract made available the technical knowledge, methods, and experience (i.e., the know-how) of the foreign corporation, notwithstanding that the instruction did involve the performance of personal services outside the United States, the payments were in the nature of royalty income for the use of know-how.

40. Double Taxation Treaty, *supra* note 7, Articles 4(1), 6(3) and 6(9).

41. I.R.C. §862(a)(4); Treas. Reg. §1.862–1(a)(4) (1957); Sabatini v. Commissioner, 98 F.2d 753 (2d Cir. 1938); Rohmer v. Commissioner, 153 F.2d 61 (2d Cir. 1946), *cert. denied*, 328 U.S. 862 (1946).

42. I.R.C. §861(a)(4).

43. Sabatini v. Commissioner, 98 F.2d 753 (2d Cir. 1938); and Rohmer v. Commissioner, 153 F.2d 61 (2d Cir. 1946), *cert. denied*, 328 U.S. 862 (1946).

44. Estate of Alexander Marton, 47 B.T.A. 184 (1942); Molnar v. Commissioner, 156 F.2d 924 (2d Cir. 1946); Rohmer v. Commissioner, 153 F.2d 61 (2d Cir. 1946), *cert. denied*, 328 U.S. 862 (1946). For allocation provisions, *see* Woodward and Matsuo, *supra*.

45. I.R.C. §862(a)(4); Treas. Reg. §1.862–1(a)(4) (1957); Rev. Rul. 17, 1955–1 Cum. Bull. 388.

46. I.R.C. §861(a)(3); I.R.C. §862(a)(3); Commissioner v. Hawaiian Philippine Co., 100 F.2d 988 (9th Cir.), *cert. denied*, 307 U.S. 635 (1939).

47. 1955–1 Cum. Bull. 388.

II. Taxation of Licensors

A. Tax Basis of Intangible Property

Three methods of transferring intangible property rights are available from the standpoint of United States income taxes: licensing on an ordinary income basis, licensing on a capital gains basis, and tax-free exchanges of technology for equity. Tax and financial factors are important in selecting between capital gains licensing and tax-free exchanges because, for the reasons hereinafter indicated, patents and know-how will have little or no tax basis. As a consequence, the entire value of these assets is vulnerable to tax at ordinary income rates. This is the crux of all tax planning in dispositions of these rights.

Research and development expenses that may culminate with a patent, invention, or know-how are specially treated under the Code. Section 174 of the Code, which came into the United States tax law in 1954, provides for an election either to deduct these expenses currently or to treat them as deferred expenses and deduct them over a period of sixty or more months. Taxpayers can be expected to deduct research and development expenses currently for two reasons. First, capitalizing and amortizing these expenses results in the disadvantage of losing a current deduction and paying higher taxes in the early years. This means lower, after-tax income without any offsetting advantage. In the one situation where the tax deduction might be lost because of insufficient immediate income or income through the carry-over period to offset a current deduction, deferring the tax write-off will prove worthwhile. Another factor favoring the current deduction is that if the taxpayer elects to defer deducting current research and development expenses, and a patent results, the taxpayer must capitalize and write off unamortized expenses over the life of the resulting patent. For both reasons, research and development expenditures from which patents and know-how are derived will be expensed. Thus, these intangible properties will have no tax basis, and the entire fair market value of any asset so acquired is susceptible to tax.

B. Tax-Free Exchanges

1. Requirements. A United States corporation ordinarily exploits its technology by manufacturing and selling products, with licensing relegated to a subsidiary role in its business activities. On the international scene this situation changes, as many forces enter to make licensing a desirable, if not the only, way by which technology can be exploited. It is well known that at least so far as strategic industries are concerned, an American corporation has not had the option of exploiting its technology in Japan except through the importation and sale of its products. With local manufacturing foreclosed as to numerous products, the transfer of technology to a Japanese licensee, whether a joint venture or an independent third party, becomes an important means by which a United States corporation can exploit its technology in that country. The methods of accomplishing the transfer that will produce tax advantages for the United States licensor are the tax-free incorporation of the technology and capital gains licensing, topics considered below.

A commonly used method of transferring patents and know-how in Japan is through the exchange of this intangible property for equity shares on a tax-free basis. This allows the American corporation to participate with its Japanese partner in the formation of a Japanese subsidiary and to transfer its technology to the joint venture without payment of United States tax on such an exchange.

Section 351 of the Code states the conditions that must be met to permit the transfer of valuable patents and know-how to a joint-venture corporation in exchange for equity stock without any tax cost: (1) The intangibles transferred must be "property"; (2) The joint venture must be 80 percent owned by the Japanese and American partners; and (3) The exchange must be solely for voting stock.

The third condition raises a special problem in Japan. Under the Japanese Commercial Code, the transfer of property to a corporation in exchange for stock first requires an appraisal of the property by a court-appointed appraiser.[48] To avoid this cumbersome procedure, the post-incorporation sale is used to transfer technology to the corporation for stock. Although two steps are involved in the transfer of cash to the corporation for shares and in the purchase of patents and know-how with the cash, the Internal Revenue Service will rule that this is a single transaction involving the exchange of property for stock.[49]

An additional requirement is a ruling from the United States Internal Revenue Service that tax avoidance is not the principal purpose of the exchange.[50] Failure to secure a favorable ruling will result in the recognition of income on the difference between the fair-market value of the technology and its basis. As a result of the Revenue Act of 1962, if the United States corporation owns more than 50 percent of the voting stock, the gain will be treated as ordinary income.[51] It, of course, is rare for this percentage of stock ownership to be held by the

48. Nakamura, Dodge, and Toyama, *infra* note 10; Ariga, *supra*.; Lyon and Doi, *supra*.

49. Private rulings have been granted qualifying the post-incorporation sale under section 351.

50. I.R.C. §367.

51. I.R.C. §1249.

American partner in a Japanese joint venture. Even though no shares are received in exchange for the contribution of appreciated property by a United States corporation to a foreign subsidiary, unless a no-tax-avoidance ruling under section 367 of the Code is secured in advance of the transfer, the appreciation of value of the contributed property will be taxable.[52]

At one time rulings on know-how transfers were difficult to obtain, for whether know-how constituted property and how it could be transferred were unsettled issues.[53] In 1960 the service discontinued rulings on know-how transfers to controlled foreign corporations pending a resolution of these issues.[54] The service continued to rule on the tax-avoidance issue, but the taxpayer had to assume the risk that the know-how was property and that the transaction effected a transfer of it. In 1961 the service indicated that guidelines would be forthcoming.[55] Subsequently, a number of revenue rulings and revenue procedures have been issued to establish the conditions under which the Internal Revenue Service will issue advance rulings under section 367 on know-how transfers to controlled foreign corporations.[56] For ruling purposes, it is now clear that secret processes constitute know-how that may be transferred in a section 351 transaction.

Section 351 is similarly available to a Japanese corporation in conducting its United States operations, and no tax-avoidance ruling is required by section 367. Thus the Japanese corporation can, if it chooses, organize its own United States subsidiary, transfer its patents and know-how to the subsidiary on a tax-free basis, and exploit its technology by manufacturing and selling its products in the United States. Alternatively, the Japanese corporation can participate in the formation of a joint-venture company to exploit its technology in the United States. Here, too, the tax-free transfer of the Japanese corporation's intangible property to the joint venture is available if the conditions of section 351 are met.

The alternative to a transaction qualified under section 351 is licensing with taxable royalty income. For the United States corporation it will be either ordinary income, or capital gains, provided the license meets the required conditions of capital gains licensing that are de-

52. Rev. Rul. 155, 1964–1 CUM. BULL. 138.

53. *See* Duffy, *Doing Business Abroad: Use of American Know-How*, N.Y.U. 20th INST. ON FED. TAX. 1269 (1962); Eckstrom & Slowinski, *Tax Planning for Foreign Licensing of United States Industrial Property Rights*, N.Y.U. 19th INST. ON FED. TAX. 969, 972 (1961).

54. T.I.R. 308, 1961 INT. REV. BULL. No. 13, at 21.

55. T.I.R. 353, 1962 INT. REV. BULL. No. 2, at 15.

56. Rev. Rul. 56, 1964–1 CUM. BULL. 133, Rev. Rul. 564, 1971–2 CUM. BULL. 179, and Rev. Proc. 10, 1973–1 CUM. BULL. (all dealing with know-how transfers under §351); and Rev. Proc. 23, 1968–1 CUM. BULL. 821 and Rev. Proc. 19, 1969–2 CUM. BULL. 288 (both setting forth guidelines for §367 rulings on know-how transfers).

tailed below. For the Japanese corporation, the royalty will be taxed at the lower treaty rate, provided the intangible property is not effectively connected with a United States permanent establishment. This income, however, will be taxed by Japan, although at a reduced rate.[57] Even though the transaction is cast as a sale, under the 1966 Act, the gains are taxable, a result not changed by the treaty.[58] Previously, gains from the sale of patents and know-how were taxable only if the foreign corporation had a United States permanent establishment, in which event they were taxable on a capital-gains basis. Now, however, if the gains are not effectively connected, they are treated as royalties and taxed. For the Japanese corporation, the 10 percent treaty rate will apply. If effectively connected to a United States trade or business, these proceeds will be entitled to capital gains treatment.[59]

2. Compared with capital gains. With the option of a capital-gains or a tax-free transaction, the tax and financial aspects of the two must be compared. Since inventions and know-how normally can be expected to have low tax bases, depreciation will not be available without a taxable transaction that produces a stepped-up basis. If the transaction is taxable, the basis of this property will be increased to its fair market value and depreciation may be taken on this new, increased basis. If the gain realized qualifies for preferred capital gains treatment by casting the transaction so that the transferee can offset payments against ordinary income, this ordinary income will have been converted into capital gains.[60]

Tax-free transfers, however, will be more advantageous where the income of the transferee is not significant. If a newly organized, Japanese, joint-venture manufacturing operation is licensed on a royalty basis and is unable to generate sufficient income against which a royalty payment can be deducted, the parties will have successfully manufactured taxable income where none existed. Thus the tax-free exchange can be expected to be the preferred approach in the formation of a joint venture, especially where the income is likely to be low in the early years. In addition to this tax advantage, the tax-free exchange has several other considerations to commend it. First, if the joint venture anticipates low income in the early years, income that otherwise would be used to pay royalties may be retained for working capital. Second, it may be preferable to receive equity over royalty. Piddling cash royalties that soon expire are not much consideration for worthwhile technology. It is far better to receive a perpetual

57. Nakamura, Dodge, and Toyama, *infra* note 10.

58. Text accompanying notes 24–30 *supra*.

59. I.R.C. §§882(a)(1) and 1201(a).

60. For an analysis of this proposition, see Dunn, *Tax Considerations in Patent Assignments and Licenses Between Related Corporations*, 16 TAX L. REV. 315 (1961).

equity interest for new concepts that will require years to develop fully. These considerations apply whether the Japanese corporation is seeking to exploit its intangible property in the United States, or the United States corporation is seeking to exploit such rights in Japan.

A consideration unique to Japan results from government restrictions on the licensing provisions, especially the royalty rate and the duration of the term. These limitations have made licensing on an exclusive basis an undesirable method of exploitation of technology in Japan by a United States company. Fortunately, the Japanese government recently began a program to relax these restrictions.[61] As a result, capital gains licensing by a United States corporation should become increasingly important in Japan, both in licensing unrelated parties, and in joint-venture licensing, provided the income is adequate to pay the royalty.

C. Capital-Gains Licensing

1. Legislative background. One of the objectives of the 1966 Act was to eliminate the use of the United States as a "tax haven" by foreign corporations for patent and know-how licensing. Previously, the foreign corporation could conduct base company licensing operations through a United States office. Under treaty rules, royalties paid to the United States base would be exempt from tax in the country where the intangible property was exploited, or the rates would be markedly lowered. If the tax rules of a foreign corporation's domicile favorably taxes foreign source royalty income, as does Japan, then royalty income obtained by a foreign corporation through licensing intangible rights outside the United States could be generated free from tax, or on a favorable tax basis. This use of the United States as a tax haven was done away with by the 1966 legislation in those cases where the royalty income is effectively connected with the United States office. As already mentioned, that legislation also taxes United States source royalty income not effectively connected with a United States trade or business, even though the income represents gain from the sale of a capital asset, and without treaty relief the tax rate for that income is 30 percent. As is evident from the 1966 Act, intangible property transactions lie in a controversial area.

Capital gains licensing has produced a long history of judicial controversy and legislation. The tax treatment of patent transactions by inventors involved a serious policy consideration for Congress. Section 1235 of the Code, which pertains to individual inventors, expressed the desire of Congress to promote creativity. This policy determination overruled the objection to the conversion of royalty pay-

61. Ariga, *supra* note 48.

ments into capital gain by making a patent license exclusive. Where the transferor is a corporation or the invention is not patented and this section is not applicable, as the cases hereinafter discussed will reveal, the courts have made the same policy determination in favor of the taxpayer.

Another and related policy consideration for Congress involved the tax treatment of transfers to controlled corporations. Should the owner of income-producing, depreciable property be allowed to sell the property to his own corporation on a capital-gains basis? If permitted, ordinary income can be converted into capital gains. There was no redeeming social value in this case such as encouraging inventions, and no difficult policy objections could be raised to revising the tax treatment that should be accorded that transaction. In the case of individuals, section 1239 of the Code was enacted to preclude the taxpayer from pursuing this route to convert ordinary income into capital gains. This section, however, does not apply to corporate transferors. Consequently, a corporation is still able to realize on its inventions and know-how on a capital-gains basis by these transfers.

Prior to the Revenue Act of 1962 (hereinafter referred to as the 1962 Act), the corporation also was in the position to exploit its foreign rights on a capital gains basis by selling these rights to its own foreign manufacturing subsidiary or its base licensing company. Congress met this problem by the enactment of section 1249 of the Code[62] to preclude capital gains on the sale of inventions and know-how to a "controlled foreign corporation."[63] The reason for section 1249 was the loophole left in the provisions of "subpart F."[64] Section 951 of the Code, as enacted by the 1962 Act, taxes to the United States parent corporation the "subpart F income" of its controlled foreign subsidiary. Included in subpart F income are royalties derived by the subsidiary from licensing of patents and know-how property acquired from the parent corporation. Since capital gains sales from the United States corporation to the subsidiary would increase the basis in the property, and payments made to the United States parent for this property were deductible, subpart F would have proved ineffectual to reach base company licensing. Following the initial hearings, Secretary Dillon appeared before the Senate Finance Committee and proposed numerous amendments to the bill. One amendment added

62. A related provision also enacted by the Revenue Bill of 1962 is section 1245, which provides for taxation as ordinary income of those gains realized on the sale of certain depreciable property (but not inventions and know-how) irrespective of the relationship between the parties.

63. This is a corporation which is more than 50 percent owned by United States shareholders. I.R.C. §957.

64. I.R.C. §§951–964.

section 1249 to provide that gain from the sale of this property to a foreign subsidiary no longer may receive capital-gains treatment. The committee accepted Dillon's proposal, and it was enacted into law. The only Congressional action pertaining to the taxation of the licensing of inventions and know-how since then has been the 1966 Act.

2. *Tax analysis.* The tax problem faced by a United States corporation in the exploitation of industrial property abroad results because of the high tax rates of the foreign country. In the case of the joint venture, for example, if it starts out profitably and its income is taxed at a high rate, the tax-free exchange will not accomplish anything. Under these circumstances, it is better to license on a capital-gains basis (provided the joint venture is not a controlled foreign corporation subjecting the license to section 1249), pay United States income taxes on the royalty income, and take advantage of the credit provisions of section 901 of the Code on the foreign income taxes paid with respect to this income. In treaty countries, including Japan, the tax rate will be reduced to the 10–15 percent range, but in any event will be below United States capital-gains rates. It is important to note here that a capital-gains licensing transaction is possible even though title to the intangible property is retained, the territory of exploitation is limited, the license is terminable should the licensee commit a breach of its terms, assignment and sublicensing are precluded, and the usual infringement provisions are included in the license.[65]

To have an effective, capital-gains transaction, the property must have a low basis and the proceeds from the transfer must receive capital-gains treatment. The conditions that must be met to achieve this goal are reviewed fully in the next section. The royalty payments also must be deductible if the technique is to work. If it develops that the licensee is acquiring a nondepreciable capital asset, the transaction would not be as favorable as ordinary licensing, for there, at least, the deduction equals the income. Fortunately, royalty payments, even in the form of capital payments, are deductible in Japan.[66] When the United States corporation goes to Japan, it is further necessary that the royalties be free from Japanese taxation other than withholding. If the United States licensor does not have a permanent establishment in Japan, treaty provisions limit the rate to 10 percent, and the reduced tax may be credited against the licensor's United States income taxes.[67]

65. As to drafting these provisions *see* Woodward and Matuso, *supra* note 44. For the Japanese regulatory measures respecting them, *see* Ariga, *supra* note 48. The United States antitrust aspects of these restrictions are dealt with in Fugate, *supra*.

66. Nakamura, Dodge, and Toyama, *infra* note 10.

67. I.R.C. §901. *See* Pugh, *Sales and Exchanges of Foreign Patents*, N.Y.U. 20th Inst. on Fed. Tax. 1305, 1314 (1962).

3. Capital asset requirement—property. The requirement for securing the capital-gains advantage under sections 1201 *et seq.* of the Code is that there must be a sale or exchange of a capital asset. This has generated enormous controversy; the various intangible property rights that may be qualified for capital-gains treatment, and what is required to effect a sale or exchange of these rights still are unsettled issues. A patent clearly qualifies as property, and analysis of whether unpatented inventions and know-how also qualify as property will be facilitated by considering the nature of the property right in the patent. A patent is an intangible, statutory right to exclude others from making, using, or selling the product or using the process. Unless he perfects his invention by patent, the inventor does not possess this statutory right. The inventor's right is to make, use, or sell the product or to use the process, and to the extent that it is secret, he can exclude others by not disclosing the invention.

Inventions, whether product or process, are "property" for tax purposes.[68] According to the cases, the property is in the invention, not the patent, and the inventor's property right arises upon the reduction of the invention to actual practice, which occurs on completion of the drawings setting forth the invention in sufficient detail to enable those skilled in the art to manufacture it without further application of the inventive act. *Dreymann*,[69] which held that an unpatented process invention constituted property, provides an important concept in analyzing the property aspects of know-how.

One form of know-how consists of services performed in transferring the invention. This is often called "show-how." The courts treat this know-how as ancillary to the assignment of the invention, with the effect that it becomes part of that capital asset. Thus, compensation for such services qualifies for capital-gains treatment. This is illustrated by the *Ruge* case[70] where the transferors of the invention agreed to provide sixty days of consulting service each year to assist the transferee in establishing and controlling its manufacturing operations. The tax court held that the 5 percent royalty paid for both the assignment and these services was entitled to receive capital gains treatment. The court reasoned that since they were required to implement the sale of an invention, the yearly consulting services were

68. Waterman v. Mackenzie, 138 U.S. 252 (1891); Franklin S. Speicher, 28 T.C. 938 (1957); Carl G. Dreymann, 11 T.C. 153 (1948); Edward C. Myers, 6 T.C. 258 (1946); Samuel E. Diescher, 36 B.T.A. 732 (1937), *aff'd sub nom.* Diescher v. Commissioner, 110 F.2d 90 (3d Cir.), *cert. denied*, 310 U.S. 650 (1940).

69. Carl G. Dreymann, 11 T.C. 153 (1948).

70. Arthur C. Ruge, 26 T.C. 138 (1956), *acquiesced in*, 1958–2 CUM. BULL. 7; Raymond M. Hessert, 6 CCH Tax Ct. Mem. 1190 (1947); Rev. Rul. 56, 1964–1 CUM. BULL. 133.

ancillary and subsidiary to the assignment of the invention. Revenue Ruling 64-56, which provides an analysis of the types of ancillary services that qualify for tax-free treatment in know-how transfers, holds that the result depends on whether the services are performed in promoting the transaction or in assisting in the start up of operations.

Services not necessary to make the transfer of the invention do not qualify for capital gains. In *Ruge*, for an additional 2 percent royalty, the transferors agreed to provide their best efforts in promoting and developing the licensee's business and to transfer subsequent developments and inventions. This additional 2 percent royalty was determined to be ordinary income. In *Spence*,[71] taxpayer sold his patents for 8 percent of the net sales for so long as he should remain head of the company. Payment thereafter was to be 5 percent of the net sales. The court held that three-eighths of the royalty payment, unlike the 5 percent royalty in *Ruge*, was paid for services rendered, and was intended as compensation over and above the royalties paid for the patents. This portion of the royalty payment was to terminate upon cessation of employment, and clearly was intended to be compensation. This result is consistent with the above ruling that even if the services are continued technical assistance, the payment for them is ordinary income.

Revenue Ruling 55-17[72] also applied this "ancillary and subsidiary" approach to the performance of personal services in connection with a know-how transfer. A nonresident foreign corporation not engaged in trade or business in the United States licensed a United States corporation to use its know-how, and agreed to provide outside the United States instructions to employees of the domestic corporation. Withholding was required if the payments were royalties for the use of property in the United States. Since performed outside the United States, withholding was not required with respect to the services. It was ruled that the entire payment was to be allocated to the know-how on the basis that in these circumstances the value is in the know-how. Specifically, the ruling provided:[73]

> The payments made under the contract are applicable both to the specific rights therein granted, that is, the right to use the "know-how," and to services performed abroad in instructing and training the employees or technicians of the domestic corporation. Such payments should therefore be allocated between the license to use the "know-how" and the personal services. Since the personal services have only nominal value apart from

71. Spence v. United States, 140 Ct. Cl. 362, 156 F.Supp. 556 (1957). *See also* Kimble Glass Co., 9 T.C. 183 (1947).

72. 1955–1 Cum. Bull. 388.

73. *Id.* at 389.

the license to use such "know-how," all but a nominal sum should be allocated to the license.

The rationale of the cases and rulings will not apply when the value of the services is significant in relation to the value of the invention or know-how. At this point the value of the proprietary position of the invention or know-how must be compared to the value of the services required to effect the transfer to determine that the services are ancillary and subsidiary to the invention or know-how. It is not difficult to imagine a case where the patent, the invention or know-how is ancillary and subsidiary to the services. Where the value of the services necessary to transfer the intangible property is small in comparison to the value of that property, this rule can be rationalized, but if this value is comparatively larger, an approach that treats these services as part of the transfer becomes more difficult to justify. Even if the services are substantial, it does not follow that the tax result must change, for it is logical to support the conclusion of the cases on the basis that the performance of these services transfers know-how, and that this form of know-how is property for tax purposes.

The foregoing analysis distinguishes between services performed as part of and services performed separately from the transfer of intangible property. The difficult question is whether the know-how constitutes property in the tax sense. Although characterization of some forms of know-how has been extremely difficult,[74] know-how in the form of a secret process has long been held to be property.[75] Sections 861(a)(4), 862(a)(4), 864(c)(4)(B)(i), 871(a)(1)(D), 871(e), 881(1)(4), and 1249 of the Code categorize secret processes as property.

In *E.I. du Pont* the taxpayer failed to obtain capital-gains treatment on a know-how sale, but this was because the property had not been transferred.[76] The unpatented secret process was conceded by the government to be property for tax purposes. This is but an extension of the *Dreymann* rule that process inventions are property. Consequently, an unpatented as well as a patented secret process is property which may be sold or exchanged.

Several revenue rulings and revenue procedures provide that

74. An exhaustive review of the judicial theories that have evolved in protecting the rights of parties in industrial property rights is contained in Lyon and Doi, *supra* note 48. As the authors observe, a secret process is protected as "property."

75. Nelson v. Commissioner, 203 F.2d 1 (6th Cir. 1953); E.I. du Pont de Nemours & Co. v. United States, 288 F.2d 904 (Ct. Cl. 1961); Franklin S. Speicher, 28 T.C. 938 (1957); Wall Products, Inc., 11 T.C. 51 (1948); Carl G. Dreymann, 11 T.C. 153 (1948); George S. Mepham, 3 B.T.A. 549 (1926).

76. E.I. du Pont de Nemours & Co. v. United States, 288 F.2d 904 (Ct. Cl. 1961). The holding of this case that the contract did not transfer the know-how is discussed at note 134 *infra*.

know-how in the form of a secret process is property for the purpose of section 351 transfers.[77] This means that the transfer of a secret process in exchange for stock in a foreign subsidiary can qualify as a tax-free exchange of property for stock. Revenue Ruling 64-56 specifically provides that[78]

> the term "property" for purposes of section 351 of the Code will be held to include anything qualifying as "secret processes and formulas" within the meaning of section 861(a)(4) and 862(a)(4) of the Code and any other secret information as to a device, process, etc., in the general nature of a patentable invention without regard to whether a patent has been applied for . . . and without regard to whether it is patentable in the patent law sense. . . . Other information which is secret will be given consideration as "property" on a case-by-case basis.
>
> The fact that information is recorded on paper or some other physical material is not itself an indication that the information is property. . . . It is assumed for the purpose of this Revenue Ruling that the country in which the transferee is to operate affords to the transferor substantial legal protection against the unauthorized disclosure and use of the process, formula, or other secret information involved.

It is not beyond doubt that Japanese law affords such legal protection, but certainly in a proper case the Japanese courts would not deny the owner of a secret process a remedy that would prevent an unauthorized disclosure or use of the process.[79] In any event, for ruling purposes the United States Internal Revenue Service has accepted the proposition that know-how is sufficiently protectible in Japan to be treated as property.[80]

According to the courts, a process need not be secret to qualify as property. In the *Heil* case,[81] the know-how was not secret. A lump-sum consideration of $1,000,000 was paid for the patents and for the know-how necessary to the manufacture of the patented products. On reasoning similar to that in *Ruge*, the tax court rejected the commissioner's position that a substantial part of the consideration was for the performance of personal services, and held that the know-how "was an incident of the patents, took on the nature of such property,

77. Note 56 *supra*.

78. 1964–1 CUM. BULL. 133.

79. As indicated by Lyon and Doi, *supra* note 48, no Japanese judicial precedent supports this position, but the authors suggest that the Japanese courts would protect secret processes.

80. Although no published rulings have been issued indicating that Japan affords such legal protection, the United States Internal Revenue Service has granted private rulings permitting tax-free know-how transfers into Japan on the basis that Japan does afford the owner of a secret process protection against unauthorized use or disclosure.

81. Heil Co., 38 T.C. 989 (1962), *acquiesced in*, 1963–1 CUM. BULL. 4.

and constituted a long term capital asset."[82] Conceptually, this language is very close to the proposition that this form of know-how, even though not secret, constitutes property in the tax sense. The position of the Internal Revenue Service is contrary, and a favorable ruling may not be obtained under Revenue Ruling 64-56 and Revenue Procedure 69-19 unless the know-how is secret. In fact, the latter requires representations that the know-how is known only to confidential employees who have a need to know, adequate safeguards have been imposed to guard against unauthorized disclosure, and it is original, unique, and novel. Until a judicial determination is made that nonsecret know-how is property, the taxpayer proceeds with a capital-gains transaction involving this intangible at substantial risk of challenge.

To classify know-how as property for tax purposes if and only if it is secret is a doubtful proposition. Secrecy is only a matter of degree, and whether know-how is to be considered "secret" creates a large penumbra of definitional problems. Also, it is very probable that in most instances secret know-how can be obtained by sufficient expenditures of money and resources. However, it will often be more advantageous for this information to be purchased rather than developed. Moreover, the right to legal protection of know-how turns importantly on the relationship between the party seeking protection and the party threatening to disclose the information, together with the facts and circumstances of the particular case.[83] Serious questions are therefore raised by any proposition that only secret designs, processes, and formulas should qualify as an intangible property.

The property concept developed in the cases dealing with other intangible property rights provides a better basis of determination of what know-how constitutes property than does either the "ancillary and subsidiary" or secrecy rationale. Intangible rights such as goodwill, life estates, partnership interests, leases, exclusive agencies, franchises, and similar intangible rights can qualify as capital assets. An analysis of the cases, in the opinion of the Second Circuit in *Commissioner* v. *Ferrer*[84] shows that whether the intangible right comprises property turns on whether it provides the right to income or the "opportunity" to earn income. This distinction is exemplified by the exclusive agency and franchise cases, which hold that even though the right may be not much more than an opportunity, nevertheless it may

82. *Id.* at 1003.

83. Lyon and Doi, *supra* note 48; Ladas, *Legal Protection of Know-How*, 7 PAT. T. M. & COPYRIGHT J. OF RES. & EDUC. 397 (1963).

84. 304 F.2d 125 (2d Cir. 1962), *rev'g in part* 35 T.C. 617 (1961).

furnish the basis for a capital-gains transaction. In fact, it has been settled by Congress that even an agreement to terminate an exclusive agency is the sale of a capital asset.[85]

Although overturned by section 1253 of the Code, enacted into law by the Tax Reform Act of 1969, the *Dairy Queen* franchise cases furnish support for the proposition that a process can be property whether or not it is secret.[86] These cases involved patented freezing machines and a trade name. The owner of an exclusive territorial franchise entered into agreements granting exclusive subfranchises of the right to use the patented machine and the trade name. The tax court held the transactions were not sales because of the numerous restrictions respecting such matters as title to the machines, quality control, the facilities to be provided, and record keeping. The Courts of Appeals for the Fourth, Fifth, and Tenth Circuits reversed the tax court on this issue. All held that these were capital transactions, the court in *Gowdey* defining the property as the exclusive right to the use of the machine (but not the patent rights), the trade name, and the formula mix for the specified territory. These rights were more than an "opportunity" to earn income, and thus qualified as property on the basis of the distinction made in *Ferrer*.

These cases involved both payments of fixed amounts—part down and part payable in installments—and payments based on the gallons of mix used for the term of the franchise. In *Moberg* the tax court held that the fixed payments as well as the gallonage payments were ordinary income.[87] The fifth circuit court reversed, holding that the fixed payments were proceeds from the sale of property, and remanded the case for a determination of whether gallonage payments also should be considered as part of the sales price of the subfranchise.[88] On remand, the tax court held that gallonage payments not limited by a fixed dollar amount should not be considered part of the sales price of the subfranchise.[89] This holding, which was the sole issue on appeal, was affirmed by the fifth circuit.[90] The opinion of the court of appeals

85. The court in Commissioner v. Starr Bros., 204 F.2d 673 (2d Cir. 1953) *rev'g* 18 T.C. 149 (1952), held that the cancellation was not a sale or exchange. This decision was reversed by section 1241, which provides that in cases where the distributor has a substantial capital investment in the distributorship, amounts received for the cancellation of the agency are to be deemed received in exchange therefor.

86. Gowdey's Estate v. Commissioner, 307 F.2d 816 (4th Cir. 1962), *rev'g* 20 CCH Tax Ct. Mem. 555 (1961); Moberg v. Commissioner, 305 F.2d 800 (5th Cir. 1962), *rev'g* 35 T.C. 773 (1961); Dairy Queen of Oklahoma, Inc. v. Commissioner, 250 F.2d 503 (10th Cir. 1957), *rev'g* 26 T.C. 61 (1956).

87. 35 T.C. 773 (1961).

88. 305 F.2d 800 (5th Cir. 1962).

89. 22 CCH Tax Ct. Mem. 1483 (1963).

90. 365 F.2d 337 (1966); *accord*, Gowdey's Estate v. Commissioner, 307 F.2d 816 (4th Cir. 1962). *Contra*, Dairy Queen of Oklahoma, Inc. v. Commissioner, 205 F.2d 503 (10th Cir. 1957).

emphasized the contractual characterization of the gallonage payments as being "in the nature of a royalty" and the separation of the gallonage payments from the sales price clauses in the contract. Thus when spread out for the life of the subfranchise, the gallonage payments represented the retention of an interest in future earnings. This concept was incorporated into section 1253 in denying capital gains treatment to contingent periodic payments.

The *Moberg* decision that the method of payment was relevant in determining whether it was part of the sales price is important in determining whether the payment is for property. The *Dunn* case provides good reason to distinguish the tax treatment between a sale made on a lump-sum basis and one made for periodic payments based upon the use of the property.[91] Although the method of payment has been held not to be relevant in determining whether there has been a sale or exchange,[92] the method of payment could be a useful factor in classifying know-how as property. Where one pays an agreed, fixed price for know-how, and assuming no substantial services are involved, it is conceptually difficult not to categorize the particular know-how as property, although it does not follow that the use of periodic payments makes the know-how less than property. The property and sale or exchange issues are so interrelated that formulation of a general rule applicable in every situation is not possible. A review of the decided cases suggests that the requirements that have to be met in making a sale or exchange of the know-how resolve the property issue also.

4. Must not be held for sale. In order to qualify as a capital asset, the invention or know-how must not be held primarily for sale to customers. For the individual licensor of patents and inventions, enactment of section 1235 of the Code settled this issue in favor of the inventor with the elimination of the distinction between the professional and the amateur.[93]

This issue was raised in relation to a corporate owner of patents in the *Allied Chemical, Armco* and *Norgren* cases.[94] Resolution of this issue begins with the Supreme Court's interpretation of "primarily" in the *Malat* case.[95] It was there determined that this word means "of first

91. Dunn v. United States, 259 F.Supp. 828 (W.D. Okla. 1966), *aff'd*, 400 F.2d 679 (10th Cir. 1968). *See* note 151 and accompanying text *infra*.

92. *See* notes 109–13 and accompanying text *infra*.

93. Thomas H. McClain, 40 T.C. 841 (1963), *acquiesced in*, 1964–1 CUM. BULL. (Pt. 1) 5; Roland Chilton, 40 T.C. 552 (1963) *acquiesced in*, 1961 CUM. BULL. (Pt. 1) 4.

94. Armco Steel Corp. v. United States, 253 F.Supp. 749 (S.D. Ohio 1967); Allied Chem. Corp. v. United States, 66–1 U.S. Tax. Cas. ¶9212 (S.D. N.Y. 1966), *aff'd*, 370 F.2d 697 (2d Cir. 1967); C.A. Norgren Co. v. United States, 268 F.Supp. 816 (D. Colo. 1967).

95. Malat v. Riddell, 383 U.S. 569 (1966).

importance" or "principally," not "substantially" or "essentially." In determining whether patents were held for sale, the courts have held the following factors to be important: the reason for the licensing activity; whether the corporation's activities are devoted principally to the development of patentable and salable products rather than the development of salable patents; the continuity and frequency of the licenses; the substantiality of the sales when compared to other sources of income; and the method of payment.

When patents are acquired by a corporation with the expectation of employing the invention in its own manufacturing operations, it would seem obvious enough that they are not held primarily for sale to customers. Thereafter, it may be determined that there are products that the corporation will be unable or unwilling to exploit and territories into which it is not ready or able to move. In these situations licensing may be desirable or even necessary. But this is a secondary method of realizing upon new discoveries. The *Allied Chemical* case illustrates this proposition. There, the district court decided that the patent was not held for sale where the transfer was made because Allied Chemical did not possess sufficient expertise to fully exploit the invention internally.

In the *Armco* case five foreign licensing transactions were before the court. These licenses were granted to British, French, Belgian, Swedish, and Japanese companies because Armco was unable to exploit this licensed technology abroad by any other method. Additional factors were that while the royalties for the three years at issue exceeded $5,000,000, this amount was less than 2 percent of Armco's sales during these years, and Armco's licensing transactions were infrequent. In *Norgren*, the taxpayer found it necessary to license a British company to manufacture and sell its products in several foreign countries. In view of these factors and because the licenses were granted for the reason that there was no other practical way to exploit these foreign markets, the courts found that the patent rights were not held for sale.

Another basis for these holdings is that if all substantial rights in a patent are transferred, there has occurred a disposition of property that cannot be replaced. This property is not like "stock in trade" or "inventory" or "property held . . . primarily for sale to customers." When foreign manufacturing becomes impractical because the corporation does not possess sufficient expertise or capital or it is not practical to enter a particular geographic market, exclusive licensing of the relevant patents is more akin to the transfer of property held for use in the business. The sale of such property produces a capital gains transaction under section 1231 of the Code. Accordingly, the sale of patent rights in such circumstances should not result in the determination that these rights were held for sale.

The foregoing decisions and analysis may not decide the issue in cases involving know-how or the unpatented invention, but they are pertinent. A basic difference exists between the exclusive license of a patented invention and the exclusive license of an unpatented invention or know-how. The exclusive patent license transfers the right to exclude others from making, using, or selling the product or using the process. The disposition of this right of exclusion does not necessarily occur in the sale of an unpatented invention or know-how. It can, however, if the licensor possesses the legal right of exclusion and the contract precludes him from making, using, or selling the product or using the process.[96] If the license contract does this, it is submitted that the rationale of these two decisions on whether foreign patent rights were held for sale should establish the basis for determination of whether the unpatented invention or know-how is held for sale.

Two English cases involving the issue of whether the taxpayer was trading in know-how support this position. In *Evans Medical Supplies*,[97] the taxpayer, which was engaged in the chemical and drug business throughout the world, sold to the government of Burma the know-how to establish a pharmaceutical factory, commence production, and manage the business. The issue in the case was whether the transfer of the secret processes was a nontaxable, capital transaction.[98] This turned on whether the taxpayer was trading in know-how, i.e., acquiring and disposing of know-how in the ordinary course of business. Although several companies did have the necessary knowledge, only a few of them used it to prepare such products, and until this agreement, taxpayer had never communicated these secret processes to others. For that reason the House of Lords determined that, since the taxpayer was not engaged in the business of trading in know-how, this was not a taxable capital transaction.

In *Rolls Royce*,[99] the House of Lords held that the taxpayer was not only a manufacturer of aircraft engines, but was also in the trade of teaching others how to manufacture them. The basis for the decision was that over an eight-year period taxpayer entered into numerous agreements to supply others with the necessary know-how to manufacture aircraft engines. Moreover, no restrictions were imposed on

96. As pointed out in notes 79–80, *supra*, whether the owner of unpatented industrial property rights has the right to prevent the unauthorized use or disclosure is not settled in Japan.

97. Moriarty v. Evans Medical Supplies, Ltd., [1957] 3 All E. R. 718 (H. L.).

98. A secret process is property that can be sold in a nontaxable transaction under the rule of Handley Page Ltd. v. Butterworth, 19 Tax Cas. 328 (H. L. 1935).

99. Rolls-Royce, Ltd. v. Jeffrey, [1962] 1 W. L. R. 425.

taxpayer by the licensees that prevented the disclosure of this know-how to third parties who, in turn, could use it in competition with the licensees.

On the basis of the patent cases the decisions in both instances would have been the same had they resolved the slightly different question of whether the know-how was held for sale to customers. Since the nature of know-how permits multiple transactions in the same know-how in the same territory, to prevent a determination that this property is being held for sale, the contract should preclude the subsequent transfer of the know-how in the territory encompassed by the license.[100]

5. Sale or exchange requirements. Major problems connected with the capital-gains treatment of royalties from the licensing of inventions and know-how derive from the issue of whether there has been a sale or exchange of this intangible property. Substantial litigation has resulted from the characterization of a transaction as a "license," from retention of title, and from the royalty method of payment. As for the characterization of the transaction as a "license," however, *Watson* v. *United States*[101] held flatly that the use of the term was not controlling. There the court stated:[102]

> The calling of the instrument a license agreement, and the denomination of the parties thereto as licensor and licensee, respectively, did not fix, limit, or qualify the scope and effect of the grant. The legal question whether the instrument constituted an effective assignment or was a license must be determined by considering together the several provisions contained in the instrument, not its title or the manner in which reference was made to the parties.

In many instances the licensor will retain title to the patents, but this does not preclude a sale or exchange.[103] Retention of title provides substantial advantages, particularly in the case of foreign licensing, for a variety of contractual requirements may be imposed on the licensee without disturbing the capital-gains treatment of the royalty, and title retention makes them more meaningful.[104] Related to title retention is the right to cancel. Coupling these two provisions can be of real value in transfers to joint ventures and unrelated parties. A risk is removed if the transferor is in position to recoup all rights in

100. The antitrust implications of territorial restraints in know-how licensing are considered in Fugate, *supra* note 65.

101. 222 F.2d 689 (10th Cir. 1955).

102. *Id.* at p. 691.

103. Storm v. United States, 243 F.2d 708 (5th Cir. 1957); Kronner v. United States, 126 Ct. Cl. 156, 110 F.Supp. 730 (1953). *Cf.* Eterpen Financiera Sociedad. v. United States, 124 Ct. Cl. 20, 108 F.Supp. 100 (1952), *cert. denied*, 346 U.S. 813 (1953).

104. *See* Woodward and Matsuo *supra* note 44, for guidance in the preparation of contractual provisions.

the event of a breach. The courts have held that the right to cancel the license in any of the following events did not disqualify the license as a sale: nonperformance by the licensee,[105] bankruptcy or insolvency of the licensee,[106] governmental interference with the licensee's business,[107] or failure of the licensee to use its best efforts to market the invention.[108] The theory is that the right to cancel is a "condition subsequent." Consequently, retention of title together with the right of forfeiture does not prevent the transfer of all substantial rights to the invention.

Payment for patents, inventions, and know-how may be on a lump-sum basis, or for a royalty measured, for example, by selling price or units of production, or pursuant to a formula based on profits, production or use. The determination that the method of payment is not relevant to the issue of whether the transaction effects a sale has been settled by section 1235 of the Code, and by court decisions where that section is not applicable. This question was raised in 1942 when it was first contended that this method of payment disqualified the transaction for treatment as a sale or exchange. It was held, however, that the critical determination was whether the patent owner had parted with all substantial rights in the patent.[109] If he had done so, a sale had occurred notwithstanding the method of payment.

The issue was raised again in 1946, and the tax court again held that an exclusive license of the invention qualified as a sale for tax purposes, even though it was paid for with a royalty measured by the use of this property.[110] An acquiescence was filed in 1946, but in 1950 a nonacquiescence was substituted.[111] As a result, section 1235 was enacted to assure capital-gains treatment on the royalties received under a license, provided that the individual inventor parted with all substantial rights to his patent. A later ruling announced that only payments made following the statutory enactment would qualify for capital-gains treatment, but this position also was reversed by congressional action.[112] If the transaction cannot be brought within the ambit of section 1235 because, for example, the invention is not patented or

105. Watson v. United States, 222 F.2d 689 (10th Cir. 1955); Allen v. Werner, 190 F.2d 840 (5th Cir. 1951); Golconda Corp., 29 T.C. 506 (1957), *acquiesced in*, 1958–2 Cum. Bull. 5.

106. Commissioner v. Celanese Corp., 140 F.2d 339 (D.C. Cir. 1951); Carl G. Dreymann, 11 T.C. 153 (1948).

107. First Nat'l Bank v. United States, 136 F.Supp. 818 (D. N.J. 1955).

108. Kronner v. United States, 126 Ct. Cl. 156, 110 F.Supp. 730 (1953).

109. Commissioner v. Hopkinson, 126 F.2d 406 (2d Cir. 1942), *aff'g* 42 B.T.A. 580 (1940).

110. Edward C. Myers, 6 T.C. 258 (1946).

111. Mim. 6490, 1950–1 Cum. Bull. 9. Rev. Rul 353, 1958–2 Cum. Bull. 408, reversed this position.

112. I.R.C. §1235(c) overturned Rev. Rul. 58, 1955–1 Cum. Bull. 97.

the licensor is a corporation, it is now settled law that the method of payment is not determinative of whether the transaction is a sale.[113]

6. *Transfer of all substantial rights.* To effect the sale or exchange of an invention, there must be a transfer of all substantial rights in the invention. The following test as to what constitutes such a transfer in the case of patents was formulated by the Supreme Court in 1891:[114]

> The monopoly thus granted is one entire thing, and cannot be divided into parts, except as authorized by those laws. The patentee or his assigns may, by instrument in writing, assign, grant, and convey either, 1st, the whole patent, comprising the exclusive right to make, use and vend the invention throughout the United States; or, 2d, an undivided part or share of that exclusive right; or, 3d, the exclusive right under the patent within and throughout a specified part of the United States. . . . A transfer of either of these three kinds of interests is an assignment, properly speaking, and vests in the assignee a title in so much of the patent itself, with a right to sue infringers. . . . Any assignment or transfer, short of one of these, is a mere license, giving the licensee no title in the patent, and no right to sue at law in his own name and for an infringement.

Section 1235 of the Code, and the regulations issued pursuant thereto, provide for capital-gains treatment of proceeds from the transfer of all substantial rights to a patent by a "holder" as defined in subsection (b).[115] In the enactment of this section, Congress intended to adopt the test laid down by the courts in determining whether the transfer was a sale or exchange. Consequently, these guidelines, while they do not apply to a corporation, nor to one other than a "holder," should be consulted in ascertaining whether a particular transaction effects a sale or exchange.

A sale or exchange requires the grant of the exclusive right to make, use and sell the invention. This test may be applied readily with respect to a product invention, but not where the invention is a process. The substantial rights here are to use the process and to commercialize any resulting product. Thus an exclusive license covering a manufacturing process may only provide the licensee with the right to manufacture and sell the resultant product. Whether the failure to grant the right to use the product precludes a sale depends on the specific circumstances. In one case, *Rollman* v. *Commissioner,*[116]

113. Golconda Corp., 29 T.C 506 (1957), *acquiesced in,* 1958–2 Cum. Bull. 5; Leonard Coplan, 28 T.C. 1189 (1957), *acquiesced in,* 1958–2 Cum. Bull. 4; Franklin S. Speicher, 28 T.C. 938 (1957), *acquiesced in,* 1958–2 Cum. Bull. 7; Arthur C. Ruge, 26 T.C. 138 (1956), *acquiesced in,* 1958–2 Cum. Bull. 7; Vincent A. Marco, 25 T.C. 544 (1955), *acquiesced in,* 1958–2 Cum. Bull. 6.

114. Waterman v. MacKenzie, 138 U.S. 252, 255 (1891).

115. For an interpretation of "holder," see Elmo Meiners, 42 T.C. 653 (1964), *acquiesced in,* 1967–2 Cum. Bull. 3.

116. 224 F.2d 634 (4th Cir. 1957), *rev'g* 25 T.C. 481 (1955); *accord* Flanders v. United States, 172 F.Supp. 935 (S.D. Cal. 1959); *cf.* Broderick v. Neale, 201 F.2d 621 (10th Cir. 1953).

the fourth circuit court held that the substantial rights in a footwear process were to manufacture and to sell shoes, reversing the tax court's holding that the failure to grant the right to use the product was fatal. In another, *E. I. du Pont de Nemours & Co.* v. *United States*,[117] the taxpayer exclusively licensed eight Brazilian process patents for the manufacture of nylon, but retained the right to sell into Brazil. The third circuit court held that because this right was without value, its retention did not prevent the transfer of all substantial rights in the patents.

In the case of a product patent, whether the right to manufacture or use or sell is substantial also depends upon the nature of the invention. *Lawrence* v. *United States*[118] involved the license of a product patent. The licensee was given the exclusive rights to manufacture and to use and to lease the product to others, but sale of the product was contractually precluded. The question was whether the transfer qualified under the provisions of section 1235. The invention, a device for removing obstructions from oil wells, was classified in the trade as a service tool that was not sold. The inventor did not want the tool sold because it required trained operators to use it, and if improperly operated, the result would be failures or damaged wells. Neither party considered the right to sell the tool a substantial right. The fifth circuit court held on these facts that all substantial rights had been transferred.

Suppose, however, that there is a complete transfer of the right to make, use, and sell, but that the licensee is precluded from making all possible uses of the invention, from exploiting it in the entire territory within the scope of the patent, or from using it in other than a specified industry. What if the transfer is subject to prior outstanding licenses?

It is settled law that "for capital gains purposes, a taxpayer may sell a partial interest in an invention."[119] In *Laurent*,[120] the license was exclusive only insofar as the invention could be applied to a specific product of the type manufactured by the licensee, and the tax court held that the transaction was a sale. Subsequently, the tax court again held in *Rouverol*[121] that notwithstanding separation of a patent into

117. 432 F.2d 1052 (3d Cir. 1970).

118. 242 F.2d 542 (5th Cir. 1957).

119. Bell Intercontinental Corp. v. United States, 381 F.2d 1004, 1014 (Ct. Cl. 1947). *Cf.* Mros v. Commissioner, 493 F.2d 813 (9th Cir. 1974) *rev'g* 30 CCH Tax Ct. Mem. 519 (1971) and Fawick v. Commissioner, 436 F.2d 655 (6th Cir. 1971) *rev'g* 52 T.C. 104 (1969) which held that a field of use limitation precluded capital gains treatment under §1235 of the Code.

120. Milton P. Laurent, Sr., 34 T.C. 385 (1960), *nonacquiescence*, 1961–2 CUM. BULL. 6.

121. William S. Rouverol, 42 T.C. 186 (1964), *nonacquiescence*, 1965–2 CUM. BULL. 7.

different fields of use by the transfer of each field of use to a different licensee, each transaction qualified as a sale or exchange. The third circuit court held in *Merck & Co.* v. *Smith*[122] that the grant by the inventors of sulfa drugs of an exclusive license to make, use, and sell sulfadiazine only, which was but one of the claims in their patent, constituted a sale. In a license covering a brake patent, the sixth circuit court held in *Kavanagh* v. *Evans*[123] that the retention by the inventor of the rights under the patent to manufacture, use, or sell power brakes did not preclude the transfer from constituting a sale. A license under taxpayer's Brazilian process patents to manufacture nylon retained the dacron rights also covered by the patents, but the third circuit court held that "patent rights are divisible between different industries and different products."[124]

The potential significance of a corporation's licensing activities abroad is illustrated in many of the cases cited and reviewed in this article. In some cases millions of dollars were added to profits by the exploitation of intangible rights through foreign licensing. Foreign licensing necessitates a distinction between licenses of unpatented inventions and know-how on the one hand and patented inventions on the other. An exclusive license under a patent in only a specified portion of the granting country will transfer the patentee's right to exclude others from making, using, or selling the product or from using the process in that territory. Since these are all the patentee's rights in that part of the country, there has been a sale to the extent of that area.[125]

In the license of an unpatented invention or know-how, the licensor can transfer only the right to make, use, or sell, but not the right to exclude others insofar as they may independently have acquired the same invention or know-how. Since neither an unpatented invention nor know-how have such circumscribed territorial limitations, any transfer on less than a worldwide basis carves up this intangible property. This will not preclude a tax-free exchange under section 351, and by analogy should not prevent a sale or exchange unless, of course, the transactions are so frequent that a court determines that this property is being held for sale. As hereinafter noted, however, Revenue Ruling 64-51 does require the licensor to transfer to the licensee the right to prevent others, including the licensor, from using the know-how in the country of use.

A related kind of limitation is illustrated in *United States* v. *Car-*

122. 261 F.2d 162 (3d Cir. 1958).
123. 188 F.2d 234 (6th Cir. 1951).
124. E.I. du Pont de Nemours & Co. v. United States, 432 F.2d 1052 (3d Cir. 1970).
125. Vincent A. Marco, 35 T.C. 544 (1955), *acquiesced in*, 1958–2 CUM. BULL. 6.

ruthers,[126] which held that an exclusive license of processing equipment limited to the tuna-canning industry qualified as a disposition of all substantial rights in the invention. The court of appeals reasoned that in the context of this issue, there was no difference between a transfer limited as to industry and either one limited to area or a transfer of a partial interest in the patent or invention. Thus an exclusive license, even though limited, can qualify as a sale, whether that limitation is product (scope of use), area, or industry.

Previously granted licenses can exist as in *Bell Intercontinental Corp. v. United States*,[127] where the transfer was subject to a cross-licensing agreement among aircraft manufacturers providing for use of each other's inventions. Taxpayer not only granted its license subject to this prior commitment, but also retained the right to receive the royalty. The court of claims held that this outstanding license did not prevent the sale of taxpayer's patent rights. The court, however, distinguished this case from *Allied Chemical*,[128] where the retention of the right to grant a nonexclusive license to a third party prevented the sale of all substantial rights.

Limitations on assignment and sublicensing, which allow the licensor to select only qualified parties to exploit the technology, do not preclude a sale. The reasoning of the courts is that the requirement that the licensee obtain the consent of the licensor to make an assignment only protects the rights of the parties, and does not prevent the vesting in the licensee of all substantial rights in the invention.[129]

Licensing transactions must anticipate both third-party infringement suits against the licensee and infringement activities by others. In the situation where infringement suits are against the licensee, ordinarily the contract provisions allow, or perhaps even require, the licensor to defend the action, and royalty payments may be suspended or escrowed pending the outcome. The requirement that the licensor defend or aid in the defense of infringement actions protects the interest of the licensee, and is similar to a covenant to defend title. This covenant does not prevent a sale because, although it provides the licensor with the opportunity or the obligation to defend his interest in continued royalty payments, no interest in the intangible property is retained.[130]

126. 219 F.2d 21 (9th Cir. 1955).

127. 381 F.2d 1004 (Ct. Cl. 1967).

128. Allied Chem. Corp. v. United States, 370 F.2d 697 (2d Cir. 1967).

129. E.I. du Pont de Nemours & Co. v. United States, 432 F.2d 1052 (3d Cir. 1970); Rollman v. Commissioner, 244 F.2d 634 (4th Cir. 1957); Watson v. United States, 222 F.2d 689 (10th Cir. 1955); Bell Intercontinental Corp. v. United States, 381 F.2d 1004 (Ct. Cl. 1967); Golconda Corp., 29 T.C. 506 (1957), *acquiesced in*, 1958–2 CUM. BULL. 5; First Nat'l Bank v. United States, 136 F.Supp. 818 (D. N.J. 1955).

130. Watson v. United States, 222 F.2d 689 (10th Cir. 1955); First Nat'l Bank v. United States, 136 F.Supp. 818 (D. N.J. 1955).

Infringement actions against third parties are necessary to protect the interest of the licensor in continued royalty payments. This is particularly true where patents are involved, as unrestrained infringements cast doubt on their validity. These suits also are required to protect the licensee from the competitive disadvantage of being the only payor of royalties. For both reasons, properly drafted license contracts should and do deal with the problem of handling litigation against infringers.

An exclusive license that passes the right to sue on to the licensee is consistent with a sale. Even where the licensor retains control of the litigation, the courts have held that such retention is nonetheless consistent with the transfer of all substantial rights in the invention. The rationale of the decisions is that the retention of the right to sue only protects the licensor's interest in the royalties; it does not withhold any right in the invention. In an early case, the board of tax appeals held that retention of the right to sue, with each party to share equally in the cost of litigation and any recoveries, did not prevent a sale of all substantial rights.[131] More recently, the tenth circuit court held that a contract obligating the parties to act jointly in resisting any infringement, and fixing the manner of dividing any damages recovered, was designed to protect and safeguard the rights of both parties and was not at variance with the sale of the invention.[132] Where the transaction was cast in the form of a sale rather than a license, the same result was reached where the right to sue infringers was retained by the transferor.[133] In this case the transferor even had the first option of bringing the infringement suit and to retain all the recovery as part of the consideration. In the event the transferor failed to exercise timely the option, the transferee was permitted to conduct the litigation, retaining the proceeds of any award.

E.I. du Pont[134] involved the issue of whether there has been a transfer of all substantial rights in know-how. The taxpayer entered into a know-how license covering a secret process. The licensee agreed to keep the process secret for five years, but no restrictions were placed on further disclosures, and subsequently similar rights were granted to another. It was held that the know-how had not been sold because the right to prevent further disclosure had not been transferred. The court of claims analogized the requirement that the transferor not divulge the secret to others to the right of the transferee of a patent to

131. Parke, Davis & Co., 31 B.T.A. 427 (1934), *acquiesced in*, XIV–1 CUM. BULL. 15 (1935).

132. Watson v. United States, 222 F.2d 689 (10th Cir. 1965).

133. Thornton G. Graham, 26 T.C. 730 (1956), *acquiesced in*, 1958–2 CUM. BULL. 5.

134. 288 F.2d 904 (Ct. Cl. 1961).

prevent its infringement. Therefore, to transfer all substantial rights to know-how, the transfer of exclusivity is required.

Pickren[135] involved an unsuccessful attempt to secure capital gains on the sale of a secret process because a term limited to twenty-five years prevented the transfer of all substantial rights.

Revenue Rulings 64-56 and 71-564, which came after these cases, set forth the position of the Internal Revenue Service as to the requirements that must be met for a know-how transfer under section 351 of the Code. The former provides that "The unqualified transfer in perpetuity of the exclusive right to [the know-how] within all the territory of a country . . . will be treated as the transfer of all substantial rights in the property in that country." The latter holds ". . . that an unqualified transfer of the exclusive right to use a trade secret until it becomes public knowledge and no longer protectible under the applicable law of the country where the transferee is to operate is a transfer of property for purposes of Revenue Ruling 64-56."

In the context of *du Pont* and *Pickren,* these rulings require that the license have a "perpetual" term, that the licensor not disclose the secret process to others for use in all the territory of the country, and that this obligation be enforceable under the law of the country of use. To constitute property under the former ruling, the licensee must be afforded the "substantial legal protection against the unauthorized disclosure and use of the process."[136] Although this legal protection no doubt is available in Japan,[137] there may be a situation where a proper disclosure is made to a third party for use elsewhere, and that third party discloses the process to other Japanese parties. Conceptually, if secret processes are to be analogized to patents, the transfer of all substantial rights to the process would require an agreement on the part of the licensor not only to disclose the process to others for use in the territory, but also to extract such a contractual commitment from subsequent licensees for the benefit of the licensee. Revenue Rulings 64-56 and 71-564 do not go so far.

Thus, to meet the requirements for a sale, the cases and the rulings require that the transfer be for the life of the know-how, that is, in "perpetuity." Revenue Ruling 71-564 defines that to be only so long as it remains secret and protectible.

In summary, capital-gains licensing may be conducted to provide substantial protection to valuable foreign rights in inventions and know-how. Retention of title and the right of forfeiture, limitations on the scope of use and territory, and restrictions on assignment and

135. Pickren v. United States, 378 F.2d 595 (5th Cir. 1967).

136. Note 78 and accompanying text *supra.*

137. *See* notes 79–80, 96, and accompanying text *supra.*

sublicensing should furnish substantial protection for these rights. As a result, considerable latitude is available in drafting an exclusive license without disturbing the capital-gains treatment of the royalties. A few of these restrictions and limitations can raise antitrust issues, whether the licensee is an American or a Japanese corporation,[138] and in the latter situation, the restriction or limitation may provide grounds for disapproval of the license by the Japanese government.[139] Therefore, in planning a licensing transaction between Japan and the United States, these as well as the tax aspects of the transaction need to be considered.[140]

III. Taxation of Licensees

A. Payments for Intangible Property

1. Methods of payment. Payment for the use of intangible property normally is on a royalty basis. Payment for the acquisition of such property usually will be with a royalty, but occasionally, patents and know-how will be purchased for a lump sum. A variety of formulas exist for establishing royalty and purchase arrangements, and careful attention must be paid to the drafting of these obligations. For the draftsman, the tax impact of the method of payment will be an important consideration, particularly in licenses acquiring know-how.

Patent licensing does not generate substantial tax problems because the licensee may either expense the royalty payment for the use of the patent or depreciate its cost. Selection of the method of payment, especially where patent rights are acquired, however, does provide a significant opportunity for tax planning. This is because under the installment method of reporting available under section 453 of the Code, gain realized on the "sale" of patent rights need not be reported until received, even though a depreciation deduction is currently available to the licensee. Thus deferred, fixed, lump-sum payments for patents provide the tax advantage of postponing the tax on the gain, yet permitting the deduction of the purchase price through the depreciation allowance.

Payments for the use of know-how similarly are deductible under section 162 of the Code, but the right to deduct payments for the *acquisition* of know-how is uncertain. The rule may be stated fairly that a lum-sum payment made to purchase know-how is a nondepreciable capital expenditure. Under the *Dunn* decision,[141] however, royalty

138. Fugate, *supra* note 65.
139. Ariga, *supra* note 48.
140. *See* Woodward and Matsuo, *supra* note 44.
141. Dunn v. United States, 259 F.Supp. 828 (W.D. Okla. 1966), *aff'd*, 400 F.2d 679 (10th Cir. 1968).

payments for the purchase of know-how may not be deductible, and this results in a tax treatment of know-how that differs from that of patents.

2. *Valuation for fixed-price sales.* The practical disadvantage of the fixed-price sale is the difficulty of establishing the value of the patent, invention, design, process, or formula. A special problem exists if the transfer is made other than at arm's length, and fixed-price sales to subsidiaries are subject to the following provisions of Treasury Regulation section 1.482-2(d):

> [W]here intangible property or an interest therein is transferred, sold, assigned, loaned, or therwise made available in any manner by one member of a group of controlled entities (referred to in this paragraph as the transferor) to another member of the group (referred to in this paragraph as the transferee) for other than an arm's length consideration, the district director may make appropriate allocations to reflect an arm's length consideration for such property or its use.

If there have been transfers of the same or similar property under the same or similar circumstances to unrelated persons, the standards established in those transactions control. If not, the regulations list a dozen factors to be taken into account in arriving at the appropriate consideration for the intangible property. The regulations apply to payments for the use of as well as for the purchase of intangibles, and they are very important in intercompany licensing.

One reason for buying intangibles on a royalty basis is that estimating value is a highly speculative proposition. The only time that courts have been called upon to pass on this method of valuation followed soon after the enactment of the income-tax laws. At that time valuation of these intangible rights was required to establish a basis for depreciation purposes. Early cases held that the capitalization of income method was the correct method of valuing patent rights, but capitalization of royalties was not rejected.[142]

The capitalization of income method requires a determination of the expected profits, an assessment of the risks affecting the profits, and a discount to take into account these risks and the fact that the profits are deferred. This formula is difficult to apply because expected profits will depend greatly on trying to estimate correctly the growth of the business. The rate of capitalization of these future profits not only must take into account the risks affecting the profits, but also must reflect the value to be assigned to the management and

142. Standard Conveyor Co., 25 B.T.A. 281 (1932), *acquiesced in*, XI–1 CUM. BULL. 6 (1932); Prophylactic Brush Co., 25 B.T.A 676 (1932), *acquiesced in*, XI–2 CUM. BULL. 4 (1932); Syracuse Food Prods. Corp., 21 B.T.A. 865 (1930), *acquiesced in*, X–2 CUM. BULL. 69 (1931).

organization necessary to promote, exploit, develop and operate the business.[143]

Another method of valuation is to discount to present value the royalties which reasonably might be expected for the life of the property. Although this valuation method has never been judicially accepted, where inventions and know-how are to be exploited by licensing, this approach to value seems appropriate.

3. Deduction of "royalty" payments. Royalty payments for the use of patent rights are currently deductible as ordinary and necessary business expenses.[144] Payments for the purchase of patent rights, on the other hand, are nondeductible capital expenditures.[145] However, the cost of patents used in a trade or business or held for the production of income are subject to an allowance for depreciation under section 167 of the Code. Treasury Regulation 1.167(a)–6 provides for a depreciation allowance for patents as follows: "The cost or other basis of a patent or copyright shall be depreciated over its remaining useful life. Its cost to the patentee includes the various Government fees, cost of drawings, models, attorneys' fees, and similar expenditures. . . . If a patent or copyright becomes valueless in any year before its expiration the unrecovered cost or other basis may be deducted in that year."

The depreciation rules are more easily stated than applied where patent and other intangible rights are paid for on a royalty basis. The following two questions arising out of patent licensing transactions required court decision: (1) Where a license to make, use, and sell a product or use a process is based on more than one patent, how is depreciation taken? and (2) Where the intangible right is acquired on a royalty basis, how is the depreciation to be calculated?

The first issue was raised very early when the commissioner contended in a number of cases that depreciation had to be separately computed for each patent.[146] All the cases, however, allowed the taxpayer to lump his patents into one group and to take his depreciation accordingly. The controversy and outcome are illustrated in *Syracuse Food* where the commissioner contended that the allowance for depreciation had to be computed separately for each patent, and that a

143. Standard Conveyor Co., 25 B.T.A. 281 (1932), *acquiesced in*, XI–1 CUM. BULL. 6 (1932).

144. Raytheon Prod. Corp., 1 T.C. 952 (1943), *aff'd*, 144 F.2d 110 (1st Cir.), *cert. denied*, 323 U.S. 779 (1944); Nestle Co., Inc., 22 CCH Tax Ct. Mem. 46 (1963).

145. Polak's Frutal Works, Inc. 281 F.2d 261 (2d Cir. 1960); Davis & Son, Inc., 5 T.C. 1195 (1945).

146. Syracuse Food Prods. Corp., 21 B.T.A. 865 (1930), *acquiesced in*, X–2 CUM. BULL. 69 (1931); Lanova Corp., 17 T.C. 1178 (1952), *acquiesced in*, 1952–1 CUM. BULL. 3; Prophylactic Brush Co., 25 B.T.A. 676 (1932), *acquiesced in*, XI–2 CUM. BULL. 8 (1932); Union Metal Mfg. Co., 4 B.T.A. 287 (1926), *acquiesced in*, VI–2 CUM. BULL. 7 (1927).

depreciation deduction should be denied on the grounds that the taxpayer had not proven the separate value of each patent. The board of tax appeals rejected these contentions, since the patents were interdependent, and in the hands of separate owners each would have been of little value. In the opinion of the board,[147] "[u]nder a single ownership they represent a valuable property right, and it is this right which is being gradually exhausted. Under less compelling circumstances, the Board has not found any obstacle to determining the allowances for exhaustion of patents upon the basis of a group value and the average life of the group. . . ."

The royalty payment, that is the contingent payment for intangible property, is the amount to be taken into account for the purpose of the depreciation allowance. *Associated Patentees*[148] involved an agreement obligating the taxpayer corporation to pay to the transferors of an invention 80 percent of all sublicensing royalties. The commissioner argued that taxpayer should be allowed only a proportionate part of this amount as a depreciation deduction, with the balance prorated over the succeeding years of the lives of the patents. While this approach would have given the taxpayer the opportunity of recovering its ultimate total cost, the practical result would have been entirely inadequate allowances for depreciation at the beginning of the term and excessive allowances for depreciation at the end. The taxpayer argued that the payment made each year was deductible in full because it was the cost pertaining to that year. In upholding the taxpayer, the tax court held that this method of computing depreciation provided a reasonable method of recovering the cost of the invention.

4. *Deduction of know-how payments*. Payments for the use of know-how, are deductible under section 162 of the Code, provided they are ordinary and necessary expenses incurred in carrying on a trade or business. Even payments made for the acquisition of know-how may be deductible if made periodically on the basis of use. In the *Nelson* case it was clear that the agreement licensing the secret process was on a year-to-year basis, and thus was not a sale, but in *Wall Products* the transaction was exclusive. Both cases allowed the taxpayer to deduct the payments for the secret processes.[149] Nonetheless, it is not clear from these decisions that periodic royalty payments based on use which are made to purchase know-how are deductible.

147. 21 B.T.A. 865 at 890.

148. Associated Patentees, Inc., 4 T.C. 979 (1945), *acquiesced in*, 1959–2 CUM. BULL. 3; Best Lock Corp., 31 T.C. 1217 (1959).

149. Wall Prods., Inc., 11 T.C. 51 (1948); Nelson v. Commissioner, 23 F.2d 1 (6th Cir. 1953).

The reason the deductibility of royalty payments made for the purchase of know-how is uncertain is because of the limitation of section 263 of the Code, requiring that the cost of capital expenditures be recovered as depreciation, not as an expense, and the limitations of Treasury Regulation section 1.167(a)–3 on depreciating intangible property. Although under section 167, property with a life of more than one year is subject to an allowance for depreciation if it is used in the trade or business or held for the production of income, this regulation requires that an intangible property have a determinable use life to be eligible for depreciation. It provides as follows:

> If an intangible asset is known from experience or other factors to be of use in the business or in the production of income for only a limited period, the length of which can be estimated with reasonable accuracy, such an intangible asset may be the subject of a depreciation allowance. Examples are patents and copyrights. An intangible asset, the useful life of which is not limited, is not subject to the allowance for depreciation. No allowance will be permitted merely because, in the unsupported opinion of the taxpayer, the intangible asset has a limited useful life. No deduction for depreciation is allowable with respect to goodwill. . . .

A lump-sum payment to acquire know-how will be a capital expenditure and will be subject to depreciation only upon the taxpayer being able to establish that the know-how has a determinable useful life. If the taxpayer is unable to make such a showing, the allowance for depreciation is not available. When know-how with no determinable useful life is acquired on this basis, no depreciation is allowable under this regulation. This position is amply supported by the cases prohibiting any depreciation allowance for items such as goodwill and franchise rights. The difficult issue arises when the payments for the intangible property are made periodically and are measured by the use of the property. Under these circumstances, is the taxpayer to be permitted to take the depreciation deduction even though he is unable to establish a determinable useful life of the property?

In the patent cases where there is a sale on a royalty basis, the courts permit the licensee to deduct the annual periodic payments as depreciation.[150] The reason is that depreciation based on annual royalty payments, in fact, provides a "reasonable allowance" for depreciation. The same logic can be applied where the intangible property is a secret process. Where the parties in an arm's length transaction provide for this, the determination should fix the tax attributes unless the other attendant considerations require a different result. One such

150. John A. Nelson Co., 28 B.T.A. 529 (1933), *aff'd on other grounds*, 75 F.2d 696 (7th Cir. 1935), *rev'd on other grounds*, 296 U.S. 374 (1936); Associated Patentees Inc., 4 T.C. 979 (1945), *acquiesced in*, 1959–2 CUM. BULL. 3; G. R. Fouche, 6 T.C. 462 (1946), *acquiesced in*, 1946–1 CUM. BULL. 2.

consideration would exist if the rights continued indefinitely after discontinuance of the payments.

The failure to allow the licensee to deduct periodic royalties for an intangible property in those cases where the transaction is cast as a sale will establish differing tax patterns for license transactions without differences in economic substance. *Dunn* v. *United States*,[151] however, did exactly that. Previously, it had been held that the transfer of the intangible property (a franchise) was a sale of a capital asset by the transferor, and at issue in this case was the transferee's right to deduct, as depreciation, the cost of the acquired capital asset. The commissioner successfully contended that even though the payments were made periodically on the basis of use (consumption of gallons of mix), the depreciation deduction was unavailable because the usefulness of the franchise was indefinite. The district court rested its decision on the numerous cases disallowing depreciation deductions on lump-sum payments for franchises. This result is a radical departure from the "flow of income" position taken in the patent cases, and adverse economic effects could have resulted from the *Dunn* decision.[152] However, this controversy over the tax treatment of franchising transactions was settled by the enactment of section 1253 of the Code as part of the Tax Reform Act of 1969. Under the provisions of the new law, contingent periodic payments for franchises are deductible if made after 1 January, 1970. This issue as it relates to know-how, that is, assumption of know-how with periodic payments based on use, has not been settled by an Internal Revenue Service ruling or by the courts.

151. 259 F.Supp. 828 (W.D. Okla.), *aff'd*, 400 F.2d 679 (10th Cir. 1968). This case was the other side of Dairy Queen of Oklahoma, Inc. v. Commissioner, 250 F.2d 503 (10th Cir. 1958).

152. Saltoun & Meyer, *Depreciation of Intangible Assets with Unascertainable Useful Life*, 45 Taxes 538 (1967).

Japanese Taxation of Patent and Know-How Licensing

SEIICHI NAKAMURA, KOZO TOYAMA, AND JOSEPH M. DODGE II

I. Introduction

A. Structure of Corporate Taxation System

The Corporation Tax Law (*Hōjin-zeihō* of Japan[1] provides that a domestic corporation is liable for a corporate tax, in respect to a given accounting period,[2] imposed upon the net income for such accounting period.[3] The net income for an accounting period is in turn computed by deducting the total pecuniary losses from the total pecuniary receipts for said period, rather than by figuring the gain or loss for particular transactions.[4]

A domestic corporation (one which has its head office in Japan)[5] is subject to the national corporation tax on worldwide income,[6] while a foreign corporation (head office not in Japan)[7] is only taxed on

1. Law No. 34, March 31, 1965, 4 EHS No. 4100 (hereinafter cited as CTL). Articles and sections of the statutes, tax circulars, treaties, and the like in this paper are effective as of *January 1, 1975*. Tax laws and circulars thereunder are often modified and revised in Japan. No court decisions are referred to in this paper, because of lack of appropriate or important decisions.

2. An accounting period may be less than twelve months; most businesses have either one or two accounting periods a year. *See* CTL arts. 13–15.

3. CTL art. 21.

4. *See* CTL art. 22(1), (2) and (3). In practice, especially for transactions involving the sale of assets, standard accounting methods, resulting in the computation of gain or loss for each such transaction, may be used. CTL art. 22(4). The authors nevertheless feel that a discussion in terms of the principles of the tax law itself, *i.e.*, that pecuniary receipts and pecuniary losses are aggregated separately, better emphasizes the fact that all transactions, barring the application of special provisions, are treated alike, there being no distinctions among types of assets or types of gains or losses.

5. CTL art. 2(iii).

6. *See* CTL art. 21.

7. CTL art. 2(iv).

Japan-source income,[8] and then only if it has a "permanent establishment" in Japan.[9] A foreign corporation not having a permanent establishment in Japan may nevertheless be liable for tax under the income tax law on income received in the nature of, *inter alia*, royalties, rentals, dividends, interest, and remuneration for services (if performed by a service enterprise).[10]

The national corporation tax rates applied to the taxable income of domestic corporations are shown below:[11]

tier	undistributed net income	net income distributed as dividends
first 7 million yen[12] (about $23,333)	28%	22%
over 7 million yen	40%	30%

As noted, the distribution of dividends is favored; this feature, however, is not available to foreign corporations.[13]

In addition to the national tax, there are two local taxes on the corporate income of a domestic corporation that should be mentioned in passing: (1) the enterprise tax,[14] which is imposed upon the corporate net income at a 12 percent rate,[15] and (2) the inhabitant tax,[16]

8. CTL arts. 4(2) and 138. *See* notes 76–93 and accompanying text *infra*.

9. CTL art. 141(i), (ii) and (iii). There is an exception in art. 141(iv) for a limited range of transactions which do not involve patents or know-how. For the definition of "permanent establishment", see note 83 and accompanying text *infra*.

10. *Shotokuzeihō* (Income tax law) arts. 5(4), 161(ii)–(vii), (ix)–(xi), and 178 (Law No. 33, March 31, 1965), in 4 EHS No. 4050 (hereinafter cited as ITL). *See* notes 88–93 and accompanying text *infra*. The most likely reason for the imposition of the income tax rather than the corporation tax on certain transactions by foreign corporations not having a permanent establishment in Japan is administrative; such a firm would not keep books for purposes of tax accounting in Japan, would not have an accounting period known to Japanese tax collectors, and would not have assets to fasten a tax lien upon; the income tax, on the other hand, is ideal for resolving this problem by means of the mechanism of withholding income at the source. *See* ITL arts. 212–215.

11. CTL art. 66. *Sozei tokubetsu sochihō* (Special tax treatment law) art. 42(1) (Law No. 26, March 31, 1957), in 4 EHS No. 4031.

12. The lower rates apply only to a corporation whose paid-in capital is 100 million yen (about $333,333) or less. CTL art. 66(2). Also, the 7 million yen cut off is proportionally reduced if the accounting period is less than 12 months. CTL art. 66(4) and (5).

13. *See* CTL art. 143(1) and (2). *See also* note 11 *supra*.

14. *Chihōzeihō* (Local tax law) art. 72–22 (Law No. 226, July 31, 1950).

15. For corporations whose offices and factories are located in only one or two prefectures, lower rates are applicable for tiers up to 3.5 million yen, which, however, is only about $11,666. *Id.*

16. *Id.* arts. 51, 52, 312 and 314–6.

which consists of a nominal flat fee plus about 17 percent[17] of the national tax amount.[18] These local taxes are also applied to a foreign corporation's taxable net income which is attributable to its offices or places of business in Japan.

B. Types of Industrial Property; Types of Transactions

Under Japanese tax law, patents, patent applications, rights to use patents, such as the right to license them, [altogether hereinafter referred to as patent rights], and know-how[19] are all considered to be "industrial property rights and rights concerning technology."[20] Patents are treated as intangible assets.[21]

There are five types of transactions involving patent rights and know-how: sale, gratuitous assignment, exchange for other patent rights or know-how, exchange for stock and, finally, licensing (both exclusive and nonexclusive).

The first four involve the transfer of all of the transferor's rights in the patent rights or know-how, and thus can be described by the word "assignment." It should be pointed out here that the Japanese corporation tax law does not admit of "capital-gains" treatment, so that the items of income from the various types of transactions described above do not receive any deduction or reduction in tax rates because of the nature of the assets involved, and, by the same token, there is no problem relating to capital losses.[22] A licensor, on the other hand, retains ownership of the property and merely gives the transferee various rights in respect to the use thereof. An assignment involves both pecuniary receipts and, where a basis for expenses exists, pecuniary loss, while a license usually involves the payment of "royalties," which consist simply of the consideration (cash plus the value of assets and services) received in exchange for the license.

17. To be exact, 17.3 percent is the usual rate; the allowable maximum rate is 20.7 percent.

18. This paper does not further mention these local taxes, as their structure generally reflects the national corporation tax and also the national income tax.

19. "Know-how" refers to the right to adopt a manufacturing process using special unpatented techniques, such as technical knowledge which has been used repeatedly in manufacturing products or otherwise in the business and includes original inventions, methods adopting special materials, machine and tool designs, and other secret knowledge which has technological value. *Tsūtatsu Shōwa 45 Chokushin (Sho) 30* (Basic Income Tax Circular) art. 161–22 (July 1, 1970).

20. *See* CTL art. 138(vii)(a); ITL art. 161(vii)(a).

21. CTL art. 2(xxiii) & (xxiv); *hōjin zeihō shikōrei* (Cabinet order implementing the corporation tax law) art. 12 and 13(viii)(e)–(h) (Cabinet Order No. 97, March 31, 1965) (hereinafter cited as CTL Cabinet Order).

22. *See* CTL art. 21 *et seq.* Some capital gains treatment is permitted by ITL art. 33, but that provision is not applicable to corporations, *see* ITL arts. 5(1), 21 *et seq.*, 174, 178.

II. General Principles for Taxing Patent and Know-How Transactions

A. Basis of Property

1. Acquired by research and development. In general, research and development costs of a Japanese corporation can either be debited to a deferred expense account[23] and amortized over a period not exceeding five years[24] or charged as expenses in the year incurred.[25] "Costs of research" include expenditures incurred for the manufacture of new products and in carrying on research and experiments regarding new inventions. "Development costs" include expenditures incurred in adopting new technology or a new managerial organization, in developing resources and markets, and in starting up a new business.[26] Such costs, needless to say, are of the type resulting in the accumulation of patent rights and know-how, but they do not form a basis, therefor, except as noted below.

Upon the issuance of a patent, assuming the election has been made to defer and amortize the expenses of research and development, the right to so amortize forthwith ceases in respect to those research and development expenses that are allocable to the patent, and the basis thereof is established as the sum of such unrecovered research and development costs. Expenses, including legal fees, incurred in applying for and registering the patent, may constitute the basis or be deducted forthwith at the option of the company.[27] The basis is depreciated over an eight-year period.[28]

A mere patent application resulting from a company's research and development effort does not have a basis; rather, a basis is fixed, as described above, when the patent is issued upon the application.[29]

Know-how so developed likewise has no basis, although the cost incurred in developing it can, as noted above, be amortized over a period not exceeding five years or expensed currently.

2. Acquired by assignment or license. Where patent rights or know-how

23. CTL art. 2(xxv); CTL Cabinet Order art. 14(1)(iv) and (v).

24. Commercial Code art. 286–3.

25. *Id.*, CTL Art. 32; CTL Cabinet Order art. 64(1)(i).

26. CTL Cabinet Order art. 14(1)(iv) and (v).

27. *Id.* art. 54(1)(ii); *Tsūtatsu Shōwa 44 Chokushin (hō) 25*, (Basic Corporation Tax Circular) art. 7–3–14. (May 1, 1969) (hereinafter cited as "CTL Basic Circular").

28. *Genka shōkyaku shisan no taiyo nensūto ni kansuru shōrei* (Ministerial order regarding the useful life of depreciable assets) art. 1(1)(iii) (Ministry of Finance Ministerial Order No. 15, March 31, 1965). The eight-year period does not correspond to the useful life of the patent, as a patent is valid for fifteen years in Japan.

29. Should the company, however, decide to give up a given research effort, because, for example, it has failed to produce a patentable invention possessing potential for profitable exploitation, any unrecovered expenditures in connection therewith can be deducted forthwith.

are acquired by purchase and not by the company's own research and development, the basis therefor, not surprisingly, is the value of the consideration given plus necessary expenses specifically allocable to the acquisition.[30] However, if a patent right or know-how is obtained gratuitously, the basis is the fair-market value of the patent or know-how.[31] A third possibility, acquiring patent rights or know-how by exchange, fixes the basis as the value of the assets exchanged plus necessary expenses incurred in connection with the exchange.[32] It follows that patent rights or know-how acquired in exchange for stock will be given a basis equal to the aggregate value of the stock, plus expenses related to the transaction; however, should the basis so computed exceed the fair-market value of the patent rights or know-how received, then the latter figure is the basis.[33] In the special case of a company's exchanging assets, including patent rights or know-how, for 95 percent or more of a newly established corporation's stock, the basis of the assets (other than cash) so transferred when in the hands of the parent, may be assumed by the subsidiary, even where the transaction is really based upon the relative market values of the assets and the stock;[34] such an accounting may be imposed by a parent corporation desiring to avoid the reckoning of profit on the transfer of its assets until it distributes the acquired stock, at which time, if the distribution is in the nature of a dividend, the distributees rather than the corporation may have to recognize some gain.[35]

The right to use patent rights and know-how acquired through a license takes a basis which can be depreciated over a five-year period.[36] The basis is generally the sum of the costs incurred in acquiring the license, such as the contract fee or other fixed lump-sum payments.[37]

B. Realization of Gain or Loss

1. Sale (assignment) for consideration. The gain or loss in respect to a particular transaction is not figured as such, but rather the value of

30. CTL Cabinet Order art. 54(1)(i).
31. *Id.* art. 54(1)(vii).
32. *Id.* art. 54(1)(i).
33. *Id.* art. 54(1)(vi).
34. CTL art. 51; CTL Cabinet Order arts. 93–95. The subsidiary realizes no profit or loss despite the disparity between the value of its stock and the basis of the assets acquired by it; in effect, the transaction itself fixes the value of the stock as being equal to said basis. Such a transaction also comes under the more general principle that no profit or loss accrues to a corporation as the result of increases or decreases in its capital. CTL art. 22(2) and (5).
35. For a more detailed explanation of tax consequences to the parent and to distributees of the stock, see notes 52–59 and accompanying text *infra*.
36. CTL Basic Circular arts. 8–1–4, and 8–2–3.
37. *Id.* art. 8–1–4; *see* notes 97–105 and accompanying text *infra*.

the consideration received is included in pecuniary receipts, and the basis is included in the pecuniary loss for the accounting period in which the assignor's right to receive the consideration accrues.[38] As for commissions, it does not matter if they are specifically allocable to the particular transaction, as they are nonetheless all includible in the pecuniary loss for the period in which they accrue.[39] In the rare case of an assignment of the limited rights acquired by a license, the same principles apply, the basis being the undepreciated amount of the contract fee;[40] for an assignment of rights acquired, on the other hand, by a license requiring the payment of royalties, the basis of such rights is zero.

Where an assignment is paid for by installments, gain rather than separate receipts and expenses, is recognized and allocated to succeeding accounting periods in which installments are due, if the statutory conditions and requirements are met.[41] To be specific, a "deferred payment conditioned transfer of assets"[42] can be treated as follows: the gain accruing in an accounting period bears the same ratio to the gain from the whole transaction (value of consideration received less basis and less commissions) as the sum of installment payments receivable (plus payments received before maturity) in the accounting period bears to the sales price of the assignment.[43] A procedural prerequisite for obtaining installment treatment is that the company must elect to follow the installment method of tax accounting for installment sales of non-inventory[44] assets not only in the current period but also in each subsequent one, and such election must be made during or before the first accounting period in which such sales occur; otherwise, the company is precluded from adopting it and must use the pure accrual method.[45]

2. Gratuitous assignment. Where a corporation gratuitously assigns patent rights or know-how to others, it is deemed to have received imputed income equal to the fair-market value thereof at the time of

38. Japanese tax laws generally employ accrual method. *See, e.g.*, CTL Basic Circular art. 2–1–1 *et seq.*

39. *See* CTL art. 22(3), and note 4 *supra*. *But see* CTL art. 22(4).

40. *See* note 37 and accompanying text *supra*.

41. CTL art. 63.

42. Such a transfer is characterized by the following: i) payment must be made in three or more periodical installments; ii) the period between the transfer of the assets and the due date for the last installment must be at least two years; and iii) payments due by the transfer date must not exceed two thirds of the transferee's total liability under the contract. CTL art. 63(2); CTL Cabinet Order art. 126.

43. CTL art. 63(1); CTL Cabinet Order art. 124.

44. Installment sales of inventory are separately regulated under closely similar provisions. *See* CTL art. 62.

45. CTL art. 63(1); CTL Cabinet Order art. 125.

transfer, and the net basis of said assets is reckoned into pecuniary loss.[46] However, the imputed receipts in respect to gratuitous assignments made during the accounting period can be offset by a deduction up to the aggregate amount thereof or the maximum limits for the deduction for such period,[47] whichever is the lesser amount.[48] At best, therefore, the gratuitous assignment will merely be cancelled out for tax purposes; it will never result in a net deduction, except for the rare case in which the fair-market value of the assigned patent rights or know-how is less than their basis.

Even if valuable consideration is received for the assets, but the value thereof is substantially lower than the transferred assets' fair-market value, such part of the difference between the fair-market value of the assets and the value of the consideration as is fairly considered to be a gift to the transferee is treated as a donation, and is accounted for pursuant to the principles mentioned above.[49] Thus, some transactions superficially appearing to realize a net loss may be neutralized or partially turned around to result in a net profit for tax purposes.

3. Assignment by exchange. If a corporation assigns patent rights or know-how in exchange for property of another person or company, the fair-market value of the property received is added to pecuniary receipts, and the net basis of those given up is figured as a pecuniary loss.[50] There is no need, therefore, to ascertain whether a given transaction involving both an exchange of property and the receipt by one or both parties of money or other property is essentially an exchange or a sale, as the controlling principles for all such transactions are the same.[51]

4. Assignment for stock. The computation of profit is not different in any material respect from the cases described above when the corporation assigns patent rights or know-how in exchange for the stock of the transferee; that is, the aggregate value of the stock[52] obtained is

46. CTL art. 22(2) and (4).
47. CTL Cabinet Order art. 73(1).
48. CTL art. 37(2).
49. CTL art. 37(6).
50. CTL Cabinet Order art. 54(1)(vii). *Cf.* INT. REV. CODE of 1954, §1031(a) (hereinafter cited as I.R.C.), which gives tax-free treatment for exchanges solely of property "of a like kind" held for productive use in a trade or business or for investment; where property not of a like kind (including cash) is also received in a like-kind exchange, then gain, if any, but not loss, from the transaction is recognized, but not in excess of the value of the not-of-a-like-kind property. I.R.C. §1031(b) and (c).
51. *See* note 39 and accompanying text, *supra*.
52. The scope of this paper precludes a discussion of methods of valuing stock of corporations.

added to pecuniary receipts, and the net book value of the patent rights or know-how assigned is included in pecuniary loss.[53] Special treatment, however, is available[54] for contributions by a domestic corporation of property other than money to a new corporation if the former acquires at least 95 percent of the latter's stock.[55] Pecuniary receipts are increased by the value of the stock received,[56] while pecuniary losses are increased by the basis of the assets transferred plus a special deduction equal to the "gain" realized by the transaction. The basis of the stock acquired by the parent is not the value of the assets transferred, even though such value may have formed the inducement for the transaction, but rather the (lower) basis of the assets transferred.[57] Thus, there is no practical necessity of undertaking the difficult task of valuing the stock received, as whatever gain there may be to the transferor of the assets is cancelled out by the special deduction of the same amount.[58] If the stock is subsequently distributed to the shareholders of the parent, then the amount calculated pursuant to the following formula will be considered to be dividend income to the distributee.[59]

53. *See* CTL art. 22(2).

54. CTL art. 51(1).

55. The subscription price of the stock held by any person other than the transferor of the assets, *e.g.*, the statutory promotors (COMMERCIAL CODE art. 165), must not be disproportionately low. CTL Cabinet Order art. 93.

56. If CTL art. 51(1) does not apply, the stock is given a basis equal to the fair market value of the assets transferred. CTL Cabinet Order art. 38(1).

57. CTL art. 51 also applies where the parent owns all of the stock of a subsidiary which was established by the promotors' investing money rather than other forms of property in order to avoid the inspection required by Commercial Code arts. 173(1) and 168(1)(v), if the parent assigns its assets to the new corporation in exchange for cash, and if such exchange was scheduled as of the date of incorporation to be effected within one month thereof and actually was consummated within such period. CTL Basic Circular art. 10–7–1; CTL Cabinet Order art. 38(3).

58. *Cf.* I.R.C. §368(a)(1)(D), 354, and 355. If there would have been, without the application of CTL art. 51, a net loss, which would be unlikely, CTL art. 51 is not applied, and the loss is recognized as such by the parent, which also acquires a basis equal to the fair market value of the assets transferred in an arm's length exchange. CTL Cabinet Order art. 38(1)(v). For tax consequences to the transferee of the assets in a CTL art. 51 transaction, see note 34 and accompanying text *supra*.

59. CTL arts. 24 and 25. Of course, a dividend can be paid only if the requirements of law are satisfied, *see Commercial Code* art. 290, and the corporation can acquire its own stock in limited situations. COMMERCIAL CODE, arts. 210, 212 and 377. Dividend income may receive a favorable tax treatment if certain requirements are met. *See Sozei tokubetsu sochihō* art. 8–4 (overiding ITL art. 22(2)(i), 89, 91 and 165). The Convention between Japan and the United States of America for the Avoidance of Double Taxation and the Prevention of Fiscal Evasion with Respect to Taxes on Income, March 8, 1971, 23 U.S.T. 967, T.I.A.S. 7216 (hereinafter cited as Double Taxation Treaty) art. 12 fixes the tax rate for dividends as fifteen to ten percent for a United States resident unless the resident has a permanent establishment in Japan and the shares with respect to which the dividends are paid are effectively connected with such permanent establishment.

$$\text{Total value of the distributed stock} - \left(\text{Total amount of capital and capital reserves} \times \frac{\text{Number of parent-stock owned by the distributee}}{\text{Number of outstanding parent-stock}} \right.$$

5. Licenses. Royalties received are includible in pecuniary receipts when the right to receive them accrues.[60] Since a licensor, as opposed to an assignor, retains ownership of the patent rights and the know-how, his basis therein, if any, is not recoverable otherwise than by depreciation or amortization.[61]

C. Litigation Expenses and Settlement Proceeds

All expenses incurred in litigating a patent infringement suit, including legal fees, court costs, and payments of damages or lost profits incurred in a settlement, are currently deductible.[62]

Amounts received by a corporation as a result of the successful prosecution or settlement of a patent infringement action, whether in the form of damages or lost profits, are includible as ordinary income.[63]

D. Special Rules for Overseas Transactions by a Japanese Corporation

1. Exclusion of a portion of foreign-source receipts. As a special inducement for the export of Japanese technology, a corporation[64] which accrues income from international transactions involving technology[65] acquired by the company's own endeavor and per-

60. CTL art. 22(2); *see* note 38 *supra.*

61. CTL arts. 31 and 32.

62. *See* CTL art. 22(3)(ii). Contrast the "defense of title" regulation in United States tax law, Treas. Reg. §1.212–1(k) (1957), under which litigation expenses of defending infringement suits should be added to the basis of the patent and can be recovered only through depreciation over the remaining life of the patent. I.R.C. §167 and 1016(a)(2).

63. There is no distinction between a recovery for lost profits and a recovery for damages to assets, perhaps because the notion of capital gains is not found in the Japanese corporate tax law. *See* note 22 and accompanying text *supra.*

64. This provision only applies to a corporation which files a "blue return," the privilege of so doing being conditioned primarily upon the company's undertaking to follow prescribed accounting methods. Since many tax concessions are available only to those filing blue returns, most companies of any appreciable size file them. *See* CTL arts. 2(xxxx), 121 and 146.

65. This naturally includes the furnishing of non-Japanese customers with patent rights, know-how and other technical information.

formed during accounting periods beginning on or before March 31, 1976, can deduct from the pecuniary receipts of the relevant accounting periods 70 percent of such income up to a maximum of 50 percent of the company's pecuniary receipts for each such period.[66]

2. *Special reserves.* For overseas transactions involving technology which do not fall under the immediately foregoing paragraph, establishment of a special reserve account may be allowed.[67] Under this rule, a certain portion of income arising from the relevant overseas transactions may be credited for corporation tax purposes, and therefore, the same amount can be added to the pecuniary loss.[68] This amount, however, must be debited and added back to the company's pecuniary receipts equally in the succeeding five year period.[69] Thus, this reserve sets forth a tax deferral rather than an exemption of income from tax.

3. *Foreign tax credit.* Taxes paid to foreign governments[70] can be credited against the Japanese corporation tax up to the limitation for the accounting period, which is the corporation tax payable multiplied by the ratio of foreign-source income to total income.[71]

E. Special Rules for a "Family Company" (Closely Held Corporation)

A family corporation is defined in terms of its control by a limited number of shareholders.[72] The main consequence of being a family company is that the tax authorities can reconstruct transactions between the company and its shareholders in order to reflect more clearly the values exchanged and thus recompute the corporate tax.[73] This provision could be applied to assignments and licenses between companies and subsidiaries or joint ventures; therefore, care should be taken that such transactions appear to be at arm's length. A treaty

66. *Sozei-tokubetsu-sochihō* art. 58(1); *Sozei-tokubetsu sochihō-shikōrei* (Cabinet Order implementing Special Tax Treatment Law) art. 34(1) (Cabinet Order No. 43, March 31, 1957).

67. This reserve is called Reserve for Overseas Markets Development. *Sozei-tokubetsu-sochihō*, art. 54. *Sozei-tokubetsu-sochihō-shikōrei*, art. 32.

68. *Sozei-tokubetsu-sochihō*, art. 54(1).

69. *Id.* 54(6).

70. The liability for such taxes may itself be affected by a tax-treaty between Japan and the taxing state. For example, the treaty between Japan and the United States, *supra* note 59, as it applies to a United States exporter of technology to Japan, also benefits a Japanese corporation which exports technology to the United States.

71. CTL art. 69(1).

72. A family company is a corporation where 50 percent or more of its issued shares are held by not more than three shareholders. A "shareholder" includes the shareholder together with all relatives and dependants and corporations controlled by them. CTL art. 2(x); CTL Cabinet Order art. 4.

73. CTL art. 132. This is in effect similar to I.R.C. §482.

provision provides somewhat analogous treatment to transactions between a joint venture and an American stockholder or partner therein, including a stipulation that both parties would be affected by any readjustment of income which is made.[74]

Of less interest to the topic of this paper, a personal family company (i.e., a company determined to be a family company by disregarding all corporate shareholders which are not themselves family companies) is subject to a provision levying a surtax, ranging from 10 to 20 percent, on such company's undistributed profits in excess of a certain amount.[75]

III. Tax Effects on American Corporation That is Assignor or Licensor[76]

A. General Rule

Under Japanese law, disregarding any treaty provisions to the contrary, a foreign corporation[77] must pay corporation and/or income tax only when it has Japan-source income[78] and sometimes only upon various categories of Japan-source income,[79] depending, in the case of the corporation tax, upon the nature and scope of the corporation's activities in Japan.[80]

B. Source Rule for Income in Respect to Patent Rights and Know-How

Proceeds from the transfer or rental or rights concerning technology to a company carrying on a line of business in Japan to which the rights or know-how pertain is deemed to be Japan-source income.[81] Such a definition clearly encompasses both gains from the assignment of patent rights and the sale of know-how as well as the rental thereof in return for royalteis.[82]

74. Double Taxation Treaty, *supra* note 59, art. 11.

75. CTL art. 67. The excess-profits deduction is the larger of i) 35 percent of the income of the accounting period, ii) 10 million yen on an annual basis, or iii) an amount necessary to increase earned surplus to one-fourth of paid-in capital.

76. We consider only the case of American corporations so that detailed reference can be made to the Double Taxation Treaty, *supra* note 59.

77. This is defined as a corporation whose head office is not located in Japan. CTL art. 2(iii) and (iv).

78. CTL art. 141; ITL arts. 5(4) and 178. The computation of corporate net income for foreign corporations is virtually the same as that for domestic corporations, see notes 38–75 and accompanying text, *supra*, and the tax rates are the same, except that there is no provision for lower rates in respect to profits distributed as dividends. CTL arts. 142 and 143.

79. For the categories, *see* CTL art. 138 and ITL art. 161.

80. *See* CTL art. 141.

81. CTL art. 138(vii)(a); ITL art. 161(vii)(a).

82. Double Taxation Treaty, art. 14(1), sets forth a source rule for royalties as follows:

C. Permanent Establishment

Since tax rates applied to Japan-source income depend upon the existence and type of the American corporation's "permanent establishment" in Japan, it is necessary to define that term. A permanent establishment exists in Japan if the American company: (1) has in Japan a branch, office, factory, workshop, warehouse, mine, or quarry or other place of extraction of natural resources, or a building site or construction or installation project that exists for more than twenty-four months; or (2) has an agent in Japan who has and habitually exercises the authority to conclude contracts on behalf of the corporation.[83]

D. Applications

1. Gain from assignment of patent rights or know-how. As a general rule, it will be recalled that income from the assignment of patent rights or know-how is reckoned into pecuniary receipts for purposes of computing the corporation tax.[84] However, the Double Taxation Treaty states:[85]

> Industrial or commercial profits of a resident of a Contracting State shall be exempt from tax by the other Contracting State unless such resident is engaged in industrial or commercial activity in that other Contracting State through a permanent establishment situated therein. If such resident is so engaged, tax may be imposed by that other Contracting State on the industrial or commercial profits of such resident but only on so much of such profits as are attributable to the permanent establishment.

The tax on "industrial or commercial profits" obviously includes the

"Royalties derived from sources within a Contracting State by a resident of the other Contracting State may be taxed by both Contracting States."

The term "royalties" is defined in the same art. 14(3) as follows: "(a) Payment of any kind made as consideration for the use of, or the right to use . . . patents, designs or models, plans, secret processes or formulae, trademarks, or other like property or rights, or know-how . . . , and (b) Gains derived from the sale, exchange, or other disposition of any property or rights referred to in subparagraph (a) of this paragraph to the extent that the amounts realized on such sale, exchange, or other disposition for consideration are contingent on the productivity, use, or disposition of such property or rights."

83. Double Taxation Treaty, art. 9, which is similarly echoed in CTL art. 141(i), (ii) and (iii), and ITL art. 164(i), (ii) and (iii). Consult Double Taxation Treaty art. 9 for further details of this definition. Obviously, the scope of "permanent establishment" under Double Taxation Treaty is much narrower. Consequently, Double Taxation Treaty operates to favor an American company. It is a general principle of Japanese law that a treaty is superior to even a subsequently-enacted contradictory statute. It should be noted, however, that any provision in Japanese tax or other laws, which confers upon an American company more favorable tax benefits than those under the Double Taxation Treaty, would be applicable. Double Taxation Treaty, art. 4(2).

84. CTL art. 22(2).

85. Double Taxation Treaty, art. 8(1).

Japanese corporation tax on gains from the sales of assets including patents or know-how if such gains are effectively connected with a permanent establishment.[86]

It should be noted further that once a United States corporation is taxable on the profits from the sale of assets, it may deduct, pursuant to the Double Taxation Treaty, "expenses which are reasonably connected with such profits, including executive and general administrative expenses, whether incurred in the Contracting State in which the permanent establishment is situated or elsewhere."[87]

Further, Japan-source income accruing from sale of patent or know-how may be taxed in Japan even if the United States company does not have a permanent establishment.[88] Tax on such capital gains, however, is imposed in Japan only when the gains have in substance the nature of royalties as defined in the Double Taxation Treaty.[89] It follows that capital gains arising out of a genuine and complete assignment of patent rights or know-how are not taxed in Japan, but in the United States.[90]

2. *Royalty payments.* Royalties received by a United States corporation from a Japan source are specifically not exempted from Japanese taxes by the Double Taxation Treaty even where the United States company has no permanent establishment in Japan.[91] Where the United States company has no permanent establishment in Japan, Japan may tax such royalties at a rate not exceeding 10 percent.[92]

Where a United States corporation does have a permanent establishment in Japan, and if the right giving rise to such royalties is effectively connected with such permanent establishment, the Japanese corporation tax will be fully imposed on royalties attributable to the permanent establishment.[93] In this case, the royalties are deemed to constitute industrial or commercial profits for purpose of the Double Taxation Treaty.

IV. Tax Effect on Japanese Corporation That is Assignee or Licensee

A. Capitalization vs. Expense

As mentioned above, the costs of acquiring patent rights and know-how from another person or corporation are capital expendi-

86. *Id.* art. 8(5).
87. *Id.* art. 8(3).
88. *See* note 82, *supra.*
89. Double Taxation Treaty, arts. 16(2) and 14(3) (b).
90. *Id.* art. 16.
91. *Id.* art. 8(5).
92. *Id.* art. 14(2).
93. *Id.* art. 8(1) and (5).

tures not currently deductible[94] and are depreciable ratably over a fixed period.[95] On the other hand, royalties paid for the right to use such property are deductible currently upon the due date for each royalty payment.[96]

B. Recovery of Investment

The basis[97] of a patent acquired by assignment is fully depreciated by the straight line method over eight years from the date of its acquisition (or less, if it expires within eight years).[98] A patent application so acquired is handled in exactly the same manner until the patent is issued,[99] at which time the book value of the patent becomes then the net book value of the patent application plus expenses incurred in registering the patent; this revised book value is then eligible for depreciation in the manner described in the preceding sentence. Should the application be abandoned, withdrawn, refused, or voided, however, its remaining undepreciated book value can forthwith be included in pecuniary losses.[100] If know-how is acquired by assignment, the purchase price is capitalized and amortized over a five-year period.

In the case of a license agreement,[101] an advance or down payment that is paid at the time the agreement is made is chargeable to a separate deferred expense account and is amortizable over five years (or less, if the term of the agreement does not exceed five years and it is obvious that another down payment or advance will be paid at the time of the renewal of such license).[102] This treatment is the same whether the agreement provides for a running royalty or not. However, if the agreement provides that for a certain period no royalty is to be paid, the amount that would otherwise be charged as royalty during that period can be excluded from the amount of the down

94. *See* notes 30–37 and accompanying text *supra*.

95. *See* notes 97–105 and accompanying text *infra*.

96. *See* CTL art. 22(3)(iii).

97. For the rules which determine the basis, see notes 23–37 and accompanying text *supra*.

98. CTL Cabinet Order art. 48(1)(iii); *Genkashōkyaku shisan no taiyōnensūtō ni kansuru shōrei* (Ministerial order regarding the useful life of depreciable assets) art. 1(1)(iii), CTL Basic Circular art. 7–1–6.

99. CTL Basic Circular art. 7–3–15.

100. If a patent should be about to become obsolescent, etc., before the eight-year (or less) period of depreciation, accelerated depreciation pursuant to a complex formula will be allowed, upon application to the tax bureau and acceptance thereby, for a corporation filing a blue return during the period beginning with the accounting period in which the application for the special depreciation is approved and ending with the period in which the patent is deemed to have become obsolete. CTL Cabinet Order art. 60–2.

101. Actually, the present provisions only refer to know-how license agreements; nevertheless, they are also applicable to license agreements involving patent rights.

102. CTL Cabinet Order art. 14(1)(ix)(c), CTL Basic Circular arts. 8–1–4 and 8–2–3.

payment or advance and can be deducted as an expense in the relevant accounting period.[103] A running royalty provided by such an agreement is fully deductible.

Depreciation charges in respect of patent rights or know-how, amortizations of down payments, allocation of prepaid expenses, and running royalties themselves—in other words almost everything—can be charged to costs of manufacturing inventory.[104]

If a license agreement is terminated, the unamortized down payment or advance is computed into pecuniary loss.[105]

103. CTL Basic Circular art. 8–1–4.
104. *Id.* art. 5–1–4(5) and (6).
105. *Id.* art. 8–3–4.

Index to Cases Discussed

1. JAPANESE

2. AMERICAN

General Index

LIST OF CONTRIBUTORS

MICHIKO ARIGA received her LL.B. from Tohoku University in 1932. She is a lecturer of Law at Chuo University and serves as president of the Licensing Executives Society, Japan Branch. She is the author of *Dokkinho to tokkyohō tono sesshoku ni tsuiteno kokunaiteki-kokusaiteki shomondai* [Domestic and international problems relating to interrelationship of the antimonopoly and patent laws] and the co-author of "The Antimonopoly Law of Japan and Its Enforcement," 39 *Washington Law Review* 437(1964).

DAVID G. CONLIN received his J.D. from Georgetown University in 1971 and is presently a partner in the Boston law firm of Dike, Bronstein, Roberts, Cushman & Pfund. He has been a lecturer in continuing legal education courses for the Patent Resources Group for several years and formerly served as technical advisor to Judge Baldwin of the U. S. Court of Customs and Patent Appeals. He is a co-author of the treatise *Patent Preparation and Prosecution Practice* (P. R. I., Washington, 1976) and of "Patentable Subject Matter under National and Multinational Systems," 2 *Law and Politics of International Business* 479(1970).

JOHN J. COOPER received his LL.B. from Stanford University in 1951 and his LL.M. in taxation from the University of Southern California in 1964. He is now general counsel and secretary and member of the board of directors of Varian Associates. He is the author of "Tax Aspects of Corporate Exploitation of Inventions and Know-How," 38 *Southern California Law Review* 206(1965) and "Tax and Antitrust Aspects of Foreign Licensing Transactions," 13 *UCLA Law Review* 25(November 1965).

JOSEPH M. DODGE II received his LL.B. from Harvard University in 1967. He is now an attorney practicing in the United States.

TERUO DOI received his LL.M. from Waseda University in 1954 and his M.C.L. from Tulane University in 1956. He is now a professor of law at Waseda University and serves as a member of the Copyright Council of the Japanese government. His most recent publications include *Kokusaishihō* [Private international law] (1970) and *Interekuchuaru puropati* [Intellectual property] (1972).

MARCUS B. FINNEGAN received his J.D. degree from the University of Virginia in 1955 and his LL.M. degree from George Washington University in 1957. He served as U.S. Patent Advisor to Japan in Tokyo from 1957 to 1959. He is presently a partner in the law firm of Finnegan, Henderson, Farabow, and Garrett in Washington, D.C. and a professorial lecturer in law at George Washington University. Among his publications is "The Burgeoning Development of the Common Market Competition Rules and Its Impact on International Licensing," 27 *Mercer Law Review* 519(Winter 1976).

WILBUR L. FUGATE is a member of the District of Columbia Bar. He received his LL.B. from the University of Virginia and his LL.M. and S.J.D. from the George Washington University. He was for a number of years chief of the Foreign Commerce Section of the

Antitrust Division, U.S. Department of Justice and a U.S. Delegate to the OECD Restrictive Business Practices Committee. He is the author of *Foreign Commerce and the Antitrust Laws* (1st ed., 1958; 2d ed., 1973).

YUTAKA KUBOTA received his LL.B. from the University of Tokyo in 1950 and his LL.M. from Harvard Law School in 1961. He is currently an attorney at law. His recent publications include "Patent Infringement and Temporary Injunction," 1171 *Tokkyo Kanri* [Patent Administration] 24(1974); "On the Relation between Federal Arbitration Act and State Arbitration Laws in the U.S.," *Journal of the Japan Commercial Arbitration Association*, vols. 7, 8, and 9 (1975); and "On Arbitration Agreement between Japanese and American Companies," *Journal of the Japan Commercial Arbitration Association*, vols. 5 and after (1976).

EUGENE LEE received his J.D. and LL.M. degrees from the University of Washington in 1966 and 1968, respectively. He was honored with a Fullbright Scholarship to Tokyo University in 1969. He is now a professor of international business at Sophia University and president of International Investment Consultants Limited in Tokyo. He is the co-editor of *Foreign Investment and Japan*.

JOHN D. LYON received his J.D. from the Harvard Law School in 1960. He is currently executive vice-president of the Oil Shale Corporation in Los Angeles.

KAZUKO MATSUO received her LL.B. from the University of Tokyo and her M.C.J. from New York University. She is an attorney and a patent attorney and serves as a lecturer on industrial property laws at St. Paul University.

SELICHI NAKAMURA received his LL.B. and LL.M. degrees from Waseda University in 1959 and 1964, respectively, and in 1970 received an LL.M. from the University of California at Berkeley. He is now an attorney of law.

WARREN L. SHATTUCK received his LL.B. degree from the University of Washington in 1934 and his J.S.D. degree from Yale University in 1936. He retired from the University of Washington law faculty in 1973 and is now Professor of Law, University of California, Hastings College of the Law, San Francisco. He is the co-editor of the recent publication *Trade and Investment in Taiwan* (1973).

KEIKO SOMENO, professor at Yokohama Commercial College, received her bachelor of economics from the University of Tokyo. Her unpublished theses include "The Scope of Protection of Patented Inventions" and "General Thought of Invention," both written in 1969.

YOSHINOBU SOMENO, professor of law at Nihon University, received his LL.B. from Nihon University. He has published *Commentary on the Laws of Industrial Property* (1960) and *Patents and Trade Marks* (1961).

ROBERT A. STENZEL, an international patent lawyer employed by the Xerox Corporation, received his J.D. in 1967 from the Washington College of Law of the American University. His significant publications include "Effective Prior Art Date of a United States Patent," 16 *American University Law Review* 335 (March 1967) and "The Budgetary Process and the Appropriations Committees," U.S., Congress, Senate, *Congressional Record*, 89th Cong., 2d sess., 1966, 112, no. 99:12929-41.

KOZO TOYAMA received his LL.B. from the University of Tokyo in 1963 and his M.C.L., from the University of Illinois in 1973. He is currently an attorney at law.

KOE TOYOSAKI, professor of law at Gakushuiin University, received his LL.B. and LL.D.

degrees from the University of Tokyo. He is a member of the Industrial Property Council of the Japanese Government and has published *Kōgyōshoyūken-hō* [Industrial property law], (rev. ed., 1975).

WILLIAM R. WOODWARD, who received his LL.B. from Harvard Law School in 1938, was a leading member of a group that standardized licensed agreement language for the Western Electric Company, of which he was later General Patent Attorney (1960–69). He was general patent counsel of Allied Chemical Co. in 1969–70 and now is a member of Flynn & Frishauf, P.C. of New York City. He is the author of the annually updated chapter "Sales of Patents and Copyrights" in Lasser's *Income Tax Techniques* (1965) and of the forthcoming "Protection of Successive Inventions of a Research Organization by Co-pending U.S. Patent Applications."